Friedrich Pollock

Historical Materialism Book Series

The Historical Materialism Book Series is a major publishing initiative of the radical left. The capitalist crisis of the twenty-first century has been met by a resurgence of interest in critical Marxist theory. At the same time, the publishing institutions committed to Marxism have contracted markedly since the high point of the 1970s. The Historical Materialism Book Series is dedicated to addressing this situation by making available important works of Marxist theory. The aim of the series is to publish important theoretical contributions as the basis for vigorous intellectual debate and exchange on the left.

The peer-reviewed series publishes original monographs, translated texts, and reprints of classics across the bounds of academic disciplinary agendas and across the divisions of the left. The series is particularly concerned to encourage the internationalization of Marxist debate and aims to translate significant studies from beyond the English-speaking world.

For a full list of titles in the Historical Materialism Book Series available in paperback from Haymarket Books, visit: www.haymarketbooks.org/series_collections/1-historical-materialism.

Friedrich Pollock

The Éminence Grise of the Frankfurt School

Philipp Lenhard

Translated by
Lars Fischer

Haymarket Books
Chicago, IL

First published in 2024 by Brill Academic Publishers, The Netherlands
© 2024 Koninklijke Brill NV, Leiden, The Netherlands

Published in paperback in 2026 by
Haymarket Books
P.O. Box 180165
Chicago, IL 60618
773-583-7884
www.haymarketbooks.org

ISBN: 979-8-88890-555-5

Distributed to the trade in the US through Consortium Book Sales and Distribution (www.cbsd.com) and internationally through Ingram Publisher Services International (www.ingramcontent.com).

This book was published with the generous support of Lannan Foundation, Wallace Action Fund, and the Marguerite Casey Foundation.

Special discounts are available for bulk purchases by organizations and institutions. Please call 773-583-7884 or email info@haymarketbooks.org for more information.

Cover art and design by David Mabb. Cover art is a development of *Long Live the New! no. 43, Kazimir Malevich drawing on Morris & Co. design*, paint and wallpaper on canvas (2016).

Printed in the United States.

Library of Congress Cataloging-in-Publication data is available.

Contents

Preface to the English Edition VII
Acknowledgements VIII
Prelude IX
List of Figures XI

Introduction 1

1   Origins 5

2   A Friend for Life 14

3   Failed Revolution 26

4   'Scientific' Marxism 41

5   The Quest 69

6   Dusk 82

7   Practical Relief Work 97

8   Émigré 117

9   A New Order? 133

10 Dinner at the White House 161

11 Return? 178

12 New Old Germany 198

13 Automation 210

14 On Old Age 222

    Epilogue 236

Chronology 239
Archives 241
References 244
Illustrations 263
Index 274

Preface to the English Edition

The publication of this revised English edition of my Pollock biography seems particularly appropriate in light of the Frankfurt School's own transatlantic history. In the last half century, US academics have produced crucial works on the history of Critical Theory. That the relevant Anglophone and German-language literature all too often lead independent lives is not least down to issues of translation. It is all the more gratifying to see my book come out in English just as I myself relocate from Bavaria to California. I should like to thank the many friends, colleagues and institutions who have made this possible.

In the first instance, I am grateful to the editors of the Historical Materialism Book Series, notably Sebastian Budgen and Loren Balhorn, for agreeing to publish my book, Danny Hayward for assistance and Simon Mussell for his copyediting. At Brill, Athina Dimitriou, Jennifer Obdam and Jason Prevost have been enormously helpful throughout. I am grateful to Nora Mercurio and Elena Cascio of the Suhrkamp Verlag for their unwavering support in facilitating this English-language edition. I am also indebted to Martin Jay for acting as an independent reader. Not least, I thank Lars Fischer who, by rendering not only an excellent translation but also making numerous helpful suggestions, has gone far beyond the call of duty.

The publication of this book would have been impossible without the generous financial support of the History Department at the Ludwig Maximilian University in Munich. Indeed, the department has played an indispensable role in recent years in facilitating, fostering and advancing my research. I am particularly grateful, to single out just one of my colleagues, to Wolfgang Piereth. I owe an abundance of intellectual stimulation and academic experience to my colleagues and students in Munich, notably to Michael Brenner, Daniel Mahla, Julia Schneidawind and Evita Wiecki ז״ל at the Institute of Jewish History and Culture. Finally, I am grateful to Detlev Claussen, Peter Mischung, Jörg Später, Pollock's 'godson' Stephan Kux and Horkheimer and Pollock's lift boy at the Kurhotel Badischer Hof in Baden-Baden for sharing further knowledge and impressions of Pollock with me since the publication of the German edition.

Munich/Berkeley
November 2022

Acknowledgements

I would have been unable to complete this book without a great deal of help from various quarters. Above all, I owe a huge debt of gratitude to Michael Brenner for his many years of support. My stay as a visiting scholar at the University of California in Berkeley, funded by the DAAD, was of crucial importance to this project. I am enormously grateful to Martin Jay for our many engaging discussions about Friedrich Pollock and, far from least, for his granting me access to his private collection. I was also able to spend a significant amount of time at the Deutsches Literaturarchiv in Marbach, allowing me to consult the papers of numerous relevant individuals and devote a significant amount of time to the manuscript. I particularly thank Caroline Jessen for her support in this context.

Throughout the years I have spent working on this book, Mathias Jehn, Oliver Kleppel and Stephen Roeper of the Archivzentrum at the University Library in Frankfurt/Main have met my every need. Furio Cerutti, Carlo Campani and Maria Enrica Vadalà helped me with the still relatively unknown corpus of Pollock's papers now held by the University Library in Florence. I am also indebted to Carol A. Leadenham of the Hoover Institution in Stanford; Robert Bierschneider of the Munich State Archive; Jochen Rees of the Baden-Württemberg State Archive; Hans-Peter Widmann of the State Archive in Freiburg (Breisgau); Claudius Stein of the University Archive in Munich; Melissa McMullen of the special collections and archives section at SUNY Albany; and the colleagues of the New York City Municipal Archives, the Leo Baeck Institute in New York and the Asociación de Genealogía Judía de Argentina. Christine Broit, Liliana Ruth Feierstein and Carlos Abraham Weil assisted me in tracing the Argentinian Pollocks.

I thank John Abromeit, Nicola Emery, Jan Gerber, Sander Gilman, Jürgen Habermas, Dirk Heißerer, Hans Dieter Huber, Doris Maja Krüger, Johannes Platz, Gregor-Sönke Schneider, Bernd Serger, Andrea Sinn and Jörg Später for a variety of helpful pointers. Alex Gruber, Hartmut Lenhard, Janina Lenhard, Niklaas Machunsky and Elisabeth Uebelmann were kind enough to read parts of the manuscript at different stages, and I am enormously grateful for their valuable comments.

Prelude

The large, heavy wooden table in the middle of the dining room is laid out for seventeen. It is just before eight on the evening of Friday, 5 February 1943. The location is central D.C. It is freezing outside, but the room is well heated. The flickering of the candles is reflected in the sparkling wine glasses, the napkins, artfully turned into standing fans, now lie, folded casually, next to the plates. Staff are serving the various courses – oysters, roast ham with pineapple, various vegetables as side dishes, salad and cheese – and the aroma of good food lies in the air. One of the guests has clearly made an effort to dress for the occasion. He is wearing a three-piece suit and a bow tie. Through his black-rimmed spectacles his gaze rests on the woman sitting opposite whom he seems to be quietly lecturing. He reinforces his words with hand gestures designed to demonstrate his confidence. Even so, he does not seem to be entirely at ease. Looking at him amicably with her blue eyes, his interlocutor is listening attentively and occasionally nods in agreement. She is wearing a loosely fitting but high-necked dress and pearls. Occasionally, the resolute woman, who is nearing sixty, looks to the right where her husband is absent-mindedly eating his meal. Her husband is the 32nd President of the United States, Franklin Delano Roosevelt. It was his wife Eleanor who invited the guests now attending the plush dinner party. Her nephew and the Roosevelts' daughter-in-law, Ruth Josephine, are also in attendance.[1]

The group includes four naturalised German guests who seem oddly out of place. They have come to present their plans for post-war European reconstruction. Also in attendance is Vice President Henry A. Wallace, who subsequently noted that two of the guests, 'Lowe and Polak', were Jews. It is unclear how or why he knew this. He acknowledged, however, that both were excellent economic statisticians.[2] 'Polak' was in fact called Pollock, but the names can admittedly be difficult to distinguish in American pronunciation.

For Pollock, the man in the three-piece suit and bow tie, this evening in February 1943 marked the zenith of his endeavours.[3] His friend Max Horkheimer

---

1 Franklin D. Roosevelt Day by Day, 5 February 1943, http://www.fdrlibrary.marist.edu/daybyday/daylog/february-5th-1943/. My account draws on the information Pollock provided in a letter to Max and Maidon Horkheimer two days later (Fondo Friedrich Pollock, Università degli Studi di Firenze, 2.1.1., 2) and on photographs from similar events.
2 Morton (ed.) 1973.
3 Eleanor Roosevelt's telegram to Pollock of 2 February 1943 implies that he wore a business suit, Fondo Friedrich Pollock, Università degli Studi di Firenze, 2.1.1, doc. 1.

congratulated him on this extraordinary 'opportunity to listen in on conversations of historical importance'.⁴ Pollock was certainly pleased. The now decades-long quest for a better place had taken him from tranquil Freiburg (Breisgau) through half of Europe all the way to the White House. He now had an opportunity to present his ideas and plans to the most powerful man on earth – even if, as yet, only his wife was actually paying attention. He explained at great length that only the creation of a 'true democracy' in Germany would secure peace in the long term. He appreciated that some in the State Department and the armed forces would rather establish a military administration, yet this would offer only a short-term solution. In the long run, there was a risk that Europe would turn 'either Communist or fascist' once the occupation forces withdrew.

The First Lady listened attentively but the President was evidently irked by Pollock's preachiness. Back home, Trude Lash, one of Eleanor Roosevelt's closest associates and, like Pollock, a native of Freiburg, told her husband that

> The Germans were not as clear and good as last time. The White House, the Vice President *and* the President proved too much. Their manner was too professorial and in the end the President asked them to prepare school books – thus treating them as school masters which distressed Pollock especially.⁵

As it turns out, she need not have been all that concerned: Pollock was invited back.

So how did Friedrich Pollock of all people come to be invited to dinner at 1600 Pennsylvania Avenue NW? What kind of life had led him from an apartment located above a small shop for women's apparel in central Freiburg to the heart of twentieth-century political power?

---

4 Max Horkheimer to Friedrich Pollock, 10 February 1943, in Horkheimer 1996a, pp. 420–5, p. 421.
5 Lash 1982, p. 428.

List of Figures

1 Groundplan of the Casas Horkheimer and Pollock in Montagnola   263
2 Pollock's Birthplace in Freiburg   263
3 Pollock's Gravestone on the Jewish Cemetery in Bern   264
4 Lucille Weil   265
5 Logo of the NordPol suitcase factory   265
6 Pollock's drawing of Adolph Lowe   266
7 Self-portrait, 1920   267
8 The Pollock Family, 1898   267
9 The Pollock Family, 1902   268
10 The Pollock Mansion   268
11 Max Horkheimer and Friedrich Pollock as Soldiers   269
12 Friedrich Pollock, 1929   270
13 Max Horkheimer and Friedrich Pollock, 1928   270
14 Friedrich Pollock, early 1930s   271
15 Friedrich Pollock, early 1940s   271
16 Andrée and Friedrich Pollock, 1939   272
17 Group Photo of the First Marxist Work Week, 1923   272
18 Dée Pollock looks at the NYC skyline   273
19 Carlota Pollock, 1948   273

Introduction

In 1963, Max Horkheimer published a short article in West Germany's most prestigious daily, the *Frankfurter Allgemeine Zeitung*, to mark the seventieth birthday of his closest associate and lifelong friend Friedrich Pollock. 'That Friedrich Pollock ... is known only as a scholar', he wrote,

> can be explained only by his profound modesty. However useful his scholarly legacy may prove in assessing crucial economic and social issues, his practical impact on the emergence, evolution and renewal of the social sciences in Germany, not least in saving individual social scientists in the years of persecution, amounts to a significant chapter in the history of this long-neglected discipline. A detailed account of the life he devoted in so much greater measure to duty than to his own wellbeing, notably in supporting theoretical endeavours and institutions, would make a valuable contribution to our understanding of intellectual developments in the last half century.[1]

The words Horkheimer chose to express his profound respect for Pollock may have a hagiographical undertone, but they nevertheless make for an entirely appropriate point of departure for this book.

Of course, Horkheimer's claim raises the question of why, then, this is the first biography of the man. The explanation lies not least in Pollock's aforementioned 'profound modesty'. As West Germany's foremost political weekly, *Der Spiegel*, noted in its obituary for Pollock following his death on 16 December 1970,

> The co-founder of the Frankfurt Institute for Social Research consciously stayed in the shadows of his great friend Max Horkheimer whose lifelong helper and majordomo he was. As the institute's organiser and financial administrator, he established branches in London, Geneva and Paris in the early 1930s, thus securing the institute's ability to continue working after Hitler came to power. ... Pollock was an economist and his publications earned him a reputation as an expert on Marxist economics. In retirement, he was Horkheimer's neighbour in Montagnola. He died there on Wednesday before last.[2]

---

1 Horkheimer 1985d, p. 265.
2 'Register', *Der Spiegel*, no. 53, 27 December 1970, p. 94.

To be sure, *Der Spiegel* did credit him with 'a reputation as an expert on Marxist economics'. Even so, Pollock the scholar – according to Horkheimer supposedly the only capacity in which he was known – plays only a marginal role in this obituary. It portrayed Pollock primarily as an organiser and financial administrator, a neighbour and majordomo, and it is in just these terms that he has, for the most part, been profiled in the historiography of the Frankfurt School. In this light, Horkheimer's appreciation seems to amount to no more than one friend doing another a good turn, a close companion's gushing praise. In this book, I show that Pollock was indeed infinitely more than a majordomo, that he helped shape the intellectual profile of the institute in decisive ways both theoretical and practical and, far from least, that he was instrumental in saving and assisting dozens of German-Jewish intellectuals seeking to flee Nazi Germany and Nazi-occupied Europe.

Like all individuals who merit a biographer's attention, Pollock was a man of various small and not so small contradictions: he was the son of a factory owner yet wanted to abolish private property; a professor who did not publish extensively; an economist who incurred substantial losses on the stock exchange; a man from the German province of Baden who eventually felt at home only in American English; a communist who considered Marxism anachronistic; a Jew who wanted nothing to do with Judaism or Jewish peoplehood; and, finally, a critical intellectual who believed that his lifelong friendship covenant with Horkheimer provided a space for the anticipatory realisation of the good life. Far from trying to smooth over these contradictions, I do my level best to portray him warts and all, presenting both his strengths and weaknesses and the turns, twists and false starts that shaped the often convoluted course of his life.

I have endeavoured to provide sufficient political, cultural and intellectual context to allow readers to understand Pollock as (in Marx's terms) the ensemble of social relations he, like all individuals, was. That said, important as context is for the interpretation of an individual's specific decisions, actions and ways of thinking, neither are individuals merely a cross section of omnipotent impersonal forces. The havoc wrought by modernity may have profoundly fractured the individual, but my account remains committed to the assumption that individuals maintain the ability to deviate from and transgress established norms and express their individuality by setting themselves against the mainstream. Mine is not the kind of biography that supposedly accounts for an entire century on the back of a single individual. Instead, I focus emphatically on the life of one extraordinary individual in an age of enormous catastrophes, conflicts and transformations and his sometimes idiosyncratic responses to these shocks and wider developments more generally.

No student of the history of German sociology, Western Marxism, the so-called Frankfurt School or the German-Jewish émigré community in the United States will be oblivious to Pollock. His name constantly pops up in the relevant literature and, even more so, in the primary source material, and yet Pollock has continued, to quote Wiggershaus, to be the final enigma among the members of the Frankfurt School.[3] When Wiggershaus made this diagnosis in 1994, he hoped it might draw attention to Pollock, but little has been added to his brief biographical sketch in the intervening years, nor is Pollock really much better known now than he was then. He continues to be overshadowed by the stars of Critical Theory, foremost among them Theodor W. Adorno, Walter Benjamin, Max Horkheimer and Herbert Marcuse. Only diehards are familiar with at least some aspect of his theoretical work, and he rarely makes it out of the footnotes even of works on the Frankfurt School. It is high time indeed to do justice to his significant contribution, both theoretical and practical, to the development of Critical Theory.[4]

This desideratum is all the more startling insofar as Pollock, as co-founder and deputy director, was absolutely central to the institute's development, even in purely formal terms. The six-volume edition of his collected works, whose publication began in 2018, will hopefully help intensify interest in his work.[5] The publication of Horkheimer's collected works in the 1980s and 1990s has done wonders in this respect. Such editions also help create a better balance between context and immanence, between the external influences and internal dynamics, the continuities and discontinuities that shaped an individual author's thought over time. This makes it easier to profile their specificity as an original thinker who both influenced, and was influenced by, their peers in (in Pollock's case) the field of Critical Theory and a number of other significant authors.

No longer reduced to the auxiliary role of throwing light on his better-known colleagues, Pollock's life turns out to be every bit as exciting and fascinating as that of his more prominent peers. He was torn between two continents, between revolutionary yearning and realpolitikal scepticism, between theoretical pessimism and a utopian lifestyle, between cosmopolitan self-definition and being identified by others as a Jew, between the desire to implement his ideas, convictions and dreams and the need to confront an increasingly hostile environment. It was the need to make sense of, and come to terms with, these

---

3 Wiggershaus 1994b.
4 Among the few relevant studies are: Dubiel 1975; Gangl 1987; Campani 1992; Heerich 2007; Emery 2023.
5 Pollock 2018a; Pollock 2021a.

tensions that motivated, drove and sustained the symbiotic covenant of friendship between Pollock and Horkheimer that invariably has to take centre stage in any account of Pollock's life and work.

These tensions are also reflected in Pollock's version of Critical Theory. Pollock was keen to theorise on a broad empirical basis and in a way that made it possible to anticipate emerging social trends. This exposed him to a far greater risk of being disproven than run-of-the-mill social scientists who simply work descriptively. Some of his prognoses have turned out to be wrong or at least overblown. Others may have sounded like something straight out of science fiction at the time and yet they are as acute today as they ever were. The 'revolution of the robots' is a case in point.[6]

They may originate in a different age that will strike many as strange and distant, but many of Pollock's ingenious and highly prescient analyses regarding issues such as the increasing economic superfluousness of human individuals, accelerating automation and expanding bureaucracies, issues whose import was only partially discernible at the time, speak in a helpful way to some of our most important current concerns.

Pollock very much hoped that his legacy might help future scholars make sense of the world in substantive ways. In this sense, I hope that this biography can do more than draw attention to an individual owed far greater engagement as a historical figure than he has hitherto received. Ideally, it will help do what all works of intellectual history ultimately should: bring the intellectual contribution of its subject back into contention.

---

6 For recent examples, see Michael Sainato, 'Grapes, Berries and Robots. Is Silicon Valley Coming for Farm Workers Jobs?', *The Guardian*, 8 September 2022, https://www.theguardian.com/environment/2022/sep/08/california-agriculture-technology-farm-workers; Joe Pinkstone, 'Will a Robot Take Your Job? These are the Roles at Greatest Risk from the Robo-Revolution', *Telegraph*, 13 April 2022, https://www.telegraph.co.uk/news/2022/04/13/will-robot-take-job-roles-greatest-risk-robo-revolution/; Taylor Nicole Rogers, 'Covid Speeds Up Automation of Low-Wage Jobs', *Financial Times*, 1 September 2021; Jane Humphries and Ben Schneider, 'I, Robot Worker: Employment, Growth and Problematic Technology', *TLS*, 25 June 2021, pp. 24–5; Benanav 2020.

CHAPTER 1

Origins

At the time of Friedrich Pollock's birth on 22 May 1894,[1] Freiburg (Breisgau) was a medium-sized provincial city in the southwest German region of Baden with a university and a population of 50,000. It was large enough for city life, entrepreneurial knowhow and scientific innovation to flourish yet small enough to allow its traditional social structures to withstand radical political and economic change. The Albert Ludwigs University, established in 1457, was one of Germany's oldest and most prestigious institutions of higher education, and its 2,000 students (women were first admitted in 1899) maintained a palpable presence in the city. Predominantly liberal and bourgeois in character, Freiburg reaped considerable benefits from the annexation of Alsace following the Franco-Prussian war of 1870/71, especially thanks to the newly constructed rail line to Colmar. The city's increased prosperity was also reflected in its architecture and infrastructure. A horse-drawn bus service was introduced in 1891, an electric tram service a decade later. A significant number of new properties inspired by historicist concepts transformed the cityscape. Given the rapid increase in the city's prosperity and cultural significance, the population, boosted notably by wealthy citizens from the Ruhr region and from Hamburg – many of the latter fleeing from the cholera epidemic of 1892 – grew to more than 80,000 on the eve of the First World War.

At the time of Friedrich Pollock's birth, the city's small Jewish congregation had roughly 1,000 members. As we will see, Jews only began to settle in Freiburg again in earnest in the 1860s. The city's budding Jewish congregation was initially taken care of by the neighbouring district rabbinate based in Sulzburg. While its congregations were beacons of rural Jewish traditionalism, Freiburg's Jews tended to be more reform-oriented. In 1885, a new district rabbinate was established in Freiburg. It subsumed the former district rabbinate of Breisach and, in 1887, following the death of district rabbi Mendel (Emanuel) Dreyfuß the year before, the district rabbinate of Sulzburg too.[2] None too surprisingly, the traditionalists were not best pleased. As the orthodox journal *Der Israelit* (The Israelite) lamented,

---

1 State Archive Ludwigsburg, Stuttgart passport files, card index, F 201 Bü 415/19.
2 Paulus 1984, p. 50.

> The Freiburg congregation is strictly – impious. An organ plays both on Shabbat and the holidays: hence, right-minded and genuinely observant rabbis were prevented from applying [for the new district rabbi position]. In accordance with the old saying that a congregation gets the rabbi it deserves, Freiburg too now has a rabbi who, in terms of his 'persuasion', is a perfect fit. We are sufficiently tolerant not to begrudge Freiburg's Jews their rabbi; all we want is not to have him imposed on us.[3]

The insufficiently pious rabbi in question, Freiburg's first rabbi in the modern era, was Adolf Lewin. Originally from Posen (Poznań, then part of Germany), he was a graduate of the renowned Jewish Theological Seminary in Breslau (now Wrocław) who, before assuming his position in Freiburg, had gathered plenty of experience as a rabbi, first in Koschmin (now Koźmin), then in Koblenz. During his 24-year tenure in Freiburg, he exerted a profound influence on the congregation and the way services were celebrated in Freiburg's first synagogue of the modern era, inaugurated in 1870. Among the new rules he enforced was a dress code predicated on bourgeois standards of respectability.

> Those who attend the synagogue are expected to turn up in suitable, preferably dark clothing. ... On Saturdays and the holidays, married members of the congregation must wear a black top hat. Adults should wear dark hats.[4]

By contrast, the use of prayer shawls and loud praying by individuals were prohibited. Lewin's liberal Judaism was fused to an ostentatious German patriotism which he articulated with great self-confidence, especially in disputes with antisemites who accused Jews of insufficient loyalty to the fatherland.[5] Lewin shared this stance with many members of his flock. Bourgeois in outlook, many were selective in their religious observance and some abandoned religious practice altogether. This by no means automatically implied that they officially left the congregation, however. Judaism no longer exerted any great influence on their daily lives, but they still vigorously defended themselves against attacks on their Jewishness.

Friedrich Pollock's parents seem to have belonged to this group. A photo from 1902 shows the family in an almost classic bourgeois pose. Julius Pollock

---

3 *Der Israelit. Ein Central-Organ für das orthodoxe Judenthum*, 27.96, 9 December 1886, p. 1657.
4 Quoted in 'Die neue Freiburger Synagogenordnung', *Der Israelit*, 35.84, 29 October 1894, pp. 1557–9, p. 1558.
5 Dolfe (Lewin) 1891, pp. 24–7.

(1866–1937), as the pater familias, sports a Kaiser Bill moustache and is by far the tallest figure in the picture. He stands at the centre of the family, his gaze directed outward towards society. Elisabeth 'Elsa' Pollock (1867–1930), the mother, wearing a high-necked dress, looks sideways at Hans Pollock (1895–1973), the younger son. Both Hans and Friedrich Pollock are wearing sailor suits – given widespread enthusiasm for the imperial navy, they were all the rage at the time – yet Friedrich stands slightly apart on the right-hand side, almost as though he has already taken his first steps towards the independence he later asserted. That said, he is holding on to his mother's arm, even as she looks the other way.

Family portraits of this kind were typical for the middle classes and they were, of course, largely staged by the photographers. They tended to be exhibited in a prominent position in the drawing room to display the merits of the bourgeois nuclear family that emerged as the social norm in Imperial Germany. In this respect, Jewish and Christian families hardly differed. There is nothing in the Pollock family photo to suggest that they were Jewish. Evidently, their Jewishness was not integral to the way in which they wished to present themselves to the world. Friedrich Pollock remained close to his mother until her early death. She came from Cologne, where her birth family, the Francks, were well established.[6] Her parents 'still attended synagogue on the holidays', Pollock later recalled, 'but they were already liberal Jews and my mother confirmed that she never went, she no more attended synagogue than I did'. We know nothing about Julius Pollock's religious orientation. His son later described him as an 'antisemite' who 'did not really want to socialise with Jews'.[7] It would seem, however, that his animosity was principally reserved for Jews who did not conform to his bourgeois standards – such as the more traditional Jews from Sulzburg. In contrast to his brother Isidor Louis (later: Hans Ludwig) Pollock, Julius Pollock never formally left the congregation and was buried in the Jewish section of the Prag Cemetery in Stuttgart.[8]

Friedrich Pollock's paternal grandfather, Salomon Pollock (1834–1899), originally came from the small locality of Rust, located 30 kilometres northwest of Freiburg, where a Jewish community had existed since the seventeenth century. In the mid-nineteenth century, Rust's Jews (who made up roughly one tenth of the overall population) fell on hard times and increasingly migrated to urban locations.[9] The Code Napoléon, the civil code enacted in Baden in

---

6 State Archive Ludwigsburg, Stuttgart passport files, card index, F 215 Bü 39.
7 Ernst von Schenck, interview with Pollock and Horkheimer, transcript, 1965/66, Horkheimer Archive, University Library Frankfurt/Main, MHA X 132a, pp. 53, 153.
8 Hahn 1992, p. 170.
9 Debacher 1988.

1810, allowed Jews to settle legally in Freiburg again for the first time in more than four hundred years. As the economic circumstances of the Jews in the surrounding rural localities deteriorated, the number of Jews in Freiburg very gradually increased. Yet even by the middle of the century, given the remaining legal restrictions, a mere 20 Jews lived in Freiburg.[10] Only once Jews were granted more or less full freedom of trade and settlement in 1862 did the Jewish community begin to grow in earnest.[11]

This decisive change also paved the way for Salomon and Pauline Pollock's (1839–1912) move to Freiburg. On 18 October 1862, within a fortnight of the 'Gesetz über die bürgerliche Gleichstellung der Israeliten als Gemeindebürger im Großherzogtum Baden' (Law Regarding the Civil Normalisation of Israelites in the Grand Duchy of Baden) receiving grand-ducal assent, and only three days after its coming into force, their men's apparel store offering 'German, French and English fashion' opened its doors on Schustergasse.[12] Announcing the opening in the *Freiburger Zeitung*, Salomon Pollock expressly pointed to his 'varied experience in all branches of this business'. Following his formal recognition as a citizen of Freiburg in 1864, he not only announced that, 'by popular demand, alongside my men's apparel business the most refined and modern women's coats and jackets' would henceforth be offered.[13] He also acquired the residential property Eisenstraße 6 in central Freiburg, a stone's throw from the minster (with its infamous denunciatory juxtaposition of *synagoga* and *ecclesia*) and just two blocks from the first prayer house run by the new Israelite Religious Society established in 1864.[14] At the time, 35 Jewish families lived in Freiburg, and the Pollocks were among the congregation's founding members.[15] Yet their ties to the congregation soon loosened and they became increasingly lax in their attendance of services.[16] Above all, they ran a business and wanted

---

10   Lewin 1890, p. 101.
11   Lewin 1909, p. 335.
12   See *Freiburger Zeitung*, 19 October 1862, p. 4. I am grateful to Bernd Serger for this reference.
13   See *Freiburger Zeitung*, 29 September 1865, p. 4. Once again, I am grateful to Bernd Serger for this reference.
14   *Freiburger Adreß-Kalender für das Jahr 1865*, http://dl.ub.uni-freiburg.de/diglit/adr1865, p. 77.
15   'Aus dem Badischen', in *Allgemeine Zeitung des Judenthums*, 28.37, 6 September 1864, p. 579; Lewin (1909, p. 385) gives an even lower number of only 17 families for the same year.
16   They did not, however, leave the Jewish congregation. See, e.g., entries for Friedrich Pollock's grandmother, Pauline Pollock, née Weinheim, on 25 March 1880 and just before Salomon Pollock's death in 1899. Freiburg Jewish congregation register of births, deaths and marriages, State Archive Freiburg, J 386 Bü 194, 1 and 195, 6.

to participate in the city's bourgeois life. Salomon Pollock became a 'Fasnet' (the local carnival) enthusiast and actively supported the Carnival Association, one of the 'well-respected, positively upper middle-class associations' among whose members 'factory owners and entrepreneurs, solicitors and architects' featured prominently.[17] In October 1873, Salomon Pollock added a Shoe and Boot Emporium to his apparel store. It was located close to the family home on Eisenstraße 1–2,[18] but does not seem to have been a success. In 1880, he stopped selling shoes and turned all his attentions to the apparel business again, which was now located on the ground floor of the family home.

When Salomon Pollock retired in 1887,[19] his sons Emanuel (later Emil, 1864–1920) and Julius Pollock took over the running of the business, reorienting it exclusively to women's apparel. That it took two years following Salomon Pollock's death for his estate to be settled definitively suggests that there may have been some wrangling between the two elder brothers as to who should inherit the Damenkonfektionsgeschäft S. Pollock (Ladies' Apparel Store S. Pollock) as it now was.[20] In the end, Julius Pollock took over the enterprise. In 1902, Emanuel Pollock, who was presumably paid out, moved to Dresden to join his new wife.[21]

Yet the family business in Freiburg evidently did not exhaust Julius Pollock's ambitions. In 1900, with considerable financial support from his parents, he joined forces with his brother-in-law Sigmund Nördlinger (1868–1942) – he was married to Julius Pollock's sister Rosalia (1871–1942) – to establish a substantial leather and travel goods factory, Nördlinger & Pollock, in Stuttgart (located 130 kilometres northeast of Freiburg as the crow flies and 200 kilometres by road).

According to Werner Sombart, in Germany, the leather industry 'was already more developed in the mid[-nineteenth] century than any other branch of

---

17   Kalchthaler 2017.
18   *Freiburger Zeitung*, 19 October 1873, p. 3; *Adreßbuch der Stadt Freiburg für das Jahr 1878*, http://dl.ub.uni-freiburg.de/diglit/adr1878/0004?sid=be4b498b40a3b6d6432df55fff81a8e c, p. 54.
19   *Adreßbuch der Stadt Freiburg für das Jahr 1887*, http://dl.ub.uni-freiburg.de/diglit/adr1887/0202?sid=dc7cd9c033c042a91f74172b1a15e5c4, p. 202; *Adreßbuch der Stadt Freiburg für das Jahr 1888*, http://dl.ub.uni-freiburg.de/diglit/adr1888/0209?sid=1449062413709c6f5b48f6a135c4081e, p. 209.
20   State Archive Freiburg, Hinterlassenschaftsakte S. Pollock, H Nr. 18904.
21   Johanna Dorothea Marie Pollock, née Prielipp (1871–1955), was a Protestant. Marie and Emanuel/Emil Pollock had two sons: Karl (b. 1903), who was a policeman (sacked in 1933) and musical entertainer, and Rudolf Gerhard Werner (b. 1906), who was a graphic designer. At the time of the German minority census of 1939, Marie Pollock and her two sons were registered in Saßnitz on the Baltic island of Rügen. It is unclear what happened to the two sons after that but as 'half Jews' whose Jewish parent had died when they were still young, they may well have survived.

industry at the time'.[22] Yet by the turn of the century, competition between the German leather producers, of whom there were 551 in 1846,[23] had led to a marked decline in their numbers. Hence the need for Julius Pollock to find a partner if he wanted to become a serious player in the industry. In this sense, the creation of Nördlinger & Pollock was in itself a reflection of the extraordinary intensification in capitalist competition following the Great Depression of 1873–1896.

Friedrich Pollock's father was now involved in running two prospering businesses. In Freiburg, his decision to focus exclusively on women's apparel paid off and, in 1905, the business was awarded the title 'by appointment of the Archduke of Baden'. Nördlinger & Pollock too was a considerable success, but Pollock and his family continued to live in the apartment above the shop in Freiburg for another decade. Consequently, he was forced to commute which was no mean feat, given that cars were still an extraordinary luxury at the time. Whenever possible he took the train to Stuttgart, but Freiburg remained his main home.

Only in 1910 did Julius Pollock finally decide to move the family to Stuttgart to be closer to the factory. The following year, he took Adele Rüdenberg, a former employee, on board as his partner in the apparel store, allowing him to concentrate fully on the leather goods business.[24] Pollock eventually sold his remaining share in the apparel business to Rüdenberg in 1914,[25] when Nördlinger & Pollock shifted its focus to goods needed by the military and massively expanded its production capacity. For all the sense the partnership with Sigmund Nördlinger made in economic terms, it also altered Julius Pollock's role. In Freiburg, his father Salomon and then he himself had borne sole responsibility for all their (sometimes controversial) business decisions. In Stuttgart, he was accountable to his partner.

Not that this in any way diminished his status as pater familias and the dominant spouse in the marriage. In return for the prospect of a promising future running the family business, he expected submission, diligence and obedience from his sons Friedrich and Hans. Daily life in the family home was shaped not so much by love, warmth and good humour but primarily by a 'puritanical

---

22 Sombart 1902, p. 453.
23 Sombart 1902, p. 452.
24 As a Jew, Adele Rüdenberg (b. 1871) was forced to sell the business in 1935. Following its 'aryanisation', it was called Modehaus Wohlschlegel & Cie. Facing an increasingly hopeless situation, Rüdenberg committed suicide on 21 August 1938. State Archive Freiburg, commercial register file S. Pollock, G 540/5 no. 3829 and State Compensation Office, Freiburg branch, personal file F 196/1 no. 14938.
25 State Archive Freiburg, commercial registration S. Pollock, G 540/5 no. 15023.

mindset' concerned exclusively with hard work and the acquisition of wealth.[26] Even after they moved to Stuttgart with its 300,000 inhabitants and lively cultural scene, the parents showed little interest in, or respect for, intellectual pursuits.[27] They were relatively plain people and, despite being middle-class and well off, owned none of the sophistication and classical education of the urban bourgeoisie.

In 1961, Alice Nägele-Nördlinger, the daughter of another (unrelated) Jewish businessman in Stuttgart, recalled a very different experience:

> Although my father's health gave them a good deal of cause for concern, my parents were very open-minded and sought to give us children access to all the cultural opportunities Stuttgart had to offer, so we had a great childhood. As well as the *Neue Tageblatt*, one read the *Beobachter* and the *Frankfurter Zeitung*, went to the theatre and held a subscription for the symphony concerts, and regularly went to the Fine Arts Society and the Association for Commercial Geography.[28]

If the Pollocks occasionally attended such events they did so principally out of a sense of social obligation. They were more enthusiastic about joint rambling excursions with other families to the Swabian Jura and the Rems Valley. Their enthusiasm for nature was part and parcel of their local patriotism which coexisted quite harmoniously with their sense of Jewishness. While Alice's father considered himself 'not a Swabian Jew but a Jewish Swabian' and maintained his affiliation with the Israelite Religious Society as a matter of course, Julius Pollock kept his distance from the life of the congregation.[29] While Alice's father, who lived just two minutes from the Pollocks, remained partially observant, attended synagogue on the holidays and served the congregation in a number of voluntary roles, Julius Pollock had abandoned Judaism altogether.[30] Friedrich Pollock's father was an entrepreneur first and then a German and a husband and father. He did not deny his Jewish background, but neither did it shape his sense of self. And yet, his immediate social circle, both professional and private, was almost exclusively Jewish. Not overly concerned with

---

26   Ernst von Schenck, interview with Pollock and Horkheimer, transcript, 1965/66, Horkheimer Archive, University Library Frankfurt/Main, MHA X 132a, p. 46.
27   State Archive Freiburg, residents' registration card Julius Pollock.
28   Alice Nägele-Nördlinger, 'Erinnerungen', Stuttgart Municipal Archive, Special Collection 172, M–R, quoted in Rueß 2009, p. 191.
29   Ibid.
30   Friedrich Pollock, letter to Martin Jay, 24 March 1970, Martin Jay private collection.

issues beyond his own business interests, he was a conservative by inclination and despised the liberal haute bourgeoisie with its aesthetic leanings. For him, the fine arts, religion and philosophy, even medicine, as Friedrich Pollock later recalled, were pointless indulgences:

> I know from my own family that all professors who were not scientists, medics included, were met with contempt. It was proper businessmen who actually achieved something. While they work ... the others read![31]

This attitude may have been reinforced by the competitive edge of Julius Pollock's relationship with his much younger brother Isidor Louis (1873–1939) who had decided not to go into business and instead trained as a urologist. Following the completion of his medical doctorate in 1898, he called himself Hans Ludwig Pollock.[32] Fully integrated into Freiburg society, he – unlike his brother – officially left the Jewish congregation.[33] In Julius Pollock's eyes this meant that his brother had chosen the path of least resistance. He himself might have turned his back on Judaism but would not have dreamt of abandoning the Jewish congregation. For him, this was simply a matter of self-respect.

If in the previous generation it had been the youngest brother who chose a different path, this time it was the older son who 'strayed', and it fell to Pollock's younger brother Hans (born on 9 September 1895) to become an entrepreneur and took over their father's business. The brothers do not seem to have been particularly close and Friedrich tended to look down on his little brother who, as he saw it, lacked the courage to make his own decisions. Like his father, Hans married the daughter of a Jewish businessman, Ida Stern, née Joseph (1892–1982), a war widow whose first husband, Emil Stern, was killed in 1916. In 1922, Hans adopted her daughter from her first marriage, Liselotte (Lilo, born in 1913).[34] When life in Nazi Germany became intolerable, the family fled first, in 1936, to Amsterdam and then to Buenos Aires, where Hans Hispanicised his first name, changing it to Juan. Friedrich and Hans Pollock's mother died in 1930, their father in 1937, and contact between the brothers remained minimal during the war. Only at an advanced age did Friedrich Pollock develop a more pronounced sense of family.

---

31   Ernst von Schenck, interview with Pollock and Horkheimer, transcript, 1965/66, Horkheimer Archive, University Library Frankfurt/Main, MHA X 132a, p. 25.
32   *Jahresverzeichnis der an den deutschen Universitäten erschienenen Schriften* 14: *15. August 1898 bis 14. August 1899*, p. 82.
33   Clausing 2005, p. 60, n215.
34   Leo Baeck Institute New York, Auerbach Family Collection, AR 11 847, III/56.

Yet for now, all this lay in the distant future. The process by which Friedrich Pollock distanced himself from his family and its values was gradual. From an early age, his parents sought to prepare him for his prospective role in the family business. He attended the humanistic secondary school in Freiburg, graduating with a qualification that made him eligible for the so-called voluntary one-year form of military service. Friedrich did not shine at school, and it is little wonder that the higher secondary school in Stuttgart refused to admit him when the family moved there.[35] Since it was never envisaged that he would go to university, his parents saw no need for him to qualify for university admission. They assumed it was much more important for him to gain practical experience both in his father's firm and with entrepreneurs abroad with whom his father was in business. The sons of prosperous entrepreneurs and merchants were frequently trained in this way (daughters were rarely given the same opportunity), thus acquiring their management skills on the job. Internships abroad allowed them to hone their language skills and network with international partners. If they were really lucky, they might even find a suitable future wife while abroad.

Friedrich Pollock's existence was comprehensively foreordained, then. He would be a successful entrepreneur, marry, have one or two children and be a loyal citizen serving his fatherland. That his life took an entirely different turn resulted not least from a very special, lifelong friendship that, from his youth to his death, shaped his existence even in its most intricate details: the friendship with Max Horkheimer.

---

35   Abromeit 2011, p. 23.

CHAPTER 2

A Friend for Life

When the Pollocks moved to Stuttgart in March 1910, Friedrich was fifteen. Forced to leave his friends in Freiburg behind, he now had to find his bearings in the new city. His friends organised a small send off for him and gave him a transcript of the gathering as a farewell gift. A plentiful musical offering (including works by Bach, Vivaldi, Mozart, Schumann and Wagner) alternated with the recitation of poetry. As Horkheimer's biographer Ernst von Schenck has noted, the assemblage of selected texts can be seen 'as a kind of group manifesto: Rückert's "Chidher, the ever youthful", Schiller's "The Pledge", Hamlet's monologue, Lessing's ode, "A Friend's Farewell"'.[1] Pollock – known to his friends as Pollux – enjoyed reciting poems and reading plays in character. The prologue to the transcript of his farewell do stressed his skills in adopting a variety of voices: 'Who was it who above all others gave each role a new guise, a new character?'[2] At school, Pollock seems to have been good in maths, and there is also mention of his extraordinarily good memory. After a visit to the opera – 'be it Walküre, Tiefland, Strauss' – he always knew the main tunes by heart.

Yet none of this was enough to get him into the higher secondary school (Gymnasium) in Stuttgart. His marks were too low, and he was sent to a commercial college, which suited his father's plans better anyway. Here, the classes were socially more diverse than they were at the elitist, culturally more aspirational Gymnasium.

Friedrich Pollock was suspicious of the children from the families with whom his parents socialised and wary of their inflated sense of self. Adolph Löwe (1893–1995), whom he would later befriend, is a case in point. The son of a wealthy businessman, he was one year older than Friedrich and attended the Realgymnasium (a form of Gymnasium that focussed less on the classics and placed greater emphasis on maths and modern foreign languages) in Stuttgart. On 18 January 1911, now in his final year, Löwe spoke at a ceremony to mark the fortieth anniversary of the creation of the Imperial German state. In his pompous address, he waxed lyrical about the Germans' 'liberating awakening from a long, leaden dream': 'The various parties were reconciled, finally we were

---

1   Ernst von Schenck, Biographie von Max Horkheimer (typescript), Fondo Friedrich Pollock, Università degli Studi di Firenze, 2.2.3, p. 8.
2   Ernst von Schenck, Biographie von Max Horkheimer (typescript), Fondo Friedrich Pollock, Università degli Studi di Firenze, 2.2.3, p. 9.

one people again.'³ Friedrich would not have dreamt of engaging in this kind of conformist swagger. Much to the annoyance of his parents, he wanted little to do with the bourgeois children of their neighbours and became increasingly introvert and defiant. Of course, this may also have been a response to the overall change in circumstances resulting from the move to Stuttgart. The family's relative prosperity notwithstanding, their new residential arrangements were inferior to those they had previously enjoyed. In 1908/1909 the Pollocks had finally vacated the flat above the store in central Freiburg and moved into a villa, located on Dreikönigstraße 13 in the much more prestigious Wiehre district south of the river. In Stuttgart, they lived in a flat again, located on Reinsburgstraße, in the immediate vicinity of the travel goods and suitcase factory on Reuchlinstraße.⁴

In the winter of 1910, Friedrich Pollock received the following entirely unexpected and oddly stilted letter, addressed to 'Dear Mr. Pollock'. 'Since we began to establish our dance class', it read,

> we had hoped that you too might participate in our little winter amusement, yet back then our hope was in vain since, from what I understand, you assumed that you would not be in our beautiful city at the time. A few days ago, I heard from Mr. Eisenmann that you will now be here this winter after all and might not be averse to the idea of spending one evening a week with us learning to dance. ... I hope this might be so and that we might welcome you to Olga House tomorrow evening at quarter to nine, Yours Max Horkheimer.⁵

Max Horkheimer was the only son of Kommerzienrat (literally: counsellor of commerce, an honorary title awarded to prominent businessmen) Moriz Horkheimer, a respected pillar of bourgeois society and observant member of the Jewish congregation, making him, in Pollock's eyes, one of those spoilt scions from a respectable family whom he viewed with suspicion. They had never met, though they might have seen each other from a distance once or twice, given that their parents were loosely acquainted. Horkheimer's friend

---

3 Quoted in Krohn 1996, p. 12.
4 *Adreß- und Geschäfts-Handbuch der Königlichen Haupt- und Residenzstadt Stuttgart* 1911, p. 573. The factory was originally on Urbanstraße. The new, larger building came into play when Julius Pollock moved to Stuttgart. State Archive Ludwigsburg, commercial register, 5 December 1900, F 303/II Bü 344 (doc. 2).
5 Quoted in Ernst von Schenck, *Biographie von Max Horkheimer* (typescript), Fondo Friedrich Pollock, Università degli Studi di Firenze, 2.2.3, p. 39.

Walter Wolf, who originally suggested Pollock as a possible participant in the dance class, likewise came from the refined haute bourgeoisie.

Pollock had hardly been yearning for a dance class, not least given the extent to which dancing lessons were 'a mark of the refined middle classes' he had begun to despise so intensely.[6] To make things worse, the participants were all sons of prominent members of the Jewish congregation and, though a Jew by birth, he had no interest in Judaism, let alone in its institutionalised form. When, in the event, he did give the dance class a try, he took an instant dislike to Max Horkheimer: 'He drove me mad. And I joined forces with a number of discontents and we were in the process of setting up our own dance class and leaving him and two or three of his chums behind.'[7]

When he became aware of the conspiracy, Horkheimer, who was not used to this kind of rejection, was deeply upset. He went to see Pollock – who at this point still lived in a recently constructed western suburb of Stuttgart – and asked him for an explanation.

> And he said to me: 'So, listen, I am, of course, aware of what you're planning, and this is all down to the fact that you don't really know me. I'm not at all the person I seem to be. I'm an extremely desperate person and if someone doesn't help me soon, I am going to go mad'.[8]

Pollock was totally surprised to see before him not the overbearing son of the Kommerzienrat he had previously met but an entirely different, weak and profoundly human Horkheimer who was vulnerable and sought help. Even so, Pollock remained suspicious and merely agreed to give the matter some thought. Shocked by the renewed rejection, Horkheimer left.

Had he not, after careful further consideration, given Horkheimer another chance after all, Pollock's life would likely have taken an entirely different course. They became friends and soon entered the fray as the inseparable duo they would henceforth be. In a first joint act, they were now the ones who sabotaged the dance class by turning their backs on all the other participants. Before long, they decided to place their friendship on a robust footing in the form of a friendship contract. It is presumably no coincidence that, as the sons of entrepreneurs, they created a contract to assure each other of their mutual loyalty and dependability. Yet there was much more to this contract they regu-

---

6 Lowenstein 2005, p. 162.
7 Ernst von Schenck, interview with Pollock and Horkheimer, transcript, 1965/66, Horkheimer Archive, University Library Frankfurt/Main, MHA X 132a, p. 46.
8 Ibid., p. 47.

larly renewed and supplemented in subsequent decades with memoranda and psychological reports they wrote about themselves and each other. At its core was a utopian programme. 'We consider our friendship', they wrote in the original document which, unfortunately, has been lost, 'to be the highest good. That it lasts until death is inherent in the concept of friendship. Our conduct shall reflect this relationship of friendship and all our principles will take it into consideration before all else.' For them, the contract reflected 'a critical and human zest' that sought to 'create solidarity among all human beings'.[9] It laid out in detail how they would lead their shared life, including specific times of the days for discussion.

In reality, the life of the two friends continued to be rather more prosaic for the time being. While the Horkheimers' great wealth was occasionally reflected in the lifestyle of their son Max, for the most part, the two new-found friends' daily lives did not differ substantially from those of their peers. They gathered around a bench in town or in a café to discuss 'the pointlessness of our parents' lives'.[10] The gathering revolt against their parents was typical of many growing up in respectable well-to-do families whose ability to gain autonomy depended, in good oedipal fashion, on their ability to challenge the dominance of their fathers. As the children saw it, their parents led one-dimensional lives, 'constantly preoccupied with how to amass yet more money'.[11] To this capitalist ideal the two young friends juxtaposed a moral vision of equality, truth, fidelity and solidarity they were intent on implementing in their friendship. Implied was, not least, an extraordinary level of exclusivity. 'I'll be in Stuttgart on Thursday', Horkheimer, on holiday in Bregenz, wrote in September 1912. 'I'll call you as soon as I get home so we can arrange to meet. If I might ask a favour: don't tell anyone I'm coming, I want to be able to spend the first couple of evenings just with you and not end up having Stuttgart's *jeunesse dorée* dropping by.'[12]

The next step of the revolt consisted in reducing their exposure to their parents. In 1912, both Pollock and Horkheimer faced the prospect of being apprenticed in their parents' businesses and set on the very career path they so desperately wanted to avoid. They found a way out by suggesting that they should begin their training by gaining professional experience and language

---

9   Quoted in Gumnior and Ringguth 1973, p. 13.
10   Ernst von Schenck, interview with Pollock and Horkheimer, transcript, 1965/66, Horkheimer Archive, University Library Frankfurt/Main, MHA X 132a, p. 47.
11   Ibid.
12   Max Horkheimer to Friedrich Pollock, 3 September 1912, Horkheimer Archive, University Library Frankfurt/Main, MHA VI 30, 484.

skills as interns abroad, and their parents eventually agreed. The parents vetoed the den of vice that was Paris and would have much preferred to send them to Manchester as a true industrial metropolis. In the end, they agreed on Brussels as a compromise. Horkheimer was assigned to a manufacturer of ready-made clothing and Pollock to the substantial *À l'innovation* department store, his father's principal Belgian customer. Receiving what was for interns a handsome monthly stipend of 400 Belgian Francs, they were able to live comfortably in Brussels.

Having come to Brussels first, Horkheimer booked lodgings in adjacent guest houses and waited impatiently for Pollock to arrive. On 10 May 1913, Pollock wrote from Stuttgart how happy he was 'that we are now making our getaway together'.[13] Four days later, Horkheimer replied that 'I don't want to wake up again until you arrive, but what can I do, there's another twelve hard days to go.'[14] Some formulations in their correspondence would not be out of place in a love letter, and there is no doubting its homoerotic overtones. It would seem that, in this regard, Horkheimer occasionally went too far for Pollock's liking. He knew, Horkheimer wrote on one occasion, 'that you do not like it when I write like this, but I am sick & it helps me'.[15] They by no means limited their enthusiasm to each other or the same sex, however. Horkheimer, for example, was infatuated with his childhood friend Alice Rosenstraus who, alas, had no idea 'just how much I care for her'.[16]

Pollock too used the opportunity to gather first experiences with the opposite sex. The two friends regularly took young women out for dinner, frequenting high-class establishments such as the Taverne Royale in the Saint-Hubert arcade. The women tended to be young shop assistants whose salaries barely sufficed to make ends meet and who would never have been able to go to the theatre or to restaurants unless invited out. As the sons of prosperous entrepreneurs who cut a rather dashing figure at that, the role of the suave and generous gentleman came naturally to Pollock and Horkheimer. Pollock had a fling with the much older housekeeper of his landlord Dr. Moskowitz. She 'promptly fell in love with the slim and evidently still quite inexperienced young man'. One day, she placed a finger on his mouth and told him

---

13   Friedrich Pollock to Max Horkheimer, 10 May 1913, Horkheimer Archive, University Library Frankfurt/Main, MHA VI 30, 481.
14   Max Horkheimer to Friedrich Pollock, 14 May 1913, in Horkheimer 1995a, pp. 9–11, p. 10.
15   Ibid.
16   Ibid.

he should come with her. And he went with her, and she led him to a door and told him to look through the keyhole. And there he saw Dr. Moskowitz amusing himself with a female patient.[17]

At a time when sexual activity was still much more of a taboo than it is today, encounters of this kind were doubtless quite formative for Pollock.

In the event, then, Brussels was not so much where they implemented the 'solidarity of all human beings' outlined in their friendship contract but mainly a social space in which the two young men were able to gather new experiences and escape their parents' repressive sexual mores. While discussing what a more meaningful existence might look like and searching for it in literature, they conducted themselves much as one might expect of wealthy bachelors who can afford to ignore the misery around them. They were particularly attracted to naturalist and symbolist literature. Its anti-bourgeois tenor and negation of traditional gender roles ideally suited the sensibility of their intimate and devoted union. Henrik Ibsen's plays emerged as an important focal point for their quest. They positively devoured *Enemy of the People*, first published in 1882. Its main protagonist refuses to go with the flow and denounces society as being founded 'upon a quagmire of lies and fraud', insisting that the prevailing 'compact, liberal majority' was 'the most dangerous foe to truth and freedom'.[18] For Pollock and Horkheimer, the 'enemy of the people' was a role model: he was despised by the masses but unwavering in his crusade for truth and freedom.

No less appealing to them was Ibsen's portrayal, in *Ghosts*, of the family as a veritable prison, based on domination and repression. Its main protagonist is haunted by the ghosts of the past who will not release her and eventually destroy her life. Ibsen's *Wild Duck*, moreover, expressly treats the relationship between two friends. One of the two main protagonists, Gregers Werle, wants exactly what Horkheimer and Pollock too are trying to create: a friendship founded on truthfulness that is free of lies and deceit and oblivious to the charm of vapid trinkets; a friendship in which each is at all times willing to sacrifice his life, at a drop of a hat, for that of the other. Narratives of this kind allowed Pollock and Horkheimer to idealise their hedonistic lifestyle. They thought of themselves not as two spoilt scions of the ruling class but assumed they were making a difference by conducting themselves as they did. For them,

---

17   Ernst von Schenck, interview with Pollock and Horkheimer, transcript, 1965/66, Horkheimer Archive, University Library Frankfurt/Main, MHA X 132a, p. 49.
18   Ibsen 1890, pp. 205, 187.

Brussels was the counter-location to the factory. Where Stuttgart stood for the narrow-mindedness, tyranny and deceit of bourgeois society, the Belgian capital embodied a life of freedom, pleasure and truth.

While some political statements expressing disdain for oppression and exploitation, notably by Horkheimer, do exist from this early period, the two friends were principally concerned with their own lives at this time. Disagreements with their parents and their attempts to assert their intellectual independence from them overshadowed all else. They neglected their internships but eagerly learnt French with their private tutor, Monsieur Calle, a retired civil servant from the Loire region whom they adopted as something of father figure. Yet that was not all. Pollock led the way in making the first forays into philosophy. Browsing in a bookshop with nothing particular in mind, he came across a number of reduced philosophical classics. 'This was Spinoza, as a Jew I knew something about him; then Kant's *Critique of Pure Reason* and Schopenhauer's *The Wisdom of Life*.'[19] He began to read, but neither Spinoza nor Kant resonated with him. 'And then I read Schopenhauer and here was suddenly someone who spoke plain German and treated issues of concern: what an individual is, what an individual stands for etc.'[20] Enthused, he presented the book the Horkheimer. 'You're always giving so much thought to the world', he said, 'perhaps this will interest you.'[21] A few days later, Pollock acquired six leather-bound volumes of Schopenhauer's collected works in the city's German bookstore, and the great pessimist of German philosophy henceforth accompanied Pollock and Horkheimer for the rest of their lives.

Yet their interest in philosophy was, as yet, limited. Schopenhauer spoke to them primarily because he unflinchingly pointed to the meaninglessness of life. Yet far from embracing misanthropy, they continued to consolidate their friendship as an alternative, ostensibly meaningful life plan. It is unclear how much the parents knew of their sons' conduct, but the business partners for whom they worked presumably reported back to them. In late 1913, the respective parents decided that Friedrich Pollock and Max Horkheimer should leave Brussels and go to Manchester – the European textiles capital – where they were expected to find new internships and learn English. They tried to revive as much of their Brussels lifestyle in Manchester as they could, yet this was easier said than done. Other than their long walks – now along the Mersey – and their profound deliberations about the meaning of life or lack thereof, the

---

19 Ernst von Schenck, interview with Pollock and Horkheimer, transcript, 1965/66, Horkheimer Archive, University Library Frankfurt/Main, MHA X 132a, p. 49.
20 Ibid.
21 Horkheimer 1985e, p. 320.

hypocrisy of bourgeois society and the barely concealed materialism of their parents, there was little they could simply emulate in Manchester, and they soon grew bored of the city. Culturally, it had little to offer that appealed to them and its overwhelmingly proletarian character, all their empathy for the exploited workers notwithstanding, simply did not resonate with them.

Of course, Pollock and Horkheimer were not alone in nurturing ambivalent feelings towards the working class. Leo Löwenthal later expressed this ambivalence as follows:

> To the extent that they still exist, proletarian ways of life by no means offer a desirable model. Post-proletarian, i.e., petit-bourgeois, ways of life are not really all that much better, but they do, in terms of their essential core, imitate upper-class ways of life. ... I would go as far as to say that luxury is an anticipation of utopia. Marx too might have been able to formulate some thoughts in a better and more differentiated manner, had he not been so poor.[22]

Pollock and Horkheimer's contempt for bourgeois society and its materialism certainly did not translate into a yearning for asceticism or some kind of simple life, and they became increasingly convinced that the goal surely needed to be the equal distribution of the material surplus so that all could share in the benefits it afforded. It was wrong to monopolise and enjoy one's undeserved privileges without giving them another thought, to be sure, but it would be much worse still for the privileged to go around in sackcloth and ashes, thus mocking the desperate desire of the poor and exploited to share in society's wealth. This first, crucial step towards a critical theory of society was, however, still closely connected to the anti-bourgeois thrust of naturalist literature and lacked any kind of substantive grounding in philosophy, let alone in the critique of political economy. Schopenhauer and Nietzsche were exceptionally gifted polemicists who identified contemporaneous social trends with great acuity. Yet they were also nihilists who showed little interest in the question of how the world might sensibly be organised – the very question that increasingly crept up on and unsettled Pollock and Horkheimer. In this regard, the literature they were reading certainly offered no answers.

Having spent less than two months in Manchester, Pollock and Horkheimer moved to London where they rented a small flat in Hampstead which, at the time, was up and coming but nowhere near as exclusive as it is today. It was the

---

22   Löwenthal 1980, pp. 225–6.

exact opposite of Manchester: a fashionable spa in the eighteenth century, it was now a leafy suburb with excellent connections, both by overground and, since 1907, by underground, to central London and its many attractions. The move to London also marked a caesura in that a young woman now joined their covenant. On a trip to Paris that Horkheimer undertook on his own while they were still in Brussels, he had fallen head over heels in love with Suzanne 'Suze' Neumeier, a distant French relative. In subsequent months, he repeatedly visited her, and he continued to do so after they had moved to England. Horkheimer offered a record of the short but intense encounter with Neumeier in an avowedly autobiographical novella, appropriately called *L'île heureuse*. Bearing in mind that he doubtless stylized the experience in the novella, it nevertheless complements what we can glean from other sources about the episode.

It was not long before he urged Pollock to allow her to become part of their compact. Fearing that a third party, and a woman at that, might stand between them, Pollock was sceptical. He 'was sullen and cold as the ocean bed' and nearly drove Horkheimer to despair.[23] Yet when Horkheimer's enthusiasm was still unbroken three days after his most recent date with Neumeier, Pollock relented. Neumeier had repeatedly told Horkheimer that she felt like a prisoner in her parental home and found society's norms and expectations crushing.[24] The two friends had assumed they alone felt this way and they were surprised to discover that another person shared their sentiments and yearning. Even so, Pollock was uncertain whether this commonality was sufficient to underpin the principles laid out in their friendship contract.

Pollock apparently suggested that Horkheimer should write Neumeier a long letter explaining once more the conditions attached to admission to their covenant, which Horkheimer did. 'There could no longer be any misapprehension, I had told her absolutely everything and revealed every last secret about us.'[25] Neumeier responded in a letter she signed with her blood. 'I am your body and your soul' – your plural. Thus, her decision to join the covenant became, to stick with the contractual terminology, legally valid. In May 1914, Pollock and Horkheimer took the train from London to the northern French coastal resort of Fort-Mahon and met with Neumeier.

The title of Horkheimer's account, *L'île heureuse*, was taken from a poem by the French-Jewish symbolist Éphraïm Mikhaël (1866–1890) that Emmanuel

---

23   Horkheimer 1987, p. 303.
24   See Max Horkheimer to Suzanne Neumeier, 7 September 1913, in Horkheimer 1995a, pp. 11–13, p. 12.
25   Horkheimer 1987, p. 303.

Chabrier, the 'new Offenbach', had set to music and greatly impressed Horkheimer. Its final stanza reads: 'But yonder, under the sun / the precious and radiant red land appears / from whence the song of a joyous new dawn sounds; / This is the happy island in the cloudless sky / where, among the unfamiliar lilies / in the orchards, I will sleep / in your embrace.'[26] The affinity between the hopeful and alluring, almost Messianic mood expressed in Mikhaël's poem and Horkheimer's portrayal of the atmosphere among the three friends in Fort-Mahon is palpable:

> Here we sat, on the hot sand of the dunes, our eyes blissfully taking in the deep blue sea stretching out before us, our souls filled with unbounded joy and our chests bursting with love beyond words for this glorious, radiant nature and for ourselves who were free and had shed all that was alien or base. Nothing now stood between us, no interest, no reservation, no honour, no dignity and no duty: each saw the other only as the totally free human individual whose innermost character they had come to know, to whom they were forever joined and with whom they had attained these heights. We must ascend yet further, learn to understand and enjoy the world more intensely, conduct ourselves more and more in a way that is good and true.[27]

No less palpable is the affinity between Horkheimer's use of the literary metaphor of the happy island with its occasionally enraptured visions and contemporaneous life reform movements of the kind that met in the tiny hamlet of Monte Verità in Ticino, where anarchists, vegetarians, theosophists and artists of various stripes assembled and engaged in newly invented rituals to celebrate the unity of body and soul, spirit and nature.[28] In marked contrast to those who gathered on the Mountain of Truth, Pollock, Neumeier and Horkheimer's island got by without eurythmy, working the land and the rock of Valkyrie, but central tenets of the life reform movement are nevertheless clearly discernible in Horkheimer's account. 'The fact that Suze was a woman [Weib] rendered our connection more coherent, self-sufficient and whole. We could devote our entire humanity to our covenant, our soul, intellect and body were no longer beholden to the outside world, every aspect of us, even our common urges, were assuaged among us since Suze took pleasure in being able to gift us her

---

26   Mikhaél 1890, p. 102.
27   Horkheimer 1987, p. 295.
28   See Green 1986.

sensual beauty.'²⁹ Far from least, inspired as it was by libidinous fantasies of wholeness, their covenant also amounted to an erotic adventure, to be sure, but their worldview – Horkheimer occasionally referred to it as 'our religion' – nevertheless amounted to rather more than the sublimation of sexual fantasies. The development of an independent consciousness and options for a good and truthful life continued to form its centre piece. They passionately discussed and planned, often until dawn, what they wanted their new life to be like. At one point they considered running a farm in South Africa and subsisting purely on what the land yielded. This yearning for a simple, earthy existence pervaded the entire spectrum of life reform movements, from völkisch German to Zionist, regardless of the individual groups' specific ideological orientation. Given that it was soon unable to compete with Pollock and Horkheimer's penchant for their privileged lifestyle, their rejection of their parents' values notwithstanding, this new and ultimately uncharacteristic programmatic tenet was short-lived, however.

The ménage à trois fully came into its own in June 1914, when Neumeier really did manage to get away from her parents and joined Pollock and Horkheimer in London. They were finally reunited and free to live as they pleased on their *île heureuse* – albeit not for long. Neumeier had left her parents a farewell letter explaining her intentions. Alarmed, they immediately contacted Horkheimer's parents, who, in turn, alerted Pollock's parents to what was going on. Pollock's mother, who knew no English, took her son's address on Castle Road to mean that he was in prison (*Kastell* being a German word for a fort). She wrote to him, affirming how much she loved him and promising to stand by him no matter what he had done.³⁰

Julius Pollock was altogether less understanding. Together with Moriz Horkheimer and Neumeier's father he travelled to London and even involved Scotland Yard in his search for the unruly youngsters. One evening – Neumeier and Horkheimer had gone out and only Pollock was at home – the doorbell rang unexpectedly. He opened to find two 'sinister-looking' policemen at the door who informed him that an arrest warrant for what was then called the white slave trade, i.e., the trafficking of women, had been issued against him. Pollock was not in fact arrested, but he was prevented from leaving the flat and questioned. Fortunately, the three fathers soon arrived, followed not long after by Horkheimer and Neumeier, and the matter was resolved. Pollock and

---

29 Horkheimer 1987, p. 311.
30 Ernst von Schenck, interview with Pollock and Horkheimer, transcript, 1965/66, Horkheimer Archive, University Library Frankfurt/Main, MHA X 132a, p. 53.

Horkheimer were forced to return to Stuttgart and enter their respective family businesses. Neumeier burnt all their letters and declared that she no longer wanted anything to do with their covenant. Pollock and Horkheimer were profoundly shocked. That their shared life in a European metropolis had come to an end was bad enough, but it was the treachery (as they saw it) of Suzanne Neumeier's abrogation of their friendship covenant that profoundly wounded them and impressed its mark on their future lives.[31]

---

[31] See Abromeit 2011, pp. 26–7.

CHAPTER 3

Failed Revolution

Following the London incident, Julius and Elisabeth Pollock wanted nothing more than a return to (what they considered) normality. They wanted Friedrich Pollock to abandon his fantasies and grow into his commitments. The professional routine in the factory would surely knock some sense into him. Yet within a month of Friedrich Pollock's return to Stuttgart, something occurred that few had expected until very recently: on 1 August 1914, Germany declared war on Russia; two days later a declaration of war against France followed. With the war, supposedly required to defend Germany's honour, came new priorities. In this hour of need, the economy was expected to serve the nation and subordinate all self-interest to the common weal.

Julius Pollock instantly realised that he would be able to combine such ostensibly altruistic commitments with the attainment of healthy profits. Finally selling his remaining share of S. Pollock in Freiburg, he threw all his energy into shifting production in Stuttgart towards products required to support the war effort, notably holsters and ammunition pouches. Given the enormous demand for such products, he was quickly able massively to grow not only the concern's production capacity but also its profits. Given that Nördlinger & Pollock had thus been turned into an enterprise of strategic significance, Friedrich Pollock, for all his resentment of his father's activities and the family business, was not initially called up. As not least Julius Pollock's acquisition, in 1916, of a stylish villa in prime location, on Lessingstraße, just five minutes by foot from the Horkheimers, indicates, he now became a seriously wealthy man.[1]

Friedrich Pollock still resented working in the family business where he felt he was wasting his time. Like millions of his peers, though in marked contrast to Horkheimer, he believed the official propaganda that presented the conflict as a just war of defence against the tyrannical tsar. On 17 July, as war seemed increasingly likely, Horkheimer, who was staying at a health resort in Villingen, noted that he did not understand 'where people are finding their so-called enthusiasm'.[2] Repulsed by the burgeoning nationalism, he wrote:

---

1 See the *Adreß- und Geschäfts-Handbuch der Königlichen Haupt- und Residenzstadt Stuttgart* for 1915 for the old, and the issue for 1916 for the new address (p. 303 in both instances).
2 Max Horkheimer to Friedrich Pollock, 27 July 1914, in Horkheimer 1995a, pp. 13–15, p. 13.

The peoples are avaricious & envious & deceitful, all it takes is a coincidence – some arbitrary incident – conflict ensues & the whole thing goes off. The German is convinced he's right and screams blue murder; the Frenchman is convinced he's right and screams blue murder; the Russian is convinced he's right and screams blue murder & on and on it goes. The Serbian too is convinced he's right and screams, like all the others, that he must defend his 'national honour'. Which of the squabbling parties really is more evil than the others I do not know, but I am confident that there is little difference between them since war is always a matter of the 'people' and the herd is always equally foolish. What is so outrageous about the current issue is the profligate human delusion that it would be good and just to sacrifice the lives of hundreds of thousands of human beings for two lives that have been lost.[3] It demonstrates the foolishness & wantonness of society which, alas, is in evidence in the majority of human actions. And yet – one says, 'needs must' & consoles oneself with this contention.[4]

On this issue, then, Horkheimer and Pollock were fundamentally at odds. Pollock inclined more towards the stance of the Majority Socialists. German Social Democracy had long considered tsarist Russia one of the principal obstacles to progress in Europe. In 1907, the late Social Democratic leader August Bebel had called Russia a 'bastion of cruelty and barbarism', suggesting that 'this old boy would still be ready to shoulder a rifle and go to war against Russia'.[5] Pollock was motivated not so much by nationalism but primarily by the desire to join, in the name of humankind, the fight against the autocratic regime in St Petersburg. In his fictitious exchange of letters, 'War', written at the time, Horkheimer summarised the ideology of the internal truce (*Burgfrieden*). All social distinctions had supposedly been transcended, 'worker and prince, beggar and millionaire, Jew and Christian' stood united against the external enemy.[6] In his initial enthusiasm, Pollock would seem to have subscribed to this point of view.

In the spring of 1915, Pollock was called up but not sent to the front. Instead, he was sent to barracks closer to home than the front, where his enthusiasm

---

3 The two lost lives were those of the Austro-Hungarian heir presumptive, Archduke Franz Ferdinand, and his wife, Sophie, Duchess of Hohenberg, whose assassination in Sarajevo on 28 June 1914 – though it was in no meaningful sense the cause of the war – triggered the so-called July crisis that led to the First World War.
4 Max Horkheimer to Friedrich Pollock, 27 July 1914, in Horkheimer 1995a, pp. 13–15, pp. 13–14.
5 *Protokoll über die Verhandlungen des Parteitages der Sozialdemokratischen Partei Deutschlands. Abgehalten zu Essen vom 15. bis 21. September 1907*, Berlin: Vorwärts, 1907, p. 255.
6 Horkheimer 1988a, p. 21.

soon dissipated. The awful news from the front undermined the official propaganda, and the monotonous routine on the base hardly struck him as healthy. Whenever possible, he ducked orders. 'Partly for genuine organisational reasons, partly due to my bad faith',[7] he was stationed with a transport logistics unit in Ludwigsburg. Given how close Ludwigsburg was to Stuttgart, he was frequently able to go home. His leave seems to have been fairly generous and it is conceivable that he may have bribed his superiors to get additional time off. As Leo Löwenthal later recalled, this was not at all unusual in regiments where 'the boys from respectable well-to-do families served'.[8] Horkheimer's attempts to convince Pollock that the reports issued by the General Staff were fictitious and that the war was pointless gradually made inroads. This made it all the more difficult to rejoin the unit after a night or two spent in Stuttgart. Pollock was far removed from the suffering and death at the front. Of these he knew only from the heavily censored reports in the press and the accounts of returnees from the front. The war offered him no 'inner experience' of the kind Ernst Jünger romanticised in the war diaries he published in 1920;[9] but neither did he suffer the indignities many of his peers confronted.

In his predominantly proletarian regiment based in Hanau, Leo Löwenthal, for example, was confronted with antisemitic 'banter'. He later likened his time as a soldier to being in a 'concentration camp avant la lettre'.[10] Pollock was spared this particular Jewish experience of the First World War, often associated symbolically with the military census specifically targeting Jews (*Judenzählung*) of 1916, though it should be noted that the census did not necessarily impact Jewish soldiers at the front in the same way as their brethren back home.[11] Pollock neither recorded any antisemitic insults nor seems to have been concerned by the census. He was, above all, bored and frustrated and yearning for a very different 'state of emergency' – the *île heureuse*.

Even so, the summer of 1915 did bring an exciting new encounter in the form of a date with a French woman four years his junior, Andrée Woog (1898–1939), known as Dée, with whom he subsequently began to go out.[12] Originally from Paris, she had moved to Stuttgart some years before, when her mother Adrienne Salomon (1876–1928) remarried following the untimely death of her

---

7   Ernst von Schenck, interview with Pollock and Horkheimer, transcript, 1965/66, Horkheimer Archive, University Library Frankfurt/Main, MHA X 132a, p. 54.
8   Löwenthal 1980, p. 52.
9   Jünger 2014.
10 Löwenthal 1980, p. 53.
11 See Ullrich 2019, pp. 58–84; Geheran 2020, pp. 12–34; Rosenthal 2007.
12 The date of birth given in the passport records of the State Archive Stuttgart is 10 April 1898 (F 201 Bü 509).

first husband Raoul Woog (1868–1899).¹³ Andrée's stepfather Sigmund Kahn (1872–1953) – who, on Pollock's account, could be 'narrow-minded and petty' – was a well-to-do, respectable member of the city's haute bourgeoisie and thus acquainted with the Horkheimer family. Adrienne Kahn-Woog was hellbent on marrying her daughter to Max Horkheimer whom she considered an eminently eligible and highly desirable bachelor. Horkheimer's mother Babette, determined to see her son marry 'at least a Jewish princess', thought little of the idea.¹⁴ Nor was Max Horkheimer inclined to go on a date with her since he had recently fallen for his father's private secretary Rose 'Maidon' Riekher (1888–1969), his future wife. He and Andrée were childhood friends, and he was only too happy to see his best friend, who had been interested in her for some time, take his place at the pre-arranged date.¹⁵ The young woman was stunned when Pollock turned up instead of Horkheimer and told her point-blank:

> Look, Andrée, here's the thing ... The thing with Max is an error, he likes you a lot, but he's got a girlfriend whom he is going to marry one day. But I care a lot for you too. So, let's discuss the possibility of our going out.¹⁶

The matter-of-fact and entirely unromantic language Pollock deployed on this occasion (at least according to his own recollection) is reminiscent of that of his friendship contract with Horkheimer. It was now up to Woog to make a decision in his favour. This was a far cry from the enraptured infatuation that had characterised Horkheimer's numerous flings. Woog had not swept Pollock off his feet, he 'cared for her' and therefore proposed that she be his girlfriend. She agreed and spent the rest of the day at home with him (his parents happened to be away).

As Horkheimer had done with Neumeier, Pollock, assuming what he took to be his duty as an urbane gentleman, now took it upon himself to 'educate' his girlfriend. He informed her about the meaninglessness of life and laid out the tenets of his and Horkheimer's 'religion'. The deep connection that developed between Pollock and Woog in subsequent years hinged in no small measure on her willingness to acknowledge the significance of his special bond with

---

13   New York City Marriage Records, 1829–1940, FHL Microfilm 1,674,299, New York City Municipal Archive.
14   Ernst von Schenck, interview with Pollock and Horkheimer, transcript, 1965/66, Horkheimer Archive, University Library Frankfurt/Main, MHA X 132a, p. 54.
15   See Max Horkheimer to Andrée Woog, 1 September 1910, Horkheimer Archive, University Library Frankfurt/Main, MHA VI 30, 469.
16   Ernst von Schenck, interview with Pollock and Horkheimer, transcript, 1965/66, Horkheimer Archive, University Library Frankfurt/Main, MHA X 132a, pp. 54–5.

Horkheimer. Nothing in the preserved papers suggests that she was in any way dissatisfied with the role she played in Pollock's life relative to Horkheimer. Pollock's feelings for Woog were real enough, but he maintained a clear distinction between this particular kind of love and the attachment on which his covenant with Horkheimer rested.

In 1917, as his still vague political interests gradually intensified, he suggested to Woog that she would be better off with a different partner. Determined to become a politician after the war, he could not afford to be 'weighed down by a wife', he later recalled, least of all 'if she is as apolitical as Andrée'.[17] Clearly, Pollock's feelings for Woog were at odds with his rational, entrepreneurial and foresighted outlook. Pollock was part single-minded businessman, part rebel on a quest for the good life. The contradictions between these two dimensions of his personality sometimes led him to behave in extraordinary ways. His perfectly serious suggestion that Woog, who worked as an auxiliary nurse during the war, should marry the Jewish lieutenant Julius Marx (1888–1970), is a case in point.[18] On his account, he told her that 'You need to get out of your step-parents' home, away from your domineering mother, or you'll perish. So marry.'[19] In tears, she vowed to marry Marx yet for the time being, Marx was still at the front and Woog and Pollock continued to go out and conduct themselves like a couple. At the end of August 1918, with the end of the war in sight, Pollock was able to spend a weekend in Stuttgart again. Although he and Woog had not seen each other for three weeks and one might have thought they would have better things to do than go out, they spent one of the evenings attending a performance of Johann Strauss's operetta *The Bat*.[20]

The war dragged on although everyone knew it could no longer be won. Horkheimer was called up in 1917 but he was soon deemed unfit for service and referred to a clinic in Munich. Pollock therefore had little opportunity to

---

17 Ibid.
18 Marx was born into a traditional rural Jewish family in Freudental (located 30 kilometres north of Stuttgart). In 1913, he settled in Stuttgart where he established a flourishing business for car parts and accessories. The fact that Horkheimer addressed him with the familiar *Du* strongly suggests that both he and Pollock had known, and been friendly with, him since their youth. See Max Horkheimer to Julius Marx, 27 November 1948, in Horkheimer 1996a, pp. 1036–9. Marx served valiantly throughout the First World War and was extremely proud of his role as a German Jew in the German army. On Marx, see Nebel 1994.
19 Ibid.
20 Friedrich Pollock to Max Horkheimer, 24 August 1918, Horkheimer Archive, University Library Frankfurt/Main, MHA VI 30, 471.

discuss the epoch-making caesura of the October Revolution with him.²¹ The Bolsheviki had 'ended the war, stand for freedom and bread and no longer want to conform', Horkheimer noted with initial enthusiasm, yet he was soon troubled by the fact 'that Lenin had the entire royal family killed'.²² He considered the execution of an entire family barbaric and felt that it compromised the communist promise of 'a more humane society'. Pollock, by contrast, defended the measure, pointing to the risk of the Whites reconquering Petersburg and then restoring the monarchy. This disagreement notwithstanding, they were initially united in broadly welcoming the Communist experiment.

Having spent three weeks together in Munich in September 1918, the two friends next met in November. Before leaving for Munich, Pollock met with Woog to say farewell to her. Utterly distraught, she confessed that she had accepted Marx's proposal and acknowledged that this was the sensible thing to do, but she simply could not marry the man since it was Pollock she loved. She had become ill, suffered from a fever and was dreadfully lovesick. Pollock consoled her but remained firm and convinced her to go ahead with the marriage.²³

On 8 November 1918, Pollock went to his superior, Ernst Ritter von Brunner, pointed out that the war had been lost, no matter what, and asked for leave. Rather remarkably, his request was granted, and Pollock immediately made his way to Munich. There, the two friends were caught up in the convulsions of the November Revolution. They witnessed the storming of public buildings by revolutionary forces and were eager observers as the Free State of Bavaria proclaimed by Kurt Eisner took shape. On the morning of 8 November 1918, the entire first page of the *Münchener Neueste Nachrichten* was taken up with a declaration announcing the revolution:

---

21   Friedrich Pollock to Max Horkheimer, 24 August 1918, Horkheimer Archive, University Library Frankfurt/Main, MHA VI 30, 470.
22   Ernst von Schenck, interview with Pollock and Horkheimer, transcript, 1965/66, Horkheimer Archive, University Library Frankfurt/Main, MHA X 132a, p. 37.
23   Woog and Marx married in 1920. Marx's business was a great success, and he was able to establish branches in several European countries. In 1925, the couple moved from Johannesstraße in the city centre to a villa in the illustrious Hohengeren neighbourhood and from there, two years later, to an equally well appointed property on Stafflenbergstraße. Marx liked to keep the company of artists and intellectuals and dabbled as a poet and playwright. In his memoirs, he wrote that 'Andrée, my first wife, was well known not only at the theatre in Stuttgart but in the city at large. She managed to turn our villa ... into a meeting place, indeed, into a centre for local actors, directors and musicians; so much so that we soon found quenching the thirst of all these darlings of the muses for alcohol a challenge.' Marx 1970, p. 65.

To the Population of Munich! The awful fate that has befallen the German people has set Munich's workers and soldiers in motion. A provisional workers', soldiers' and peasants' council took up its work in the premises of the state parliament in the night of 7/8 November. Henceforth Bavaria is a Free State.

The 'democratic and social republic' vowed to secure as bearable a peace settlement for Germany as possible but also addressed social issues. 'The old tension between town and countryside will disappear. The exchange of foodstuffs will be organised in a rational manner.'[24] Pollock and Horkheimer were seriously impressed. Overnight, the passive and enslaved workers had become political subjects. As yet, they had no idea what their role in the new society might be, but Pollock and Horkheimer watched the political developments with glowing interest.

They moved into a shared flat at Von-der-Tann-Straße 22, close to the university. First, they completed the *Abitur*, the school-finishing qualification required for university admission that their parents had deemed unnecessary, given that they were destined to run their respective family businesses. Given the havoc the war had wreaked on the education of many young men, the qualification was offered in a pared-down version. Alongside their studies for the *Abitur* the two friends immersed themselves in the city's vibrant and restive cultural life. Various artists and scholars, authors and philosophers, anarchists and esoterics congregated in cafés and pubs in the Schwabing district. An extraordinary historical moment had turned Munich into a European metropolis of culture that attracted writers and intellectuals from the four corners of the earth.[25]

They socialised with artists and acquired innovative works of art including a well-known watercolour by Franz Marc (they were on friendly terms with Marc's widow Maria). As the case of the photographer Germaine Krull illustrates, the line between the city's cultural and political scenes was fluid. She was one of Pollock's most important contacts in Munich. In her memoirs, Krull wrote that Pollock had become her lifelong 'big brother'. Pollock, conversely, considered himself 'a kind of father figure'.[26] Pollock and Horkheimer likely met Krull in the house of the psychiatrist and Communist sympath-

---

24 'An die Bevölkerung Münchens', *Münchener Neueste Nachrichten*, 71.564, 8 November 1918, p. 1, https://digipress.digitale-sammlungen.de/view/bsb00131382_00111_u001/1.
25 For a compelling account of Schwabing at the time, see Heißerer 2008.
26 Krull 2015, p. 80.

iser Dr. Wilhelm Maier in Schwabing's Georgenstraße.²⁷ Its bourgeois appearance notwithstanding, communists regularly gathered in Maier's residence where Krull, Pollock and Horkheimer were frequent guests. It was, however, Katja Walch-Lux who formally introduced them. Walch-Lux, who later converted to Judaism in protest against the ever more pervasive antisemitism, was a dance teacher whom Horkheimer bumped into by chance in a Schwabing bookstore. Close to the radical author and, at one point, chair of the Bavarian Independent Socialists (USPD), Ernst Toller, she was, at this time, Krull's best friend. In 1917, Krull established a studio on Schellingstraße where she produced portraits not only of Pollock but also of luminaries such as Thomas Mann, Kurt Eisner and Ricarda Huch. In addition to being a great artist – in the 1930s, Benjamin placed her on a par with August Sander – Krull was an eminently political individual deeply immersed in the activities of the radical left.²⁸

Lovingly called Zottel by her friends, Krull had seen some tough times. Her father left the family when she was fifteen. Her strict mother, who ran a guest house in Munich, showed her little love. When Krull fell pregnant at eighteen, her mother forced her to have an abortion. Her plan to leave home by going to university was thwarted by the fact that she lacked the requisite qualification for university admission. Hence, she applied to Munich's Teaching and Experimental Institute for Photography where her instructors were impressed by her extraordinary talent and enthusiasm for photography. With the support of her friends, she was eventually able to open her own studio. Not short on ambition, she wanted to be 'the queen' and make her studio 'the meeting place of all of Schwabing' – and various artists, writers and politicians did indeed come.²⁹ Here, Krull's friends 'Fritz and Max' met Else Eisner – the wife of the Bavarian Prime Minister Kurt Eisner – Communists such as Jakob Heck (b. 1898) and, according to Krull's recollection, the authors Stefan Zweig and Rainer Maria Rilke.³⁰

Pollock later claimed that he and Horkheimer considered the subsequent Soviet Republic a 'calamity' from the outset. According to Krull's memoirs, Pollock in particular argued that the time was not yet ripe for a communist revolution. This was a prevalent Social Democratic viewpoint in line with Karl

---

27 Staatsanwaltschaften 2296: trial of Anton Aschauer, witness statement Georg Embritzer, State Archive Munich.
28 Benjamin 1999, p. 526.
29 Sichel 1999, p. 17.
30 Sichel 1999, p. 16. On Heck, see Mallmann 1996, p. 110.

Kautsky's critique of the October Revolution.[31] Pollock had called the proclamation of the Soviet Republic 'totally idiotic' and wanted Toller to be 'arrested immediately'.[32] He saw that the communists lacked the support not only of the population at large but of the workers too and therefore feared a bloodbath. 'We attended all kinds of gatherings, I still remember how one speaker, his name was Unterleitner, said in one of the large assemblies that, if the government should send the Prussians, Bavaria would rise up united. They formed their own Freikorps.'[33] On balance, Pollock and Horkheimer nevertheless sided with the republic and accused the Social Democratic government that had retreated to Bamberg of lying. 'Don't believe the lies about Munich', Horkheimer wrote to Maidon Riekher on 19 April 1919, just twelve days after the proclamation of the Soviet Republic. 'The liars want to engage in murder – murder for money's sake; we are *not* in the grip of madness and injustice.'[34] While the two friends played no role in the short-lived Soviet Republic, they did feel an urgent desire 'to salvage what might be salvaged' once it had been quashed. This was the wellspring of their first foray into something resembling active political engagement.[35]

In May 1919, at the request of the Social Democratic Bavarian Prime Minister Johannes Hoffmann, whom the communists had chased out of Munich, the Social Democratic German defence minister Gustav Noske sent 30,000 regular and irregular Reichswehr soldiers – including the far-right Freikorps led by Franz von Epp and Ernst Röhm (the subsequent head of the SA) – to occupy Munich. Some of Pollock's new-found friends and acquaintances now had to fear for their lives. 'And now a "white terror" ensued such as no German city, not even Berlin in March, had yet experienced. For a whole week the conquerors were at liberty to shoot, and everyone "suspected of Spartacism" – in effect Munich's entire working-class population – was fair game.'[36] More than 600 actual or alleged communists were literally hunted down and murdered in the

---

31 Kautsky 1918.
32 Quoted in Krull 2015, p. 83.
33 Ernst von Schenck, interview with Pollock and Horkheimer, transcript, 1965/66, Horkheimer Archive, University Library Frankfurt/Main, MHA X 132a, p. 37. The speaker was likely Hans Unterleitner (1890–1971), an Independent Socialist who served as welfare minister under his father-in-law Kurt Eisner. Following the November Revolution, the central government in Berlin effectively had no significant security forces under its direct control and instead relied on the Freikorps ('Prussians') – counterrevolutionary militias consisting mainly of right-wing and far-right former Wehrmacht soldiers – to do its dirty work in quashing any further revolutionary endeavours.
34 Max Horkheimer to Rose Riekher, 19 April 1919, in Horkheimer 1995a, pp. 55–6, p. 55.
35 Ernst von Schenck, interview with Pollock and Horkheimer, transcript, 1965/66, Horkheimer Archive, University Library Frankfurt/Main, MHA X 132a, p. 37.
36 Haffner 1972, p. 175 (translation amended).

streets, thousands were arrested and tortured. 'The White troops marched into Munich', Krull later recalled.

> From the window of Max and Fritz's flat we saw the red flags burning. Then they were replaced by the blue-and-white Bavarian flag. They were patrolling the streets, everywhere there were arrested workers with their hands tied behind their heads. The Whites were determined to find the ringleaders responsible for Toller's folly – at any price. Having failed to detect even one, they decided to go district by district, beginning with the working-class quarters. None of the leaders were found. A sense of fear and torment prevailed. I stayed with Max and Fritz since they lived in a distinctly bourgeois area where it was less dangerous than it would have been in my studio in Schwabing.[37]

Travelling by train to Garmisch, Max Horkheimer found himself in the Whites' crosshairs when Freikorps fighters assumed he was Ernst Toller and arrested him. Given Toller's prominent role in the Soviet Republic, a reward of 10,000 Reichsmark had been offered for his arrest. Following the brutal execution of Gustav Landauer, the Whites were frantically searching for Toller in order to make an example of him too. Horkheimer was able to convince his captors that he was not Toller and they sent him back to Munich where, on arrival, he was detained and accused of being Toller yet again. 'We arrived in the evening', Horkheimer later recalled, 'where I was taken to a military arrest facility in the station where the officer explained that these two [Freikorps] hussars would take me somewhere in town. Night had fallen in the meantime and now I was afraid; I did not want to be "shot while trying to abscond", as the saying went.'[38] Fortunately, this did not happen, but the experience certainly put the fear of God in Horkheimer.

Pollock and Horkheimer witnessed at close quarters of what the soldiers and paramilitary forces – some of whom were already strutting around with swastikas on their helmets – were capable. Soon after Horkheimer's close shave with the Freikorps, one of their acquaintances was killed during a shootout on Odeon Square. They also offered a fugitive they knew, Elia Pupko, refuge in their flat for a night, claiming that he was Pollock's brother although 'he barely spoke German and had a thick Eastern accent'.[39] Pupko, who originally came from

---

37 Krull 2015, p. 83.
38 Horkheimer 1985f, p. 447.
39 Ernst von Schenck, interview with Pollock and Horkheimer, transcript, 1965/66, Horkheimer Archive, University Library Frankfurt/Main, MHA X 132a, p. 32.

the Russian city of Lida (now in Belarus) and read philosophy in Munich, was a close associate of the head of the Soviet Republic, Eugen Leviné, who was executed on 5 June 1919.[40] Communist circles began to take note of Pollock as someone with a talent for clandestine transactions who 'always knows all the political gossip' but of whom, alas, one was never quite certain 'on which side he stood'.[41]

Pollock and Horkheimer also supported Tobias Akselrod, the former Bundist and now director of the Bolshevik Russian government's press operations in Germany who served as deputy finance commissioner in the Bavarian Soviet government, hiding him in their flat for several days. When the situation became increasingly critical, Krull asked Pollock to let Akselrod use his papers to flee the country. Krull and Akselrod, along with Willi Budich, who had also been a member of the Soviet Executive in Munich (he went on to serve as a high-ranking KPD official), left Munich in the dead of night, intending to cross the Tyrolian Alps into Austria.[42] On the evening of 10 May 1919, they reached Eben am Achensee where they took rooms in the Pletzachalm Inn. Yet, eavesdropping on her guests, the landlady heard them talk about Munich. In addition, they had conversed partly in Russian, which made her all the more suspicious.

> She therefore informed the gendarmerie post in Pertisau of her suspicions, whereupon the gendarmes brought the two suspects to this station. The lady had supposedly travelled to Innsbruck to acquire a change of clothes. One of the gentlemen called himself Friedrich Polloch, claiming to be a businessman from Munich and in charge. He had on him a residential registration issued by the municipal authorities in Munich, stating that he was born in Freiburg (Baden) on 22 May 1894; he was carrying 2,000 Marks and 25 Crowns. ... Since the authenticity of the documents was in question and they had none of the entry documents currently required, it was decided, in accordance with the directives issued by the district authorities in Schwaz ... to send them back across the border.[43]

---

40 Ludwig Maximilian University Munich, Central Archive, Personenstandsregister winter 1918/1919, p. 128.
41 Staatsanwaltschaften 1939: trial of Tobias Akselrod, Hans Kain to Anton Aschauer, 1 August 1919, State Archive Munich.
42 For accounts of the flight, see Krull 2015, pp. 86–92; Vatlin 2014 does not mention Pollock. On Akselrod's role in the Soviet Republic, see Brenner 2022.
43 Staatsanwaltschaften 1939: trial of Tobias Akselrod, Res. no. 11, 'Axelrod und Genossen, Spartakist, Aufgreifung', 16 May 1919, State Archive Munich.

One can imagine the refugees' panic at this point, given that Akselrod and Budich were charged with treason and likely faced the death penalty should they be forced to return to Bavaria. With little to lose, they decided that attack was likely the best form of defence: 'When they were informed about this decision, Polloch claimed that he was a foreign agent and had information of great importance to the Austr. state. He would divulge this information only to an Austr. government official, however, and demanded to meet one.'[44] While the request was denied, the detainees were given permission to send several telegrams requesting a diplomatic intervention. One of them went to the Austrian foreign minister, the Austro-Marxist Otto Bauer, another to the Hungarian embassy in Vienna, explicitly asking for a radiogram to be sent to Moscow. Admitting that the documents he had provided were false, Akselrod signed this latter telegram with his actual name.

Eventually, the three detainees really were deported and taken back to Munich. Akselrod was court-martialled and sentenced to fifteen years penitentiary. Horkheimer and Pollock followed his case closely. They turned to various associates, including commercial contacts, to mobilise support. Eventually, the Russian government intervened on behalf of its 'diplomat', and Akselrod was able to return to Petrograd, where he took up work for the Communist International. Germaine Krull and her fiancé, the Ukrainian Communist Samuel 'Mila' Levit, soon joined him. His direct involvement in Akselrod's abortive attempt to escape notwithstanding, there is nothing in the relevant police files to suggest that Pollock was ever questioned about this episode.[45] Perhaps, like many who tried to help those who needed to flee at the time, he had simply reported his passport stolen.

This unrelenting succession of dramatic events forced the two friends to abandon what remained of their inward-looking adolescent mindset. Their support for the persecuted revolutionaries was motivated by a new-found political consciousness born of the upheaval in Munich. To be sure, they had previously adopted Schopenhauer's normative concept of compassion and were in thrall to the principle of human solidarity, but only now did society come into focus as a category worthy of examination in its own right. Their turn to the social sciences, in the widest sense of the word, followed directly from their novel experiences in Munich. As Horkheimer later recalled, they had 'come to know the bohemian scene in Schwabing and eventually I thought: well, would it

---

44 Ibid.
45 Neither the institutional nor the individual Freikorps or police records held by the War Archive of the State Archive Munich contain any references to Pollock.

not be a good idea to go to university. Humankind is an odd sort of community, after all, and I ought to know more about it and the world at large.'[46]

In the summer semester they enrolled at the University of Munich, Pollock to study what would today be called political studies (*Staatswissenschaft*, literally: science of the state) and Horkheimer to read philosophy.[47] Pollock's urging notwithstanding, Horkheimer was not overly conscientious when it came to attending lectures and seminars, and Pollock was by far the more diligent student. He took a broad range of courses, from economics, politics and history to philosophy and sociology. He listened attentively as the great sociologist Max Weber – whose sociology remained a lifelong point of reference for Pollock – lectured on 'The Basic Concepts of Social Knowledge'. Walther Lotz, a liberal economist interested in social questions, introduced him to another topic he would come back to time and again: 'The Theory of Money and the Currency Question. Banking, Stock Exchanges, Trade and Exchange Policies'. The statistics lectures by Georg von Mayr, an ultra-conservative economist who was the university's vice chancellor at the time, while altogether less inspiring, later stood Pollock in good stead, not least when it came to the empirical studies undertaken by the Institute of Social Research. He also attended a seminar on the history of the newspaper offered by Sebastian Hausmann, a professorial teaching fellow in political studies who focussed principally on historical topics. He accompanied Horkheimer to the survey lecture course on 'modern philosophy' offered by Clemens Baeumker who was essentially a medievalist and, in 1916, had published a widely acclaimed monograph on Roger Bacon. Horkheimer, in turn, joined his friend on a survey course on the political foundations of the state given by Karl Rothenbücher, a liberal Catholic and expert on state and canon law. Finally, Pollock also attended Konrad Cosack's lecture course on 'The Socialisation of Civil Law as a Result of the Revolution'.[48] It is tempting to interpret this diversity of subjects as a precursor of Critical Theory's emphatic crossdisciplinarity, but it may also reflect no more than a yearning for intellectual orientation.

It is important to note that Pollock's budding interest in social theory was not limited to the academic sphere. He was an avid reader of Franz Pfemfert's expressionist-libertarian cultural journal *Aktion* and, especially, of *Die*

---

46 Horkheimer 1985f, p. 446.
47 Belegblatt 4° H. lit. 2858, University Archive, Munich.
48 Ludwig Maximilian University Munich, Central Archive, Fritz Pollock's index card for the summer semester of 1919; Ludwig Maximilian University Munich, *Verzeichnis der Vorlesungen Sommer-Halbjahr 1919*, https://epub.ub.uni-muenchen.de/1151/1/vvz_lmu_1919_sose.pdf.

Rote Fahne (The Red Flag).[49] His appetite for Marxist theory had been whet yet he soon found the Communist propaganda he encountered too superficial and simplistic. Consequently, he turned to the original sources: Marx's *Capital*, Engels's *Anti-Dühring* and Lenin's *State and Revolution*. Horkheimer initially took a more skeptical approach but, in August 1919, in light of Pollock's sustained preoccupation with Marxism, they read Nikolai Bukharin's *Programme of the World Revolution* together and it greatly impressed Horkheimer.[50] 'Rather than fight for "democracy"', Bukharin clarified in his preface to the Hungarian edition (which was included, in translation, in the German version), 'we proclaim the class dictatorship of the proletariat. Rather than engage in piecemeal reform, we turn the entire capitalist economic order on its head.'[51] This would ultimately lead to the 'abolition of the money system'. 'Society is being transformed into one huge labor organization or company to produce and distribute what is already produced without the agency of gold coinage or paper money. The end of the power of money is imminent.'[52]

Pollock and Horkheimer were enthralled with the radicality of Bukharin's demands. That a world in which the imperialist powers could wage wars that cost millions their lives, in which the proletarian masses were enslaved by wage labour and the accumulation of capital trumped all other concerns needed to be comprehensively transformed instantly resonated with them. For them, the massacres in Munich were a palpable reflection of the class struggle, and they were only too familiar, of course, with the hardship faced by the working class. They had long detested their parents' single-minded preoccupation with the extraction of profit but now recognised that it was an expression not of materialism per se but of bourgeois class interest. Passages such as the following must have taken the words right out of their mouths:

> The rich classes who even now have an abundance of money can live at their ease. In towns, traders, merchants, capitalists and speculators: in the country the 'kulaks' (rich peasants), the sharks and sweaters who have fattened on the war to an incredible degree, having saved hundreds of thousands of roubles. Things have reached such a pitch that some buried their money in the ground in boxes or glass jars.[53]

---

49 Die *Rote Fahne* was established on 9 November 1918 when the Spartacus League occupied the premises of the *Berliner Lokal-Anzeiger*. When the KPD was formed on 31 December, it adopted the paper as its flagship periodical.
50 Max Horkheimer to Rose Riekher, 14 July 1920, in Horkheimer 1995a, pp. 57–61, p. 60.
51 Bukharin 1918, [p. i].
52 Bukharin, 1920, p. 70.
53 Bukharin 1920, p. 66.

Pollock's father too owed his wealth to the war. Now that Marxism had opened his eyes, he despised his father even more than before. For all his faith in the utopian project of his friendship with Horkheimer as a foreshadowing of the good life, he sensed that they could not proceed in isolation from society. The world was in urgent need of change and, as the failed revolution had just shown, one first needed really to understand it to bring about that change. Horkheimer and Pollock therefore decided to move to the calmer city of Frankfurt where it would be easier to concentrate on their studies.

CHAPTER 4

'Scientific' Marxism

Following all the excitement they had encountered in Munich, the two friends were yearning for calm and keen to find their bearings again. They stayed at the Oranien guest house in the Westend for several weeks and then bought a house in nearby Kronberg im Taunus. They had borrowed most of the requisite funds from Pollock's parents and his brother Hans who was now a co-signatory in the family business. In addition, they sold the works by Franz Marc, Paul Klee and Marc Chagall they had acquired in Munich at a profit. The return is likely to have been relatively modest but at least it gave them the sense that they were not entirely dependent on family money, given that, for them, it embodied oppression and exploitation.

While their new domicile allowed them to revive the *île heureuse*, in the event, Maidon Riekher only moved in with them in the winter of 1921 because Pollock and Horkheimer decided to spend the summer semester of 1920 and the winter semester of 1920/21 at Freiburg university where Horkheimer was keen to attend the lectures of the great phenomenologist Edmund Husserl.[1] The seminar of Husserl's assistant Heidegger, which they also attended, evidently made no lasting impression on Pollock who was enrolled in the legal and political studies faculty. Apart from occasionally going to Heidegger's seminar and attending Husserl's lectures, he studied political economy with Karl Diehl and Robert Liefmann.

Back in Frankfurt, they were finally able to establish their triple alliance with Maidon. This constellation differed from that in London, however, since Maidon, in contrast to Neumeier, was unambiguously Horkheimer's partner while Pollock was best friends with both of them. Writing to her in April 1921, when she was still in Stuttgart, he called her 'the most enviable of women' – enviable because she was in a relationship with his best friend.[2] Even so, he signed the letter 'Yours (in part) – F.' That Pollock loved her, even though a

---

[1] See Studien- und Sittenzeugnis, Friedrich Pollock, 6 September 1921. University Archive Freiburg/Breisgau, B 44/51/655. In Germany, it used to be common practice for students to move around in order not to limit themselves to the expertise available at just one university.

[2] Friedrich Pollock to Rose Riekher, 21 April 1921, Horkheimer Archive, University Library Frankfurt/Main, MHA VI 30, 448.

sexual relationship between them was inconceivable, is also demonstrated by another letter from this time, which he signed 'Yours with krisses – Friedrich'.[3] Next to the misspelt word krisses – a combination of greetings and kisses – he scribbled in pencil: 'Freud???' This was not a conventional *ménage à trois*, then. Moreover, while Maidon henceforth played an integral role in Pollock and Horkheimer's life, she was neither admitted to their covenant nor party to the decision-making process when it came to the realisation of its ideals.

Pollock enthusiastically embraced his studies in economics but found the introductory lectures by the classical economist Paul Arndt rather disappointing. Franz Oppenheimer and Adolf Weber, despite neither of them being well-versed in Marxist theory, were more to his liking. Oppenheimer – an impassioned Zionist – was an expert in economic theory whose broad knowledge and grasp of historical context attracted the brightest students. His portfolio included lectures on the history of socialism. Two of his assistants later became collaborators in the context of the Institute of Social Research: the Marxist theoretician Fritz Sternberg and the psychologist Kurt Goldstein. Horkheimer's aforementioned school friend Adolph Löwe – who later worked closely with the institute – and the theologian Paul Tillich – one of Pollock's closest friends in the United States – had studied with Oppenheimer when he was still in Berlin. Beginning in 1922, one Theodor Wiesengrund was also among his students.

As an 'avowed theoretician and universalist', Oppenheimer cut a distinct figure among his colleagues.[4] The University of Frankfurt grew out of the Senckenberg Institutes and the city's commercial academy and it was still 'strongly oriented towards the training of practical commercial skills', as Oppenheimer recalled in his memoirs. Indeed, a large part of the student body 'intended to enter a commercial or some other practical profession as soon as they graduated'.[5] *Prima facie*, even Pollock and Horkheimer matched this profile. Yet they were only keeping up appearances to assuage their parents. Not that either of them knew what they wanted to do after graduation. Occasionally, Pollock contemplated taking the easy path his father had paved for him after all. Even so, they certainly did not organise their studies in a way that would have equipped them with the practical skills required to go straight into the private sector after graduation.

---

3   Friedrich Pollock to Rose Riekher, 15 April 1921, Horkheimer Archive, University Library Frankfurt/Main, MHA VI 30, 447.
4   Oppenheimer 1964, p. 252.
5   Ibid.

In contrast to Oppenheimer, Adolf Weber (not to be confused with the sociologist Alfred Weber), who soon left Frankfurt again, was an adherent of economic liberalism and unambiguous opponent of socialism. His vantage was frequently shaped by Max Weber's sociology, however, and he was interested in welfare issues, the social problems of large urban centres and the history of labour relations.[6] Pollock's main reservation regarding Weber was that he proposed no remedies for the problems he identified. In this respect, he found the Marxist authors whose works he had begun to read in Munich much more compelling. Yet Marx, let alone Lenin or Rosa Luxemburg, were not taught at the University of Frankfurt.

In the winter semester 1921/22 a new academic popped up in the course register who became an important point of reference for Pollock: Siegfried Budge. A nephew of one of the Jewish patrons of the university, Henry Budge, he had just completed his postdoctoral qualification under Oppenheimer's supervision and offered two tutorials on Marx and one on the classical economist David Ricardo.[7] His core specialism was monetary theory from Turgot to Ricardo and Marx, and Pollock became his star student. It was not long before the plan emerged for Pollock to write a doctoral thesis on Marx's concept of money under Budge's supervision. This project led Pollock into the inner sanctum of political economy. Alongside Oppenheimer's works and those of Joseph Schumpeter he closely studied Rathenau's lecture on production policy of October 1920;[8] the first volume of Böhm-Bawerk's *Kapital und Kapitalzins* (Capital and Interest, first published in 1884);[9] the first volume of Karl Diehl's *Theoretische Nationalökonomie* (Theoretical Economics, 1916);[10] Friedrich Julius Neumann's important essay, 'Wirtschaftliche Gesetze nach früherer und jetziger Auffassung' (The Past and Present Understanding of Economic Laws, 1898);[11] Heinrich Dietzel's classic, *Theoretische Socialökonomik* (Theoretical Socioeconomics, 1895)[12] – and he kept coming back to Marx's *Capital*.[13] In addi-

---

6 Weber 1907; Weber 1908; Weber 1910.
7 *Vorlesungsverzeichnis der Universität Frankfurt a. M.: Winterhalbjahr 1921/22*, https://publikationen.ub.uni-frankfurt.de/opus4/frontdoor/deliver/index/docId/11222/file/1921_wv.pdf, p. 44.
8 Rathenau 1921.
9 Böhm-Bawerk 1884; Böhm-Bawerk, 1890.
10 Diehl 1916.
11 Neumann 1898.
12 Dietzel 1895.
13 See the notebook, 'Extracta zu Marx IV' (1921), Horkheimer Archive, University Library Frankfurt/Main, MHA XXIV 1, 2.

tion, he read the leading Marxists of the age: Karl Kautsky, Rosa Luxemburg, Rudolf Hilferding and Lenin.[14]

On 15 March 1923, 'Fritz' Pollock was able to submit his thesis *Zur Geldtheorie von Karl Marx* (On Karl Marx's Monetary Theory) to the examination board of the economics and social sciences faculty.[15] At the same time, Horkheimer completed his thesis *Zur Antinomie der teleologischen Urteilskraft* (The Antinomy of Teleological Judgement) under the supervision of the Neo-Kantian philosopher Hans Cornelius. They both passed with top marks (*summa cum laude*). Pollock had originally intended to publish his thesis but another author working on a closely related topic had managed to bring his book out first and Pollock was forced to abandon his plan. Consequently, the typescript gathered dust in the university library and made no discernible impact. It does, however, offer an interesting indication of his scholarly preoccupations in the early 1920s and helps position him within the Weimar era left.

In his thesis, Pollock did more than offer a detailed reconstruction of the concept of money Marx developed in *Capital* and the *Grundrisse*. He engaged in the critique of ideology, a relatively new approach pioneered at the time by Isaac Rubin, Georg Lukács and Evgeny Pashukanis in writings not yet known to Pollock.[16] Like them, he sought to recover the critical potential of Marx's theory that had been submerged by Social Democratic dogmatism. Deemphasising the theories of revolution and class that were at the centre of orthodox Marxism, Pollock, Lukács, Rubin and Pashukanis placed Marx's concepts of ideology, reification and fetishism centre stage. In light of the failed revolutions of 1918/19, mechanisms of ideological delusion were an obvious focal point. Evidently, world revolution was not, as orthodox Marxism claimed, the necessary and inevitable product of the laws of history. That the revolution had failed even though not only intellectuals but sections of the proletariat too had supported it, needed to be explained and the critique of ideology in Marx's vein had the potential to do just that.

As Marx explained in the first volume of *Capital*, capitalism was a mode of production that concealed its true character. The workers were indeed exploited but the ideological mechanism of commodity fetishism prevented them from appreciating this. As early as 1902, in *What is to be Done?*, written in exile in Munich, Lenin had discussed why spontaneous labour movements invariably led to no more than 'mere trade-unionism', 'and trade-unionism

---

14   See the file with excerpts, Horkheimer Archive, University Library Frankfurt/Main, MHA XXIV 2.
15   Pollock 2018a.
16   Lukács 1971; Pashukanis 2002; Rubin 1973.

means the ideological enslavement of the workers by the bourgeoisie'.[17] This assumption led Lenin to believe that Communist parties needed to act as an avantgarde and assert the interests of the proletariat, if need be, in ways few proletarians would immediately understand or condone. Yet the anticipated world revolution had failed to materialise, forcing the regime in the nascent Soviet Union to resort to increasingly counter-intuitive and disconcerting measures to defend the revolution.

The KPD, controlled ever more closely by Moscow, held the SPD responsible for the failure of the revolution. As they saw it, the Social Democrats had betrayed the workers. Conversely, intellectuals critical of Moscow increasingly questioned Lenin's revolution theory.[18] Focussing on epistemological issues, Pollock doubtless belonged to the second group. The task of the scholar, he argued in his thesis, was to identify that which the seemingly obvious in fact covered up – for example, in the case of money, that it reflected not 'material realia', as the economist Walther Lotz, whose lectures Pollock had attended in Munich, claimed, but a social relationship.[19]

The distinction between essence and appearance also underpinned Pollock's materialist critique of the legal system. The exploitation of labour was 'concealed by bourgeois legal norms implying that human beings interact as free and independent subjects while obscuring the relations of dependence in the process of production'. Real-life individuals only ever witnessed various forms of competition and one could not possibly gain any genuine 'insights into the structure of the social reproduction process' simply by describing the legal forms that facilitated capitalist exploitation on their own terms.[20] Individuals only ever judged the daily cut and thrust in terms of the categories right and wrong. Individual conduct under the condition of competition was thus reduced to a moral issue, making it impossible to appreciate the significance of the overarching economic framework structuring social relations. The key to understanding society lay not in the legal and moral assessment of the consequences of competition but in the analysis of its economic foundations.

Pollock sought to implement this agenda in two ways: firstly, by reconstructing Marx's theory of capitalism and, secondly, with a critique of contemporaneous scholars of political economy. He rejected the prevalent uncritical characterisation of money as simply a neutral means of payment. It was in fact an expression of systematic exploitation, he insisted. To be sure, exploitation too is

---

17 Lenin 1960, p. 384.
18 Anderson 1976, pp. 29–33.
19 Pollock 2018b, p. 34.
20 Ibid.

a moral category, but Pollock sought to characterise it in 'scientific' terms.[21] The fundamental principle of capitalist exploitation, he explained, was that workers provided more labour than absolutely necessary, indirectly robbing them of part of their lifespan. In theory, workers' wages covered all they needed to sustain themselves, yet this did not change the fact that they produced more goods than they would need to turn out in order to cover their own needs. In short, the workers were constantly rendering surplus labour that exclusively benefitted the capitalist.

A fictitious pre-capitalist model illustrates what for Pollock was the crux of the matter. We spend four hours a day growing turnips and potatoes but do not farm the large meadow next to the field because we are easily able to make ends meet with the harvest we have. Then someone convinces us not to while away half the day and instead use all our assets to maximise our turnip and potato harvest. We now work eight hours a day and harvest twice as many vegetables. Since our own consumption has not increased, we barter the surplus to obtain, say, a new table or a beautiful vase. Yet then, our small enterprise confronts its first crisis, because the farmer next door is willing to barter more turnips for a beautiful vase. The turnips it has taken so much effort to grow now perish because no one wants them. For the length of a season, we have wasted four hours a day for absolutely nothing – when we could have spent that time reading a good book or, as Adorno later put it, 'lying on the water and looking peacefully at the sky'.[22]

In this simplistic, purely illustrative example, no great harm is done. We can simply go back to only working four hours a day and producing no more than we need ourselves. In a world that is profoundly shaped by a complex division of labour and in which few people own their own field or factory, the problem becomes altogether more serious. Where most are forced to make a living

---

21 The German term *Wissenschaft* encompasses both the STEM disciplines and the Arts and Humanities. Hence, ethnomusicologists and historians of the medieval book are considered 'scientists' in the same way as nuclear physicists or evolutionary biologists, which obviously does not correspond to standard Anglophone usage. In the Arts and Humanities, it is therefore generally more appropriate to translate the term as scholarship. The case of 'scientific' Marxism is more complex, however, insofar as Marxists consciously adopted the label scientific precisely to indicate that, as they saw it, Marxism was no less of an exact and reliable science than any of the STEM subjects (how exact and reliable they themselves really are is, of course, another matter altogether). A similar conceit presumably underpins the term social sciences. The inverted commas ('scientific' Marxism) are designed to mediate between this conceit and what tends to be familiar to Anglophone readers.

22 Adorno 2005, p. 157.

by working for others, those for whom they work dictate the conditions. Within the constraints of the law, the capitalist sets the working hours and ensures that the workers produce a sufficient surplus during those hours. In order to guarantee that he gets his money's worth from the labour he buys the capitalist imposes a regime of obedience and discipline. The workers' fortunes, meanwhile, may fluctuate but ultimately, their status is always precarious, and they constantly face the threat of poverty and destitution should they not be productive enough. All they can do is join forces with their peers to try and attain better working conditions. To this end, they can pursue one of two options. They can join the *revolutionary* struggle that seeks to subvert the very principle of wage labour and takes issue with the private ownership of the means of production (factories, land etc.); or they can support a *reformist* approach that does not question that principle and, instead, reflects moral concerns about insufficient wage levels and excessive working hours.

Arguing from a scholarly point of view and without drawing any immediate political conclusions from his analysis, Pollock inclined towards the revolutionary response. As he saw it, the reformist approach was based on a fundamental fallacy. What was exploitative was not the fact that wages were too low, but the fact that capitalism was predicated, as a matter of principle, on the extraction of surplus labour, i.e., on workers rendering more labour than was 'objectively' necessary to sustain them. The capitalists, as the sole owners of the means of production, claimed to be engaging in a fair exchange when in fact they were stealing the workers' time. In short, when it came to wage labour, the reformists failed to discern the distinction between essence and appearance. In purely formal terms, the employment contract did seem to codify a fair exchange. Paid for their labour, workers were able to spend their wages as they saw fit. Yet on closer inspection it transpired that for the workers, the exchange was only ever a zero-sum game. While the capitalist profited from the surplus labour, wages never did more than replenish what the workers needed to sustain themselves. Just how much that was depended on the state of the class struggle. Consequently, the workers would never be able to rise above their inferior position and always continued to be dependent on the capitalist – unless they were able to take control of the means of production.

The class struggle as the trade unions and reformist Social Democrats pursued it, primarily as a matter of appropriate wage levels, was of little interest to Pollock. On the one hand, it reminded him of the wage bargaining he had encountered in the hated family business, on the other, his big-picture identification with the proletariat did not stretch this far. This did not register with him as a lack of empathy, for him it was simply a mark of the radicality of his position. Ultimately, his fundamental question was how a barter economy could systematically produce inequality, and he saw the key to answering it in Marx's concept of money. The entire extensive and intricate process of commodity exchange, Pollock argued, transpired through money in the form of wages and payments for machines, factories, storage facilities and commodities.

Not that Pollock was in any way inclined to acknowledge the demonisation of money as a valid critique of capitalism. Its specific function in capitalism 'already presupposes the capital relation'.[23] The systematic, state-driven expropriation of small leaseholders in early modern England was a case in point. It proletarianised the former leaseholders and helped precipitate the creation of two clearly distinguishable classes: those who own the means of production and the proletarians who own nothing but their labour. Above both stood the state. It ensured that the capital relation was maintained. Pollock was one of the first explicitly to make the point that the emergence of money could not be explained simply in terms of an evolving barter economy and system of payment in kind; it was intrinsically dependent on what Marx called 'state compulsion'.[24] Whoever is not willing to talk about the state should also keep quiet about money.

In his discussion of international money transfers, Pollock again pointed to the fact that the value of currency depended on state coercion. 'The state's power to render relatively "worthless" objects legally valid tender too', he noted, 'ceases at its borders'.[25] The state can determine what qualifies as money only for the territory it controls. Pollock thus rejected liberal theories maintaining that money had simply emerged as a rational means of exchange and that the state merely functioned as the proverbial nightwatchman who guaranteed that all parties stuck to the rules supposedly agreed in some mythical primeval past. Pollock might have identified this notion of a social contract, developed by Thomas Hobbes in the seventeenth century at the beginning of the bourgeois age, as a necessary illusion indispensable to the capitalist order, i.e., a form of bourgeois ideology, yet this is not a line of argument he developed. The relish with which he mocked the bourgeois economists who ignored all relations of force and compulsion in the economic sphere to paint a picture of harmony and consensus demonstrates how critical he had become of conventional political economy.

Pollock also touched on crisis theory in his thesis, an issue that continued to preoccupy him for decades. Following Marx, he defined capitalist crises in

---

23   Pollock 2018b, p. 89.
24   Marx 2010a, p. 139 (translation amended); Pollock 2018b, p. 85, n52.
25   Pollock 2018b, p. 87.

terms of the existence of an 'abundance of commodities that no one wants to buy'.[26] Ordinarily it then seemed as though the crisis were caused by a lack of disposable funds. Consequently, the state responded by printing more money which, in turn, led to inflation. It should be borne in mind that Pollock wrote his thesis against the backdrop of steadily mounting inflationary pressures in Germany and completed it just as the hyperinflation of 1923 began to gather pace. Sounding more like an adviser than a critic of the government, Pollock pointed to the wrongheadedness of printing ever more unsupported paper money. It would be much better to bring in 'a boatload of gold' because what was lacking was not tender per se but sufficient means of payment (in the specific Marxian sense of the term). Pollock's prescription was not that far removed from the measures eventually taken to bring the crisis under control. Alongside the securing of a range of international agreements that allowed the government to attract substantial American loans, it was the introduction of the Reichsmark, which was pegged to the gold standard, that temporarily stabilised the situation, paving the way for the so-called Golden Twenties, even if the years of relative stability from 1924 to 1928 no longer look all that golden with the benefit of hindsight.[27]

Other topics discussed by Pollock in his thesis included the nexus between the amount of money in circulation and the prices of commodities, the velocity of money and 'the fate of money that is surplus to requirement in the sphere of circulation'.[28] His principal achievement, however, lay in his reconstruction of Marx's theories of money and value and the methodological and epistemological questions they raised. His study created a crucial foundation for the Marx reception of the Frankfurt School and in the Institute of Social Research, he was rightly considered the in-house expert for the critique of political economy. When Hans-Georg Backhaus, who studied at the institute in Frankfurt in the 1960s and one day, to his great surprise, found a first edition of Marx's *Capital* in the library of his halls of residence, had questions about Marx's theory of value, Horkheimer and Adorno promptly sent him to Pollock as the obvious expert in such matters.[29]

Given that it was not published, the scholarly reception of Pollock's thesis was virtually non-existent. It may well have been known in Marxist and communist circles, however. One way or another, Pollock soon enjoyed a reputation for being intimately familiar with Marx's thought. In his first year at Frankfurt,

---

26 Pollock 2018b, p. 90.
27 See Schulz 1987, pp. 68–78.
28 Pollock 2018b, p. 95.
29 Backhaus 1997, pp. 29–30.

he had befriended his fellow student Felix José Weil (1898–1975), the son of the German-Jewish wheat trader Hermann Weil whose business in Buenos Aires had made him a millionaire several times over. His father had sent him to Frankfurt when he was nine to ensure that he received a solid education and benefitted from sound commercial training.[30] Having gained the requisite qualification to enter higher education, Felix Weil, who, as an Argentine citizen, was not called up during the war, had gone straight on to study political economy. The revolutionary turmoil of 1918/19 also affected Frankfurt and, as an enthusiastic supporter of the insurgents, he found himself, though more by accident than by design, defending one of their positions with a weapon in his hand. In the summer semester of 1919, following the failure of the revolution, he switched to the University of Tübingen to study with the Marxist Robert Wilbrandt who eventually suggested he develop one of his seminar papers into a doctoral thesis. Alas, his political record got in the way of this plan when, in October 1919, Weil was temporarily detained and then expelled from the province of Württemberg (where Tübingen was located). He returned to Frankfurt where he did then embark on a doctorate. His thesis, *Sozialisierung: Versuch einer begrifflichen Grundlegung nebst einer Kritik der Sozialisierungspläne* (Socialisation: Towards a Conceptual Foundation for, and Critique of, the Socialisation Plans), supervised by Adolf Weber, was eventually published in a series edited by the ultraleft communist theoretician and activist Karl Korsch.[31] During the November Revolution, the Council of People's Commissioners, dominated by the Social Democrats, had appointed a socialisation commission chaired by Karl Kautsky and tasked with the nationalisation of certain industries.[32] As well as Weil's former teacher Wilbrandt, it assembled some of the most prominent economists of the age – including Joseph Schumpeter, Emil Lederer, Max Weber and Rudolf Hilferding – to debate relevant ways and means. Politicians and industrialists, including Walther Rathenau, weighed in on the debate, as did the far right which supported certain forms of nationalisation. Weil was the first to review and systematise the debate and offer a clear outline of the diverging concepts.

Weil had noticed Pollock and Horkheimer because they were the only students in the seminars who openly articulated socialist positions. The three of them became friends, went on to spend a great deal of time in each other's company and started making plans together. Weil maintained relations to various

---

30   Felix Weil, 'Erinnerungen (Fragment)', Institute for the History of Frankfurt, S 5/421, pp. 20–1.
31   Weil 1921.
32   Behrend 1998.

prominent Marxist intellectuals and readily introduced Pollock to them. It is unclear whether Pollock knew that Weil had started working as an informer – codename Lucio or Beatus Lucio – for the Communist International in Buenos Aires in 1921 and submitted numerous reports on the Argentinian left that went straight to Lenin's right-hand man Grigori Zinoviev.[33] Not that it would have drawn his friendship with Weil into question if he had known. Far from it. Pollock had big plans, and Weil's connections and his financial resources were most welcome.

Weil had been contemplating the possibility of using his father's money and the funds he had inherited from his mother (who died young) to create a Marxist institute to explore and promote socialism on a scholarly basis and unconstrained by party-political dogmatism.[34] With the input of Kurt Albert Gerlach, a professor of economics with anarchist leanings and former member of the Independent Socialists who had just moved from Aachen to Frankfurt, the plan was now revived. Unclear about how exactly to go about implementing it, the initial brainstorming took place on a park bench close to Pollock and Horkheimer's house in Kronberg.[35] What then really set the process in motion were the plans of Karl Korsch, who held a precarious position at the University of Jena at the time, to convene a conference on 'scientific' Marxism.

Pollock and Weil enthusiastically welcomed Korsch's initiative, envisaging the conference as their institute's inaugural event. The friends turned to Hermann Weil, who was seriously ill and had returned to Frankfurt, asking him to fund both the conference and their planned institute for which Pollock suggested the innocuous name Institute of Social Research. Hermann Weil had for some time been concerned about the growing virulence of antisemitism in Germany and thus they included research on antisemitism in the prospective institute's mission statement.[36] Motivated not least by the hope that his patronage might earn him an honorary doctorate from Frankfurt University, Hermann Weil agreed to fund the construction of the institute building and provide an annual subsidy of 120,000 Reichsmarks (a modest amount by his standards). In addition, he promised to endow a chair for social philosophy at the university to be held ex officio by the institute's director, thus creating a firm link between the institute and the university. On 1 November 1922, Felix Weil and Friedrich Pollock established the Society of Social Research. Hermann Weil was the notional chair, Felix Weil his deputy.

---

33 Heufelder 2017, pp. 36–7.
34 Walter-Busch 2010, pp. 16–17.
35 Herhaus 1970, p. 42.
36 See Claussen 2008, p. 80.

Gerlach unexpectedly died of diabetes before he could take up the position of academic director. The acclaimed Engels biographer Gustav Mayer, who held a personal chair in the history of democracy and socialism in Berlin, proved too much of a diva and presumably never seriously contemplated giving up the position he had finally secured in Berlin after the war.[37] In the end, Carl Grünberg was appointed as the institute's first director. He previously held the chair in political economy at the University of Vienna, edited the *Archiv für die Geschichte des Sozialismus und der Arbeiterbewegung* (Archive for the History of Socialism and the Labour Movement, generally known simply as Grünberg's *Archiv*), and was well respected in Marxist circles. He was known as a congenial scholar primarily interested in historical and sociological issues rather than Marxist theory. An avowed Marxist, he kept his distance from the Communist party and seemed the ideal director for a pluralist and non-dogmatic Marxist institute.[38]

The institute would have its own building and be academically independent, its affiliation with the university notwithstanding. Arthur Oppenheimer, a notary and business associate of Hermann Weil, led the negotiations with the university. There was, after all, a substantial amount of money and the endowment of an externally funded chair at stake. There were politically motivated reservations on the part of the university, but the negotiations were successfully completed all the same. On 3 February 1923, the institute was officially established; construction work on its purpose-built premises on Viktoria-Allee, close to the university, began a month later.

In the meantime, preparations for an eight-day conference directed by Korsch and Weil, the First Marxist Study Week – which took place in May 1923 – were rapidly advancing.[39] Twenty young Communists gathered in a station hotel in Geraberg (Thuringia) to discuss the ongoing social crisis in the Weimar Republic and a range of research questions and methodological issues relating to 'scientific' Marxism. Korsch and Weil had asked Richard Sorge – Gerlach's former assistant and a member of the KPD – to select the participants. Illustrious figures such as Georg Lukács, Karl August Wittfogel and Konstantin Zetkin (the son of the veteran Communist activist Clara Zetkin and erstwhile lover of Rosa Luxemburg) accepted his invitation.[40] Felix Weil's wife Käthe Weil, née Bachert, also took part.

---

37   See Prellwitz 1998, pp. 194–9.
38   Wiggershaus 1994a, pp. 36–40.
39   In the older literature it was occasionally suggested that the conference took place in 1922. The original invitation which Susanne Alexander found among her mother's papers has confirmed the correct date, however. Alexander 1985.
40   On the participants, see Buckmiller 1988.

The conference focussed on three main themes. Eduard Alexander, a lawyer who originally came from the Ruhr region and was, at the time, a municipal KPD deputy in Berlin (he was later elected to the Reichstag), ran the first section on ways of dealing with the current crisis – a topic Pollock had just treated in his thesis. Korsch and Lukács then led the discussion on Marxist methodology – here too Pollock was able to make a valuable contribution. The final section on organisational aspects of Marxist research was directed by the Hungarian philosopher and Communist Béla Fogarasi. The participants all considered the conference a great success – with one exception: Weil lamented that only intellectuals had taken part and that the gathering had rendered no practical results. He failed to appreciate what the conference had in fact achieved. Communist intellectuals, most of them party members, had gathered informally, unconstrained by party discipline, to discuss essential Marxist concerns. That Pollock and Weil took part, despite neither being nor intending to become party members, indicates just how fundamentally the gathering differed from leftist party congresses and propaganda events.

This was just the undogmatic, free-spirited approach in which Weil and Pollock wanted to shape the institute. The public inauguration ceremony took place on 22 June 1924. In his address, Carl Grünberg confirmed that the institute would be devoted above all to research. Teaching, by contrast, would be no more than an indulgence.[41] 'After the ceremony, while the last guests were still wandering around the building', Weil later recalled, 'Pollock and I walked up to the institute's notice board and attached the announcements of our first course':[42] 'Imperialism, run by Dr. Felix Weil'. The lead instructor was the aforementioned Fritz Sternberg, a member of the Zionist labour party Poale Zion who had worked as Franz Oppenheimer's assistant for three years before leaving the academy after a dispute with his mentor. He was an unaffiliated Marxist intellectual and later joined the German Socialist Workers' Party (SAPD) that split from the SPD in 1931 and called for a united front with the Communists to combat fascism. He fled Germany in March 1933, supporting resistance activities against the Nazis first from Czechoslovakia and then from Switzerland. In 1939, he was able to move to the USA where he regularly contributed to the institute's *Zeitschrift für Sozialforschung* (Studies in Philosophy and Social Science). In the 1920s, Sternberg was regularly involved in the institute's work and made quite an impression on the students. 'He was an unusually fat Jewish man with a mop of black curls, and he had really beautiful eyes', Nelly Held, one of

---

41 Grünberg 1924, p. 7.
42 Felix Weil, 'Erinnerungen (Fragment)', Institute for the History of Frankfurt, S 5/421, p. 173.

the institute's students at the time who regularly took part in Pollock's seminar, later recalled.[43] 'Fritz Sternberg was big fan of Rosa Luxemburg, whom Lenin and the party more generally had criticised for some of her theories. ... Fritz Sternberg wrote a big book, *Imperialism*, which I obviously read.'[44] His evolving conceptualisation of imperialism, eventually presented in this book, published in 1926 by Malik in Berlin, caused quite a stir among Marxists, and Weil ensured that it was discussed early on at the institute.[45]

The completion of his doctorate notwithstanding, Weil never really settled into academic life. Not least because of his father's illness, he vacillated between the family business and leftist patronage. He frequently travelled to Argentina, which was the focal point of his commercial activities, but his political activities were increasingly centred on Berlin. He was strongly invested in the reorganisation of the Malik publishing house under the commercial auspices of Julian Gumperz who later completed his doctorate under Pollock's supervision and worked for him at the institute. The publisher introduced the likes of Upton Sinclair, Leo Tolstoi and Maxim Gorki to the German public. Weil also generously supported George Grosz and other avantgarde artists.

Grünberg and Pollock, who was concerned with the institute's administration, were perfectly happy when Weil soon took an increasingly hands-off approach to its day-to-day running, his enthusiasm for the institute notwithstanding. This made it easier to shape the institute as they saw fit. In his memoirs, Weil later took issue with the contention that he had supported the institute only financially but not participated directly in its work. Yet the sources show just that. He stayed in touch but systematically wound down his active involvement, although he certainly continued to be consulted on crucial decisions. Pollock took charge of the administration and Grünberg determined the academic profile. The reliability of Weil's account is doubtful, then, which means that the following anecdote relating to the institute's inauguration too needs to be taken, at the very least, with a pinch of salt. According to Weil, Pollock asked him whether they should 'each inaugurate our offices too. I have a bottle of sparkling wine in my coat just in case'. Weil then looked at his watch and, seeing that it was only noon, insisted that 'one inaugurates an office by working in it'. 'Fine by me', Pollock had answered, and thus the institute's first working day began.[46]

---

43 Drechsler 1990, p. 31.
44 Ibid.
45 Sternberg 1926.
46 Felix Weil, 'Erinnerungen (Fragment)', Institute for the History of Frankfurt, S 5/421, p. 172.

Weil had just written his first official letter, expressing his gratitude to Erich Wende, an enormously helpful administrative official of the Prussian Ministry of Education, when there was a knock at his door.

> Three young men entered and introduced themselves. One of them was as political studies student, the other two were metal workers. They wanted to know how the admission to our tutorials and seminars worked.[47]

The first seminars offered by Carl Grünberg, Henryk Grossman and Karl Korsch were exceptionally well attended. 'When I think back to the institute's seminars between 1924 and 1929', Weil later reminisced,

> I remember one thing above all: the crowds. Far more students and workers wanted to attend than we were able to accommodate. They even came in droves from abroad. I still remember various Americans and especially an Indian, Manabendra Nath Roy, who later played a role in the Communist Party of his country.[48]

Pollock too was involved in teaching. His first institute-internal seminar dealt with 'The Problem of Workers' and Salaried Employees' Leisure Time'.[49] Yet his main role was managerial.

Teaching may have featured more prominently than Grünberg had envisaged, but research was nevertheless at the heart of the institute's work. To this end, not only offices but a reading room and an excellent library too were required. In close coordination with Grünberg, Pollock and Weil, Rose Schlesinger (who had married Karl August Wittfogel in 1921) built up a substantial library that comprised 42,000 books and subscriptions to 412 journals (123 of them from abroad) and 40 newspapers.[50] The library was run by a man called Huber. As well as Schlesinger, Richard Sorge's wife Christiane also worked in the library (until the couple, both of whom were Soviet spies, disappeared in October 1924), as did Siegfried Kracauer's future wife Lili Ehrenreich, Clara Mackauer and one Mrs. Weisser. That the employees in the library, except for the director, were all women while the academic staff consisted entirely of men

---

47 Felix Weil, 'Erinnerungen (Fragment)', Institute for the History of Frankfurt, S 5/421, p. 173 A.
48 Felix Weil, 'Erinnerungen (Fragment)', Institute for the History of Frankfurt, S 5/421, p. 173 C. Roy was a Comintern envoy to China and involved in the establishment of the Communist parties in India and Mexico. See Roy 1997.
49 International Institute of Social Research 1935, p. 12.
50 Felix Weil, 'Erinnerungen (Fragment)', Institute for the History of Frankfurt, S 5/421, p. 178.

was doubtless owed to the social and familial obstacles women who wanted to pursue an academic career still faced at this time. Yet it also speaks to the nonchalance with which our radical critics of society, now and in subsequent decades, continued to enjoy their patriarchal privileges. We may recall that Pollock and Horkheimer, as young adults, took it for granted that they would need to 'educate' their future wives. In this sense, it is no coincidence that the institute's senior academic positions were held exclusively by men, even as women became increasingly emancipated. Not that this was in any way unusual in the German academy in the first half of the twentieth century. Far from it. It was the norm.

As the case of Hilde Weiss demonstrates, female academics certainly did feature in the institute's work early on. She came to the institute in 1924 as a doctoral student working under Grünberg's supervision, left again following the completion of the doctorate but returned in 1930 as Pollock's research assistant.[51] It may be tempting to cite her example as evidence for the fact that the suitability of women for academic careers was never in doubt for Pollock and his colleagues. Alas, when Weiss later sought to rejoin the institute in exile she was rejected in no small measure on sexist grounds. In a letter to Horkheimer, Adorno pointed to her, as he saw it, unduly aggressive character. Pollock's no doubt well-meaning suggestion that she might work as a nanny until she found a suitable position likewise throws a shocking light on the critical theoreticians' concept of gender roles.[52] The institute was, from the outset, an essentially male domain.

The institute's five-storey building comprised eighteen offices, seminar rooms, the library with its own stacks and several guest rooms for doctoral students and fellows.[53] For an independent research institute, these were unusually generous facilities. Compared to similar institutions, such as the Forschungsinstitut für Sozialwissenschaften (Research Institute for the Social Sciences) that had recently opened in Cologne, the institute also employed a significant number of permanent staff and associates. As we saw, Pollock was the general manager. Grünberg had arranged for his former mentee and close friend Henryk Grossman, who was facing serious political persecution in Poland and urgently needed to leave the country, to join the institute. As a young activist, Grossman, who originally came from Cracow, had played a leading role in the Jewish Social Democratic Party of Galicia (ŻPS). The ŻPS was active in the part of Poland that came under Austrian control in the course of the Polish

---

51   See Weiss 2006, p. 107.
52   Ibid.
53   Pollock 1930, p. 353. See Voigt 2016.

Partitions and formed the counterpart to the better-known Bund, the General Jewish Labour Bund, which operated in the part of Poland under Russian control and in Russia itself. He subsequently acquired his postdoctoral qualification in Vienna where Grünberg was his mentor. Returning to Poland in 1921, he joined the Communist Party.[54] He was an expert on Marx's crisis theory but ultimately a relatively conventional Marxist and, in his book, *Das Akkumulations- und Zusammenbruchsgesetz des kapitalistischen Systems (Zugleich eine Krisentheorie)* (The Law of Accumulation and Breakdown of the Capitalist System, Being also a Theory of Crises) – published in 1929 as the first volume in the institute's book series – predicted the inevitable collapse of capitalism.[55]

In 1925, Karl August Wittfogel (who switched from the Independent Socialists to the KPD in 1920) took up a permanent position at the institute. Alongside his work for the institute, he was also involved in the Marxist Workers' Academy (Marxistische Arbeiterschule) established in Berlin in 1926 by Hermann Duncker, where Korsch also taught, and he co-edited its publication series jointly with Duncker and Alfons Goldschmidt. In addition to this core staff, numerous doctoral and postdoctoral scholars were fully integrated into, and in some cases funded by, the institute. Four of these scholars merit closer attention insofar as they became friends and colleagues who went on to play an important part in Pollock's life: Leo Löwenthal, Paul Massing, Kurt Mandelbaum and Julian Gumperz.

Löwenthal, a secondary school teacher by training, joined the institute in 1926 as a fellow working on a *Soziologie der deutschen Novelle im 19. Jahrhundert* (Sociology of the German Novella in the Nineteenth Century).[56] Born in Frankfurt in 1900 to a Jewish family (his father was a physician), he was initially a supporter of the labour Zionist cause. At the time, he was closely associated with Ernst Simon whose many connections in the Jewish community opened various doors for him (Simon went on to become a prominent Israeli educationalist). At one point, Löwenthal worked for the welfare bureau for Eastern European Jewish refugees, and he occasionally gave lectures at Franz Rosenzweig's Free House of Jewish Learning. From early 1925 to early 1926, he and Simon co-edited the Frankfurt-based orthodox weekly, *Jüdisches Wochenblatt*, but it turned out that the periodical was unable to sustain two editors. In 1920, he met Erich Fromm and Siegfried Kracauer, both of whom were later associated with the institute, among those who flocked to the charismatic rabbi Nehemias Anton Nobel. Kracauer, in turn, introduced him to his best friend,

---

54 On Grossman, see Jacobs 2015, pp. 37–40; Kuhn 2007.
55 Grossman 2021.
56 Wiggershaus 1994a, p. 31.

Theodor Wiesengrund-Adorno, and the three of them became good friends. In 1925, Löwenthal's increasing disillusionment with Zionism led him to abandon the movement. Having completed his doctorate on Franz von Baader's philosophy of religion in 1923, Löwenthal now focussed primarily on his studies again and successfully applied to join the institute.[57]

Paul Massing, whose father was a land registry administrator, was two years younger than Löwenthal and one of the few non-Jews to work for the institute. He initially conformed to Oppenheimer's description of the typical Frankfurt student. Following his graduation in economics, he acquired a business diploma at the Commercial College in Cologne. Yet, rather than go straight into the private sector, Massing went to Paris to study for a further year and then, in 1928, joined the institute and completed his thesis on nineteenth-century agronomy under the supervision of the economist Wilhelm Gerloff. Having become an orthodox Marxist in the meantime, he subsequently moved to Moscow to work at the International Agricultural Institute. He did not return to Germany until 1931 and then worked not for the institute but for the Central Committee of the KPD in Berlin.[58]

Kurt Mandelbaum was born into a Jewish family in Schweinfurt in 1904, his father too was a physician. He joined the institute in 1927 on Korsch's recommendation.[59] A member of the KPD since 1922, he was one of the many 'ultra-leftist sectarians' expelled, together with the likes of Heinz Langerhans, Werner Scholem and Karl Korsch, from the now staunchly Stalinist party in 1926. Mandelbaum read economics and philosophy in Würzburg, Munich and Berlin. In 1926, he was one of the first scholars to complete his doctorate under Grünberg's supervision in Frankfurt with a thesis on debates among German Social Democrats about imperialism, *Die Erörterungen innerhalb der deutschen Sozialdemokratie über das Problem des Imperialismus (1895–1914)*. When Pollock was promoted to deputy director of the institute the following year, he employed Mandelbaum as his assistant.

Julian Gumperz was the oldest of the doctoral scholars associated with the institute. He came from a family of German-American-Jewish industrialists and was born in New York in 1898. He had come to Germany as a young adult and begun to study economics in Halle. Yet his attentions soon shifted to the Expressionist and Dadaistic cultural scene and, specifically, to one of its journals, *Der Gegner* (The Adversary), which he coedited, first with Karl Otten, then

---

57   See Krüger 2015.
58   See Wyrwa 2017.
59   See Jay 1979.

with Wieland Herzfelde.[60] In 1921, he published a selection of Karl Liebknecht's articles and speeches and joined the editorial team of the KPD's flagship periodical, *Die Rote Fahne*. He also became increasingly involved with the aforementioned Malik publishing house, which was loosely associated with the party and, in 1923, brought out Georg Lukács's path-breaking *Geschichte und Klassenbewußtsein* (History and Class Consciousness), a work of crucial significance for the interpretation of Marx.

According to the memoirs of Hede Massing (who was married to him from 1926 to 1933), Gumperz was asked in 1925 'to supervise all of the German Communist party publishing' for the Communist International. Once an ardent supporter of the Soviet Union, Gumperz had become increasingly disillusioned, however. Hede Massing recalled that,

> As part of his responsibility, he went fairly often to the Soviet Union ... When he came back from those short trips there was none of the glow and enthusiasm for Russia that I had seen in him after his first trip in 1923. ... He was coming to dislike it more and more. He did not tell me, at the time, what it was that so disappointed him, but he did quit the job very suddenly, and without much explanation.[61]

In 1927, as the Stalinisation of the Soviet Union gathered pace, Gumperz stopped working for the party and abandoned Bolshevism altogether.

Felix Weil started funding the Malik publishing house in a big way in 1925. In conjunction with Weil's engagement, Pollock joined the publisher's supervisory board alongside the cultural studies scholar Eduard Fuchs and Malik's founder Wieland Herzfelde.[62] In this capacity, he worked closely with Gumperz whom he had already met – and taken a shine to – at the Marxist Study Week. When he was looking for a new professional opportunity following his departure from the Communist movement, Pollock invited him to join the institute. Gumperz accepted the invitation and became Pollock's closest collaborator. What Pollock could not know was that, in 1928, Richard Sorge recruited Gumperz's wife Hede as a Soviet agent. Gumperz's marriage soon broke down and in 1929, his wife moved in with Paul Massing who was also a Soviet spy.[63] It seems

---

60   Wiggershaus 1994a, p. 31.
61   Massing 1951, p. 55.
62   Felix Weil, 'Erinnerungen (Fragment)', Institute for the History of Frankfurt, S 5/421, p. 240.
63   Her first husband was the KPD official Gerhart Eisler who later chaired the East German national broadcasting committee. The composer Hanns Eisler and Ruth Fischer, who stood at the helm of the KPD in 1924/25, were his siblings.

remarkable that four – or, if one includes Felix Weil's stint as an informer, five – individuals involved with the institute – Hede Gumperz, Paul Massing, Christiane Sorge and Richard Sorge – were Soviet agents. This constellation speaks to the permeability of the dividing lines between the various factions of the Weimar left and to the ambivalent feelings of many leftists vis-à-vis the Bolshevik regime.

In this respect, Pollock and Horkheimer were no exception, although it is hard to imagine that either of them would have agreed to spy for the Soviet Union. Initial sympathies with the Soviet Union rapidly dissipated once Stalin managed to make himself the uncontested leader, and many were appalled by the Stalinisation of the Communist parties elsewhere. Yet this was an incremental and by no means linear process. Many tried, for the longest time, to ignore, minimise or rationalise the mounting terror. As early as 1922, Pollock and Horkheimer's friend from their time in Munich, Germaine Krull, had informed them of her unsettling experiences in the 'promised land of the workers' where she had been arrested as a 'spy and counter-revolutionary'. 'You know', she wrote in a letter to them, 'that I am a truthful person; so you can imagine that I did not turn into a vehement opponent of these people for petty personal reasons. It is now clear to me that it would be a misfortune for the world and the working class in particular if Bolshevism came to the West.'[64] Responding to her letter, Pollock and Horkheimer expressed their empathy for Krull yet at the same time, writing to his wife, Horkheimer drew the grounds for Krull's anti-Bolshevik turn into question. 'There are objections of principle against the social revolution that I respect; but I have always hated the notion of "learning from *experience*" that emanates from her letter like the stench of putrefaction – & be it the experience of physical death!'[65]

Maidon Horkheimer may well have wondered what 'objections of principle' her husband had in mind if the threat of being tortured to death did not count. One can only speculate that it was his frustration at the way the Soviet Union was developing that engendered this kind of cynicism. Yet Pollock and Horkheimer's critical solidarity increasingly turned into fundamental rejection and eventually they became card-carrying anti-Bolsheviks. Committed to the original aspirations inherent in Marx's theory all the same, the institute thus became a preferred refuge for those who turned their back on Bolshevism.

To be sure, the institute's non-Jewish collaborators Sorge, Wittfogel and Massing remained loyal to party Communism for the time being, but the over-

---

64   Germaine Krull to Friedrich Pollock and Max Horkheimer, 12 January 1922, in Horkheimer 1995a, pp. 80–1, p. 80.
65   Max Horkheimer to Rose Riekher, 23 January 1922, in Horkheimer 1995a, pp. 81–2.

whelming majority of its (mostly Jewish) associates turned away from the Communist movement in the course of the 1920s, shifting their attention to scholarly research on Marxism and the further development of Marxist theory. According to an internal report by Frankfurt's police chief of 1926, it had been 'demonstrated irrefutably that Prof. Grünberg's former assistants at the Institute of Social Research, Dr. Friedrich Pollock and Dr. Felix Weil, and all the institute's employees are Communists'.[66] In Pollock's case this was certainly not the whole truth. Like the Communists, he subscribed to Marx's critique of capitalism but even in his doctoral thesis, he had not drawn out its revolutionary implications and instead focussed on its potential for the critique of ideology; and, personal contacts notwithstanding, he certainly had no dealings with party Communism, especially after Stalin's ascent in the Soviet Union and the Bolshevik purge of the KPD.

If Pollock and his colleagues distanced themselves from the Communist movement, they did so not on the understanding that they were changing their position but that it was the movement that had mutated. The so-called Schlageter policy adopted in 1923 committed the KPD to a nationalist agenda that was diametrically opposed to Marx's internationalism.[67] Under Ernst Thälmann's leadership, the party became a Bolshevik outpost and anathematised councillist and other undogmatic Marxist or Trotskyite positions; and Stalin transformed the Soviet Union into a totalitarian society governed by terror and oppression. It took quite something to be sufficiently deluded on ideological grounds to ignore this development.

As an episode that has hitherto drawn insufficient attention illustrates, this transformation also made itself felt in the institute. Following the October Revolution, the Central Committee of the Communist Party in Russia decided to create an institute for the collection and preservation of the Marxist heritage and the production of both popular and scholarly editions of the writings of Marx and Engels. The Marx Engels Institute (MEI) undoubtedly served propaganda purposes too, but the appointment of its first director indicated an ideological open-mindedness that would have been inconceivable under Stalin. The appointment went to David Borisovich Riazanov, a Jewish Marxist, born in Odessa in 1870, who, prior to the First World War, had sympathised with the Socialist Revolutionary Narodniki before shifting his allegiance to the Marxist labour movement. He was chosen for the position because, although its publication was ultimately prevented by the turmoil of the war, he was well

---

66 Quoted in Felix Weil, 'Erinnerungen (Fragment)', Institute for the History of Frankfurt, S 5/421, p. 203.
67 See Flechtheim 1969, pp. 177–9.

respected for his edition of the minutes and documents of the First International. Riazanov had long wanted to publish an edition of the complete works of Marx and Engels (MEGA), an endeavour that initially garnered enthusiastic support from the Bolshevik Central Committee.[68]

The principal challenge for Riazanov lay in the fact that Marx's manuscripts and documents were dispersed across Europe and partly in private ownership. A significant part of the material was owned by the SPD archive and Karl Kautsky, whose relationship to the Russian Communists was ambivalent at best. Riazanov therefore needed an ally who could mediate between the MEI and the SPD. Given that Riazanov and the exceedingly well connected Grünberg had a long-standing working relationship, the Institute of Social Research seemed the ideal candidate for this role. On 20 August 1924, just after its inauguration, the institute signed a cooperation agreement with the Marx Engels Institute Publishing Company Ltd. It was run by Felix Weil and Friedrich Pollock. Riazanov's former colleague, Boris Ivanovich Nikolaevsky, who, as a leading Menshevik, had left the Soviet Union in 1922 and was now based in Berlin, coordinated the inventorisation, production of photographic copies and collation of the material on behalf of the Moscow institute and became Pollock and Weil's principal point of contact.[69]

For several years, Pollock, Weil and Nikolaevsky, joined in 1925 by Hans Jäger, invested a great deal of energy into acquiring the documents and sending photocopies to Russia. 'The photostatic copying of the Marx Engels Papers', Weil later recalled, 'also happened in the institute with the approval of the SPD executive'. A staff of six, working in two shifts, was tasked with copying the 150,000 pages in the institute's basement. A courier then collected the copies and transported them to the Soviet embassy in Berlin. 'From there, they went by diplomatic courier to the Marx Engels Institute in Moscow. All the papers were copied in this way. The Marx Engels Institute then prepared the volumes for publication by the Marx Engels Archive publishing enterprise which was initially based in Frankfurt.'[70] The first issue of the supplementary journal, *Marx Engels Archiv*, came out in 1925, and the first part of the first MEGA volume – containing *Werke und Schriften bis Anfang 1844 nebst Briefen und Dokumenten* (Works and Writings up to Early 1844 as Well as Letters and Documents) – was published in 1927.[71]

---

68 See Hecker 2009.
69 See Nenarokov 2011.
70 Felix Weil, 'Erinnerungen (Fragment)', Institute for the History of Frankfurt, S 5/421, p. 199.
71 Riazanov 1925; Marx and Engels 1927.

The publication date was intentionally chosen to mark the tenth anniversary of the October Revolution, celebrated in Moscow with much ado. On Riazanov's recommendation, Pollock was invited to attend the official ceremony, which was quite a privilege. He arrived in the capital of the 'Workers' Fatherland' on 25 October 1927 and stayed for an entire month. The MEI put him up in a hotel and let it be known that he should consider himself a guest of the institute.[72] On 7 November 1927, along with numerous other Western authors, cultural figures and academics supportive of the Soviet cause, Pollock witnessed a huge parade organised by the regime on Red Square. The parade was followed by a march of 600,000 workers sporting banners, pennants and flags. Reflecting on this event, the expressionist poet Armin T. Wegner resorted to religious metaphors, characterising it as a 'pilgrimage to the red Jerusalem'.[73] The author Joseph Roth had attended the official May Day rally in Moscow the year before. Even though he hardly sympathised with the Bolsheviks he penned an enthusiastic report: 'This march-past is the most forceful military spectacle of our age and likely since Napoleon. Repeated so and so many times, it loses none of its force and is always fresh.'[74]

Yet unlike many other Western communist intellectuals, Pollock was no mere political tourist. Inspired by Felix Weil's research on socialisation, he had developed an interest in problems pertaining to the planned economy and decided to study the Soviet economic order.[75] His stay in Moscow offered him the rare opportunity to observe institutions involved in the planning process at close quarters, consult practitioners and gather a wealth of relevant source material. He took copious notes on everything he heard and observed and amassed a substantial collection of pamphlets, directives, internal memoranda, flyers, scholarly publications and economic plans. The MEI and Riazanov in particular made every effort to support his research and opened quite a few doors for him that would otherwise presumably have remained closed.

What he observed was a serious and sincere attempt to graft a planned industrial economy onto the semi-feudal relations of production in a country significantly lagging behind technologically and characterised by mass poverty and recurring famines. Could this endeavour succeed? How did the dictatorship of the Communist party impact the small leaseholders and farm labourers who still formed the majority of the population? What might one learn in

---

72   Marx Engels Institute to Friedrich Pollock, 10 October 1927, quoted in Hecker, Sperl and Vollgraf (eds.) 2000, p. 364, n566.
73   Wegner 1979, p. 29.
74   Roth 1995, p. 174.
75   For a systematic analysis, see Campani 1992.

the West from the Soviet project? When Pollock left Moscow, he had not yet reached a judgement. The letter he wrote to Riazanov following his return of Frankfurt to thank him for his support during his stay in Moscow clearly indicated that he had gone to the Soviet Union not to indulge romantic notions regarding the revolution or the workers but to undertake research. 'Having arrived in Frankfurt safe and sound', he wrote, 'I would like to assure you and your wife of my sincere gratitude for your warm welcome and emphatic support in Moscow. Without your help I would surely have been unable to gain such a thorough overview over the evolving Soviet economy in the few weeks I was able to spend in Moscow.'[76]

Pollock had finally identified a suitable topic for his postdoctoral thesis that would allow him to be appointed to a chair, and he did not intend to waste any time. Grünberg enthusiastically welcomed the prospect of a rigorous analysis of the Soviet planned economy. He suggested Karl Eman Pribram, a Jewish economist who originally came from Prague and had recently taken up a position in Frankfurt, as second supervisor, and Pribram agreed.[77] Bursting with energy, Pollock began to work on an outline, analysing the statistical data and primary source material and familiarising himself with the relevant secondary literature. Walter Biehahn, an associate of the institute with Trotskyite leanings, assisted him, and the Odessa-born student Rudolf Selke, who had also recently been expelled from the KPD as a Trotskyite, helped with translations.

Numerous Soviet officials whom Pollock had met in Moscow sent him additional material and were happy to answer his queries. Pollock took care to maintain his contacts to Soviet officials and economists, and they repeatedly shared valuable information with him that was not readily available in Germany. In November 1928, Roman Efimovich Vaisberg, who worked for the Soviet planning authority, sent a copy of his recently published book on problems connected to the prognostics involved in drawing up the Five-Year Plan to 'My Dear Comrade Pollock with best wishes'. The following year, Aron I. Gaister, the deputy head of the State Planning Commission forwarded a copy of his book on the collectivisation of Soviet agriculture to 'Comrade Dr. Pollak'.[78]

Consequently, Pollock was able to draw on an extraordinarily rich source base for his postdoctoral thesis, a work that is still of interest to Soviet histor-

---

76 Friedrich Pollock to David Riazanov, 22 November 1927, in Hecker, Sperl and Vollgraf (eds.) 2000, p. 373.
77 Chaloupek 2019, pp. 403–19.
78 These two and a third volume by Gleb Krzhizhanovsky, dedicated to 'Comrade Pollock, Yours Ever', were held by the Staatsbibliothek Berlin following their theft by the Nazis. They were among 536 books finally returned to the institute in 2018.

ians. In March 1929, it was published as the second volume in the institute's book series, as *Die planwirtschaftlichen Versuche in der Sowjetunion 1917–1927* (The Attempts to Construct a Planned Economy in the Soviet Union, 1917–1927). As Pollock emphasised in the introduction, his was the 'first attempt by a non-Bolshevik party to offer at least a general economic history of Russia in the last ten years'. Contrary to the claims of the Bolsheviks' opponents, economic policy was 'discussed controversially and with the greatest openness, both in Soviet literature and at party congresses and conferences'. Consequently, the records of these debates provided excellent source material. Conversely, he had not studied the publications of the Communist International, given the extent to which they bore 'the imprint of political propaganda'.[79]

On Pollock's account, Soviet economic policy was experimental in nature. It was driven by clearly identifiable concepts taken from the writings of Marx, Engels and, especially, Lenin, but their implementation was anything but straightforward. Given how far Russia lagged behind in its industrial development, a phase of transition was clearly required to move from a still largely feudal system to Communism. Pollock distinguished two phases in the development towards Communism to date. In the initial phase of War Communism (from 1917 to 1921), economic policy had been dictated by the hardship caused first by the World War and then by the Civil War. The party could hardly be held responsible for the catastrophic supply and hunger crisis of these years, given that it resulted from global political and economic circumstances. Yet Pollock took issue with the fact that leading Bolsheviks had sought to make a virtue of necessity and presented War Communism as the shortest path to Socialism. The elimination of the market without putting in its place a carefully thought-out and well-functioning administration could not but lead to a catastrophe. 'When the peasants' grain is requisitioned without any substantial compensation and the village consequently returns to the most primitive form of closed household economy; when the feudal corvée is resurrected to compel labour for the purposes of timber procurement; when industry is administered to death and the entire economy eventually grinds to a halt', Pollock concluded, it was hard to see in all this 'a kind of economy superior to the exchange economy'.[80]

Lenin had recognised this and, in 1921, introduced what was then still the current phase in the development towards Communism, the New Economic Policy (NEP). It facilitated the partial reintroduction of market-based commerce, an

---

79　Pollock 1929, p. v.
80　Pollock 1929, p. 99.

easing of the supply crisis and a carefully bounded measure of social liberalisation. For Pollock, it was this policy that marked the genuine shift towards a planned economy. This may seem like a paradoxical contention, given the legalisation of private commerce the new policy entailed. Yet Pollock interpreted it against the backdrop of Lenin's concept of state capitalism as the transitional stage that would pave the way for Communism. On a pragmatic level, the reintroduction of private commerce was designed to ease the supply crisis, but the new policy was also meant to integrate private commerce into the planned economy and subordinate it to the plan. This form of state capitalism was a considerable improvement over the false radicalism of War Communism which had depressed living standards. Crucially, however, the politically dictated and scientifically implemented economic plan would always take precedence, while allowing, say, peasants who produced more than the plan required to sell the surplus privately. This fostered productivity and offered peasants a practical means of making a better living for themselves. It was important to acknowledge that the contentment of the population was a central concern for Communism. Substantial landowners (*kulaks*), on the other hand, who were held responsible for the misery created by the feudal system and on whom the Bolsheviks had declared war, would continue to be constrained in their economic activities. Pollock could hardly be expected to anticipate that Stalin would have large numbers of actual or ostensible opponents identified as kulaks murdered some years later. Conversely, in light of his positive reception of the New Economic Policy it is obvious that he could interpret Stalin's policies in the years 1928 to 1933 only as a return to the false radicalism of War Communism.[81]

It should be noted that Pollock was far more interested in the technical than the political aspects of his topic. He wanted to know whether and how a planned economy worked and what pitfalls needed to be avoided if one were to introduce it, say, in Germany. The crash of 1929 was not far off and anyone who paid close attention could sense that capitalism was on the verge of a fundamental crisis. As we saw, while Pollock was writing his postdoctoral thesis, his colleague Henryk Grossman was working on *The Law of Accumulation*, also published in 1929.[82] For all his criticism of Grossman's book, Pollock did share his colleague's assumption that capitalism was unavoidably heading for a substantial crisis.

---

81   It is all the more surprising that Pollock defended Stalin's dekulakisation policy in his 1932 essay 'Socialism and Agriculture'. Cf. Pollock, 'Sozialismus und Landwirtschaft', in: GS 1, esp. pp. 284 f.
82   Grossman 2021. For a detailed discussion, see Kuhn 2007, pp. 113–60.

On Grossman's account, this crisis would need to coincide with a major imperialist war that would lead to the massive destruction of goods and infrastructure which, in turn, would rewind the accumulation clock. Whatever one may make of the way in which Grossman deployed his evidence in detail, his acuity in predicting the imminent Great Depression and Second World War was certainly remarkable. Pollock shared his colleague's fears but assumed that war and destruction might yet be averted if the mounting crisis engendered the insight that a planned economy was superior to the market economy. As he saw it, the future belonged to the planned economy, and one needed to be intimately familiar with its workings, the opportunities if offered and the problems it raised. This explains Pollock's generally sympathetic evaluation of the Soviet planned economy, various individual criticisms notwithstanding.

One of the contemporaneous reviewers was spot-on when he suggested that Pollock's 'charitable approach to Socialist construction' resembled the 'inquisitiveness of an observer who displays a great deal of interest in the Soviet experimentation but ultimately remains a sceptic'.[83] Pollock was particularly concerned that the planning method was insufficiently evidence-based. He also criticised the excessive bureaucratisation and attendant corruption. He also raised a number of more general issues resulting from the pioneering nature of the Bolshevik experiment. Yet, 'all these transitional challenges' were dwarfed

> by the fact that the attempt is being made to establish Socialism in an agrarian country. Whether Socialism can be established, rather than on an international scale, merely in one country is already a moot point. In an agrarian country, however, several crucial prerequisites are definitely missing.[84]

All his sympathies in principle notwithstanding, Pollock ultimately questioned the very possibility of establishing socialism in Russia, then. From the vantage of the Communist Party this was an extraordinary provocation.

Meanwhile, rather fittingly, the cooperation between the Institute of Social Research and the Marx Engels Institute was drawing to a close. 'Dear Comrade Riazanov!' Pollock wrote in a letter dated 16 July 1928, perhaps 'you will consider whether comrade Czobel [the deputy director of the MEI] might come here on or after 10 August so we can discuss all the issues concerning the dissolution

---

83 Wainstein 1931, pp. 197–8.
84 Pollock 1929, p. 366.

of our "marriage" in detail'.[85] Both parties had reasons for wanting to terminate the cooperation. Having obtained copies of most of Marx and Engels's papers, Moscow wanted to take full control of the MEGA. The institute in Frankfurt, on the other hand, under pressure for supposedly being too close to Moscow (we may recall the internal report by Frankfurt's police chief of 1926), was not at all unhappy to cap its actual connections with the MEI. Relations were further complicated by the fact that Grünberg suffered a massive stroke in January 1928, leaving Pollock to run the institute's affairs as acting director.

The termination of the cooperation agreement coincided with the domestic transformation of the Soviet Union. The Communist party viewed the MEGA, the close relations to Social Democrats such as Eduard Bernstein the work on the edition entailed and Riazanov himself with increasing suspicion. In 1930, the MEI was purged: 131 of its 243 employees were dismissed. On 15 February 1931, Riazanov was arrested, accused of being involved in a Menshevik conspiracy and exiled to Saratov. He was initially able to continue with his scholarly work, but the Great Terror eventually caught up with him. Re-arrested in July 1937, he resolutely refused to confess to any crimes or implicate anyone else. He was executed in January 1938. The MEGA, of which only a handful of volumes had been published, was aborted.

At this point, the institute's Marxist period, in the narrower sense of the word, ended. Grünberg's stroke had left him severely incapacitated, and Pollock, who was now in charge of the institute, paved the way for Grünberg's replacement by a close associate: his friend and housemate Max Horkheimer. To be sure, Pollock continued to draw on Marxian concepts for the rest of his life but the critical distance he had put between himself and the orthodox party Communism of the KPD was a crucial prerequisite for the subsequent development of an undogmatic critical social theory.

---

85   Friedrich Pollock to David Riazanov, 16 July 1928 (excerpt), in Hecker, Sperl and Vollgraf (eds.) 2000, pp. 387–8, p. 388.

CHAPTER 5

The Quest

For Pollock, breaking with the Communist movement marked a more significant caesura than it did for Horkheimer, who was already an established academic and heading for a chair. Pollock too had recently completed his postdoctoral qualification but ultimately, it was still unclear what he wanted to spend his life doing. While Grünberg's incapacitation suggested certain options, Germany's palpable shift to the right made it increasingly unlikely that Pollock would be able to secure a chair. By focussing on Marxian theory and socialist economic models Pollock had marginalised himself academically and his connections to the Soviet Union made him suspicious in the eyes of the authorities. 'In the police files marked "confidential" or "secret"' that were created in connection with the investigations of the political police as to whether the institute had been infiltrated by Communists, 'one name in particular' featured most prominently among those suspected by the authorities, and this from the very beginning: that of Friedrich Pollock.[1] When it came to Grünberg's succession, Pollock was therefore automatically out of the running and it fell to Horkheimer to secure the position. That said, both then and later, Pollock readily admitted to himself and others that Horkheimer was in any case the more gifted intellectual and therefore better suited to the position.

Pollock was unsure what to do. Should he really give absolute precedence to Horkheimer's academic career? Was the academy actually the right place for him or should he return to the private sector as his father, who, given his age, had since retired from the family business, had hoped all long? The business was now run by Hans Pollock who would doubtless have welcomed his brother back. Or was this just his father's voice belatedly asserting itself after a prolonged phase of adolescent rebellion? Perhaps his mourning the untimely death, early in 1930, of his mother, with whom he had enjoyed a good relationship, made him yearn for a closer relationship to his family? Yet he dismissed these considerations. The 'religion' of his covenant with Horkheimer was real, he remained committed to the underlying norms of loyalty, solidarity and truthfulness. But what might this mean in practice?

It was still unclear, then, what Pollock ultimately wanted to do with the freedom he had gained by turning his back on his birth family and the bour-

---

1 Migdal 1981, p. 98.

geois concepts of marriage and family life. After the war, he had flirted with the idea of going into politics but in the meantime, he had dismissed this option to which he would doubtless have been well suited. What alternatives were there that were both viable and justifiable in terms of the standards enshrined in the friendship contract? Pollock's long-drawn-out quest for a clear purpose finally came to an end in 1930, when Horkheimer became Grünberg's successor, inaugurating an entirely new phase in Pollock's life. *Prima facie*, his role in the institute barely changed as a result. As Grünberg's assistant and secretary of the Society of Social Research, he was responsible for the institute's administration and finances. As acting director during the interregnum that lasted from Grünberg's stroke in 1928 to Horkheimer's appointment in 1930, his role had largely stayed the same. Now, as deputy director, he was again the administrative head of the institute. In this capacity, he was responsible for crucial decisions, for example, when it came to the establishment of the institute's branch in Geneva or the prescient transfer of the foundation's capital abroad that he arranged in coordination with Felix Weil. The institute's profile was entirely Horkheimer's responsibility, however. To be sure, the two friends worked hand in glove and Pollock was consulted on all new appointments. Even so, he had made a conscious decision henceforth to play the second fiddle to Horkheimer. It was now up to him to secure the material and organisational conditions required to maintain a protected interior sphere within which they might be able to lead the good life to which their covenant aspired.

The institute henceforth mediated between *intérieur* and *extérieur*, between the world of their covenant and the outside world. In a sense, the institute on Viktoria-Allee marked the boundary between Kronberg and the world. Now that the two friends were in charge, they could ensure that the values of the *intérieur* also prevailed, at least to some extent, at the institute. On the other hand, they appreciated the Marxist critique of life reform and other utopian movements and understood that their *île heureuse* was just that, a resplendent island of peace in the stormy capitalist ocean governed by altogether different norms. As Horkheimer observed in the aphorisms he wrote between 1926 and 1931 and published in 1934 under a pseudonym (Heinrich Regius) as *Dämmerung* (Dawn), it was an ideological delusion to assume that one's own norms were entirely unaffected by those of society. It would take 'a radical transformation of an individual's social circumstances' for it to 'grasp how many socially determined elements still inhered even in the love, friendship, respect and solidarity it encountered'.[2] In short, their *île heureuse* was located in a hostile

---

2 Regius 1987, p. 322. The aphorism, 'From the Interior to the Exterior', is not included in Horkheimer 1978.

ocean that constantly flooded its beaches and covered them with its mud. Yet for this very reason the two friends eschewed the option of escapist withdrawal and boldly defended the commitments of their covenant against the outside world.

To this end, they maintained Grünberg's dictatorial style of leadership. If disagreements occurred, the final decision always lay with the director, i.e., with Horkheimer in consultation with Pollock. All important decisions, including those on the future profile of the institute and its stance on Marxism, were made jointly by Horkheimer and Pollock. In keeping with the commitments of their covenant, it was crucial that the political distance they developed in their dealings with orthodox Marxism not amount to some form of betrayal. As they saw it, it was they who were the true guardians of the Marxian legacy which they were defending against its doctrinaire cannibalisation by the Communist International. On the one hand, in the Communist movement, 'barring an urgent reversal, loyalty to the tenet of materialism is in danger of turning into a mindless and contentless cult of literalism and personality', Horkheimer wrote in one of his aphorisms. On the other hand, 'the materialist content, i.e., knowledge of the real world, is the preserve of those who have become disloyal to Marxism', i.e. reformist Social Democracy.[3] This juxtaposition offered a framework allowing the institute to continue its engagement of Marxism and, indeed, to present Critical Theory as an undogmatic continuation of Marx's theory while keeping their distance both from Bolshevism in its increasingly totalitarian guise and from reform-oriented Social Democracy.

Few individuals were quite as assured of Pollock and Horkheimer's contempt as turncoats. To be sure, they acknowledged that tactical conduct could be beneficial on occasion. Nor did one always have to reveal the whole truth. To act in contravention of one's own convictions and switch allegiances depending on the circumstances, however, was something they considered morally reprehensible. As young adults they had struggled with their fathers who met their contempt for the bourgeois lifestyle and its attendant norms with utter incomprehension. Analogously, they expected everyone else to unfetter themselves from obsolete authorities and be accountable only to their own reason.

That said, Pollock too looked to certain role models, and his attempts to emulate them occasionally took on a bizarre quality. Especially in its more formal aspects, his constantly palpable commitment to his special bond with Horkheimer sometimes struck a comical note with observers. Not that any of them knew of the friendship contract or Pollock's setting himself in scene as

---

3 Horkheimer 1978, p. 64 (translation amended).

the covenant's 'ministre d'extérieur' which, in part at least, was ironic in nature. Close friends and colleagues certainly did notice, however, that Horkheimer and Pollock sometimes behaved like an old married couple. In his memoirs, the philosopher Ludwig Marcuse – who ran the features section of the *Frankfurter General-Anzeiger* from 1925 to 1929 – wrote that he encountered Horkheimer as a 'charming man, overflowing with warmth' who had his 'restrained, seemingly much sterner friend Friedrich Pollock' in tow wherever he went.[4] They were inseparable and existed only as a 'package'. In 1930, Pollock and Horkheimer put Theodor Wiesengrund-Adorno up in Kronberg – where, as he later recalled, they led 'a secluded life characterised by a palpable dislike for furnished rooms' – for several weeks, so he could work on his Kierkegaard book in peace.[5] Adorno was fascinated by their lifestyle and enjoyed the time he was able to spend with them yet, in a letter he wrote to Kracauer on 12 May 1930, he also made fun of Pollock and Horkheimer, referring to them as the 'chums Lenin and Trotzky'.[6]

This was quite an epithet. But whom was Adorno identifying as Lenin and whom as Trotsky? Did he see Horkheimer, who was about to take control of the institute, in the role of Lenin and Pollock, who, in his capacity as 'People's Commissar for Foreign Affairs, War, Nutrition, Transport and Publishing', took charge of the institute's administration and the everyday concerns of the *intérieur*, as doing Trotsky's job? Maybe. The similarities between the style of leadership in Lenin's 'party of new type' and the institute are certainly striking. Yet Pollock himself might well have been more inclined to think of two other chums: Karl Marx and Friedrich Engels.[7] In their case, the congenial division of labour was even more clearly established than it was between Lenin and Trotsky. As we saw, it took Pollock some time to decide which of their respective roles he wanted to adopt: that of the prominent critic of society engaged mainly in theoretical study, or that of the loyal companion of the great thinker who devoted his life to the cause but stood back as an intellectual in his own right. These roles, and the strict distinction between the public sphere and the study, were, of course, foreshadowed in their friendship contract from the outset.

His preparatory work for a biography of Marx demonstrates that, in the course of his decision-making process, Pollock also contemplated choosing him as his role model. In 1920, he worked on a detailed reconstruction of Marx's

---

4 Marcuse 1960, p. 114.
5 Adorno 1998a, p. 156.
6 Adorno and Kracauer 2020, p. 141 (translation amended).
7 On their respective roles, see Herres 2018.

life path and familial relations. It seems noteworthy that Marx's Jewish background featured prominently in this context. Marx's grandfather Marx Levi, he noted, was a rabbi in Trier; as was Marx's uncle, Samuel Marx, another son of Marx Levi and Eva Marx, née Moses; and Samuel's son, Karl Marx's cousin Moses Marx, was, whatever he may eventually have done, at one point a rabbinical trainee in Gleiwitz.[8] Pollock noted that the birthname of Karl Marx's father, Heinrich Marx, was Hirschel, and that he had converted only in 1829.[9] To this note he added an asterisk and, adopting Heinrich Heine's well known formulation, wrote in the margin: 'entrance ticket to European culture', presumably to indicate that Heinrich Marx had not converted from religious conviction. He also noted that the rabbinic ancestry of Karl's mother Henriette, née Pressburg, stretched back for centuries.

Having established the coordinates of Marx's life path, Pollock proceeded to write short summaries of Marx's works. Here, not only *Capital* but 'On the Jewish Question' too featured prominently. His discussion of this text was prefaced by the following note: 'Moses Mendelssohn tolerated by F.[riedrich] I as book-keeper to one of the privileged money Jews.' Pollock's succinct excerpt then reads as follows: 'Political & human emancipation | Bourgeois society is of a completely Jewish character, therefore the Jew can claim pol. emancipation | Human emancipation only possible in new society.' Having taken on board the contention that Mendelssohn was tolerated only because he enjoyed the protection of the king who wanted his realm to benefit from the wealth of Bernhard Isaak who, in turn, employed Mendelssohn as the bookkeeper of his silk factory, Pollock assumed that the emancipation granted to the Jews of Imperial Germany when it was established in 1871 merely amounted to a continuation of the old system. It was owed not to rational or moral insight but to the emergence of capitalism. The early modern 'money Jews' were proto-capitalists and precursors of a new social order. Since the consolidation of capitalism had turned the Christians too into 'money Jews' – i.e., into merchants, bankers and entrepreneurs – there was no longer any reason to treat Jews any differently from Christians. As the prosperity and respectability of Pollock's family illustrated, the Jews' *political* emancipation was well under way. *Human* emancipation, by contrast, was yet to come for Jews and Christians alike who now jointly suffered the yoke of the capitalist order. Human emancipation was

---

8   Friedrich Pollock, 'Extracta zu Marx I', Horkheimer Archive, University Library Frankfurt/Main, MHA XXIV 1, 1.

9   Once the French were no longer in charge of the Rhineland, Marx's father would no longer have been able to continue practising as a solicitor, had he not converted. He did so at some point between 1816 and 1818, most likely at the earliest opportunity.

about far more than legal equality, it promised material and intellectual contentment to all – and this promise had yet to be fulfilled.

Yet it was not only the content of Marx's thought that appealed to Pollock, so too did his character. As is well known, Marx devoted all of his energy – and all the funds he inherited – to the communist cause but he did not eschew life's pleasures. The son of an industrialist, Engels was not only able to live comfortably off his family's fortune; he was also unwavering in his support of Marx who spent much of his life alternating between modest comfort and regular visits to the pawnbroker. Occasional donations from various sections of the communist movement aside, it was Engels above all who made it possible for Marx to keep up at least the appearance, for the most part, of maintaining a bourgeois lifestyle. Marx's travel, both for leisure purposes and to spend time in prestigious spa resorts such as Karlsbad (Karlovy Vary), likewise belies what some might associate with the cliché of a sullen and embittered revolutionary.[10] Marx was no bon viveur and, for the most part, tended to be 'patriarchal, prudish, bourgeois, industrious, independent (or trying to be), cultured, respectable, German, with a distinct patina of Jewish background'.[11] But he knew full well why he wanted the proletariat to share in society's wealth. In this respect, he was motivated not by abstract principles but by the fact that the overwhelming majority of the population was being cheated out of a contented and fulfilled life.

Pollock no more inclined towards asceticism than Marx. This had not changed since his time in Brussels, when he and Horkheimer spent their nights out on the town before turning their attentions to the dire state of the world again in the morning. For Pollock, distress at the world's desolate state did not preclude pleasure where it was attainable. Now, he occasionally attended Hannah and Paul Tillich's roaring parties characterised, if Friedrich Wilhelm Graf is to be believed, 'not only by freely flowing alcohol (and sometimes other drugs too), but also by partner swapping and excessive erotic abandon'.[12] Pollock himself was hardly given to excess, however. Indeed, the former institute employee Gerhard Meyer, on Martin Jay's account, remembered him as being 'steady, even obsessive'.[13] The moderation typical of the German-Jewish bourgeoisie was very much Pollock's preferred modus. He did not share his father's aversion to luxury and excess, but neither was he comfortable with the pub-

---

10 See Krysmanski 2014.
11 Sperber 2013, p. 500.
12 Graf 2015, p. 114.
13 Jay 1996, p. 7.

lic transgression of sexual norms, even when it took place in the house of a close friend and was merely semi-public. He consistently struck strangers as being not exactly uptight but certainly restrained. Generally known as an earnest, helpful and friendly man, his determination could make him seem aloof and pernickety. Overall, not entirely by coincidence perhaps, he seems to have resembled Marx rather more than Engels, the bon viveur. Marx's theory, after all, sprang not from an abstract juggling with concepts but from careful reflection on personal experiences.

One of these experiences was absolutely central to Pollock's thought too: what drove human beings to political activism was not poverty or desperation but the contradiction between that which is and that which would be possible. It followed that the world needed to be judged not on the basis of abstract ideals but in terms of what, taking into account the current circumstances, it had to offer humankind. Theory's task was to work out how to close the gap between the actual and the potentially possible state of play. Like Pollock, Marx had witnessed the failure of a revolution at close quarters. Yet, unlike many other former revolutionaries, he did not turn to reactionary politics. Instead, he took a fresh look at the theory that had just been disproven by reality. The result of this process of reflection was *Capital*. Published in 1867, it gave socialism a new direction, one that hinged on the critique of ideology. As we saw, Pollock's doctoral thesis focussed on *Capital*, and it was a work he studied, time and again, for many years. Unlike, say, Herbert Marcuse, who foregrounded the materialist anthropology and humanistic theory of alienation of the early Marx, Pollock always stuck with the 'mature' Marx. Perhaps it was up to Pollock to write a new *Capital* for the twentieth century? Or should he rather let Horkheimer don the mantle of the new Marx and serve as his guardian angel? As we saw, he eventually chose the second option. Arguably underestimating its significance, he henceforth assumed his own scholarly work to be auxiliary in nature, designed merely to feed into Horkheimer's scholarship proper. Yet, as we will see, this in no way detracted from his continued ambition to develop a cutting-edge form of Marxist theory.

Needless to say, neither was Horkheimer Marx, nor Pollock Engels. Even so, their unusually productive friendship offered an extremely inspiring model. In the end, Pollock's Marx biography did not come to fruition but in 1926, he was able to draw on the material he had gathered to this end to articulate his long-standing sympathy with both the theoretician and the human being Karl Marx by tearing into Sombart's revised (tenth) edition of his monumental two-volume *Der proletarische Sozialismus ('Marxismus')* (Proletarian Socialism ['Marxism']). *Sombarts 'Widerlegung' des Marxismus* (Sombart's 'Refutation' of Marxism), published as a supplementary volume to Grünberg's *Archiv*, was Pollock's first stand-alone publication.[14] 'At age 30', he wrote, Marx had 'established his philosophical and sociological concepts with such clarity that he did not need to correct himself in any substantial respect for the remainder of his life. Few knew the meaning of lifelong loyalty as well as he did.'[15] When he wrote these lines, Pollock himself was 32, and it is surely no stretch to suggest that he identified with the strength of character on Marx's part that he praised so effusively. Overall, his treatment of Marx in this slim volume was strongly hagiographical in nature. Marx and Engels, he wrote, 'enjoyed an absolutely perfect 38-year friendship of the most intimate kind. He joined the Communist League in 1847 and, from then on, undeterred by all the unpleasantness, undeterred by the "most awful destitution" in which he was forced to live for many years, fought tirelessly for the proletariat until death took him.'[16]

The prominent sociologist Werner Sombart, once a Social Democrat, now a conservative nationalist and proponent of the corporatist state, was an extremely influential scholar and public intellectual.[17] He held the prestigious chair in political economy at the Friedrich Wilhelm University in Berlin and enjoyed considerable acclaim – even among some leftists – as an economic historian of capitalism. Surprisingly well disposed towards Marx in the first instance, his antisemitism increasingly got the better of him and he began to rant about the rootless and truculent 'negator' Marx. Not unlike Richard Wagner who, in *Das Judenthum in der Musik*, castigated the Jews for supposedly being incapable of true creativity, Sombart claimed that Marx had lacked the 'capacity to generate productive and feasible ideas'.[18]

Nor was Marx Sombart's sole target. He also had plenty of vitriol to spare for Rosa Luxemburg, whom he characterised as 'bloodthirsty and venomous'. As he explained at length, radical Marxists were radical because they were envious of those who managed to find a place or at least accepted their station in life. The worse an individual's resentment of those they envied, the more 'bloodthirsty and venomous' they became. What chance, then, was there for Rosa Luxemburg who, as Sombart would have it, was addled by 'four forms of invidiousness: as a woman, as a foreigner, as a Jew and as a cripple'.[19]

---

14   An excerpt was also published as 'Sombart als Marx-Biograph' (Sombart as a Biographer of Marx) in *Die Gesellschaft* 3.1, 3 (1926), pp. 262–75. *Die Gesellschaft* (Society) was the Social Democratic successor journal to the *Neue Zeit*, the Second International's foremost theoretical periodical.
15   Pollock 2018c, p. 218.
16   Ibid.
17   See Krause 1962. For a more charitable account, see Appel 1992.
18   Sombart 1924, p. 73.
19   Sombart 1924, p. 76.

Ultimately, Sombart's approach stood for an assault on reason itself, as was evidenced not least by his antisemitism. After all, for Sombart the Jews were responsible not only for capitalism but also for its opposite. In the family tree he constructed to establish the genealogy of 'proletarian socialism', the 'Jewish spirit' was one of the two original ancestors.[20] This inherent contradiction, which was typical of a great deal of antisemitic ideology at the time, demonstrated to Pollock that Sombart was driven not by critical inquisitiveness but by an irrational hatred that could be met only with polemical means.

Sombart became something of a permanent adversary for Pollock. If it is true that each of the critical theoreticians had their own personal 'dark' author who never ceased to challenge or provoke them – we might think of Heidegger in Adorno's case, of Schopenhauer or Nietzsche in Horkheimer's case and, in Neumann's case, of Carl Schmitt – then Pollock's 'dark' antagonist was doubtless Sombart. Having begun to read Sombart as a student, by the end of his life, he was hardly less familiar with Sombart's work than he was with his own. In one of his final interviews, he acknowledged that Sombart was the actual author of the term late capitalism, a concept that both Critical Theory and the student protest movement had appropriated.[21] Yet whatever the merits of some of Sombart's studies in economic history may have been, his radical anti-Jewish hostility was integral to his anti-capitalism, and Pollock felt compelled to take him to task, not only in order to defend Marx but also in his capacity as the son of a Jewish entrepreneur.

It was in 1911, in his book *Die Juden und das Wirtschaftsleben* (The Jews and Modern Capitalism), that Sombart first claimed that the Jews were responsible for the corrosive impact of capitalism. In the German edition, one need only take a look at the detailed table of contents to appreciate Sombart's characterisation of 'the Jews', but this is not reflected in Mordechai Epstein's partially sanitised rendering.[22] Even so, the same stereotypes still pervade the text, but one might conclude from the translation that they are cultural rather than racial characteristics. 'The intellectuality of the Jew is so strong', Sombart lamented, 'that it tends to develop at the expense of other mental qualities'. 'Fond of abstraction', Sombart posited, 'the Jew lacks the quality of instinctive understanding'.[23] Hence, the Jews 'behold the world not with their "soul" but with

---

20 Sombart 1924, p. 84.
21 Friedrich Pollock, Television interview, 15 July 1969, sound recording, Horkheimer Archive, University Library Frankfurt/Main, MHA XXIV 174. See Chaloupek 1996.
22 On Epstein's partial neutralisation of the racialising assumptions underpinning Sombart's line of argument, see Katznelson 2012, pp. 21–2.
23 Sombart 1914, pp. 339, 261.

their intellect', and 'the Jew never loses himself in the outer world', he 'will walk through the world without seeing'.[24] Moreover, he lacks 'the true conception of the personal side of life'.[25] 'Rationalism is the characteristic trait of Judaism as of Capitalism', and the Jews have consistently been 'rationalists, both in theory and in practice'.[26] In short, 'the Jew' is 'the born representative of a "liberal" view of life'.[27]

Sombart claimed that the book was a work of serious scholarship, yet the thin veneer of 'facts' and statistics barely concealed that it was in fact an antisemitic polemic. In his preface to the German edition (which was omitted from the English translation), he unambiguously set the Jews apart from the rest of humanity and identified them as the originators, agents and beneficiaries of the capitalist economic order and the liberal culture it engendered.[28] From the vantage of conservatives and reactionaries, Communists and Social Democrats alike, it was hard to imagine a worse indictment.

Pollock did not draw the numerical overrepresentation of Jews in trade and industry into question but he decried the suggestion that this reflected racial characteristics or the essence of Judaism as what it was – outlandish nonsense. Actually, the reasons were historical. In the medieval period, Jews had been excluded from agriculture and most artisanal professions. It was this historical coincidence that really had turned the Jews into the trailblazers of capitalism. In this respect, Marx's analysis in 'On the Jewish Question' had been spot-on. The critique of domination and exploitation needed to abstract from the individuals who happened to play certain economic roles and focus instead on the underlying social relations and their significance for the capitalist mode of production in its entirety.[29]

Pollock drew out this line of thought further in the notes he made for his first own seminar in the summer semester of 1928 on 'Problems of Historical Materialism'. It focussed especially on the formation of ideology in the capitalist order. Apart from Pollock's assistants Heinz Langerhans and Rudolf Selke – the latter had translated numerous Russian sources for Pollock while he was working on his postdoctoral thesis – the seminar participants included Irma Goitein, whose doctoral thesis on Moses Hess and his impact on Marx was published as a supplementary volume to Grünberg's *Archiv* in 1931, and Nelly Held

---

24   Sombart 1914, pp. 264, 265, 262.
25   Sombart 1914, p. 263.
26   Sombart 1914, pp. 206, 265.
27   Sombart 1914, p. 264.
28   Sombart 1911, p. vii.
29   See Marx 2010a, pp. 10, 88.

and her husband Ernst Held (Rosenbaum).³⁰ Horkheimer and Wittfogel attended from time to time.³¹ In her seminar paper, Julia Feinberg, a student who was 20 at the time,³² claimed that the categories 'denomination, race, ancestry and education' had the capacity to modify economic relations, for example, when it came to 'trust in capitalism'.³³ This was a sensitive issue insofar as it could be understood as a reference to the antisemitic canard of the Jewish world conspiracy and the claim that all Jews recognised and were in cahoots with each other. Not that this was what Feinberg meant, but it did seem to her that individuals' social, ethnic and religious background were sociological factors that shaped loyalties and relations of trust. One might interpret this as a watered-down version of Sombart's thesis. Pollock objected that none of these categories were genuinely fixed. Even categories such as 'race, climate etc.' were subject to man-made change, he noted.³⁴ 'Man's nature (race) & nature as it concerns him' might influence his 'proficiency', but nature was changeable: 'The temperament and disposition of peoples adjust'.³⁵

One might understand this objection not least in terms of Pollock's own Jewish assimilationism. His father had impressed on him at an early age that the Jews had ceased to be a nation and were now merely a religious denomination to which one might choose to belong – or not. For Pollock, Jewishness was an exclusively religious category. If the intense interest he had shown in Marx's ancestry and familial relations not so long ago spoke to some kind of more deep-seated attachment to Jewish culture and tradition, he was no more aware of it than it gave him cause for thought that virtually all his friends were Jewish. Needless to say, this was not a matter of biology or the climate but resulted from the fact that German Jewry in the Weimar era was about so much more than religion. One may attribute it to the similar socialisation experienced by

---

30   Drechsler 1990. The couple moved to the Soviet Union in 1932 where they were repeatedly arrested by the secret service in subsequent years. In 1949, they returned to East Germany.
31   See the attendance list in the notebook 'Probleme des hist. Mat. III', Horkheimer Archive, University Library Frankfurt/Main, MHA VIII, 10, 237.
32   In 1933, Feinberg married Pollock's aforementioned assistant Gerhard Meyer. After the war, she completed a doctorate in Chemistry at the University of Chicago before joining the School of Dentistry at the University of Illinois (Chicago), where she eventually held a chair in Oral Pathology.
33   The seminar text is attached to the notebook 'Probleme des hist. Mat. II' and 'Probleme des hist. Mat. III', pp. 27–8, Horkheimer Archive, University Library Frankfurt/Main, MHA VIII, 10.
34   Friedrich Pollock, 'Probleme des hist. Mat. I (Notizheft SoSe 1928)', Horkheimer Archive, University Library Frankfurt/Main, MHA VIII, 10, p. 21.
35   Friedrich Pollock, 'Probleme des hist. Mat. I (Notizheft SoSe 1928)', Horkheimer Archive, University Library Frankfurt/Main, MHA VIII, 10, p. 22.

the young Jewish intellectuals who mainly came from bourgeois families or to the continued impact of a latent cultural tradition, and the ostracisation they still encountered as Jews in some arenas doubtless played an important role too – the fact of the matter is that many German-Jewish intellectuals shared a profound mutual affinity and sense of solidarity. They might position themselves at opposite ends of the political spectrum and regularly engage in harsh controversies and polemics that pitted them against each other and yet, the majority of Jewish intellectuals – just like Pollock – belonged to networks that were almost exclusively Jewish. Experiences of antisemitism, however subtle, routinely reinforced their conviction that these networks needed to be maintained. Towards the end of his life, Pollock claimed not to have encountered much antisemitism prior to the rise of the National Socialists, but he certainly knew that outright polemic was the only suitable response to what was, to adopt Sombart's terminology, a 'bloodthirsty and venomous' pamphlet fancified with the 'sequins of pseudo-science', namely, Sombart's own screed.[36]

In an important sense, Pollock polemicised against Sombart primarily in his capacity as a prominent proponent of the far right, and his polemic also targeted self-avowed fascists such as the Austrian economist Othmar Spann. Certain elements of Pollock's critique of Sombart – the demolition of reactionary anti-capitalism, the leadership cult and the concept of an organic community – already prefigured the analyses of fascism later developed by the institute. His acute observations led him to appreciate that the rise of National Socialism posed a very real danger. He still hoped that the introduction of a democratically controlled form of planned economy might avert a fascist dictatorship, but the political situation looked increasingly dire.

The first couple of years under Horkheimer's directorship of the institute allowed Pollock to bring his quest for political independence and a social role to a satisfactory conclusion. As he distanced himself from his family and its business, from the Jewish community and from party Communism, the refuge of his friendship with Horkheimer had long since become utterly indispensable. He had managed to create a small world of his own in which he played a clearly defined role. In his relationship with Horkheimer, he was tasked with making ends meet and guaranteeing the constant renewal of their covenant. In the institute, he was the administrative director and Marx-inspired economic prognostician. To society at large, he was a recognised scholar and the *éminence grise* of the controversial but nevertheless widely respected Institute of Social Research. He was able to identify fully with each of these roles, and they

---

36　Sombart 1924, p. 382; Pollock 2018c, p. 250.

put him at ease with himself. Contemporaneous observers described him as a self-assured and equable character who always had his finger on the pulse of current developments. Few knew quite how protracted and arduous the process of self-reflection had been to which he owed these qualities.

CHAPTER 6

Dusk

In the summer of 1930, Germany began to confront the full extent of the Great Depression. To be sure, the situation would deteriorate yet further. Even so, given that the unemployment figures had risen to nearly five million within a year, it was clear already that this was not an ordinary recession but a major crisis that only radical measures might be able to address. The historian Richard Evans has described the mood on Berlin's streets:

> Young men roamed the streets aimlessly, sat listlessly at home, spent the day playing cards, wandering through public parks, or riding endlessly round and round on the electric trains of Berlin's Circle Line. In this situation, action often seemed better than inaction; boredom turned to frustration. Many unemployed men, even young boys and girls, tried to make a meagre living by hawking, busking, house-cleaning, street trading or any one of the number of traditional makeshifts of the economically marginal. Groups of children haunted Berlin's fashionable nightspots offering to 'look after' wealthy people's cars, a primitive form of protection racket practised in other, less innocuous forms by grown-ups, too. Informal hiking clubs and working-class youth groups easily became so-called 'wild cliques', gangs of young people who met in disused buildings, scavenged food, stole to make a living, fought with rival gangs, and frequently clashed with the police.[1]

Crime and suicide figures were on the rise, social and mental immiseration were rampant. Those who were still in work, even those who enjoyed a comfortable existence, lived in constant panic that their existence too might implode. Free market liberals and proponents of the rule of law lost all credibility, given that the very institutions tasked with averting it seemed to have created the crisis. Critical observers would have recalled the Gründer crash of the 1870s and the ensuing, earlier Great Depression, but that crisis had been a more protracted affair. The impact of the current crisis, by contrast, was much more dramatic, it was like a hurricane making landfall. It was not only the workers who rapidly lost what confidence in the rationality of the market they had

---

1 Evans 2004, p. 233.

regained after the post-war crises. As the impression gained ground that the entire Weimar system was corrupt and benefitted only a conspiring elite of war profiteers, the principles of liberal democracy, the rule of law, the separation of powers, respect for the constitution and parliamentary sovereignty rang increasingly hollow.[2] In various ways, an increasingly pronounced yearning for redemption from this veil of tears took hold of the entire political spectrum.

Against the backdrop of mass unemployment, social immiseration and political disillusionment, the parties opposed to the Weimar Republic garnered increasing support. The resignation of the Social Democratic Chancellor Hermann Müller in 1930 inaugurated the phase of cabinets by presidential appointment that were no longer able to command reliable parliamentary majorities. In the general election of September 1930, the SPD's share of the vote dropped to 24.5 per cent while the NSDAP secured 18.3 per cent of the vote, becoming the second largest party in the Reichstag. Conversely, the KPD – utterly at loggerheads with the SPD – secured 13.1 per cent of the vote, and the DNVP – the far-right party just to the left of the Nazis – lost seven percentage points to the NSDAP. Even so, the crucial point was that the democratic centre had totally collapsed. Less than five per cent of the voters opted for Stresemann's DVP. The only party to maintain its previous status was the Catholic Centre Party with twelve per cent of the vote. The inexorable rise of Adolf Hitler, who went on to secure more than a third of the vote less than two years later, had begun.

Not least in light of the violent terror the SA had meted out for years, it did not take much to appreciate where the political development was heading, and yet many leftists were convinced that the far-right's success would only be transient. Consequently, the KPD continued with its struggle against 'social fascism' – a concept introduced by Grigori Zinoviev in 1924 to encapsulate the need to fight Social Democracy because it harmed the working class by acting to stabilise the capitalist system.[3]

The conflict between the two labour parties reached its climax in May 1929. In the autumn of 1928, the Prussian Minister of the Interior, Albert Grzesinski, a Social Democrat, lifted the ban preventing Hitler from speaking at public rallies, paving the way for Hitler's triumphant tour of the capital and rabble-rousing performance in Berlin's Sportpalast on 18/19 November of that year. The KPD felt compelled to respond to this provocation by demonstrating that it was still able to command the streets in the capital and decided that May Day 1929 offered the opportunity best suited to muster such a response. Alas, the

---

2 See Eitz and Engelhardt 2015, p. 144.
3 On the varying emphases regarding this thesis within the party, see Hoppe 2007, pp. 158–63.

party clearly underestimated the likely consequences of its defiant strategy on this occasion. Although May Day assemblies were banned, the KPD was able to mobilise some 8,000 protestors. The police, resorting to what can only be called excessive force, fired more than 11,000 shots at the unarmed crowd, killing 33 protestors and injuring almost 200 more in the course of what became known as Blood May.[4] In response, roughly 25,000 workers heeded the KPD's call for protest strikes. Karl Zörgiebel, Berlin's – also Social Democratic – Police Commissioner, then retaliated by declaring what was in effect a state of emergency in the capital and used the opportunity to deal the Communists a serious blow. Numerous arrests ensued, a temporary ban was issued against the *Rote Fahne*, and the party's militia, the Rote Frontkämpferbund, was dissolved, first in Prussia and then in the rest of Germany. If relations between KPD and SPD had been troubled before, they now lay in tatters. The Social Democrats had irrevocably alienated a potential ally in the struggle against the far right, the Communists, conversely, were left totally isolated. The Nazis were the beneficiaries of this rift which all but ruled out effective resistance when push came to shove. Many Communists meanwhile focussed their ire more than ever on the 'social fascists'. The Nazis, by contrast, they tended to view as a movement born of misguided but ultimately justified 'petit-bourgeois protest' against the capitalist system.

Communists and National Socialists had occasionally endeavoured to join forces in the past, most notoriously in 1923, when prominent KPD officials, either from conviction or opportunism or an admixture of both, jumped on the antisemitic bandwagon. At a joint NSDAP and KPD event in Stuttgart, Hermann Remmele, then a member of the Central Committee, lashed out at the Jewish livestock traders who cheated the honest German butcher. On 31 July 1923, Franz Pfemfert reported in *Die Aktion* on a public student meeting with Ruth Fischer, the head of the KPD in Berlin, on 25 July, to which völkisch students were expressly invited. The report quoted her, as infamously declaring, in the context of her attempt to outvölkisch them, that whoever called for action against

> *Jewish capital ... is already party to the class struggle*, even if he does not know it. You oppose Jewish capital and want to get the better of the stockbrokers. *And so you should. Trample the Jewish capitalists underfoot, hang them from the lampposts.* But, gentlemen, what about the big capitalists, the Stinnes, Klöckner ...?[5]

---

4 See Hoppe 2007, pp. 140–7.
5 Franz Pfemfert, 'Die Schwarzweißrote Pest im ehemaligen Spartakusbund', *Die Aktion*, 13.27/

To be sure, these were isolated incidents, but they do point to a partial convergence of anti-capitalist, antisemitic and anti-democratic tropes deployed against the 'Weimar system' in the crisis of 1923. In the event, the republic survived. Both Hitler's coup in Munich and the Communist insurrection in Hamburg failed and both the economy and the political system recovered for the time being. It was in the short interregnum between this crisis and the Great Depression that the Institute of Social Research was created and made a name for itself, and that Pollock developed from a Marxist proper into a social scientist whose approach was shaped in no small measure by Marxian theory.

Yet circumstances had changed radically by the time the new crisis really began to bite. The country was effectively governed dictatorially by means of emergency decrees, the unemployed masses filled the streets, extreme poverty had increased exponentially, and the NSDAP was no longer a marginalised party but on the cusp of coming to power in Germany. To consider the Social Democrats the principal foe in this situation was a form of ideological idiocy. One should not exaggerate the significance of the occasional cooperation of Communists and Nazis even now – for example, during the transport workers' strike in Berlin in November 1932 – nor should one minimise the considerable extent of Communist resistance to the Nazis. Even so, there can be little doubt that the conflicts and mutual recriminations between Communists and Social Democrats only helped render the democratic order ever more fragile.

The institute sought to facilitate the continued pursuit of scholarship regardless of the thunderclouds gathering outside. Even so, the political development obviously gave considerable cause for concern. On Leo Löwenthal's account, it was on 15 September 1930, the day following the general election, that he, Felix Weil, Max Horkheimer and Friedrich Pollock gathered and made the momentous decision to prepare for the worst case by establishing a branch in Geneva, a plan developed by Horkheimer and Pollock. 'You need to provide the funds so we can now establish the branch in Geneva', Löwenthal recalled saying to Weil, 'one will not be able to stay here, we need to prepare for emigration'.[6] Pollock maintained relations with the Geneva-based International Labour Organization (ILO) and its director, Albert Thomas, who was a historian by training and a former French armaments minister. Created after the First World War, the ILO

28, 31 July 1923, p. 373. The bulk of the report was subsequently reprinted in the principal SPD daily, *Vorwärts*: '"Hängt die Judenkapitalisten." Ruth Fischer als Antisemitin', *Vorwärts*, 40.390, 22 August 1923, pp. 2–3.

6 Löwenthal 1980, p. 67.

was funded by the League of Nations and concerned with international labour law, the support of war veterans and the fostering of improved working conditions.[7]

Given that its members had worthwhile things to contribute in terms of the cultural, political, psychological and economic causes and implications of the Great Depression, it was far from implausible that the Frankfurt institute would seek to collaborate with an organisation concerned with practical issues in the sphere of labour – or at least the issue could reasonably be spun this way. Although the institute pursued the cooperation principally for pragmatic and political reasons, simply because the creation of the branch in Geneva would not have been possible without the support of the ILO, Pollock's seminars in Frankfurt demonstrate that the connection did give rise to some genuine scholarly synergies. To illustrate this, we need to take a closer look at the period between Grünberg's departure and Horkheimer's accession and the subsequent transformation of the institute's profile, given that the creation of the Geneva branch coincided with a shift in the institute's scholarly focus.

The plan was that Pollock would take on the role of director of the Geneva branch in 1932. Prior to the cooperation with the ILO, he essentially taught the Marxian critique of political economy, the history of the labour movement and general economics. These were all paradigmatic topics of the Grünberg era. For example, in the summer semester of 1929, Pollock offered a lecture course on 'The Structural Transformation of the German Economy' and tutorials on the history of German Social Democracy. The following semester, the offering was 'Reading Marx' and 'Economic Problems in Soviet Russia', followed in the summer semester of 1930 by a lecture course on 'Capitalism and Socialism' and an advanced Marx reading course. The following semester he taught a seminar on 'The History of Socialism', a modified version of his lecture course on 'The Structural Transformation of the German Economy', a seminar on 'The Theory and History of Wages' and a course in introductory economics.[8] These were all conventional topics in the field of 'scientific Socialism' and they hardly speak to the merger of disciplines on the basis of the Marxian theoretical approach that Horkheimer envisaged. Horkheimer was now the director but as yet Grünberg's spirit continued to prevail and there is nothing to suggest that Pollock was troubled by this state of affairs.

A letter Karl Korsch wrote to the Japanese economist Eiichi Sugimoto in May 1931 conveys a sense of the atmosphere in Pollock's seminars. Korsch and

---

7 On the history of the organisation, see Alcock 1971.
8 'Institut für Sozialforschung a.d. Universität Frankfurt a. M.', Horkheimer Archive, University Library Frankfurt/Main, MHA IX 51, p. 2.

Sugimoto had both attended the previous semester's advanced Marx reading course. Referring to a debate on the question of whether social demand changes a commodity's magnitude of value, Korsch wrote:

> As far as your *discussion with Mandelbaum* is concerned, I am mainly in agreement with you. I think that Mandelbaum's view amounts to a revision of Marxism. Incidentally, I already went over the same issue with him in detail last summer. At the end of that discussion, he agreed with me but subsequently seems to have reverted to his original position which he then articulated in Dr. Pollock's seminar. (By the way, I suspect that this most recent revision of Marx originates neither with Pollock's seminar nor with Mandelbaum, but with 'Boris', who is well known there, and perhaps also with the Russian economist Rubin!)[9]

Even in the post-Grünberg era, then, Marxist minutiae were still the object of heated political controversy and the reproach of revisionism continued to serve as valid tender. The representation of a broad spectrum of leftist positions Felix Weil had envisaged was certainly not a feature of Pollock's seminars, given that the political background of its participants was fairly homogeneous. They mostly stood to the left of the KPD or were at least critical of the party. In Pollock's seminar, his assistant Kurt Mandelbaum, who was expelled from the KPD in 1926 for being a member of the 'ultra-leftist Korsch group', now sat alongside Korsch. The aforementioned 'Boris', whom Korsch suspected of revisionism, was Boris Roniger, a fellow undertaking research on monopoly capitalism. He too had been expelled by the KPD as a member of the Korsch group and, like Mandelbaum, had found a refuge in the institute. He fled to England in 1938 and eventually returned, in 1945, as a US intelligence officer. The Soviet economist Korsch mentioned in his letter, Isaac Illich Rubin, a long neglected early expert on Marx, did not attend the seminar in person but might as well have done, given how prominently his publications featured in its discussions. His *Studien zur Marxschen Werttheorie* (Studies on Marx's Value Theory), published in German in 1924, held canonical status at the institute.[10] His essay, 'Abstract Labour and Value in Marx's System' (published in Russian in 1927), coincides thematically with Pollock's own doctoral research and the overlap between their positions would merit closer scrutiny.

---

9   Karl Korsch to Eiichi Sugimoto, 7 May 1931, in Korsch 2001, pp. 384–7, p. 384.
10 Rubin 1973; on Rubin, see Boldyrev 2015.

As a foreigner, Eiichi Sugimoto, who went on to pioneer mathematical economics in Japan, was to some extent the odd one out. Interested in Marxism, he had come to Frankfurt in 1930 after Wassily Leontief, a Menshevik who had recently moved to the United States and with whom he was friendly, recommended he study at the institute.[11] Sugimoto left the institute again after only one semester and how much of what he learnt in Frankfurt fed into the works with which he paved the way for further research on Marxism in Japan is a moot point. Sugimoto was one of the last scholars to encounter the old-style theoretical Marx research at the institute.

From 1932 onwards, not just Pollock's seminars moved away from the critique of political economy in the narrower sense. My contention is that this resulted not least from Pollock's role in Geneva where he needed to develop his profile as director of the newly established Société Internationale de Recherches Sociales (SIRES). This also forms the backdrop to the institute's increased interest in statistics and empirical social research. Two projects were of particular significance in this context. One was an empirical study on the psychic disposition of workers and salaried employees undertaken by Erich Fromm and Hilde Weiss in 1929. Its results were deeply depressing and not published at the time but gave rise to intense discussions among the members of the institute. The study worked with a typology – radical; authoritarian; willing to compromise/reformist; indifferent – that was later developed further for the research summarised, with Adorno's participation, in *The Authoritarian Personality*.[12] The sobering – though, for the members of the institute, hardly surprising – conclusion was that workers and salaried employees would not resist fascism because their psychic makeup disposed them towards authoritarianism.

Pollock played a more substantial role in the second partly empirical research project, *Studien über Autorität und Familie* (Studies on Authority and the Family), undertaken in the early 1930s. Here, there was a direct connection to the ILO whose international connections and extensive infrastructure the institute wanted to utilise for the purposes of the project. The study had three parts: a general theoretical section; an empirical section summarising the survey material; and, finally, a section with specific studies from a variety of disciplines. The ILO helped to facilitate the third and fourth survey. The third survey comprised interviews with experts from Austria, Belgium, France, Switzerland and the Netherlands. These experts were supposed to be relevant profession-

---

11   See Ikeo 2014, p. 20.
12   Fromm 1984.

als, i.e., family court judges, public welfare workers, clergy, youth group leaders, teachers and directors of orphanages and youth centres. As the authors Ernst Schachtel and Andries Sternheim, who worked for the Geneva branch of the institute, expressly acknowledged, it had been quite difficult to 'compile a list of experts that matched the aforementioned [representative] criteria'.[13] They owed a debt of gratitude, they added, to a number of organisations for nevertheless facilitating the successful execution of this survey, foremost among them the ILO.

The fourth survey comprised interviews with 1,000 Swiss adolescents. Here too, the support of the ILO was invaluable. Responsibility for the methodology underpinning this survey lay primarily with Käthe Leichter and Paul Lazarsfeld. Lazarsfeld was able to draw on his experiences with one of the classics of empirical sociology, the study *Die Arbeitslosen von Marienthal* (Marienthal: The Sociography of an Unemployed Community).[14] Beginning in 1937, he resumed his cooperation with the institute in his capacity as the director, first, of the Princeton Radio Research Project and then, of the Office of Radio Research at Columbia University.[15] This fourth survey, comprising just under 100 pages, as well as the fifth survey, focussing on the impact of unemployment on family life, were of particular interest to the ILO.

When the studies were finally published in Paris in 1936, Pollock was not among the named contributors, but it was he who coordinated the various parts of the study, first from Geneva, where he spent much of 1932/33 and, beginning in 1934, from New York. As Horkheimer noted in the preface: 'Friedrich Pollock drafted a fundamental essay on economics for the first section. As a result of his duties running the institute and his active participation in the preparatory research for this volume this essay has not yet been finalised.'[16] In fact, Pollock never did complete the essay in question, and his role was really that of an editor rather than a contributor. Of course, in order to organise the contributions in a meaningful way and give the volume a plausible and stringent structure overall, Pollock needed to be on top of the relevant research and scholarly debate. His review essay on family sociology, published in the *Zeitschrift für Sozialforschung* in 1932, clearly demonstrated that this was indeed the case.[17] The family study – as the first 'collective "work in progress"' of the kind Horkheimer envisaged for the institute – also impacted its teaching pro-

---

13   Horkheimer (ed.) 1936, p. 293.
14   Jahoda, Lazarsfeld and Zeisel 1972.
15   For Lazarsfeld's biography, see Wiggershaus 1994, pp. 166–8.
16   Horkheimer (ed.) 1936, p. x.
17   Pollock 1932b.

gramme in significant ways.[18] In the winter semester of 1931/32, Pollock offered a tutorial on 'The Situation of Salaried Employees in Germany'. The following semester, he ran tutorials on 'The Leisure Activities of Salaried Employees in Germany', and the following semester a seminar on 'Salaried Employees in Today's Economy'.[19]

Yet alongside the coordination of the family project and his administrative duties, Pollock also continued to pursue his own academic and political agenda. He remained convinced that only a socialist planned economy could contain the economic crisis and meet the population's needs in the long term and, thus, take the wind out of the fascist demagogues' sails. For the academic year 1932/33 he planned seminars, tutorials and a lecture course on problems associated with the planned economy. In the event, only the courses announced for the winter semester of 1932/33 were able to take place. His continued engagement of the topic was owed to the assumption that, whatever one's misgivings about real-existing Socialism, one urgently needed to ascertain what lessons might be learnt for the future from the problems the planned economy encountered in the Soviet Union. Perhaps conditions in Germany or North America were better suited to a planned economy than those in Russia, given their more advanced economic development.

In addition to Marx, Engels and Lenin, it was the Social Democratic theoretician and politician Rudolf Hilferding who challenged Pollock time and again. In his influential book, *Das Finanzkapital* (Finance Capital), which was published in 1910 and which Pollock had already studied in detail as a student, Hilferding stressed that, as the market became increasingly crisis-prone, capitalism would turn into monopoly capitalism and become increasingly dependent on the state, so much so that the state would go from being the notional to being, as Engels put it, the actual all-encompassing capitalist (*Gesamtkapitalist*).[20] Pollock agreed with this assessment in principle but rejected Hilferding's optimistic assumption that a form of monopoly capitalism underwritten and administered by the state was a necessary step on the path to socialism. This also pitted him against Lenin, who had articulated a radicalised version of Hilferding's contention in his programmatic discussion of *Imperialism as the Highest Stage of Capitalism*.[21]

---

18   Wiggershaus 1994a, p. 149.
19   Pollock was likely aware of Kracauer's book on salaried employees (1930) since Kracauer sent a copy of his study to Horkheimer.
20   Hilferding 1981. For the concept of the notional and actual *Gesamtkapitalist*, see Engels 2010, p. 266.
21   Lenin 1964.

As Pollock saw it, the monopolisation and centralisation of capital rendered capitalism increasingly immune to crises. Both economically and politically, the capitalist order was becoming not more fragile but more stable. Its increasing integration into the state rendered the proletariat less capable of resistance, and the far-right revolutionaries too, he assumed, would ultimately be unable to pose any serious threat to the monopoly capitalist order. In a letter to Adorno, Horkheimer summarised how he and, on his account, Pollock judged the political situation in Germany: 'In broad strokes', he wrote from Geneva on 30 June 1932,

> the further development seems pretty settled. How exactly the process will unfold is predominantly a matter of foreign policy developments that one cannot possibly predict. It will, however, most likely be possible to bring the interests of the various groups that are running loose in the National Socialist movement fully back under the control of big industry and thus wholly paralyze the explosive potential that inheres in the movement; unless some misguided foreign policy decision aggravates the crisis to such an extent that one will be forced to resort to the most extreme remedies. This is roughly what Pollock thinks too. There is only one thing we know for certain: the irrationality of society has reached a level that renders only the bleakest prognoses plausible.[22]

That Horkheimer's pessimistic assessment really should have reflected Pollock's opinion seems doubtful. He was more inclined to insist that, alongside all the portents, there were also positive trends that needed to be taken into account. Never before had industrial productivity been as great. Consequently, genuine hunger crises could be avoided in future. He developed this argument in detail in his contribution to the Festschrift published to mark Grünberg's seventieth birthday. 'A socialist society', he wrote, 'need fear no shortages of foodstuffs or raw materials in any foreseeable future. Instead, owing to its better organisation, it can count on wheat no longer having to be burned, coffee no longer having to be thrown into the sea, cotton no longer having to be destroyed and oil wells no longer having to be shut down under military guard and, instead, on all this wealth benefitting all of humankind.'[23]

For all that Pollock had rejected the Soviet model, he still assumed one could learn a great deal from it in terms of how to do better in future. For

---

22   Max Horkheimer to Theodor W. Adorno, 30 June 1932, in Adorno and Horkheimer 2003, pp. 13–15, pp. 14–15.
23   Pollock 1984, p. 181 (translation amended).

him, the superiority and necessity of a planned economy was not in doubt. The Great Depression clearly demonstrated that free market capitalism was doomed. To be sure, not only the Communists but the Nazis too flirted with state capitalist concepts, as did conversative forces such as the circle associated with the monthly periodical *Die Tat*. Yet as Pollock saw it, this only confirmed that the need for a planned economy was no longer in question. In dispute was merely how exactly it should be organised. Since the emergence of a postliberal economic order was inevitable, trying to romanticise an already irrecoverable past was a waste of time and all efforts should be focussed with the utmost urgency on an unsparing analysis of what needed to be done next.

The *Zeitschrift für Sozialforschung* was designed to offer a forum for just this kind of debate. The plan to replace Grünberg's *Archiv* with a periodical published directly by the institute that reflected Horkheimer's crossdisciplinary and socio-philosophical agenda, had been in the making for some time. The first double issue came out in the summer of 1932. Rather appropriately, it was devoted to the topic 'crisis'. Its table of contents rather neatly reflects the hierarchy within the institute. Two contributions by Horkheimer – the preface written in his capacity as editor and a short essay, 'Bemerkungen über Wissenschaft und Krise' (Notes on Science and the Crisis), consisting of ten succinct theses laying out the issue's agenda – led the way.[24]

These were followed by the periodical's inaugural research article, written by the institute's deputy director, i.e., Pollock, 'Die gegenwärtige Lage des Kapitalismus und die Aussichten einer planwirtschaftlichen Neuordnung' (The Current State of Capitalism and the Prospects of a New Planned Economy). Offering a general survey from the vantage of economic theory, Pollock clarified the nature of his continued interest in the Soviet Union. 'It may dismay some that we have not referred to the economic system of Soviet Russia as an option for a planned economy', he wrote in a footnote, adding: 'We are indeed convinced that a great deal can be learned, regarding both theoretical and practical aspects of the planned economy, from the Russian endeavours. However, in its current state, the Russian experiment cannot serve as a case in point suited to verify whether this kind of planned economy is *economically* ... superior to capitalism based on private ownership.'[25] He had already raised the question of whether the Soviet experiment genuinely embodied the transition to a fundamentally new order, as Lenin's successors claimed, in his postdoctoral thesis.

---

24 Horkheimer 2002a.
25 Pollock 1932a, p. 27.

There, he had arrived at the sobering conclusion that the proclaimed 'ultimate goal' of a classless society had been kicked into the long grass. Instead,

> the appropriation of state power is meant to be only the first step. According to the Bolshevik viewpoint, it is followed by a sustained period of transition, the 'dictatorship of the proletariat', that gradually paves the way for Socialism. In the economic sphere this results in a transitional configuration in which the old economic institutions – the market in particular – are disintegrating but the new institutions have not yet been fully developed.[26]

Consequently, the Socialist planned economy, while embodying a response to the crisis of capitalism, led to the abolition neither of domination and exploitation, nor of the state and money.

The ongoing havoc wreaked by the Great Depression lent new meaning and urgency to the issue of the planned economy, Pollock insisted. A broad range of observers, including many in the bourgeois camp, accepted that fundamental change was inevitable. It was widely noted that the impact of the Great Depression on the Soviet Union seemed to be limited. Pollock's question now was whether it might be possible to implement a form of planned economy based on what could be learnt from the Soviet model within a capitalist framework. The war economies during the First World War had shown that the introduction of a partial planned economic need not be a matter of socialist transformation.[27] Many now wondered whether a similar model might also be a helpful and viable option in peace time.

The first double issue of the *Zeitschrift für Sozialforschung* approached this debate from a number of vantages. 'The world now has more raw materials, machines, and skilled workers, and better methods of production than ever before', Horkheimer noted in his short introductory essay, and yet, 'society in its present form is unable to make effective use of the power it has developed and the wealth it has amassed'.[28] Building on Horkheimer's diagnosis, Pollock highlighted that never before in its history had humankind had at its disposal 'such advanced means of production and so many highly qualified workers, both in absolute terms and per capita', and yet it suffered 'a twofold form of deprivation: due to the fact that so many means of production, both material and personal,

---

26   Pollock 1929, p. 1.
27   Huhn 2003.
28   Horkheimer 2002a, p. 4.

are forced to lie fallow, and to the destruction of part of the produce.'[29] The capitalist system prevented the rational exploitation of the enormous forces of production at its disposal. Not only did this failure lead to the impoverishment of the masses, it also made it increasingly impossible for industry to work at capacity and forced enterprises to cannibalise themselves. As a result, the 'free play of market forces' ceased to function, paving the way for huge, centralised conglomerates with enormous economic and political power that simply dictated the prices of goods. In the age of the monopolies, the state no longer served merely as the proverbial night watchman but constantly interfered in labour relations and implemented various socio-political measures in order to master the crisis.[30]

That the state engages in social engineering and acts as an independent economic agent, for example, by using taxpayers' money to bail out faltering banks, now goes without saying. For Pollock, observing developments in 1932, this was a novel phenomenon that marked the transition from liberal competitive capitalism to a 'underwritten', 'bound' and 'organised' form of capitalism. Given that this process responded to a structural crisis of the capitalist system, he assumed that it was irreversible. One might be able to master the current crisis temporarily with capitalist remedies but even then, the 'only partially functional old system' would still be 'charged with so much tension that even relatively insignificant problems can engender a catastrophe whose destructive impact one can as yet barely foresee'.[31] Pollock did not explain what specifically he had in mind, but its seems clear from the context that he anticipated another world war that – by facilitating the 'massive destruction of wealth and human lives' – would once again restore some form of equilibrium between the various component parts of the economic system.[32] Given the high degree of monopolisation already attained, Pollock still assumed, however, that 'peaceful' measures might yet make an impact sufficient to ensure that the economy could be readjusted without having to resort to another world war.

Yet, as Pollock saw it, it was also this very potential to bring about a 'peaceful' resolution of the crisis that made the monopoly capitalist phase so perilous. Even as its internal contradictions persisted, an authoritarian state would be able to master the crisis in perpetuity. In contrast to Henryk Grossman, Pollock

---

29   Pollock 1932a, p. 9.
30   Pollock 1932a, p. 13.
31   Pollock 1932a, p. 16.
32   Pollock 1932a, p. 15. Pollock drew on the disproportionality crisis theory developed notably by Hilferding in *Finance Capital*. It drew on the concept of the 'long-term decline in the rate of profit' discussed at length in Marx 2010b. See Gangl 1987, pp. 168–79; Gangl 2016.

denied that capitalism was heading for some kind of automatic collapse. 'There are no purely economic grounds that necessitate its replacement by a different economic system', he maintained.[33] Of course, this meant that the issue of the economic system was ultimately not economic but in fact political in nature.

Pollock's article was followed by Erich Fromm's discussion, 'Über Methode und Aufgabe einer analytischen Sozialpsychologie' (On the Method and Task of Analytic Social Psychology), and an article on Marx's crisis concept by Grossman. Next was an essay, 'Zur gesellschaftlichen Lage der Literatur' (On the Social Situation of Literature) by Leo Löwenthal – who served as the journal's managing editor – followed by the first part of a companion piece, 'Zur gesellschaftlichen Lage der Musik' (On the Social Situation of Music) by Theodor Wiesengrund-Adorno, who had just completed his postdoctoral qualification.[34] A further article by Horkheimer, 'Geschichte und Psychologie' (History and Psychology) concluded the main section of the volume. It was rounded off by an extensive review section covering new publications in the fields of philosophy, sociology, psychology, history, social movements, social policy, economic theory and literature.

Many of the guest contributors who provided the bulk of the reviews subsequently continued to cooperate with the exiled institute. Prominent reviewers such as the psychoanalysts Karl Landauer and Wilhelm Reich, the philosopher Alexandre Koyré, the sociologist Albert Salomon, the historian Wilhelm Mackauer and the political scientist Sigmund Neumann helped establish the journal as one of the most prestigious social science periodicals in Europe. That the authors were in large part Jewish seems to have impressed itself neither on the institute nor on the wider public. They were connected only by their subject expertise, even diverging political loyalties initially played no role. In marked contrast to the state of play on the streets and in the Reichstag, Social Democrats, party Communists, those expelled from the party for diverging too far to the left or the right and various undecideds, in short, authors of all leftist creeds and none peacefully coexisted and collaborated on the pages of the journal. The institute, designed to be undogmatic and non-partisan from the outset, thus ran counter to the political disintegration of the left and did what it could, with its limited means, to create at least a scholarly united front that, alas, had little immediate political impact but fully came into its own in the struggle to survive once the Nazis came to power.

---

33 Pollock 1932a, p. 16.
34 See Sönke-Schneider 2014.

The journal soon took centre stage at the institute, and teaching found itself demoted to a more or less annoying obligation. At this juncture, one might think of the institute in terms of several concentric circles. The directors Horkheimer and Pollock were surrounded by a close circle of trusted colleagues, namely, Löwenthal, Marcuse and Fromm. Then there was an intermediate circle of associates who were not formally members of the institute, such as Adorno and Franz Borkenau and, finally, there was an outer circle comprising several dozen scholars from a range of disciplines in the humanities and social sciences. While the profile of the journal was determined by Horkheimer in close cooperation with Pollock and Löwenthal (and, later, Adorno), the involvement of a broad range of guest contributors helped the institute to establish a wider-ranging network of connections across various sections of the academy. It was this network that allowed the institute to survive in exile and, consequently, to offer urgently needed support to a substantial number of scholars. As the institute's financial administrator, Pollock played a key role in this respect and it was in large measure down to him that, between 1934 and 1944, not including a range of minor, spontaneous support measures and outright donations, the institute was able to support 116 doctoral scholars and 14 postdoctoral scholars with almost $200,000 in total (the equivalent of some $4 million in today's money).[35] The institute by no means supported only its own permanent employees. Everyone commissioned to write an article or review for the journal was remunerated, regardless of whether the texts were ultimately published or not. For some of the émigré authors, these payments were absolutely essential. Maintaining this network was hard work and it fell to Pollock to shoulder this task.

---

35   Jay 1996, pp. 114–15.

CHAPTER 7

Practical Relief Work

At quarter past eleven on the morning of 30 January 1933, Germany's president Paul von Hindenburg reluctantly appointed the 'Bohemian corporal' Adolf Hitler chancellor. Hours later, the SA descended on Pollock and Horkheimer's house in Kronberg, only to find that its owners had already left. Long before the systematic 'aryanisation' of Jewish property was officially set in motion, the brown shirts decided to turn the house into their new base.[1] That they turned up within hours of the Nazis coming to power demonstrates just how great the threat to the members of the institute was.

Hitler's appointment certainly came as no surprise to Pollock. He and his colleagues had anticipated this turn of events for the last two years. They had created the branch in Geneva as a refuge and transferred the bulk of the foundation's capital to an account in the Netherlands. The speed at which the Nazis were able to exploit the situation and transform Germany in their image may nevertheless have startled him. The mass arrests and widespread terror that followed the Reichstag fire – drawing on preparations made well in advance of the fire – finally dispelled any lingering illusions that the Nazis might not mean business. The SA ruled the streets and public spaces and routinely engaged in arbitrary arrests and assaults. Just two weeks later, on 13 March 1933, the SA occupied the institute's premises, closed the institute and handed the property over in trust to the Nazi student organisation. Not that there was, at this point, any legal basis for such measures. The expropriation of the institute was legalised retroactively only four months later by the high-ranking Gestapo official Heinrich Richter-Brohm with recourse to the Law on the Confiscation of Communist Assets – a law that had only come into force at the end of May. The confiscation, expropriation and dissolution were justified, he decreed, on the grounds that 'the institute in question fostered seditious endeavours'.[2] The old police files pertaining to the institute's cooperation with the Marx-Engels Institute in Moscow were now its undoing.

Pollock had moved to Geneva in the summer of 1932 but regularly returned to Frankfurt, not least to meet his teaching commitments there. Alas, he held only a tourist visa for Geneva. Every couple of weeks he travelled across the

---

1 Wiggershaus 2013, p. 77.
2 Quoted in Wiggershaus 1994a, p. 128 (translation amended).

French border to Bellegarde-sur-Valserine and then re-entered Switzerland on a new tourist visa. Horkheimer held a temporary residency permit but was only too aware of the fact that his position was nevertheless extremely precarious. When they were in Frankfurt, where both of them continued to teach until the end of February, they stayed at a hotel close to the city's main station. They obviously could not return to their house in Kronberg and wanted to ensure that they would be able to flee instantly if need be. When the SA seized the institute, it was clear that they indeed had only one option: to get out immediately.

In mid-May, they were stripped by public decree of their academic teaching licence and at the end of the month, their Prussian citizenship was revoked. Their old life was now definitely over. Their attempts, such as they were, to avoid unnecessary attention and conflict had come to nothing as they were very publicly uprooted, ostracised and humiliated. To be sure, they had established some provisional fallback options but in the event they were essentially powerless against the forces that destroyed their previous existence. Prescient they may have been, but one would be considerably overstating the case by suggesting that they chose to emigrate. They simply had no choice in the matter. As they embarked on what they dressed up as short-term research trips, they were forced to leave behind family, friends and colleagues and abandon virtually all their material possessions.

The threat to Pollock was twofold. If the terror the Nazis unleashed immediately on taking power primarily targeted political opponents, it soon became clear that the new regime's antisemitism was not merely rhetorical in nature either. Pollock's network of friends and associates consisted almost exclusively of Jews and more or less radical leftists – indeed, many of them were both. Clearly, there was no future for him in Germany. Nor was it a matter of speculation what it meant to stay in Germany as a leftist intellectual. Observing the situation from Switzerland, Pollock witnessed the persecution of two close associates of the institute, Karl August Wittfogel and Paul Massing.

Wittfogel was in Basle to give a lecture when the Nazis came to power. Although he knew how dangerous it was for him to return to Germany, given that he was a well-known KPD intellectual and activist, he was determined to do so in order to join the resistance against the Nazis. According to Gary Ulmen's chronicle, Wittfogel travelled to Gstaad, the posh skiing resort in the Swiss Alps, on 1 February 1933 to meet Pollock who was vacationing there. For two days, they deliberated about the new political situation and the possible future of the institute. Pollock implored Wittfogel not to return to Germany, but to no avail. When it became clear to him that Wittfogel could not be dissuaded, he pleaded with him to make his stay in Germany as short as possible. The following day, Wittfogel travelled to Zurich where he gave another lecture and met the sexologist Magnus Hirschfeld who had already fled. Hirschfeld too vehemently warned him against returning to Germany. While in Zurich, Wittfogel also received a message from Ernst Toller telling him in no uncertain terms not to return to Germany.[3]

Yet Wittfogel would not change his mind – perhaps the fact that his wife was still in Berlin also played a role – and on 5 February 1933, he crossed the German border and travelled to the capital where he immediately entered the political fray. He gave lectures, attended conspiratorial gatherings and met various comrades, including Paul Massing who, according to Ulmen, was Wittfogel's closest friend.[4] All the while, given that their flat was no longer safe, Wittfogel and his second wife, Olga Wittfogel, née Joffe, a Jewish journalist from Russia who was herself a member of the KPD, spent their nights separately, he in Moabit, she near Nollendorfplatz in Schöneberg.[5]

The Gestapo was never far behind, but it was not until Wittfogel did eventually recognize, following the Reichstag fire, how urgently he needed to get out that he was caught. On the morning of 11 March, the papers and radio stations announced that the 'infamous Communist' Wittfogel had been caught in Singen (located in southern Baden, close to the Swiss border) trying to flee the country. Initially detained in Singen and then Radolfzell, he was transferred to the Ankenbuck concentration camp in May, from there to a prison in Konstanz and then, via prisons in Heidelberg, Würzburg, Hanau and Frankfurt to the Esterwegen concentration camp (located near the Dutch border), where he arrived in September 1933. While he was imprisoned in Frankfurt, Olga Wittfogel was able to visit him several times. In Esterwegen, despite suffering from tuberculosis since his youth, he was compelled to undertake forced labour. In November, he was transferred to the Lichtenburg concentration camp in Saxony, one of the particularly brutal early camps that was later merged into Buchenwald. Immediately prior to his release, Wittfogel seems too have been in the camp infirmary, where his wife was again able to visit him.[6]

Olga Wittfogel did all she could to free him. Among the many more or less prominent individuals she approached were also Pollock and Horkheimer. They, in turn, wrote to various established academics, the university administration in Frankfurt and the education ministry in Berlin, asking them to support Wittfogel. Writing regularly to Wittfogel and sending him books and

---

3   Ulmen 1978, pp. 155–6.
4   Ulmen 1978, p. 160.
5   Ulmen 1978, p. 159.
6   Ulmen 1978, p. 167.

articles (that apparently did reach him), Pollock also sought to boost Wittfogel's morale by suggesting that his detention did not rule out 'at least some measure of scholarly activity'.[7] He also sought to provide him with what was in his situation arguably the single most important resource of all: hope. The authorities would 'ultimately arrive at the conclusion that you are of more use to Germany if you continue your great work on China than if you sit in prison', he suggested. The institute was being contacted on a daily basis by supporters whom he then encouraged to petition the German embassies and consulates. 'I know that your name is now well known in the foreign ministry in Berlin,' Pollock wrote, 'and I imagine that the relevant authorities have developed a sense of your global reputation as an outstanding scholar.'[8]

Apparently, the exceedingly well connected ultra-nationalist but anti-Nazi publicist Friedrich Hielscher was instrumental in finally convincing the regime of the political innocuousness and exploitable prestige of the acclaimed Sinologist Wittfogel.[9] Wittfogel, Pollock and Hielscher knew each other from ARPLAN, the Arbeitsgemeinschaft zum Studium der sowjetrussischen Planwirtschaft (Working Group for the Study of the Planned Economy in the Soviet Union), a research group initiated by the Soviet embassy in Berlin that brought together prominent figures of the political right (including Hielscher, Ernst Niekisch and Carl Schmitt) and the left (including Wittfogel, Grossman and Pollock).[10] Eventually, Wittfogel was released on condition that he immediately leave the country for England, where the economic historian Richard Henry Tawney had agreed to take him under his wings at the LSE. In fact, when he arrived in the UK in January 1934, he took up a position at the institute's recently established branch in London (it amounted to little more than a small office at the Institute of Sociology), but he soon moved on to the USA. From 1935 to 1937, he was in receipt of a grant from the institute that allowed him to undertake field work in China.

The forced labour and his time in Lichtenburg notwithstanding, Wittfogel had been relatively fortunate. The same cannot be said of Paul Massing. It seems likely that his partner, Hede Gumperz (as she then still was), renewed

---

7   Friedrich Pollock to Karl August Wittfogel, 27 July 1933, Wittfogel Papers, Hoover Institution, 37, 8.

8   Ibid.

9   For Hielscher's colourful account of his involvement, see Hielscher 1954, pp. 270–4. It suggests that Olga Wittfogel turned to him only relatively late in the day. On Hielscher's account, he was forced to sign a statement agreeing to be incarcerated in a concentration camp himself should Wittfogel misbehave following his release. He also claims that Olga Wittfogel eventually went into hiding with his mother.

10   Cf. Rieß (ed.) 2019.

her contact with Pollock, whom she first met in 1923 at the Marxist Study Week, when she spent some time in Geneva in 1932, trying to recruit the ILO employee Abrasha Westermann, a former student of the institute who wrote reviews for its journal.[11] (There is no suggestion, though, that she tried to recruit Pollock too.) Consequently, Pollock is likely to have been well informed about Massing's fate. Massing, who was still in Berlin, was picked up by the Gestapo on 17 July 1933 and taken to the infamous Columbia House in central Berlin, one of the early concentration camps known for its particularly barbaric treatment of the detainees. There, he was interrogated, abused and tortured for several weeks. 'I had never in my life seen so much anguish, deadly terror, despair, and suffering. I had never thought men capable of such monstrosities. It seemed to be endless', Massing wrote soon after his release in *Schutzhäftling 880. Aus einem deutschen Konzentrationslager* (Fatherland), an account of his experiences he published under the pseudonym Karl Billinger in 1935. 'We were denied the most elementary rights of common criminals', he lamented, while 'Outside, the new Germany celebrated one national holiday after another.'[12]

In mid-August, he was transferred, via the Plötzensee jail, to the Oranienburg concentration camp where he spent five months. After several weeks, a female comrade took Hede Gumperz to Oranienburg (the camp was located in plain sight in the middle of town, not far from the station) where they waited in a restaurant close to the entrance of the camp until the prisoners returning from the slave labour they were forced to undertake during the day marched past.

> When the third group of marching prisoners had come close enough for us to get up and look at them, Anna slipped her arm into mine and said from the corner of her mouth, 'Here he is. He is the second from the left in the third row. His head sticks out. The tall one.' ... It was my Paul! This white, thin, shorn, limping man. He limped. He must have been crippled from the beatings. Nothing but his eyes and his nose were the same. His mouth was a line, thin and narrow, in his pitiful shorn head.[13]

Paul Massing's brother Gustav, who served as a judge in Saarbrücken, requested permission to visit his incarcerated brother, but in vain.[14] The response to his

---

11   Massing 1951, pp. 101–2.
12   Billinger 1935, p. 55. In the UK, the book was published by Gollancz and bore the title *All Quiet in Germany*.
13   Massing 1951, pp. 127–8.
14   See Gustav Massing to Oranienburg Concentration Camp, 27 September 1933, Brandenburgisches Landeshauptarchiv Potsdam, Geheime Staatspolizei und Konzentrationslager,

request was as straightforward as it was chilling: 'Re Your letter of the 27th concerning permission to speak to your brother Paul Massing, please note that, in response to the subversive Marxist and Jewish propaganda renewed on a daily basis, both nationally and internationally, a freeze on visitor permits for prisoners in protective custody is in force until 1 November 1933. Exceptions may be granted only in urgent cases.'[15] Evidently, Massing's case was not considered urgent.

In December 1933, Hermann Göring amnestied 5,000 prisoners who had been taken into 'protective custody', and Massing unexpectedly came free.[16] He immediately fled to Paris and from there, together with Hede – who had an American passport because she was technically still married to Gumperz – to the USA. It was a condition of his release that he report daily to the police in Berlin. When he failed to do so, the SS raided his flat. Evidently, they were not minded to let someone they assumed was a leading German Bolshevik get away, but they were too late.

How committed Massing was to the cause is indicated by the fact that he returned to Germany soon after. His sense of responsibility towards those suffering persecution compelled him to venture back into enemy territory, his recent horrendous experiences there notwithstanding, to help coordinate the party's illegal work. He trusted in the Communist International's prediction that Hitler's triumph would inevitably be followed by the proletarian revolution, and unquestioningly followed the party's instructions. In 1936, he married Hede and, like her, became a Soviet agent. They were loyal party soldiers who unhesitatingly risked their lives for the world revolution they still assumed was within reach.

Yet then Massing was confronted with a set of events he would never have thought possible. In August 1936, the first of the major show trials in Moscow ended with the execution of Grigori Zinoviev and Lev Kamenev (along with many others who had allegedly conspired with them). How could it be that veteran Bolsheviks who had been Lenin's closest collaborators were being accused of betraying the revolution? And this was only the beginning. In 1937, Karl

---

Rep 35G KZ Oranienburg, 3/22/1, Bl. 397. See also 'Paul W. Massing', Warum schweigt die Welt?! Häftlinge im Berliner Konzentrationslager Columbia-Haus 1933–1936, Gedenkstätte Deutscher Widerstand, https://www.columbiahaus.de/biografien/massing-paul-w.

15   Oranienburg Concentration Camp to Gustav Massing, 28 September 1933, Brandenburgisches Landeshauptarchiv Potsdam, Geheime Staatspolizei und Konzentrationslager, Rep 35G KZ Oranienburg, 3/22/1, Bl. 296.

16   See Osterloh 2017, p. 342.

Radek was exiled to Siberia, the following year Nikolai Bukharin, one of the party's most important theoreticians, was shot. Aghast at these developments, Massing turned his back on the Communist party. He was positively traumatised by the deep-seated sense of betrayal he now felt. He had devoted his entire adult life to the party and endured the horrors he encountered during his incarceration for the sake of the Communist movement. It now seemed as though all that had been entirely in vain and quite meaningless. Consequently, by the time he settled permanently in the USA, he had capped all his formal contacts to the party Communist apparatus. Ill at ease with the den of capitalist iniquity that was New York, Paul and Hede Massing moved to an old farmhouse near Quakertown (Pennsylvania) where Pollock occasionally went to participate in discussion rounds convened by Massing. They seem to have been fairly united in their assessment of current developments and their shared status as political refugees went far in attenuating the ideological distinctions that had set differing types of Marxists apart in what now felt like the distant past of the Weimar Republic.

None too surprisingly, Massing's farewell from party Communism did not automatically place him above suspicion. Following Trotsky's murder, his secretary Joseph Hansen handed the minutes of a meeting between two high-ranking members of the Fourth International to the US Consul General in Mexico, Robert McGregor, who passed them on to the State Department. They included the following passage: 'Among GPU agents named by W. whom we should be particularly careful of: Hedda Gumperz [...] and her husband who is Paul Massing, also known as Karl Billinger (author of Fatherland).'[17] In at least one instance, following the entry of the USA into the Second World War, the Massings did revive their old contacts to facilitate the flow of information from Franz Neumann (who was working at the Office of Strategic Services at the time) to the Soviets. Of course, at this juncture one needed to be neither a Communist nor a particular friend of the Soviet Union to want to hasten Germany's defeat by optimising the flow of information within the Anti-Hitler Coalition.[18] Given that these dealings came to light only after the opening of the Soviet archives, Massing seems not to have been monitored all too closely during the war. In the end, it was Hede Massing who, in 1945, approached the FBI and turned vociferous witness for the prosecution, much to Paul Massing's chagrin. He was appalled both by her betrayal of the cause (in the wider sense of the word) and the reputational collateral damage he, who really had moved

---

17   'A Report of a Conversation with W.', in McLaughlin 1985, pp. 15–18, p. 18.
18   See Müller 2010, pp. 70–2.

on and enjoyed some success in creating a new life for himself as a scholar and political publicist, suffered due to the ensuing scandal.

Pollock arrived in New York in August 1934, roughly a month after Horkheimer and his wife, just before the reconstituted International Institute of Social Research, established with the support of Julian Gumperz and the US sociologist Robert Lynd in affiliation with Columbia University, took up its work.[19] He travelled to Europe as often as possible to supervise the work of the institute's branches in Geneva, Paris and London, each of which, at least notionally, now had its own director: Andries Sternheim in Geneva, Paul Honigsheim in Paris and Jay Rumney in London. Add to this the administrative duties he shouldered in New York, and Pollock was working around the clock with barely a minute to spare for scholarly work. Because there was not enough space in the building allotted to the institute, Pollock's office was located next door, separating him from his colleagues. Erich Fromm, Herbert Marcuse and Leo Löwenthal also arrived in the summer of 1934. The institute's core staff was now back together.

In 1936, the political and legal studies scholar Franz L. Neumann joined the team. The following year, Otto Kirchheimer, who previously worked for the Paris branch, followed and then, in 1938, Theodor Wiesengrund who, on Pollock's recommendation, henceforth called himself Theodor W. Adorno in order to conceal his Jewish background, joined them. Pollock feared that it might one day harm the institute if it were perceived as a Jewish institution. Not that Adorno needed much persuading. Adorno, who was baptised as an infant, did not think of himself as Jewish, nor was he halakhically a Jew, given that his mother was a Catholic.[20] Pollock and Adorno, who formed a close friendship in exile, wanted to be identified above all as scholars, not least because their residency permit depended on it and scholars were exempt, at least in theory, from the immigration quota system enacted in 1924. As they saw it, their Jewishness was no more than an arbitrary matter of chance. Yet, not only had the Nazis now turned it into a lethal blemish, they also sought to define what being Jewish meant.[21] Both Pollock and Adorno were keen to duck this

---

19   On the reconstitution of the institute, see Wiggershaus 1994a, pp. 143–8.
20   How close Adorno and Pollock were is demonstrated by a letter Adorno wrote to Pollock in 1964. In it, he expressly noted that he could not imagine his life without him. Theodor W. Adorno to Friedrich Pollock, 20 May 1964, Fondo Friedrich Pollock, Università degli Studi di Firenze, 2.2.4, document 4. See Lenhard 2019.
21   After the Catholic-baptized 'half-Jew' Adorno married the 'full Jew' Margarete Karplus in London in September 1937, he would have been considered a 'Geltungsjude' by the Nazis on the basis of the Nuremberg Race Laws. However, the marriage would have been legally impossible in Germany after the laws came into force in 1935. Cf. Boeckmann 2004, p. 63.

imposed identity. Yet neither would it have been wise to stress their status as political refugees, given their well-documented leftist leanings. Hence, they spoke of their move (not flight) to the New World and henceforth presented – as Horkheimer did in his famous programmatic lecture of 1936 that was subsequently published in the institute's journal, 'Traditionelle und Kritische Theorie' (Traditional and Critical Theory) – their Marx-inspired critique as Critical Theory.

Not that the members of the institute were ever in any doubt that it was the adversity they and their friends and relatives faced that drove their theorising. For all the Weberian affinities of Pollock in particular, the institute was never designed to engage in disinterested, 'objective' research. Its members assumed that theory needed to be saturated with experience and constantly re-examined in the light of changing realities. Even prior to 1933, they had grown increasingly sceptical of Marxist analytical categories. Now, faced with the realities of Nazi rule, they found it virtually impossible to reconcile their established theoretical assumptions with the events unfolding before their eyes.

What they now encountered left them speechless and, in no small measure, despondent, and several years passed before Horkheimer's increasingly desperate attempts to encourage an appropriate theoretical response bore fruit. They had been in exile for the best of three years before Horkheimer was able to present a first such response in his aforementioned programmatic essay, 'Traditionelle und Kritische Theorie'. In it, he set out a course designed to transcend both 'bourgeois theory' and traditional Marxism, not least and very clearly in its guise developed by Georg Lukács, whose loyalty to Moscow was unbroken. In his influential essay, 'Die Verdinglichung und das Bewußtsein des Proletariats' (Reification and the Consciousness of the Proletariat), the core of *History and Class Consciousness*, for all his insights born of the critique of ideology, he had positively ontologised the working class's cognitive superiority. In stark contrast to Lukács, Horkheimer insisted 'that even the situation of the proletariat, in this society, offers no guarantee of correct knowledge. .... The intellectual who is satisfied to proclaim with reverent admiration the creative strength of the proletariat and finds satisfaction in adapting himself to it and in canonising it fails to see that such an evasion of theoretical effort ... makes the masses blinder and weaker than they need be.'[22]

Pollock responded enthusiastically to Horkheimer's exposition. 'I have finally finished reading the "theory" essay (for the second time). I ought really to

---

22 Horkheimer 2002b, pp. 213, 214 (translation amended).

know it by heart', he wrote to Horkheimer. 'Nowhere on earth has "critical" theory been advanced to such an extent as it has in these pages, and the fact of its loneliness, which is explained so compellingly, must not throw us off course. It is one of our greatest responsibilities to ensure that this work is continued under the best possible conditions.'[23] For Pollock, this meant that it was his duty not just to create the space and security Horkheimer needed for his work but also to tie the scholars capable of supporting and promoting the Critical Theory project to the institute. In the first instance, this meant those scholars who had been persecuted in Europe and who had seen their own socialist or liberal illusions shattered by the nescience and defencelessness of the masses and by what Julien Benda, in an essay of 1927 that Pollock had read with the utmost interest, called the 'treason of the intellectuals'.[24] The conviction that intellectuals betrayed their task, namely 'to uphold the idea', when they 'accepted today's indifference and venality of the masses as an unalterable fact' stuck with him.[25] As he wrote to Paul Guggenheim, a Swiss scholar of international law with whom he was on friendly terms, in 1941, 'in these dreadful times, the few individuals who have an understanding of what is currently going on and may be able to participate in the construction of a better order should stick together'.[26]

Consequently, in his capacity as administrative head of the institute, Pollock did everything he could to help as many victims of persecution as possible. Most of the institute's associates were able to flee to France, the UK, Switzerland and, in particular, to the United States. This alone gives an indication of the intensity and success of these endeavours. A prospectus published in 1938 to draw attention to the institute listed Horkheimer as director, Pollock as his deputy, and Erich Fromm, Henryk Grossman, Julian Gumperz, Leo Löwenthal, Herbert Marcuse, Franz Neumann, Theodor W. Adorno and Karl August Wittfogel as regular members of staff. Wittfogel was the only non-Jew among them (although his wife Olga, as we saw, was Jewish). The picture is much the same when it comes to the institute's research associates, most of whom were affiliated with the branches in Geneva, Paris and London: Walter Benjamin, Raymond Aron, Fritz Karsen, Otto Kirchheimer, Kurt Mandelbaum and Andries Sternheim were all, in one way or another, Jewish, and their affiliation with the

---

23 Friedrich Pollock to Max Horkheimer, 16 August 1937, in Horkheimer 1995b, p. 218.
24 Benda 1928.
25 See Löwe, Tillich, Pollock, symposium on *The Treason of the Intellectuals*, 1 May 1943, Horkheimer Archive, University Library Frankfurt/Main, MHA VI 33, 546.
26 Friedrich Pollock to Paul Guggenheim, 18 September 1941, Horkheimer 1996a, pp. 137–38, p. 138.

institute offered them invaluable support in their struggle for survival as the Nazis' grip on the European continent tightened.[27]

Yet the means at the institute's disposal were, of course, limited and there was ultimately very little it could do to thwart a regime whose top priority it was to murder every last Jew within its reach. In the early 1930s, annual interest on the foundation's endowment still stood at somewhere between $75,000 and $90,000. Even in 1937, despite the considerable costs involved in re-establishing itself overseas, the institute was able to channel $30,000 into its current running costs. At the time its endowment stood at 4.5 million Swiss Francs. In 1937/38, assuming that the economic downturn would pass more quickly than it did, Pollock held on to no longer profitable shares for too long. As a result, the endowment shrunk by half a million Swiss Francs, and he was forced to make up for the loss of income by tapping into the endowment to cover the institute's running costs. Although Felix Weil added a further $130,000 to the endowment in the summer of 1939, by 1941 the endowment had shrunk to $220,000 while the basic running costs stood at $30,000 p.a.[28] Given the absolute priority, now more than ever, of the *intérieur*, of Horkheimer and Pollock's independence, the institute was forced to economise, creating a discrepancy between the harsh realities of the institute's circumstances and the lifestyle of its directors that occasionally gave rise to resentment. It should not be forgotten, however, that during the Second World War, the institute supported more than 200 refugees with salaries, stipends, scholarships, various forms of unbureaucratic assistance, travel costs, affidavits and references.[29]

Of course, given the institute's limited means, there were for every successful endeavour to help numerous cases in which it could not, ultimately, achieve anything very meaningful. The prominent examples of two of the institute's close associates, Walter Benjamin and Andries Sternheim, illustrate the very real constraints under which Pollock laboured. He received hundreds of calls for help and had to coordinate his response to them with the interests of the institute and the need to secure his and Horkheimer's own existence. Against this background, it was perhaps inevitable that some of his contemporaries began to question the integrity of his decision-making processes.

---

27 *International Institute of Social Research. A Report on its History, Aims, and Activities 1933–1938*, Horkheimer Archive, University Library Frankfurt/Main, MHA IX 51a, 4.
28 Walter-Busch 2010, p. 23; Heufelder 2017, p. 143. To make things worse, the Swiss Franc was devalued by 31.25 per cent in 1936. See Bank for International Settlements, *Tenth Annual Report, 1st April 1939–31st March 1940*, Basle: Bank for International Settlements, p. 32.
29 Heufelder 2017, p. 148.

The best-known example is Hannah Arendt's implied accusation that the institute – and its financial administrator Friedrich Pollock in particular – hung their colleague Walter Benjamin, who committed suicide in 1940 while trying to flee from France to Spain, out to dry. Before picking up the chronological thread again, it may be helpful to take a look at the controversy that erupted in this matter in the late 1960s. In the first of three articles on Benjamin published in the intellectually aspirational West German monthly *Der Merkur* in 1968, Arendt referred to 'the final, for him [Benjamin] deadly serious, conflicts with the Institute of Social Research on whom he depended for his constantly precarious livelihood'.[30] The formulation 'deadly serious' lent itself to the interpretation – and was presumably meant to imply – that the effect of the conflicts in question had quite literally been lethal, i.e., that it was lack of support from the institute that ultimately drove Benjamin to kill himself. Elsewhere in the article, Arendt pointed to the critical reception Benjamin's Marxist turn had received from both Gershom Scholem and the institute and contrasted Scholem's unwavering support to what she implied was an attempt on the institute's (and especially on Adorno's) part to force Benjamin into ideological submission.

Pollock responded to Arendt's article with a perfectly restrained letter to the *Merkur* editors in which he set the record straight. Contrary to Arendt's claims, Adorno had not, at the time, been the director of the institute. Benjamin had received a stipend from the institute and was assured of a regular position at the institute as soon as he arrived in the United States. Moreover, 'the institute underwrote the travel costs to America and provided him with all the funds required for the flight. The duration and amount of his stipend were at no point connected to disagreements concerning Benjamin's ideological orientation and depended exclusively on the means at the institute's disposal.' If need be, Pollock added, he was happy to provide 'documentary evidence' bearing out his account. In short: Arendt was simply mistaken.[31]

---

30 Arendt 1968a. The formulation in question was not contained in the version of the text she published later that year in the *New Yorker* and then in *Men in Dark Times*.

31 Pollock 1968. In one point, Pollock's statement was not entirely correct. The institute did not expressly guarantee the funds required for Benjamin to travel to the United States. Horkheimer initially asked Benjamin to bear these costs himself. When it became clear that Benjamin would likely be unable to raise the full amount, Horkheimer, while making no promises, asked Benjamin to keep him informed about the size of the probable shortfall. This surely suggests that he had not yet ruled out that the institute might yet be able to contribute to the travel costs after all. Max Horkheimer to Walter Benjamin, 14 July 1939 (excerpt), quoted in Benjamin 2000, p. 314, (annotation).

In her rejoinder, Arendt conceded 'that, all the conflicts notwithstanding, it was nevertheless the institute and the institute alone that made it possible for him to survive and that, once the war had begun, the institute did everything humanly possible to rescue him.' She also expressly acknowledged Adorno's role in the publication and promotion of Benjamin's works. Yet at the same time, she moved the goal posts, now arguing that even though the institute neither pressured Benjamin ideologically nor considered cutting him off financially, Benjamin, having been encouraged by Horkheimer to consider other sources of funding, nevertheless *assumed* both to be a possibility and that this was the source of the desperation that ultimately drove him to suicide. 'This is how it was, or at least how Benjamin saw it', she wrote.[32]

Arendt misconstrued the facts at her disposal not least because she fundamentally misunderstood the relationship between Benjamin and the institute and, notably, between Benjamin and Pollock. It was Adorno who first introduced Benjamin to the institute. Pollock and Horkheimer did indeed view his work with a certain measure of scepticism, yet they never doubted his extraordinary gifts. In the 1930s, while Adorno lamented Brecht's orthodox Marxist influence on Benjamin, Horkheimer was much more worried about his theological bent. His response to Benjamin's article on the cultural historian Eduard Fuchs is a case in point. In it, Benjamin claimed that the past was never entirely closed off. 'The injustices of the past', Horkheimer countered in a letter to Benjamin, 'have transpired and they have been concluded. Those who were slain really are dead. Ultimately, your claim is theological in nature. If one really takes the notion of incompleteness seriously, one would need to believe in the Last Judgement.' For this, he added, his way of thinking was 'all too contaminated by materialism'.[33] The Nazis' terror in Germany threw this issue sharply into relief, and Horkheimer's objection was ultimately that Benjamin's insistence on its incompleteness relativised the horror of that which had irrevocably occurred.

Yet such differences were rarely a factor when it came to questions of financial support – and they certainly played no role in Benjamin's case. One need only think of Henryk Grossman, whose agenda differed much more substantially from Horkheimer's vision than Benjamin's ever did, to understand

---

32   Arendt 1968b.
33   Max Horkheimer to Walter Benjamin, 16 March 1937, in Horkheimer 1995b, pp. 81–8, p. 83. In 1939, Pollock tried to help Fuchs and his family flee to North America. See Friedrich Pollock to Eduard and Margarete Fuchs, 6 November 1939, Nikolaevsky Papers, Hoover Institution 618, 2. Fuchs died in January 1940, but his first wife Frida, their daughter Gertrud and his second wife Margarete did eventually make it to the United States.

that those supported by the institute were not required to toe the line. To be sure, Pollock was no less irritated by Benjamin's flirtation with Brecht's orthodox Marxism than Adorno and Scholem, not least, given Benjamin's poor grasp of the critique of political economy.[34] Yet Benjamin was one of the most prolific contributors to the institute's journal – where he published four substantial essays and thirteen reviews – and he was friendly with Pollock as well as Theodor and Gretel Adorno. When Pollock was in Europe, he met Benjamin in Paris to discuss his work and financial situation.[35]

In April 1938, Pollock wrote to Horkheimer from Geneva, giving a short overview over his frantic activities:

> I had lunch ... with Lorwin, Mlle. Ginsberg (at her place), dinner once at Guggenheim's, once at Lorwin's, once with Meng and Landauer, and tonight with Saussure. I also saw Rappard ... and contacted Butler but he had to go away. I had a long chat with Hürlimann on the telephone, with Farquharson and de la Harpe Saturday afternoon, with Oprecht and Emil Walter yesterday. I am meeting Hans Mayer this afternoon. I am spending an additional day here in Geneva because there is less to do in Paris: Aron has gone away ... Given the late arrival of the boat, I was able to speak to Bouglé only on the phone, Scelle I met here ... and Halbwachs is in Turkey. I have already made arrangements to meet Benjamin, Kracauer, Venedey and Leichter tomorrow, and Schröder, of course. I will ring your parents again tonight, I promised to do so when I first called them on Thursday. I think I have managed to deal with everything to our satisfaction.[36]

Pollock and Kracauer discussed, at length, an assignment focussing on Nazi propaganda and ways in which the institute might be able to support his move to the United States.[37] Pollock and Benjamin met on 12 April 1938 in the evening. Two days later, Benjamin wrote to Scholem (who was in the USA at the time and had been introduced to Adorno by Paul Tillich just a fortnight earlier) that the meeting with Pollock had been 'as cordial as it was brief' and that it had put him at ease regarding his continued collaboration with the institute.[38] The

---

34   Friedrich Pollock to Martin Jay, 20 June 1969, Martin Jay private collection.
35   Benjamin 1991a, p. 1172.
36   Friedrich Pollock to Max Horkheimer, 11 April 1938, Horkheimer Archive, University Library Frankfurt/Main, MHA V 31, 154.
37   See Kracauer 2012 and the contextualisation of these notes by the editors, Mülder and Belke 2012, pp. 831–34.
38   Scholem (ed.) 1989, p. 217 (translation amended).

following day he wrote to Horkheimer, summarising his understanding of what had been agreed with Pollock. 'The meeting went every bit as well as I might have hoped', he confirmed. 'We spent two very pleasant hours in a small restaurant near Notre Dame. I – an old Parisian! – had to be introduced to this restaurant by Pollock.' In connection with his Baudelaire essay and the nascent Arcades project he had told Pollock 'how desirable I would consider an occasional exchange of ideas with an economist', and Pollock had agreed to put him in touch with Otto Leichter (the husband of Käthe Leichter, whom we met earlier in the context of one of the surveys carried out in cooperation with the ILO).[39] They had mainly discussed Pollock's suggestions regarding the Baudelaire essay, much as they had done back in 1935, when Benjamin was working on his outline, 'Paris, die Hauptstadt des XIX. Jahrhunderts' (Paris, Capital of the Nineteenth Century).[40]

Benjamin had in fact been loosely involved with the institute since 1930, when he was invited to give a paper, 'Zur Philosophie der Literaturkritik' (On the Philosophy of Literary Criticism), at the institute. Following his mother's death, he asked for the event to be postponed until January 1931 but in the end, the lecture seems not to have taken place. He spent much of 1932/33 on Ibiza, occasionally returning to Berlin. Forced to leave Germany once the Nazis came to power, he settled in Paris in September 1933. From the spring of 1934 onwards, the institute paid him a monthly stipend of 500 Francs (equivalent to $730 in today's money).[41] The third volume of the institute's journal contained the essay 'Zum gegenwärtigen gesellschaftlichen Standort des französischen Schriftstellers' (The Present Social Situation of the French Writer) and two book reviews by Benjamin, for which he received a fee of 110 Swiss Francs (the equivalent of almost $800 in today's money) in addition to his stipend. Since he was unable to make ends meet with the remuneration he received from the institute, he tried to generate additional income by seeking commissions from several periodicals. This endeavour was not overly successful, however. Hence, the institute increased his stipend to 1,000 Francs in January 1936, to 1,300 Francs in May 1936 and, in January 1937, to 1,500 Francs. In November 1937, the institute, increasingly feeling the pinch, began to wire him $80 (equivalent to $1,650 in today's money) a month from New York – that was not a lot but at least he received his stipend in a stable currency now. In addition, Pollock informed him that he would receive a one-off payment of 1,500 Francs to defray the costs of his move to new quarters in Paris. Pollock stressed that this was

---

39   Scholem and Adorno (eds.) 1994, pp. 555, 556.
40   Gödde and Lonitz 2006, p. 93.
41   On the figures, derived from Benjamin's papers, see Gödde and Lonitz 2006, pp. 94–5.

the utmost we can currently do for you. We request that you treat this arrangement as absolutely confidential (even in your dealings with [the branch in] Geneva). At a time when we are forced to make cuts across the board we do not want to be drawn into discussions as to why we are taking an entirely different approach in your case.[42]

Clearly, the institute did not mete out the same form or level of support to all its associates. Pollock sought to figure out how he could best deploy the available resources to best match each individual case. Thanks to Adorno's constant urging behind the scenes and Pollock's friendly relations with him, Benjamin received more than most. One can only imagine how tortuous it must have been for Pollock constantly to have to decide how to allot the limited funds, knowing full well that he could not possibly offer all of the institute's associates sufficient support.

Born in 1890, Andries Sternheim, our second example, was the son of a Jewish broker in Amsterdam's diamond industry. He joined the Dutch trade union movement and Social Democratic party prior to the First World War. Having worked as a diamond cutter for a decade, in 1914, Sternheim entered the city's municipal administration where he served in a number of roles including, eventually, in the employment office. Appointed director of the library and documentation centre of the International Federation of Trade Unions in Amsterdam in 1920, he moved to the ILO in Geneva in 1931.[43] When the institute established its branch in the city, Sternheim was one of its first employees and, following Pollock's departure for New York, he became its director.[44] He was involved in the family study and contributed numerous book reviews and an essay on leisure activities to the institute's journal. This was his final essay in the journal, however, mainly because Horkheimer and the other 'New Yorkers' thought of him as a statistician and administrator rather than a theoretician. In 1938, as the contraction of the institute's resources escalated, Pollock sought to persuade the institute's employees to seek alternative sources of funding.[45] In addition, the institute began systematically to cooperate with other organisations and foundations and assiduously applied for external funding. In this vein, Adorno, when he arrived from Oxford, initially worked part-time for Lazarfeld's Princeton Radio Research Project.

---

42 Friedrich Pollock to Walter Benjamin, 13 October 1937, in Benjamin 1991b, pp. 1351–2.
43 Mulder 1991.
44 Mulder and Nauta 1990.
45 Within a year, the assets of the Société Internationale des Recherches Sociales decreased from 4.65 million to 3.56 million Swiss Francs. See Heufelder 2017, p. 143.

In Sternheim's case, this strategic shift on the institute's part ultimately had fatal consequences. The previous branch secretary Juliette Favez took over as director in 1938, and Sternheim, his wife Gholina and their sons Leonard (b. 1924) and Paul (b. 1926) moved back to Amsterdam, where he continued to work for the institute, albeit on a salary too low to sustain them. In addition, he worked as an accountant but lost this position in December 1940, when the German occupiers barred Jews from the free professions. Yet precisely at this point, Pollock 'slashed his already reduced salary by half again'.[46] Extremely well connected, Sternheim was just about able to keep his family afloat yet following Pearl Harbour and the entry of the United States into the war, the institute was no longer able to send any funds to Nazi-occupied Europe. Towards the end of 1942, the family was ordered to move to the city's Jewish quarter.[47] Andries and Gholina Sternheim were in fact exempt from deportation for the time being because of his earlier prestigious position in Geneva (suggesting that the Germans hoped they might yet be able to barter him along with other prominent Jews in negotiations with the Allies), but they nevertheless decided to follow their sons into hiding. From May to November 1943, while in hiding, Andries Sternheim kept a well-known diary that is frequently cited as an important source relating to the Shoah in the Netherlands.[48] The Sternheims' son Leonard Sternheim was caught in August 1943 and deported, on 24 August 1943, from Westerbork to Auschwitz. He seems to have spent some time in Auschwitz III (Monowitz), where survival chances were (relatively speaking) better than elsewhere in Auschwitz, but his death was recorded on 22 April 1944. Their other son, Paul Sternheim, was caught in September 1943 and deported, on 16 November 1943, from the Westerbork transit camp to Auschwitz where his death was recorded on 31 March 1944. Andries and Gholina Sternheim themselves were caught in January 1944, taken to Westerbork and deported from there, on 3 March 1944, to Auschwitz, where they were murdered on arrival.

How much responsibility did Pollock bear for this outcome? It is worth keeping in mind that in 1938, Nazi expansionism was still firmly directed towards Central and Eastern Europe, and the Netherlands did not seem to be under any kind of immediate threat. The majority of Dutch Jews still felt safe immediately before the invasion of the Wehrmacht. Neither Pollock, whose brother had been living in Amsterdam with his family since 1936, nor Horkheimer, who in early December 1938 was still planning to bring his parents to America via

---

46 Heufelder 2017, p. 150.
47 Mulder 1991, pp. 180–3, 193–200.
48 Dagboek Andries Sternheim, National Library of the Netherlands, https://geheugen.delph er.nl/en/geheugen/view?coll=ngvn&identifier=EVDO01%3AJHM01_KBN006000001.

the Netherlands as a stopover, expected the Jews in Amsterdam to be in acute danger at that time.[49] Conversely, for all the hardship the renewed salary cut in 1940 spelt for Sternheim and his family, once the Germans had occupied the country, it would have been well nigh impossible for them to flee, regardless of the funds at their disposal. Add to this that the funds Sternheim no longer received instead benefitted other associates of the institute suffering persecution, and it becomes clear just how distressingly insuperable Pollock's task ultimately was. In this particular case, the redirected funds allowed the Geneva branch to employ the young German-Jewish literary scholar Hans Mayer, himself an émigré constantly on the verge of destitution.[50]

In October 1939, the institute was also forced to let Julian Gumperz and Erich Fromm go. Gumperz was able to secure a position as a broker with the Hermann Weil Foundation. Marcuse and Adorno in particular had been at odds with Fromm's theoretical development for some time, and his departure precipitated ugly mutual recriminations. In the end, Fromm received the extraordinary sum of $20,000 in severance pay.[51] In short: the institute found itself in a horrendous predicament and every good deed was the flipside of a regrettable decision.[52]

Nor, it should be said, were Pollock's relief efforts limited to the institute and its associates. The theologian Paul Tillich, one of the most prominent proponents of religious socialism, played a key role in facilitating cooperation and mutual support between various émigré intellectuals. Tillich, who had vehemently supported Horkheimer's appointment to his chair in Frankfurt, was also on friendly terms with Pollock. Back in Frankfurt, he held a regular discussion circle at Café Laumer whose participants included Horkheimer, Pollock and their close friend Adolph Löwe as well as Carl Mennicke, Karl Mannheim and Theodor Adorno. In New York, where he now held a chair at the Union Theological Seminary, Tillich reconvened the circle on a fortnightly basis and Pollock attended regularly. In 1935, they developed the idea of creating a mutual assistance committee that would also serve as a point of contact

---

49 Max Horkheimer to Juliette Favez, 6 December 1938, in Horkheimer 1995b, p. 519.
50 See Hans Mayer to Max Horkheimer, 29 September and 24 October 1939, in Horkheimer 1995b, pp. 637–39, 644–6, pp. 638, 645.
51 Erich Fromm to Max Horkheimer, 16 November 1939, in Horkheimer 1995b, pp. 666–7, p. 666. The severance pay was so substantial because Fromm was the only member of the institute with tenure.
52 See also Max Horkheimer to Ernst Bloch, 17 March 1938, in Horkheimer 1995b, pp. 413–14, p. 413: 'The institute's finances are in a truly desolate state. We have to make most of our fellows in America and Europe and even some regular employees redundant. This is due to the recession.'

for colleagues who were still stuck in Germany. The organisation, Selfhelp of German Émigrés (later Selfhelp of Émigrés from Central Europe), Inc., with Tillich as its president, was formally established in November 1936.[53] Alongside Pollock, two female German-Jewish scholars with doctorates in economics, Else Staudinger and Toni Stolper, served as Tillich's deputies.[54] 'The basic idea', Stolper later recalled, 'was that we recent émigrés, having been saved to a decent country, were going to institute, each one of us, a self-taxation by which we would throw in our obligations of help into this new organisation.'[55] Between 1936 and 1939, the 'taxes' raised from the roughly 300 members amounted to some $34,000 in total which allowed the organisation to operate from a small office on Broadway. Its work focussed not so much on the rescue of individuals but primarily on the creation of sustainable support networks and, during the war in particular, constructive interaction with the authorities.[56] As one of the vice presidents, Pollock played an important role in this organisation.

The institute was integral to this network and the practical assistance it offered, far from being merely a pragmatic sideshow, was an immediate expression of Critical Theory's foundational principle – solidarity with the oppressed and tormented – that likewise found its expression in its members' texts. For Pollock, this work marked a return to his Munich days when, as we saw, he sought to help communists flee the White Terror, his scepticism vis-à-vis the Bavarian Soviet Republic notwithstanding.[57] This political activism, in the narrower sense of the word, was inseparable from the role of the sober theoretician that Pollock sometimes liked to overplay. One will hardly grasp just how formative the experience of National Socialism was for Pollock's theoretical work if

---

53 Hans Staudinger, 'How Selfhelp Came About', Leo Baeck Institute New York, Selfhelp for German Refugees Collection, 1939–1977, AR 4402.
54 They are named on the organisation's letterhead. See National Archives and Records Administration, Washington DC, NARA, FDR Library, Records of the War Refugee Board, 1944–1945, General Correspondence, Box 24, Folder 1: Selfhelp of Émigrés from Central Europe, document 24.
55 Toni Stolper, interview, Leo Baeck Institute New York, Recorded Memories, Folder ME 390, p. 113.
56 Among the activities of Selfhelp Community Services, Inc. today is a programme for Holocaust survivors. See Selfhelp Community Services, Inc., Annual Report 2010, https://docplayer.net/61729502-Selfhelp-community-services-inc-and-scs-foundation-inc-seventyfive.html.
57 In the 1916 version of their friendship agreement, they outlined their shared ethical approach as follows: 'Our greatest desire is that [we] both help others'. Quoted in Ernst von Schenck, *Biographie von Max Horkheimer* (typescript), Fondo Friedrich Pollock, Università degli Studi di Firenze, 2.2.3, p. 58.

one fails to take into consideration the relief work for the victims of persecution that took up so much of his time and caused him so much anguish between 1933 and 1945.

Contemporaries encountered Pollock either as a saviour or as the bearer of bad news. Little wonder, then, that he struck many as polarising, even though he hardly shared the prominence (or notoriety) that colleagues like Horkheimer, Marcuse or Adorno acquired prior to the Second World War. Of course, there was another side to the story: Pollock's personal experience as an émigré, his carefully guarded private life, his grappling with a new country, with the loss inextricably linked to emigration and, far from least, the solace of nevertheless being able to share his life with his nearest and dearest.

CHAPTER 8

Émigré

In May 1934, in a letter to Pollock, Maidon Horkheimer enthusiastically related her first impressions of New York. 'New York is a huge city', she wrote,

> without seeing it one has no idea, it is simply incredible, unreal; Paris, London, all of Europe is a negro village. One is constantly confounded by the people, by daily life, by the atmosphere, the food, the housing etc. At one o'clock in the morning you can buy whatever the heart desires, all the shops are open + the streets and houses gleam in their light.[1]

Her account no doubt aroused Pollock's curiosity, given his long-standing fascination with all things modern and urban. Yet he was also concerned that the *intérieur*, the realm of his utopian friendship covenant with Horkheimer, might not withstand this new world. Once he arrived in the United States, he was so busy that he had little time to reflect on his new circumstances in any great detail. Occasionally, he or Horkheimer would remark on the future of their relationship but only in 1935 was he able to undertake a comprehensive revision of their friendship contract first drafted in 1911. His memorandum bore the title, 'Materialien für die Neuformulierung von Grundsätzen' (Material for the Reformulation of Basic Principles). The significance of this document is indicated not least by the fact that it is actually more detailed than the original contract. In it, Pollock fastidiously laid out rules for their new lives designed to ensure that the ideals that had governed their covenant from the outset were not sidelined by the challenges their new circumstances posed.

The six-page memorandum comprised thirteen articles in total and laid out the standards that should henceforth govern their shared life. The first article placed the 'continual conduct of relations' centre stage, acknowledging that this required 'constant concentration and a great deal time'. To this end, it was critical that both parties were at all times, even under the most difficult circumstances, intimately familiar with each other's thoughts and activities (paragraph 2). 'Lengthy separations' should be avoided if at all possible, even

---

1 Maidon Horkheimer to Friedrich Pollock, 5 May 1934, Horkheimer Archive, University Library Frankfurt/Main, MHA VI 31, 111.

if doing so entailed disadvantages for one or both parties (paragraph 3). The second article reiterated the longstanding principle that 'the *intérieur* always takes precedence over the *extérieur*', stressing that this was no 'abstract truth for Sundays and the holidays' but the guiding principle they were determined genuinely to implement in their daily lives.[2] The third article offered a truly succinct definition of the *intérieur*: '1. Our covenant; 2. Our values; 3. Our attitude towards the world: conviviality, valour, pride' (p. 381).[3] The fourth article treated the need to arrive at shared judgements in all essential matters and identify with them unconditionally. It was complemented by the fifth article which stressed the need for each party to identify unreservedly with the other and genuinely take the other seriously in all respects. It was noted, however, that 'F.'s idiosyncrasy of feeling gratification only if he is seen as a gift giver (rather than acting for the sake of the cause)' formed an obstacle in this respect (paragraph 7, p. 383).

The sixth article treated mutual assurances required to proceed under the extraordinarily precarious and hazardous circumstances they now confronted. One needed to be certain, it stipulated, 'that one is never lonely or isolated, that one can rely on the other unconditionally, not only when it comes to big concerns but also in matters of everyday life, that the other will respond to more significant issues in the same way as one would oneself – this way of life is one of the central goods that our covenant should engender' (p. 383). To achieve this, the stipulations laid out in articles four and five needed to be implemented on a daily basis. Decisions needed to be taken by consensus and acknowledged as definitive. No action could be taken until agreement was reached on the matter in question (paragraph 4). An additional clause introduced two safe words for instances in which it was impossible to discuss a controversial issue until it was resolved. 'Plein Pouvoir' meant that the other could proceed, unresolved objections notwithstanding, 'Veto' meant just that (paragraph 4b, p. 384).

The seventh article revisited the commitment to pride that was integral to their attitude towards the world. Its importance lay in the fact that it counteracted the 'bourgeois organisation of urges' acquired in the process of a socialisation designed to make individuals refrain from doing what they really wanted to do (p. 385). Closely related, the eighth article stressed the importance of psychological self-knowledge and regular mutual psychological scrutiny to

---

2   Pollock 1995, p. 380. The page references for the remaining quotations from this document are given in the main text in brackets.
3   In the German original, the final three terms are rendered in French: Gaîté, Courage, Fierté.

uncover the respective other's neurotic response patterns. These response patterns reflected the incorrect organisation of the world and were, therefore, pitted against the 'correct attitude towards society' outlined in the ninth article (p. 386). Their account of the current state of society read like a blend of Marx and the cultural critics whose texts they had read as young adults: 'In today's society, all human relations are adulterated; ultimately, none of the kindness, approbation, benevolence is meant seriously. Only competition within the class and the struggle between the classes is genuine' (p. 386). Yet their characterisation of the class struggle differed markedly from Marx's and was clearly predicated on their own experience of persecution.

> Every instance of approbation, of success, of apparently sympathetic interest is owed to jailers who let those who own neither success nor power go to rack and ruin with utter indifference or torment them without restraint. All acts of kindness are directed not at the individual person but at his position in society – this becomes brutally obvious when the person in question, due to some significant or not so significant change (stock exchange, anti-Jewish incitement), has lost his position. It is not the abstract insight, however, that matters, rather, you must always bear in mind that it is you yourself who is at their mercy once all the kind and well meaning people in your daily life became aware of the fact that you have become powerless (pp. 386–7).

Perhaps Pollock and Horkheimer addressed each other with the 'you' to whom the text appealed; more likely they were using it in the sense of 'one'. The implication could not be more obvious: 'never on a plane with the jailers, solidarity with the victims' was the motto. It was important to appreciate that even as things stood, people existed who alongside their function were also human individuals, 'especially among women' (p. 387). The final article reiterated the commitment to 'live in accordance with our insights and realise the values we acknowledge to the best of our ability' (p. 388).

It is no exaggeration to suggest that Pollock and Horkheimer's friendship covenant was ultimately totalitarian in aspiration. By way of a social experiment, they sought to transcend the territoriality and limitations of the ego by radically exposing themselves to each other and revisiting their own assumptions in the reflection of the other – a process that obviously presupposed unconditional mutual solidarity. They yearned for a good life anticipating the revolution that was nowhere to be seen, based on sensible social forms that transcended bourgeois morality and the competitiveness dictated by the capitalist order. Theirs was an experiment, then, that is radically odds with the all too popular cliché of Critical Theory's unmitigated negativity and its unrelenting refusal to countenance utopian visions of a better life.[4] Whether their covenant was really a model for society as a whole may have been a moot point but, against Adorno's endlessly cited contention that 'Wrong life cannot be lived in the right way',[5] Pollock and Horkheimer maintained throughout their adult life that some ways of leadings one's life were most certainly infinitely better than others.

Faced with radically new circumstances, a foreign language, unfamiliar social conventions and social relations that struck them as being largely superficial, their covenant served, even more than before, as a bulwark against the hazards and vagaries of the outside world. 'New York with its magnificent abundance of buildings seems to symbolise the strength that resides in this country, in this society', Horkheimer wrote to his former teacher, Hans Cornelius, in June 1934, describing his first impressions of his new surroundings. The potential impact of this strength was enormous, but it was unclear where it might be directed. Then again, in marked contrast to their European peers, Americans seemed still to trust in the ideals of the Enlightenment.

> People also seem to be younger here than in Europe. For the most part, they lack the scepticism and fundamental distrust that confronts every new thought over there. While faith in the possibility of progress that might improve the circumstances in which individuals live has almost disappeared over there, here, your average man or woman on the street aspires to an ever more sensible organisation of all relations and believes that this aspiration can be realised.[6]

Yet all the positive impressions of the first couple of months notwithstanding, they felt distinctly out of place in the United States – not least, because, given everything that had happened, they no longer shared the faith of most Americans in progress. They perceived of the USA as a country that seemed super-modern yet had in fact fallen out of time, given its fixation on ideas that had long since become anachronistic. Pollock and Horkheimer found this orientation charming and dangerous roughly in equal measure, given that this

---

4 Stefan Breuer too has noted this distinction between Adorno and Horkheimer. On his account, the latter continued to be too beholden to idealism. See Breuer 1985. On Pollock and Horkheimer's negativity, see Postone and Crick 1993. On Adorno's concept of the prohibition of the image, see Tränkle 2013.
5 Adorno 2005, p. 39 (translation amended).
6 Max Horkheimer to Hans Cornelius, 15 June 1934, in Horkheimer 1995a, pp. 128–30, p. 129.

naïve faith might well be frustrated at any point and then engender barbarism. Of course, a stereotypical German quest for genuine depth may also have contributed to their fundamental distrust of potentially encouraging appearances.

Not that the land of limitless possibilities exactly went out of its way to welcome our leftist Jewish refugees. Far from it. The FBI had a keen eye on the members of the institute in general and its directors in particular and collected hundreds of documents, reports and intercepted telegrams.[7] The bureau was particularly wary of enemy aliens and surveilled numerous European intellectuals, Pollock among them. Cryptographers examined letters and telegrams on the assumption that they contained some kind of code, and individuals involved with Pollock were questioned. Eventually, on 18 July 1941, J. Edgar Hoover personally ordered the termination of the surveillance. 'The telegram forwarded by your office contains several words that could possibly be code', he wrote. 'However, it is suggested that these word in most instances at least are the names of other German-Jewish refugees. ... It is believed that the telegram in its entirety referred to legitimate transactions of the above Institute, or projects in which the Institute is interested, and accordingly it is not desired that any additional investigation be conducted.'[8] Even so, until 'Harkheimer' *aka* 'Alright', as the agents called him (because Horkheimer frequently closed his letters to Pollock with the affirmative 'Alright'), and his 'accomplice' Pollock returned to Europe, they never dropped off the FBI's radar entirely. To what extent Pollock and Horkheimer were aware of this attention is a moot point. Rumours about the surveillance certainly circulated among German émigrés.[9]

Like other members of the institute's inner circle, Pollock has been accused of living in style while cutting other people's salaries and stipends. There is certainly no denying that Pollock and Horkheimer in particular always lived in relative comfort, and no one would suggest that they ever encountered any genuine material hardship. This was in no small measure due to the fact that Pollock, who was responsible both for the institute's resources and for Horkheimer's private assets, consistently prioritised the commitments of their covenant. To this end, not only the personal and intellectual but also the material preconditions for the preservation of the *intérieur* came before all else.

Alongside the Horkheimers and Pollock, the *intérieur* now also included Pollock's great love Andrée. It was presumably the Nazis coming to power in

---

7 See Jenemann 2007, pp. xii–xiv.
8 J. Edgar Hoover to Special Agent in Charge in El Paso, Texas, 8 July 1941, quoted in Jenemann 2007, p. xiii.
9 Bertolt Brecht being questioned about his relationship to 'Mr. Horskheimer' is a case in point. See Alexander 2000, p. 146.

1933 and the 'aryanisation' of Marx's business the following year that led the couple to reconsider their options, and they divorced amicably.[10] Now a free agent again, 'Dée' was determined to resume her relationship with Pollock and met with him in Geneva in late April 1934. They went on what was only in part a business trip that lasted several weeks – until Horkheimer gently reminded him of his duties – and included stays in Rome and Paris.[11] Back in Geneva, Dée moved in with Pollock, and he began to arrange their move to the United States. In August 1934, he took the Empress of Britain from Cherbourg via Southampton to Québec, where he met Horkheimer.[12] From there, they travelled by train to New York. By the end of the year, Pollock had already secured a permanent residency permit, and Dée was able to join him in October 1935.

Their old love had matured into an extraordinarily close bond and, as it became increasingly clear that neither of them would be returning to Europe any time soon, they decided, after careful consideration, to marry in order to regularise her residency status. For Pollock, marriage was an obsolete institution, and he certainly never saw himself marrying. For all the passion he

---

10   The couple were still married and living together in July 1932. See *Gemeinde-Zeitung für die israelitischen Gemeinden Württembergs*, 9.8, 16 July 1932, p. 1. That the divorce was amicable is also suggested by the fact that his former father-in-law Sigmund Kahn helped Marx rescue some of his assets when, having been warned of his imminent arrest, he was forced to flee to Switzerland. In Zurich, Marx (who was unable to work for the Swiss branch of his own business because he was refused a work permit) and the long-standing theatre critic of the *Frankfurter Zeitung*, Bernhard Diebold (who was a Swiss national and therefore needed no permit), created an enterprise (Thema) for the sale of film proposals based on (predominantly) high-quality literary texts to film studios. On the assumption that his account of Jewish bravery in the First World War might help counter Nazi antisemitism, Marx also used the opportunity to prepare his war diary for publication. It was eventually published as Marx 1939 but found few readers. Marx's celebration of Jewish bravery could equally well be read as a celebration of war – something in which, in 1939, only all the wrong people were interested. The book was reissued in 1964 by ner tamid, the publisher created by Hans Lamm, the culture commissioner of the Central Council of Jews in Germany, and run by Shlomo Lewin at the time. Once again, the book generated little resonance although, intriguingly, the Bundeswehr (the West German military) bought 1,600 copies. Following his flight to Zurich, Marx is also said to have passed on information to British intelligence officers. Julius Marx to Walter Huder, 9 September 1965; Julius Marx, 'Wie ich emigrierte und weiterlebte' (short autobiographical account for the PEN Centre of German-Speaking Writers Abroad), 1965, Akademie der Künste, Berlin, Huder 987, https://archiv.adk.de/objekt/2076290; Nebel 1994.
11   Leo Löwenthal to Max Horkheimer, 10 and 27 May 1934, Horkheimer Archive, University Library Frankfurt/Main, MHA VI 11, 481, 495; Max Horkheimer to Friedrich Pollock, 27 May 1934, in Horkheimer 1995a, pp. 124–7, p. 127.
12   Swiss Federal Archives, Schweizerisches Auswanderungsamt und Auswanderungsbüro. Überseeische Auswanderungen aus der Schweiz, 1910–1953, E 2175–2, Volume 51.

invested in codifying his friendship with Horkheimer, he had consistently and vehemently rejected any suggestion that he might marry. Perhaps this was one last act of rebellion against his birth family. Now, in exile and faced with innumerable inescapable constraints, this form of anti-bourgeois rejectionism imploded. On 8 November 1935, Andrée Woog, formerly Marx, and Frederick Pollock were married by the city clerk of Manhattan.[13] She was 37, he was 41. Writing to Wittfogel in China a week later, Pollock had the following to say about the ceremony: 'I could tell you quite a few amusing tales about the prosaic nature of weddings here: ... "lift your hands ... you're married now ... two dollars please." And with that the edifying ceremony was over.'[14]

It had been a long while since Pollock had anyone close whom he genuinely trusted in his life, other than Max and Maidon Horkheimer. This may have weighed all the more heavily, given that he had virtually lost touch with his birth family. Following his mother's death in 1930, he rarely spoke to his increasingly morose father whom he repeatedly urged to leave Germany. He insisted on staying in Stuttgart, however, where he died in 1937 at the age of 71. Father and son met one last time in Switzerland in 1936, but we have no information as to what transpired between them on this occasion.[15] A letter of condolence Pollock wrote to Leo Löwenthal in June 1942 may offer us a glimpse of his own feelings when his father died. 'I know', he wrote, 'that for all our detachment from our parents, the death of a father can be deeply affecting. It is therefore no mere formality when I offer you and your wife my condolences.'[16] Little did Pollock know in 1937 what horrors would have awaited his parents, had they still been alive at the beginning of the war.

What of Pollock's other relatives and close acquaintances? As we saw, his brother Hans had taken over their father's suitcase factory. Forced to leave Freiburg university once the Nazis came to power, Hans and Ida's daughter Liselotte continued her studies, supported financially by her uncle Friedrich Pollock, at the Sorbonne where she graduated in 1937. In 1935, she settled in Amsterdam, presumably following her marriage to the German-Jewish banker

---

13   New York City Municipal Archive, New York City Marriage Records, 1829–1940. FHL Microfilm 1,674,299.
14   Friedrich Pollock to Karl August Wittfogel, 15 November 1935, Hoover Institution, Wittfogel Papers 37, 8.
15   See Friedrich Pollock to Max Horkheimer, 22 April 1946, Horkheimer Archive, University Library Frankfurt/Main, MHA VI 31, 293.
16   Friedrich Pollock to Leo Löwenthal, 15 June 1942, Horkheimer Archive, University Library Frankfurt/Main, MHA VI 15, 121.

Paul Sommer (b. 1911), returning to Paris only during term time.[17] The family business was 'aryanised' in 1935, leaving Hans and Ida Pollock without a livelihood. In January 1936, Hans and Ida Pollock, along with Ida's seventy-year-old mother, Babette 'Settchen' Joseph, made their way to Amsterdam where Max Horkheimer's psychoanalyst Karl Landauer too had found refuge and was able to help them find accommodation. Given the extortionate levy raised from those who sought to leave the country, the funds they were able to take with them were minimal, and the Pollocks were dependent on support from charitable organisations and acquaintances, notably a Christian solicitor called Hallama who helped them with money time and again.

Following the German invasion in May 1940, the situation of the Jewish refugees rapidly deteriorated. Civil resistance on the part of the Dutch population notwithstanding, the Germans' anti-Jewish policies were rigorously implemented. Following the systematic expropriation of the Jewish population and a succession of other repressive measures, deportations, primarily from the Westerbork transit camp, began on 15 July 1942. Because the transports ran so smoothly and no attempt was ever made to sabotage them, deportations from the Netherlands were given precedence over other transports, so much so that from March to July 1943, the trains had to be diverted to the Sobibor death camp because Auschwitz was unable to dispose of (i.e., murder) the deportees quickly enough. By October 1943, all the Jews who had not gone into hiding had been rounded up and placed in camps. There was a short lull in deportations in the Winter of 1943/44, while Westerbork was in quarantine, but the transports to Auschwitz, Theresienstadt and Bergen Belsen then continued until November 1944. Roughly half of the 20,000 Jews who had gone into hiding were eventually caught, mostly because they were betrayed. Of the 140,000 Jews living in the Netherlands at the time of the German invasion, 107,000 were deported. Only 5,000 of them returned. No other West European country, indeed, few other European countries were as badly affected by the Shoah.

As we saw, Andries Sternheim and his family were among those murdered. So too was Karl Landauer. Initially exempt from deportation because he worked as a counsellor for the Jewish Council, he was taken to Westerbork on 20 June 1943 from where, on 15 February 1944, together with his wife, Lina Landauer, née Kahn, and their daughter Eva Landauer, he was deported to Bergen Belsen. His death was recorded on 27 January 1945 (the day on which Auschwitz was liberated). Lina Landauer was liberated in Bergen Belsen on 15 April 1945. Eva Landauer, who had left the camp with the last transport headed for Theresi-

---

17 Huber 2019, pp. 61–2.

enstadt, was liberated in Tröbitz (near Frankfurt/Oder) on 23 April 1945. After the war, they moved to New York where they were joined by Eva's siblings Suze Landauer, who had survived in hiding, and Paul Landauer, who had fled to the Yishuv.[18]

Miraculously, thanks to an exit visa Friedrich Pollock somehow managed to secure for them, the Pollocks were able to leave the Netherlands for Buenos Aires on 11 August 1941. Two days prior to their departure they were once again summoned by the currency control bureau for questioning. There, Hans Pollock later recalled, 'the official literally said to me: I see that the issue with your assets in Stuttgart has been resolved; we have your share certificates and the rest is already ours, but where are your silver caddy and your life insurance?'[19] There was no silver caddy and no life insurance, at this point everything had been taken from them – but they got out. Alas, they were unable to take Ida Pollock's now seventy-five-year-old mother, Settchen Joseph, with them. Hallama continued to take care of her but on 18 September 1942, she was deported from Westerbork to Auschwitz, where she was murdered on arrival.[20]

In most cases, it was impossible to ascertain what had happened to friends and relatives until after the war. Early in 1950, Hans (now Juan) Pollock enthusiastically informed his brother that he had discovered some of their relatives in Montevideo.

> You must remember Dr. Fritz and Paul J[acoby] and Else, she married one Dr. Windmüller. Paul who studied in Freiburg and ate with the parents almost every day, it aroused many memories in me, of the Schlossberg [Castle Mount], the Sternwald Forest, Günterstal etc. Paul saw your name in *Aufbau*, wrote to the editorial office, whether you are the F. P. from Freiburg-Stuttgart, asking to be put in touch. They lost everything, live in modest circumstances and are hoping for reparations.

'Have you been in touch with Wolf Franck', he went on, 'or with Walter and Heinz? And what about the other Pollock relatives?'[21]

---

18 The relevant information comes from the Central Database of Shoah Victims' Names, the Arolsen Archives, and https://www.joodsmonument.nl/.
19 Juan Pollock to Friedrich Pollock, 23 January 1950, Horkheimer Archive, University Library Frankfurt/Main, MHA XXIII 22, 155.
20 Juan Pollock to Friedrich Pollock, 21 July 1949, Horkheimer Archive, University Library Frankfurt/Main, MHA XXIII 22, 171.
21 Juan Pollock to Friedrich Pollock, 23 January 1950, Horkheimer Archive, University Library Frankfurt/Main, MHA XXIII 22, 155.

The well known and well connected leftist publicist and pioneering broadcaster Wolf Franck was a maternal cousin, Walter and Heinz Pollock were the sons of their father's younger brother, the aforementioned Hans Ludwig Pollock. One way or another, they all ended up in the United States. Wolf Franck, his wife, Marga Franck, née Oppenheimer, and their son Michael fled to Paris in 1933, where Franck published a still interesting *Führer durch die deutsche Emigration* (Guide to the German Émigré Community).[22] Initially interned following the German invasion in 1940, Franck was able to flee to North Africa. From there, the family set sail via Martinique to New York, where they arrived on the Saint Domingue on 10 January 1941.[23] Once they arrived in the United States, Franck worked as a radio engineer in the armaments industry. After the war, he retrained as a musicologist and librarian.[24]

Walter and Heinz Pollock left much later. Perhaps they thought they might be spared, given that their parents were no longer members of the Jewish community and they themselves had been baptised. It was following the birth of their first son Walter in 1904, that Hans Ludwig (formerly Isidor Louis) Pollock formally declared that he, his wife Alice Pollock, née Goldschmidt, who originally came from Strasbourg, and, by implication, their new-born son were revoking their membership of the congregation.[25] In 1913, there seems to have been some sort of confusion regarding Walter's status and his father again revoked his membership of the Jewish congregation.[26] Eventually, on 3 December 1916, he had both of his sons baptised.[27]

In the case of the younger son, Heinz, this story took a rather unexpected turn when, in 1931, he attended the municipal authorities to make a rather remarkable statement. 'The student Heinz Pollock, who lives in Freiburg i. Br., Günterstalstraße no. 32, appeared and made the following declaration: I revoke my membership of the Official Protestant Church and wish to join the Israelite Religious Community.'[28] Attached to the record is a statement from the district rabbinate confirming that he had 'rejoined' but also noting that a 'specific ritual' still needed to be performed to render the decision religiously

---

22 Franck 1935.
23 Saint Domingue, List or Manifest of Alien Passenger for the United States Immigration Officer at Port of Arrival, New York, 10 January 1941.
24 'Wolf Franck Dead; Anti-Nazi Teacher', *New York Times*, 11 July 1966, p. 27.
25 State Archive Stuttgart, Kirchenein- und -austritte Freiburg im Breisgau, J 386 Bü 197, 119.
26 State Archive Stuttgart, Kirchenein- und -austritte Freiburg im Breisgau, J 386 Bü 197, 143.
27 Sammlung Baden und Hessen, Deutschland, evangelische Kirchenbücher, 1502–1985 (ancestry.de).
28 State Archive Stuttgart, Kirchenein- und -austritte Freiburg im Breisgau, J 386 Bü 197, 251.

valid.²⁹ Heinz Pollock does not seem to have been married at the time, so the need or desire to accommodate his status to the wishes of a woman he was set to wed or her family presumably cannot be the explanation. Perhaps he, like other German Jews, wanted to take a clear stance in the face of the ever more prominent role antisemitism played in German political life. Of course, none of this was of any interest to the Nazis for whom the Pollocks – a family comprising two members with no religious affiliation, one Protestant and one member of the Jewish congregation – were all equally Jewish simply by descent.

As a physician and – following in his father's footsteps – officer of Freiburg's Carnival Association, Hans Ludwig Pollock had been a highly respected citizen.³⁰ Yet neither his professional and social status nor the fact that he had turned his back on Judaism protected him in a state fundamentally predicated on rabid antisemitism. Nor, it has to be said, did he really have any reason to believe otherwise, given that storm troopers promptly stood outside his practice during the nationwide boycott of Jewish enterprises on 1 April 1933. His licence to treat patients on the health service was revoked and, in 1935, he had to close his practice. He was forced to sell the property he had inherited on Günterstalstraße – now Adolf-Hitler-Straße. Eventually, all his remaining assets were confiscated, and he was allowed to draw down no more than 300 Reichsmarks a month.³¹ Hans Ludwig Pollock was one of the more than 30,000 Jews arrested during the November Pogrom of 1938 and taken to concentration camps, in his case to Dachau,³² where he contracted TB. His wife, Alice Pollock, née Goldschmidt, and their two sons were able to flee to the United States, where they became Alice, Walter and Henry W. Pons (a notable research chemist). Hans Ludwig Pollock was released in December 1939 but never recovered from the camp experience. Sick, lonely and isolated, he died just three months later, on 10 March 1939.

Friedrich Pollock's aunt, Rosa (Rosalia) Nördlinger, née Pollock, and her husband, Sigmund Nördlinger (Julius Pollock's former partner), were deported, on 15 June 1942, from Cologne to Theresienstadt, where Rosa Nördlinger perished on 1 September 1942.³³ Less than three weeks later, Sigmund Nördlinger was

---

29   State Archive Stuttgart, Kirchenein- und -austritte Freiburg im Breisgau, J 386 Bü 197, 252.
30   See Clausing 2005, p. 60 n215.
31   Kalchthaler 2017.
32   See Arolsen Archives, https://collections.arolsen-archives.org/de/search/person/13042949 5?s=pollock%201873&t=532939&p=3.
33   Theresienstadt Memorial database, https://www.holocaust.cz/en/database-of-victims/victim/26594-rosa-n-rdlinger/.

sent on to the Treblinka death camp. Of the 2,003 Jews on this transport, only one survived.[34] Friedrich Pollock's doctoral supervisor Siegfried Budge fell into destitution following the revocation of his academic teaching licence and his health soon faltered. Following his death in 1941, his widow Ella Budge, née Mayer, was deported, in July 1942, to Theresienstadt where she perished on 6 November 1943.[35]

One could continue this list of relatives, friends and associates for a while yet, but this may suffice to indicate the extent to which members of the institute were personally affected by the Nazis' annihilation of European Jewry. Writing to his brother Hans (now Juan) in 1945, Friedrich Pollock suggested that his 'personal life has been undeservedly happy and successful if one takes into account what has gone on in the world'.[36] In an important sense, this was true, of course, yet it is hard to avoid the impression that survivor guilt also led him to underestimate the extent to which he himself was affected by the catastrophic events in Europe.

This sense of guilt was perhaps best expressed by Hannah Arendt in her essay, 'We Refugees', published in the *Menorah Journal* in 1943. It reflects exactly what occasional remarks in his correspondence suggest Pollock too felt. 'We did our best', Arendt wrote,

> to prove to other people that we were just ordinary immigrants. We declared that we had departed of our own free will to countries of our choice, and we denied that our situation had anything to do with 'so-called Jewish problems.' Yes, we were 'immigrants' or 'newcomers' who had left our country because, one fine day, it no longer suited us to stay, or for purely economic reasons. We wanted to rebuild our lives, that was all.[37]

Pollock knew full well, of course, that his move to the United States had not been in the least bit voluntary, but he never described himself as a refugee or owned up, at least vis-à-vis the *extérieur*, to what Arendt described as the Jewish émigré experience:

---

34 Theresienstadt Memorial database, https://www.holocaust.cz/en/database-of-victims/victim/26595-siegmund-n-rdlinger/.
35 Theresienstadt Memorial database, https://www.holocaust.cz/en/database-of-victims/victim/7463-ella-budge/.
36 Friedrich Pollock to Juan Pollock, 8 September 1945, Horkheimer Archive, University Library Frankfurt/Main, MHA XXIII 22, 215.
37 Arendt 2007, p. 264.

> We lost our home, which means the familiarity of daily life. ... We lost our language, which means the naturalness of reactions, the simplicity of gestures, the unaffected expression of feelings. We left our relatives in the Polish ghettos and our best friends have been killed in concentration camps, and that means the rupture of our private lives.[38]

Pollock was indeed lucky. His private life, unlike that of so many others, his elective family – Max and Maidon Horkheimer and his wife – survived intact, and he was able to continue working in his profession. Yet the sense of having been spared was inextricable from a profound sense of loss. Pollock sought to cope by becoming a dyed-in-the-wool American. He adopted the manners and fashion of his new compatriots, devoured the country's relevant research literature and used the American English language wherever he could. Rather than Friedrich or Fritz, he called himself Frederick and Fred and insisted that his German colleagues do so too. Yet the theories and debates that had preoccupied him in Europe no more lost their hold over him than his personal and emotional ties to the old world.

In the United States, everyone was an immigrant, and being American meant having a hybrid identity. Given that he considered himself a German-American, it was only logical that Pollock joined the German-American Writers Association (GAWA) established in October 1938. Oskar Maria Graf was its president.[39] More surprising, perhaps, because it suggests that Pollock was rediscovering his Jewishness, is his involvement with *Aufbau*, the most significant German-Jewish émigré periodical. It was initially a small monthly published by the German-Jewish Club in New York.[40] This changed dramatically once Manfred George – one of the most prominent leftist journalists of the Weimar era who, since fleeing in 1933, had been involved in various émigré periodical projects – took over as editor in 1939 and began to transform *Aufbau* into a flagship weekly with a print run of up to 30,000 copies.[41] To this end, he formed a high-calibre advisory board with initially seventeen, later twelve members. This not only bolstered *Aufbau*'s reputation but also drew in a much broader range of contributors. On 16 May 1941, George addressed his readership as follows:

> The Editors of 'Aufbau' are gratified in finding that its reading public has further grown during the first half of the year. ... This success makes us

---

38   Arendt 2007, pp. 264–5.
39   Liebner 2001, pp. 49, 50 n71.
40   Eykman 1989.
41   See Schrag 2019.

both happy and proud. At the same time, it increases our responsibility in this epoch of ever new and growing crises and problems. In full awareness of this situation, the Editors have asked a select group of personalities, who have taken an active interest in 'Aufbau', to grant our paper the benefit of their advice and experience.[42]

The founding members included illustrious intellectuals and writers such as Albert Einstein, Lion Feuchtwanger, Nahum Goldmann, Emil Ludwig, Thomas Mann and – Friedrich Pollock, who continued to serve on the board until the end of the war. It was in *Aufbau*'s classifieds section that émigrés addressed the paper's global readership, hoping for information on their missing relatives and friends; and it was *Aufbau* that first informed most of its readers about the unfolding Shoah.[43]

In the aforementioned article, 'We Refugees', Hannah Arendt, who, in her fortnightly column for *Aufbau* also articulated her growing estrangement from Zionism, touched on the ways in which the Shoah affected its European victims but also those who had been able to flee and even drove some of them to suicide. What was unfolding in Europe was simply incomprehensible, and their own inability to do anything about it was unbearable. As late as 1961, Pollock, in a letter to his brother and sister-in-law, noted that the 'horrors of the Hitler era' were 'incomprehensible even now'.[44] Little wonder, then, that Pollock had so little to say about the Shoah. Not a single article by Pollock, not even a book review touched on the topic. What scholars, following Horkheimer's criticism of Pollock, have frequently qualified as writer's block was born of a genuine inability to find words appropriate to the devastation he was forced to witness from afar. Usually a level-headed analyst even of complex constellations that most certainly did not bode well,[45] of this, he simply could not make sense. Instead, he sought refuge from theory in practice by helping others who were persecuted.

Andrée Pollock too was badly affected by the news from Europe. Her life became bleaker yet when, just a year after their wedding, she became seriously ill. Adorno tried to cheer her up by giving her piano lessons, but they were of limited comfort to her, given the enormity of the adversity she faced.[46] Pollock

---

42 Manfred George, 'Advisory Board for Aufbau', *Aufbau*, 7.20, 14 May 1941, p. 1.
43 See Kucher 2016.
44 Friedrich Pollock to Juan and Ida Pollock, 16 February 1961, Horkheimer Archive, University Library Frankfurt/Main, MHA XXIII 22, 100.
45 See, e.g., Heerich 2007, p. 113.
46 Theodor W. Adorno to Max Horkheimer, 6 January 1939, in Adorno and Horkheimer 2004, pp. 49–52, p. 52.

tirelessly looked after her, stayed at health resorts with her for weeks on end, consulted dozens of physicians. Eventually, an oncologist diagnosed her with lung cancer. This was a profound shock for Pollock but outwardly he continued to exude optimism. Downplaying her symptoms as far as possible and no longer willing to be taken for the naïve female in need of care and instruction Pollock had rather patronisingly seen in her when they met, Dée Pollock increasingly sought contact with the *extérieur*. 'I am sitting in a glorious garden', she wrote on a postcard she sent in 1937 from Lake Placid to Wittfogel in China, 'yet what I wanted to say was that one can barely believe in the horror in the world in these surroundings! Yet we are aware of, and distressed by, them all the same.'[47]

Pollock's cancer metastasised, and she eventually succumbed to the disease in August 1939. 'I never have,' Horkheimer wrote in a private letter soon after her death,

> in any human being I know, seen such a fundamental development towards truth, as in Dée during these past two years. She has meant so much to us during this time, not to Fritz only, but also to Maidon and myself. I can still see her, a week before her end, sitting upright in bed because lying down was too painful to her. She was panting from a haemorrhage in the lungs which she had suffered, and at the same time discussed a difficult practical problem. Her thinking at this occasion was clear and precise, and she did not allow any compromise.
>
> Until her last moment she has not admitted the mere fact of her illness. This came not, however, out of a strong desire for life, but from a firm resolution to preserve her faculty of spiritual enjoyment while her faculty of physical enjoyment was decreasing without mercy. Out of this resolution or, still more, out of regard for her friends, she has literally pushed aside her notion that she was stricken with cancer. She might have taught a psychologist that Freud's theory that repression is chiefly a result of weakness when facing conflicts is too narrow. Dée has repressed her knowledge out of love.[48]

Ordinarily a beacon of steadiness and restraint, Pollock was utterly distraught at his wife's death, and the very fact that he felt duty-bound to appear equable and restrained at all times only made things worse. It was he who helped oth-

---

47   Andrée Pollock to Karl August Wittfogel, 24 August 1937, Hoover Institution, Wittfogel Papers, 37, 8.
48   Max Horkheimer to Katharina von Hirsch, 12 September 1939, in Horkheimer 1995b, pp. 631–2, p. 632. Katharina von Hirsch was the former Käthe Weil, Felix Weil's first wife.

ers – friends, colleagues, refugees – not the other way around. Finding that he himself needed support left him disoriented. He was unable to spend time by himself and moved in with the Horkheimers, who employed an émigré couple from Vienna to manage the household of their reassembled *intérieur à trois*. Pollock became even more of a workaholic, devoting all the time and energy he had previously channelled into taking care of his wife to the institute. 'The meaningful work we, unlike most human beings, are allowed to perform affords him a sense of composure and gratification', Horkheimer wrote to Karl Landauer in December 1939, adding: 'I hope that he too will be able to undertake more academic work in future than has been the case.'[49]

The sadness, anger and powerlessness he felt in connection with his wife's illness and death does indeed seem to have unleashed a particular kind of productivity in him. In the year following her death, he produced his two most significant essays. They ran to just forty pages in total but offered probing analyses of the new world order and (re)shaped the future work of the institute in decisive ways. In his analysis, he was unsparing in the scrutiny of his own presumptions and he readily accepted the risk that his conclusions might be castigated for marking a betrayal of Marxism. The paradigm shift the institute underwent at the beginning of the Second World War was, in other words, inextricably linked to Pollock's debilitating and tortuous personal crisis following the death of his wife.[50]

---

49 Max Horkheimer to Karl Landauer, 22 December 1939, in Horkheimer 1995b, pp. 681–5, p. 685.
50 See Lenhard 2014.

CHAPTER 9

A New Order?

When the synagogues burnt, Jewish businesses and homes were ransacked and Jews were beaten, humiliated and dragged off to concentration camps in Greater Germany on 9 and 10 November 1938, Pollock's parents had already died of natural causes. In a letter to Benjamin, Adorno, who had recently arrived in New York, related what his parents experienced in Frankfurt. Stones had been thrown at his parents' house, his 68-year-old father Oscar Wiesengrund was taken to the police headquarters, his 73-year-old mother Maria Calvelli-Adorno was detained for days in the women's prison on Klappergasse. Oscar Wiesengrund's wine store was ransacked and wrecked.[1] Neither Adorno nor Pollock understood what caused this antisemitic violence or what it revealed about what was happening to state and society at large. The benefit of hindsight tends to lend historical developments clearer contours than those who lived through them may have been able to recognise, given that the constant, often incremental flow of events can obscure important qualitative changes – such as, in this case, the novelty and significance of the Nazis' anti-Jewish policies.

Having already lost his Prussian citizenship, in the spring of 1939, Pollock also lost his German citizenship, and his doctorate was revoked.[2] His father's factory had effectively been expropriated, family and friends had either already left or were planning to flee. All his Jewish colleagues had lost their positions, some of his political associates were incarcerated in concentration camps or had gone underground. Before long, Hitler and Stalin agreed a non-aggression pact and on 1 September, Germany invaded Poland, starting the Second World War. The first mass executions of Jews soon followed. To be sure, the institute's members had foreseen early on that something sinister was waiting in the wings and drawn practical consequences, allowing them to flee the country in a timely manner. Yet, the events that had now unfolded in short succession and set the world ablaze nevertheless caught them off guard.

---

1 See Theodor W. Adorno to Walter Benjamin, 1 February 1939, in Adorno and Benjamin 1999, pp. 298–306, pp. 298–9.
2 Index card, annulled nationality, National Archives and Records Administration, 242.15, T355, Name Index of Jews Whose German Nationality Was Annulled by the Nazi Regime (Berlin Document Center), reel 7; 'Liste 100, Deutscher Reichsanzeiger und Preußischer Staatsanzeiger Nr. 72 vom 25.3.1939', in Hepp 1985, p. 137.

The simple truth was that the institute lacked a developed concept of National Socialism and the theoretical means to account for the unfolding catastrophe. In January 1939, the sociologist Heinz Maus, a student of Horkheimer's who later became his assistant in Frankfurt, writing to his teacher from Oslo, stressed how much of a desideratum a theory of fascism transcending the party Communist clichés was for those opposed to Hitler. 'I fully share your desire for a genuine theory of fascism', Horkheimer wrote in response.

> In one sense, I consider all our literary activities of recent years as a provisional contribution to this end. I very much hope that we will have the energy and the time to continue this work as soon as possible. We already have some ideas and I hope that it will not be all too long until we can share them with you.[3]

With 'some ideas' Horkheimer presumably meant a lengthy essay he had discussed in great detail with Pollock and hoped to finalise in September 1939. Its title was 'Die Juden und Europa' (The Jews and Europe) and it was published in the eighth volume of the institute's now trilingual journal, *Studies in Philosophy and Social Science*.[4] It was a milestone in the evolution of Critical Theory because it marked the transition from an ultimately still orthodox Marxist frame of reference to a theory built on the insight that Marx's categories were no longer adequate to the current political and economic state of play. If 'Traditional and Critical Theory' announced a programme of theoretical revision, the 'Jew essay', as it was called in the correspondence, was the first attempt to offer a comprehensive – albeit as yet fuzzy and provisional – new account of society in the face of the unfolding totalitarian terror. The essay was published under Horkheimer's name and Horkheimer likely was its sole author. Pollock's economic theory nevertheless shines through at every turn, so much so that Pollock emerges as a co-author of sorts. 'The Jews and Europe' was the point of departure for the theoretical exploration of National Socialism Pollock undertook during the war, drawing not least on his earlier examination of crisis theory in 1932/33. Apparently, the start of the Second World War, the radicalisation of the antisemitic persecution, the rapid waning of the institute's assets and the blow of his wife's death combined to form the perfect storm that drove Pollock back towards theory and made the desire to order and comprehend the chaos around him irresistible.

---

3 Max Horkheimer to Heinz Maus, 13 February 1939, in Horkheimer 1995b, pp. 555–6, p. 556.
4 Horkheimer 1989.

To this end, he needed to revisit all his concepts. He made no conscious decision to move away from Marxism, and the process was incremental and painful. It was the unfolding events and the inability of the left to explain, let alone stop, them that drove Pollock to review everything he had come to take for granted, and it took several years for his misgivings about the left to translate into a comprehensive theoretical renewal. Given the succession of serious setbacks he had witnessed, the conviction of many in the organised labour movement that Hitler's rise ultimately only made their own victory more likely irked Pollock from the outset. Leftist triumphalism in the face of a slight decrease in the Nazi share of the vote in the general election of November 1932 (from 37.3 to 33.1 per cent, still making the NSDAP the single largest parliamentary party by thirteen percentage points) was a case in point. '[T]he aura of inevitability has been destroyed, the decline has started', the aforementioned Social Democratic theoretician Rudolf Hilferding commented in *Die Gesellschaft* in January 1933.[5] In February, with Hitler already in power, Ernst Thälmann, the leader of the KPD, explained to his party's Central Committee that Hitler's accession, by 'escalating the class struggle', had provided their party with 'an important key to unlock the revolutionary potential across Europe'.[6] The Nazis' failure would pave the way for the Communist revolution. 'After Hitler It'll Be Us!' was the Bolshevik motto.[7]

Those leftist intellectuals who rejected Thälmann's Moscow-aligned course anyway found this assessment of Nazism positively ridiculous. In his study, *Der Faschismus an der Macht* (Fascism in Power), published in 1935, Fritz Sternberg, whom we met earlier as one of the institute's former instructors and who was now an active member of the SAPD and in exile in Basel, presented a merciless account of the major labour parties' political errors.[8] Giving short shrift to the KPD's social fascism theory in particular, he called for a united front. The book ran to some 300 pages, and yet the Nazis' antisemitism did not feature once in Sternberg's discussion.

Pollock published a generally positive review of the book in the institute's journal but quibbled that Sternberg's 'account of the German labour move-

---

5 Hilferding 1933, p. 4.
6 Thälmann 1977, p. 345.
7 According to his recollections, the long-standing leader of the Communist regime in East Germany, Erich Honecker, incarcerated from 1935 to 1945 for his role in the Communist resistance movement, never lost his faith in an imminent Communist victory either. At no point had he 'lost faith in the victory of the working class since we knew: progress cannot be help up'. Quoted in Sabrow 2016, p. 85.
8 Sternberg 1935.

ment in recent years ... is rather superficial'.[9] Sternberg's critique was merely directed at the party elite but failed to take into account the nexus between the proletariat's socio-economic character and its failure to play what was supposedly its revolutionary role. As we saw, the institute's empirical research had demonstrated for some years that it was an illusion to assume that its socio-economic role automatically rendered the proletariat revolutionary. The workers dreamt not of the abolition of domination but of joining the ruling class. They wanted to be profiteers, wanted to belong to the strong who keep the wretched down. Yet if this was the case, Marxism predicated on class struggle was toothless and amounted to little more than a sociological theory increasingly less able to help explain current developments.

Pollock was essentially improvising as he sought to establish some kind of correspondence between current events and his theoretical and empirical knowledge to craft a moderately adequate prognosis, and he knew full well how provisional and incomplete any such attempt would initially be. In a letter written, soon after Hitler's accession, to Karl Korsch, who had fled to Denmark, he had explained that he did not believe in the prospect of a proletarian general strike bringing down the regime. In his response, Korsch agreed unreservedly. 'I definitely believe in the regime's longevity', he wrote, 'at best there may be some (barely or poorly organised) "unrest" this winter, but even this still seems far from certain'.[10] It was perfectly clear to Korsch and Pollock even then that the proletariat would not rebel against the Nazis. Yet they had no clue as to what would happen instead. Nothing offered reliable orientation any longer – least of all one's own established theoretical certainties.

Pollock certainly never returned to the assumption that the regime might collapse or that big capital or, even less likely, a general strike of the proletarian masses might put an end to the Nazi dictatorship. Initially, he did, however, maintain that it was not in the *genuine* interest of either the workers or the bourgeoisie to support the Nazis. The regime would need to resort to manipulation and propaganda to compel their support. In this vein, he wrote to Wittfogel in 1935 that 'the Nazis do not seem to be doing all that well in Germany. The attacks directed at Jews and other foes are surely diversionary in nature.'[11] Pollock knew full well from his own research that deficit spending had in the meantime substantially ameliorated the impact of the Great Depression, and yet he continued to buy into the interpretation of antisemitism as a diversion-

---

9   Pollock 1936.
10 Karl Korsch to Friedrich Pollock, 13 October 1933, in Korsch 2001, pp. 437–41, p. 439.
11 Friedrich Pollock to Karl August Wittfogel, 9 August 1935, Hoover Institute, Wittfogel Papers 37, 8.

ary tactic. From what, then, was it supposed to divert attention? He evidently either did not ask himself this question or assumed that the answer was so self-evident that it quite literally went without saying. That the absurd conspiracy theories and crude fantasies of annihilation might be meant seriously was inconceivable to Pollock. His casual downplaying of the Nazis' antisemitism, just a month before the Nuremberg Laws were issued, was indicative of an assimilation of his perception to established standards of rationality that had in fact ceased to reflect reality and become obsolete. For the Nazis, antisemitism was an end in itself, yet from the Marxist vantage, it had to be a means to some end and, as a means, it had, by some standard of rationality, to be proportionate to the benefits bestowed by the end in question. For all his critique of orthodox Marxism, Pollock was evidently still beholden to this fundamental logic.[12]

On a second issue too, Pollock and his colleagues remained beholden to conventional Marxist logic. Their own profound scepticism about the revolutionary character of the proletariat notwithstanding, they too maintained that Hitler was the lackey of big capital who tolerated him because they wanted him to put the revolutionary working class in its place. Fritz Sternberg, Richard Löwenthal (aka Paul Sering), who was a member of the communist Neu Beginnen (New Beginning) group and Herbert Marcuse in particular were strong proponents of this assumption.[13]

Marcuse had joined the institute in Geneva in 1933. He too, like Pollock, was the son of a Jewish entrepreneur. Prior to the First World War, he had enjoyed all the privileges of an upper-class upbringing in Berlin. He too was politicised by the war but chose to join the SPD. During the November Revolution he was elected to the soldiers' council in Berlin-Reinickendorf where he supported the leftist faction inclining towards the Communists. Given its role in putting down the revolution, he left the SPD again. He read literature, philosophy and political economy, first in Berlin and then, from 1922 onwards, in Freiburg. In 1928, he became Heidegger's assistant, setting him firmly on course to gain his postdoctoral qualification and secure a chair, had the Nazis not come to power. Intoxicated with enthusiasm for the Nazis, Heidegger sabotaged his postdoctoral qualification and put an end to Marcuse's academic career in Germany. At this juncture, the institute took him under its wings.

It was certainly not clear from the outset that he would come to play a prominent role in the Horkheimer circle in New York, given that his intellec-

---

12 See Diner 1993.
13 Sering 1936.

tual background differed markedly from that of his new colleagues. It was not just the fact that he was Heidegger's student that set him apart. His understanding of Marxism also ran contrary to that of Horkheimer and Pollock. Paradoxically, the latter was in part responsible for this, given his involvement in the publication of the first MEGA volume with Marx's early writings. Marcuse devoured them with unbounded enthusiasm. For him, this was the real Marx. It was these texts, he wrote in a review, that revealed 'the original meaning of the basic categories' on which the critique of political economy was based.[14] Marcuse pitted Marx the anthropological materialist against Marx the political economist or, in more directly political terms, the revolutionary enthusiast against the 'scientific' theoretician.[15] This was obviously a far cry from Pollock's own interpretation of Marx. As we saw, in his doctoral thesis, Pollock placed Marx's late, theoretical economic writings centre stage, and he had little patience for Marcuse's philosophical and ontological inflection of Marx.[16]

Yet Marcuse's intellectual brilliance was indisputable, and his skills were well suited to the institute's requirements. Arriving in New York at almost the same time as Pollock, he was the first member of the institute to embark on the development of a Marxist concept of fascism. In 1934, his essay, 'Der Kampf gegen den Liberalismus in der totalitären Staatsauffassung' (The Struggle against Liberalism in the Totalitarian View of the State), was published in the institute's periodical. He argued that liberalism already bore the kernel of fascism within itself. In important areas, the two ideologies propagated starkly differing philosophical values, to be sure. Yet liberalism failed to live up to its proclaimed values and both ideologies were fundamentally predicated on the same socio-economic order. It was therefore no surprise that bourgeois ideologues were unable to muster any genuinely fundamental opposition to fascism. This line of argument anticipated an important tenet subsequently presented in Horkheimer's 'The Jews and Europe'. In an important sense, liberalism and fascism were siblings. Both were predicated on private ownership of the means of production and the ensuing principle of competition. The 'total-authoritarian state' merely revealed liberalism's true countenance.[17] Citing an article by Pollock in the previous issue, Marcuse explained that the progression from liberalism to fascism in fact complemented the transition from private to monopoly capitalism. 'The separation of state and society the liberal nine-

---

14 Marcuse 2005, p. 86.
15 Kellner 1984, pp. 81–91.
16 On the relationship between Pollock and Marcuse, see Lenhard 2016a.
17 Marcuse 2009.

teenth century sought to implement' was now 'abolished: the state takes over the political integration of society'.[18] It followed that the right-wing intellectuals whose texts Marcuse cited with relish – including the infamous inaugural address by his former teacher Heidegger as Nazi-appointed vice chancellor of Freiburg University – were the spin doctors of monopoly capitalism. Inspired by the critique of ideology, Marcuse's approach differed markedly from Sternberg's trite economism, and yet they both could conceive of fascism only as a new stage in the class struggle. Uncertain as Marcuse may have been about 'the fate of the labor movement', the centrality of the proletariat to his frame of reference indicates the extent to which he was still beholden to the Marxist taxonomy.[19] In a sense, Marcuse's essay was to Pollock's economic analysis what fascism was to monopoly capitalism.

Given that Marxists tended to subscribe to stark, undialectical juxtapositions of base and superstructure at the time and categorically rejected 'subjectivism', leftist observers based their analyses of fascism on the economic theories they brought to the table rather than their actual experiences and observations. Pollock had assumed for more than a decade that the forces of production had so dramatically outgrown the relations of production that private capitalism was on the way out and the future inevitably lay with some form of planned economy. Mass unemployment, the destruction of the market by the trusts and the overaccumulation crisis were unavoidable consequences of the long-term decline in the rate of profit predicted by Marx. Marx surmised that the owners of the means of production would try to raise productivity by seeking technological solutions allowing them to rely less on labour and thus save on labour costs. Yet insofar as surplus value could be extracted only from labour ('variable capital') while machines ('constant capital') merely consumed surplus value that had already been appropriated, this would gradually lead to a reduction in the rates of profit. In the long term, competition thus militated against growth, inevitably precipitating a crisis. What this meant for the future of capitalism was one of Pollock's central questions, perhaps his single greatest preoccupation. In the course of the 1920s, his interest had shifted from Marx's concept of money to the transition to a planned economy, whether by revolutionary or reformist means. He had no time for voluntaristic or pseudo-radical approaches and was interested only in a materialist exploration of whether the existing relations of production themselves engendered the prerequisites for a socialist transformation.

---

18   Marcuse 2009, p. 25 (translation amended).
19   Marcuse 2009, p. 30.

In this respect, Pollock was essentially still singing from the hymn sheet of 'scientific' socialism. The revisionists assumed that socialism would inevitably come about of its own accord and devoted themselves to the introduction of social reforms in the meantime. The radicals believed that the historical development was pregnant with socialism but depended on the revolutionary action of the working class to induce its delivery. Pollock inclined towards the radical position, but he had a hard time believing in the proletariat's revolutionary consciousness. He too agreed that the competitive free-market capitalism of the nineteenth century was nearing its end but to him, nothing suggested that it would inevitably be superseded by socialism – whether in its self-generating form or as the product of revolutionary change. What, then, would take its place?

Within a year or two of Hitler's accession, it was clear that in Germany, it would indeed be the Nazis who shaped the post-liberal era, at least in the near term. As recently as 1932, Pollock and Horkheimer had argued that – barring a war – the forces of monopoly capitalism would be able to reassert their domination over the anti-capitalist elements and the NSDAP would atrophy into a regular, if reactionary, party. Clearly, they were wrong. Well before embarking on the Second World War, the regime, deploying an admixture of terror, propaganda and economic and social policies, was able to create a *Volksgemeinschaft* (ethnically homogeneous national community) in which social antagonisms were channelled into a merciless assault on any and everything deemed un-German. The Nazis' revolutionary momentum survived the elimination of the particularly radical SA leadership and the regime's consolidation in power, in other words.[20] The *Strength Through Joy* leisure programme and the persecution of Communists, the creation of the German Labour Front and the antisemitic incitement were inextricably linked from the outset. The 'German Revolution', as the Nazis themselves called their takeover, neither abolished domination and exploitation nor was it simply more of the same.

A meaningful analysis of Nazi anti-capitalism presupposed precise knowledge of the unfolding economic development. To this end, the institute created a research group led by Pollock. Its other members were Kurt Mandelbaum, Gerhard Meyer and Julian Gumperz. Pollock's 'Bemerkungen zur Wirtschaftskrise' (Remarks on the Economic Crisis) in the third issue of the journal's second volume drew on the broad range of empirical material and statistics assembled and analysed by this research group. 'The urgent need to know where things are headed' could be met only by ascertaining the exact reas-

---

20 See Bajohr and Wildt (eds.) 2009.

ons for the economic crisis, how it might be resolved and whether the current regime was in a position to bring about the requisite resolution.[21] Finally, one needed to ask how the resolution in question would shape political realities in the near future. Pollock predicted that the Nazis would be able 'to overcome the tensions within the system without transcending its basic principles' (p. 322).

As Pollock saw it, the systemic crisis was endogenous in nature but reinforced by coincidental exogenous factors. Yet its causes being principally endogenous did not imply, as Grossman claimed, that capitalism would inevitably collapse. It merely meant that the root causes of the crisis could not be resolved by political means without fundamentally transforming the mode of production. Political means could be deployed, however, to restore an equilibrium of sorts, reinvigorate consumption and productivity and ameliorate the impact of the crisis or perhaps even avert it – until the next time. The overlap between some of Pollock's terminology – cleansing, extirpation, annihilating – and that of the Nazis is striking. Engaging in the critique of ideology, he interpreted the regime's terminology as a direct reflection of ongoing economic processes: 'The "cleansing" process, i.e., the extirpation of "disproportionalities" by stripping a share of the means of production and produce of their value or physically annihilating them is underway' (p. 323).

This cleansing process was indeed facilitating a recovery of the economic system, yet it came at an enormous social and material cost. Not only did it leave millions destitute, it was also based on the destruction of a portion of society's wealth. Pollock certainly considered the possibility that this colossal 'destruction of value' might still take the form of a war but as yet, he assumed that, in purely economic terms, the countermeasures pitted against the crisis by Roosevelt, Daladier, Chamberlain and Hitler might resolve it without requiring a war (p. 342). Capitalism had grown extraordinarily resilient and its recent transformation had led to 'a more or less far-reaching restriction of the discretion individual owners of the means of production are able to apply in determining the kind and direction of their economic activity'. That discretion was, instead, increasingly concentrated in 'the large entities or the state itself' (p. 345). This marked the end of competitive free-market capitalism as the trusts or the state dominated by them took the reins, thus bringing the protracted decline of the private owner to a close. The bourgeois individual, predicated in large measure on its authority over the means of production, was

---

21   Pollock 1933, p. 321. The page references for the remaining quotations from this article are given in the main text in brackets.

becoming historically obsolete. In this sense, the National Socialists were the executors of bourgeois society.

The vexing question for leftists was why on earth none of this aroused any meaningful resistance. If both the proletarian masses and the independent entrepreneurs were pulling the short straw, how then was a small minority able to remain in power? 'The permanence of an economic and social system', Pollock explained,

> depends not only on the 'technical' means it is able to deploy to master its economic tasks, but also on the ability of the social strata bearing the costs of the existing order to resist. Experience has shown that this ability to resist has previously been vastly overestimated. Given the altered significance of the working class in the economic process, radical changes in weapons technology and the extraordinary perfection of the mental domination of the masses such resistance seems conceivable for the foreseeable future only in the wake of the gravest of catastrophes (p. 350).

The historical experience cited by Pollock extended to much more than the Day of National Labour on 1 May 1933 when the German trade unions, hoping to rescue their skin, accommodated themselves to the new regime. It encompassed the embourgeoisement of the SPD in the late nineteenth century, its approval of the war credits in August 1914 and its defence of the status quo during the revolutionary unrest of 1918/19. Pollock expected precious little of the workers. They were hamstrung politically and weakened economically, and the state had destroyed their organisations.

The 'aryan' bourgeoisie, on the other hand, to the extent that it rejected National Socialism, its long-standing confidence in its own strength and superiority notwithstanding, acquiesced in its own demise with little more than a whimper if that. Now that it was too late, they embraced the Nazis as best they could to ensure they too were on the side of the victors. Little wonder that many Nazis saw them as opportunists. Yet it took this union of true believers and opportunists to turn National Socialism into a genuine mass movement.

Was there any hope? The principal weapon of the proletariat was traditionally the strike. As technological progress made human labour increasingly redundant, this weapon became blunt. 'Yet the *will* of the great masses to fight will also be broken, both by the modern methods of mass control and by a kind of selective integration', Pollock predicted. 'The destruction of the working class's will to resist will be completed by this separation of those unemployed individuals who may expect to be employed again from those "unreliable elements" from whom this privilege has been withdrawn, either temporarily or permanently' (p. 353, emphasis added). There was little prospect, then, of National Socialism collapsing or being toppled any time soon.

For a number of years, this diagnosis was effectively all Pollock had to say about National Socialism. Especially as far as the regime's antisemitism and persecution of the Jews was concerned, Pollock could think of nothing worthwhile to articulate. Consequently, the years between his arrival in New York and the beginning of the Second World War turned out to be his least productive as a scholar, earning him the reputation of being no more than the institute's financial administrator in this time. Hanns Eisler, for example, later claimed that Pollock's work 'was less scholarly, more about housing and property speculation'.[22] This was obviously untrue, but it reflected the perception that he had fallen silent as a scholar, and it is true that he did not publish a single substantial text between 1934 and 1940. We have already noted the enormous effort that went into taking care of his sick wife and running the institute. If one studies his correspondence from this time, it is clear that he was having very real difficulties in making sense of the political developments he witnessed. While Adorno, Marcuse and Löwenthal were primarily concerned with philosophical and cultural issues, he was still the man for diagnoses and predictions in the field of political economy. The others expected him to explain where the overall development was headed so that they might carry out their theoretical studies accordingly. Yet the further the catastrophe advanced the less he felt able to meet this expectation. He was constantly groping in the dark, vacillating between erroneous assessments and their correction which, in turn, generated new theses and antitheses. He was particularly uncertain when it came to predicting whether there would be a war.

In July 1934, following the subordination of the SA, Pollock assumed that, while the '*acute* threat of war has decreased considerably', 'nothing has changed on the long run' and England was 'definitely' arming itself against Germany.[23] A year later, on Adorno's account, Pollock was 'inclined to assume that the solidarity that pits the capitalist countries against Russia weighs more heavily than their antagonisms'.[24] It was therefore improbable that the Western powers would wage war against Germany. Germany's rapid rearmament was primarily directed against Russia, and the West was looking on impassively. That Britain and France did not respond to Germany's occupation of the demil-

---

22   Bunge and Eisler 2014, p. 18.
23   Friedrich Pollock to Max Horkheimer, 21 July 1934, in Horkheimer 1995a, p. 202 n9. The phrase 'on the long run' was written in English in the original.
24   Theodor W. Adorno to Max Horkheimer, 13 May 1935, Horkheimer 1995a, pp. 345–51, pp. 350–1.

itarised Rhineland seemed to bear out Pollock's prognosis. In 1937, against the backdrop of naval skirmishes in the Mediterranean connected to the Spanish Civil War, Pollock wrote in a telegram to Horkheimer that he remained 'convinced that current European crisis will be resolved by compromise'.[25] In a letter written on the same day, he did concede, however, that 'history is not unfolding in an overly rational manner'.[26] For the most part, Pollock met Horkheimer's methodical pessimism with calm sobriety and even optimism.[27] In this respect, the two friends were constantly at odds, regardless of the specific issue. While Horkheimer consistently assumed the worst, Pollock sought to assuage him by pointing to possible alternative outcomes. When the West responded to the German *Anschluss* of Austria in March 1938 with nothing but protest notes, Pollock again felt vindicated. There would be no war.

It was absurd. On the one hand, the very concrete threat of war could barely be more palpable. War was already underway in Spain, Ethiopia and China. Germany had annexed Austria and the formerly Czechoslovakian regions of Bohemia and Moravia and now threatened Poland. Yet the Western powers were unwavering in their pursuit of appeasement. In a letter Pollock wrote to Siegfried Kracauer a few days after the signing of the Munich Agreement, he expressed his confidence that 'peace in Europe at large' had been secured for quite some time. However, 'in the absolutely unlikely case of another foreign policy crisis in the foreseeable future', the increasingly desperate Kracauer could count on unbureaucratic help.[28] Of course, Hitler assumed that the agreement gave him carte blanche for the further expansion of Greater Germany and less than a year later, Germany invaded Poland and unleashed the Second World War in Europe.

Pollock and Horkheimer remained convinced to the last that Europe would be spared a major war because the capitalist countries ultimately shared too many interests and had too much to lose. On another issue they were less blinkered. In marked contrast to large numbers of Communists, many of whom were not only dumbfounded but profoundly shocked when Hitler and Stalin agreed a non-aggression pact in August 1939, the members of the institute were not at all surprised. Pollock had foreseen that the tyrant Stalin would grab

---

25 Friedrich Pollock, telegram to Max Horkheimer, 7 September 1937, in Horkheimer 1995b, p. 230.
26 Friedrich Pollock to Max Horkheimer, 7 September 1937, in Horkheimer 1995b, pp. 231–2, p. 231.
27 See Raulet 1986.
28 Friedrich Pollock to Siegfried Kracauer, 4 October 1938, Deutsches Literaturarchiv Marbach, Kracauer papers, 72.2835/2.

whatever opportunity he could to save his own hide, and he certainly did not credit Stalin with the integrity required to reject a pact with Hitler on ideological grounds.

Towards the end of 1938, Pollock and Horkheimer fell out with Wittfogel over this issue. The three of them met for lunch at the Tip Toe Inn, a Jewish deli on the Upper Westside Horkheimer particularly liked because one could talk there for hours.[29] Horkheimer argued that Stalin would enter into a peace agreement with Hitler at his earliest convenience, if only it were on offer. So outraged was Wittfogel by this suggestion that he shouted at his colleagues and ran out. For Pollock, this 'painful incident' clarified just how far he and Horkheimer had moved away from those of their colleagues still more or less associated with the KPD.[30] Their initial sympathies for the Bolshevik experiment had waned in the course of the 1920s and since the show trials and the Great Terror, their attitude towards the Soviet Union had become hostile. The non-aggression pact merely confirmed just how far Stalin had gone in betraying the promises of the October Revolution. Hence, there would be no war with Nazi Germany.

As Britain and France declared war on Germany following its invasion of Poland, Pollock and Horkheimer were compelled to suggest that they might – might! – conceivably have been wrong. 'If the improbable, a full-scale general war, really should come to pass the shared interest of the Central and West European powers that governed politics until the summer of this year would indeed seem to have been wiped away by differences of which we had not assumed that they were currently agenda-setting', Horkheimer suggested in a rather roundabout way in a letter of 11 September 1939 addressed to Juliette Favez in Geneva.[31]

Pollock did not feel that his assessment had been fundamentally disproven, but he now placed greater emphasis on the integration of the political into his analysis of the transformation of capitalism. As we saw, he was bursting with intellectual energy at this juncture, perhaps because he needed the distraction following his wife's death, perhaps because a great weight had fallen from him shoulders when her suffering ended. Hitler's unleashing of the Second World War evidently provided the final incentive to abandon the concept of

---

29 The legendary Tip Toe Inn features in episode 409 (The Beautiful Girls) of the television series *Mad Men*. The character Roger Sterling takes his lover Joan Holloway there because there is no risk 'of running into anyone, and of course [because of] the cheesecake'.
30 Friedrich Pollock to Karl August Wittfogel, 30 September 1949, Hoover Institution, Wittfogel Papers, 37, 8.
31 Max Horkheimer to Juliette Favez, 11 September 1939, Horkheimer 1995b, pp. 628–30, p. 628.

monopoly capitalism for good. Stifled for years by circumstances and intellectual congestion, Pollock was determined finally to develop a theory of post-bourgeois and post-liberal society capable of underpinning the struggle against National Socialism. The result was the essay on 'State Capitalism', published in the ninth and final volume of *Studies in Philosophy and Social Science*. It was followed by a second article, 'Is National Socialism a New Order?' in which Pollock addressed some of the concerns raised by the first piece.[32]

In 'The Jews and Europe', Horkheimer, drawing on Pollock's earlier articles, had charted the transition from a liberal free-market economy to a fascist command economy and stressed the decreasing significance of the sphere of circulation in the age of the trusts. Because the Jews, for historical reasons, were concentrated unduly in the sphere of circulation, i.e., in commercial professions, they had become targets. By crediting the Jews with excessive power, their actual weakness notwithstanding, the antisemites dressed up their own aggression against the Jews as a form of self-defence in the face of an alleged global Jewish conspiracy. Horkheimer's principal focus lay on the transformation of capitalism, however. His point was that – contrary to the hope of many Jewish émigrés – there could be no return to the liberal order. Marx's categories had not lost their validity, but the 'totalitarian economy' transformed their meaning. 'No revision of economic theory is required to understand fascism', Horkheimer insisted. 'Equal and just exchange has driven itself to the point of absurdity, and the totalitarian order is this absurdity.'[33]

In 'State Capitalism', Pollock argued that National Socialism embodied a variant social order distinct from both liberal and monopoly capitalism: state capitalism.[34] There were notable similarities between the economic policies pursued in Nazi Germany, the Soviet Union and the United States in terms of the increasing nationalisation of spheres previously governed by the market, including big industry and the housing and labour markets. As Pollock saw it, 'the nearest approach to the state capitalist model' to date had been achieved in the Soviet Union,[35] but the Nazis' *Strength Through Joy* scheme and the Roosevelt administration's 100-Day Plan pointed in the same direction.

He was far from alone with this assessment. According to the diary of Roosevelt's secretary of the interior, Harold Ickes, the president told him on 5 October 1933 'that what we were doing in this country were some of the things that were being done in Russia and even some things that were being done

---

32 Pollock 1941a; Pollock 1941b.
33 Horkheimer 1989, p. 78.
34 The following discussion draws on Lenhard 2016c.
35 Pollock 1941a, p. 211 n1.

under Hitler in Germany. But we were doing them in an orderly way.'[36] Needless to say, FDR meant not the persecution of Jews or political opponents but specific crisis management policies that contravened central tenets of liberal free-market theory and increasingly transformed the state into an independent economic agent in its own right. In order to conceptualise National Socialism as a form of state capitalism one needed to focus on the primacy of politics that underpinned both the New Plan Hjalmar Schacht announced following his appointment as acting minister of economic affairs in 1934 and the Four-Year Plan of 1936.

In the pre-war years, National Socialism moved further and further away from the market and recent economic historians have agreed with Pollock's characterisation of National Socialism as a centralised planned economy with private capitalist aspects.[37] Consequently, the regime seemed to have become immune to crises and no longer needed to conform to the requirements of the market. The pursuit of profit, Pollock argued, had been replaced by the pursuit of power: 'The new ruling class, by its grip on the state, controls everything it wants to, the general economic plan, foreign policy, rights and duties, life and death of the individual. Its decisions are not restrained by any constitutional guarantees but by a set of rules only, designed for maintaining and expanding its own power.'[38] The essence of the National Socialist 'new order' lay in its ability to implement political ideology without mediation. This implied what for Pollock had hitherto been entirely inconceivable: that the Nazi ideology, while striking rational observers as being schizophrenic, was not merely propaganda designed to conceal the class struggle but actually what motivated state action.

What all this meant for the interpretation of the Nazis' anti-Jewish policies remained a moot point for Pollock. It needs to be borne in mind, however, that the essay was written and essentially completed before the Nazi regime proceeded to undertake the systematic annihilation of European Jewry. Adorno first mentioned in a letter to Horkheimer of 8 June 1941 (a fortnight before the German invasion of the Soviet Union) that he had gone through a draft of Pollock's article. Horkheimer and Adorno continued to discuss Pollock's text for the next ten weeks or so. By the third week of August – when the *Einsatzgruppen* were just beginning with the systematic mass shootings of Jewish populations – they were already working with the proofs.[39] It would be a rather tall

---

36   Ickes 1953, p. 104.
37   See Diehl 2005, p. 179.
38   Pollock 1941a, p. 221.
39   Theodor W. Adorno to Max Horkheimer, 8 June 1941, in Adorno and Horkheimer 2004, pp. 138–43; pp. 139–40.

order to expect Pollock to have done justice to the crimes subsequently perpetrated against European Jewry before they had actually begun to be perpetrated. The basic insight that established models of political economy did not allow for an adequate assessment of the Nazi order was, however, a crucial prerequisite for the institute's subsequent research.

The contention that National Socialism did indeed constitute a radically distinct new order gave rise to an explosive controversy within the institute. On 23 July 1941, Franz Neumann wrote a furious letter to Horkheimer in which he offered a detailed critique of Pollock's line of argument. His criticisms repeatedly descended into ad hominem attacks drawing Pollock's integrity into question. He likened Pollock's theory to the 'bourgeois' sociology of Karl Mannheim, adding that 'I have suggested that Pollock be given the freedom of the city of Mannheim but am pleased to note that Mannheim is gradually being razed by English bombers'.[40] The emotional intensity and vehemence of Neumann's angry comments indicates that more was at stake than differing viewpoints regarding the nature of National Socialism. The controversy touched on fundamental issues of political identity. Neumann's objections consistently seemed to turn into accusations of betrayal. 'In conclusion, I would like to say that the essay marks a clear departure from Marxism. In addition, the essay is an expression of total hopelessness. State capitalism as Pollock conceives of it has millenarian potential.'[41]

Neumann's principal misgiving concerned the implication that, on Pollock's account, there were, for the foreseeable future, no grounds to expect the collapse of National Socialism. While liberal capitalism was characterised by fundamental contradictions that regularly precipitated crises, state capitalism had integrated the competing forces and eliminated the factors that triggered crises. Crucially, this also held true for the proletariat. Once considered the revolutionary subject, terror, propaganda and material concessions had integrated it too into the *Volksgemeinschaft* – and the genuinely disenfranchised, foremost among them the Jews, were far too weak to engage in effective resistance. One could only hope for a victory of the United States in the war (Pollock anticipated the entry of the USA even prior to the Japanese attack on Pearl Harbour). Germany's defeat would spell the demise of *totalitarian* state capitalism but not of state capitalism per se. Its emergence was irrevocable. The Pax Americana would be based on democratic state capitalism and mark a victory over barbarism – and yet foreclose any renewed revolutionary perspective.

---

40   Franz L. Neumann to Max Horkheimer, 23 July 1941, in Horkheimer 1996a, pp. 103–8, p. 103.
41   Franz L. Neumann to Max Horkheimer, 23 July 1941, in Horkheimer 1996a, pp. 103–8, p. 107.

Neumann was hardly optimistic in his assessment of the potential for resistance within Nazi Germany, but Pollock's pessimism seemed to him to amount to a form of capitulation. If Pollock no longer believed in the possibility of a proletarian revolution, he had clearly turned his back on Marxism, Neumann reasoned. That Marxism itself and its concept of revolutionary change in particular might have been rendered invalid by changed historical circumstances was not a notion he was willing to countenance. For him, Pollock was a dissident, a traitor, someone who had made his peace with the status quo. Max Horkheimer gave these accusations short shrift: 'Your sharp scholarly and personal statements, beginning with your "rejection" of the essay, are at times nowhere near as sharp as they look. ... I can only wish you and us that those of our associates whom you least suspect of the departure that Pollock has supposedly engaged in so "clearly" will no more turn "from one extreme to the other" than Pollock has done in his entire life to date and will do in future.'[42]

Both Horkheimer and, with certain reservations, Adorno accepted Pollock's identification of National Socialism as a specific form of state capitalism, i.e., a distinct new order in which political supremacy had essentially displaced economic power. Horkheimer stressed the essay's 'disenchanting function' and considered it 'an important step towards the manifesto we so urgently need', i.e., the manifesto he wanted to write as an up-to-date counterpart to the *Communist Manifesto* of Marx and Engels.[43] Adorno was particularly pleased with Pollock's conceptual distinction between monopoly and state capitalism which he would have liked to have seen drawn out even further.[44] However, both Horkheimer and Adorno criticised that Pollock's assessment of democratic state capitalism, i.e., Roosevelt's New Deal, was too positive.[45] For Pollock, state capitalism embodied not merely a threat but an opportunity too. If it was understood that the triumph of totalitarianism was owed to the dissatisfaction of the masses, FDR's welfare state policies might ultimately engender a genuinely rational mode of production geared not merely to the demand of the solvent but to the fundamental needs of all human beings. This struck Adorno as illusory. A 'non-antagonistic economy' was incompatible with an 'antagonistic society', i.e., a class society.[46] Yet what if the opposite were possible, if a planned economy also eliminated class distinctions?

---

42   Max Horkheimer to Franz L. Neumann, 2 August 1941; Theodor W. Adorno to Max Horkheimer, 18 August 1941, both in Horkheimer 1996a, pp. 115–20, 132–5, pp. 119, 133.
43   Max Horkheimer to Friedrich Pollock, 1 July 1941, in Horkheimer 1996a, pp. 90–3, p. 91.
44   Theodor W. Adorno to Max Horkheimer, 2 July 1941, in Horkheimer 1996a, pp. 95–8, p. 96.
45   See Braunstein 2011, pp. 145–60.
46   Theodor W. Adorno to Max Horkheimer, 8 June 1941, in Horkheimer 1996a, pp. 53–7, p. 54.

To be discussing the transition to a communist economy – which is what Pollock's vision of a mode of production geared not to demand but to need amounted to – at a time when the entire planet was being enveloped by barbarism may seem rather outlandish. The 'communism' he envisaged differed radically from the Soviet model insofar as it would be bound to a democratic state and the rule of law. Having studied possible ways of introducing a planned economy for two decades, Pollock considered this the obvious and logical direction of travel. If the market economy had failed and could not be reconstituted, then it was effectively an economic law of nature that the planned economy would come next. The reports about the US administration's new economic programmes and social policy measures he read more or less every day in the papers only confirmed his assumptions. Indeed, since his arrival in the United States, the National Planning Board occasionally consulted him, giving him the sense that he was personally influencing the very process he described.[47]

National Socialism and Stalinism might currently seem to reign triumphant, but this impression was deceptive. The question was what would transpire once the Western democracies banded together (as he optimistically assumed they would) and won the upper hand? Would they be able to return to the status quo ante? Pollock thought not, and the war economy in the United States bore out his scepticism. Maybe the world really was marching towards a non-antagonistic society. If so, one would need to side with Roosevelt's administration not only in order to support the struggle against fascism but also because it genuinely stood for a better order.

Consequently, Adorno's objection did not convince Pollock. At an informal conference that took place at Paul and Hede Massing's farm in July 1943, he stood by his contention that it was economically possible to create a 'relatively crisis-free economy within the capitalist system'. The question was merely

> whether the economic opportunities are realised *politically*. For example, all sides acknowledged that post-war economic policies urgently needed to eliminate unemployment. Otherwise starkly antagonistic groups in the USA unreservedly agreed on this, as did the USA and Great Britain. Controversial is merely the extent to which this task falls to free entrepreneurship or the government, respectively. In England the tendency to expect the lion's share from the government prevails. In the US, the opposite is currently the case. The willingness of the ruling class to pursue new

---

47   See, e.g., Lorwin and Hinrichs 1934, p. 64.

options is underpinned principally by the insight that it can maintain its power only if this problem is solved.[48]

Few agreed with Pollock's assessment. Not even Adorno and Horkheimer were entirely convinced. Giving a clear indication of the way in which the issue was discussed in émigré circles, Bertolt Brecht, who occasionally bumped into members of the institute, noted in his journal on 13 August 1942 that 'dr pollock, the economist from the institute for social research (formerly frankfurt, now hollywood) is convinced that capitalism can rid itself of crises simply by means of public works. Marx could not foresee that governments might one day build roads!'[49] Yet even the sceptics among the members of the institute, including Marcuse and Neumann, were in fact influenced by Pollock's conceptualisation of National Socialism. One did not need to agree with his conclusions to acknowledge that he had drawn attention to a crucial issue. The order National Socialism embodied and, as the war progressed, was increasingly drawing all the other states into, was something fundamentally new and if one wanted to explain rather than merely describe it, one needed new concepts.

Few went as far in the scrutiny of their previous concepts as Pollock who, in notes taken in December 1941 under the heading 'The Better Order', seems to have questioned the very purpose of human existence and referred to the need for a 'new faith'. Yet this new faith could not be invented, it had to be truth itself, he argued dialectically. The 'old faith', by which he meant bourgeois ideology, was obsolete in the world as it now was. Nobody believed in property or the individual anymore, given that the new order had ultimately perverted both concepts. Not even happiness remained unblemished insofar as one's own good fortune implied the misfortune of others. One needed to explore what underpinned reason as the 'only remaining category still taken seriously in bourgeois society'; and, crucially for our discussion here, he noted that

> there is something wrong with the Marxian concepts. One needs to ascertain, what that is. Which is not to say that one should burn one's bridges. The point is to expand upon existing theory.[50]

For Pollock and Horkheimer, this expansion began with an adequate theory of state capitalism. The issue of the institute's journal in which Pollock's 'State

---

48   [Karl Korsch], 'Protokoll von Massings Farmkonferenz Juli 1943', Horkheimer Archive, University Library Frankfurt/Main, MHA XXIV 55, 8.
49   Brecht 1993, p. 252 (translation amended).
50   Pollock 2014, pp. 3–4.

Capitalism' was published, was generally referred to in the institute as the 'state capitalism issue' and, in a letter he wrote to Horkheimer on 30 July 1941, Adorno expressly referred to his own contribution on Oswald Spengler as 'my essay on state capitalism'.[51] Horkheimer was unable to finalise the contribution he had planned for the state capitalism issue in time. It originally bore the title, 'State Capitalism', but was eventually published in 1942 in the institute's memorial volume for Walter Benjamin as 'Autoritärer Staat' (The Authoritarian State). In it, Horkheimer systematically drew out the implications of Pollock's concept of the 'transition from monopoly to state capitalism'.[52]

Franz Neumann, Otto Kirchheimer, Arkadij Gurland and, to a lesser degree, Herbert Marcuse continued to insist that National Socialism was the most advanced form of monopoly capitalism.[53] They rejected the contention that the primacy of economics had been superseded and politics now dictated economic processes. Yet in his still instructive study *Behemoth*, the first comprehensive source-based account of the structure and functioning of National Socialism, Neumann by no means concealed that the National Socialist state had indeed become an economic agent in its own right and was capable of making economic decisions independently of the interests of big capital. Neumann interpreted National Socialism as a polycratic order that was characterised by internal contradictions and multiple competing power centres positively fostering chaos. The notion of state capitalist *elements* fit well into this scheme. Hence, the section on the 'Totalitarian Monopolistic Economy' also contained a chapter on the 'The Command Economy'. Rather strikingly, this chapter takes up almost half of the entire section. Yet if the command economy, on his own account, played such a significant role, why was Neumann not swayed by Pollock's arguments?

In part, the problem was that Neumann misinterpreted, or at least overinterpreted, Pollock's claim as though he had argued that private capitalism would disappear altogether. Pollock had expressly presented his concept of state capitalism in the form of an ideal-typical model, i.e., an abstract representation that threw essential processes sharply into relief without claiming to offer a comprehensive account of society in its entirety. Pollock never suggested that the state would necessarily be the sole owner of capital. His argument was that the state would emerge as the dominant agent who determined the role played by other owners of capital and who, if need be, could expropriate them without

---

51 Wiggershaus 1994a, p. 282; Theodor W. Adorno to Max Horkheimer, 30 July 1941, in Adorno and Horkheimer 2004, pp. 172–6, p. 174.
52 Horkheimer 1973, p. 3.
53 See Dubiel 1975, p. 17; Bast 1999, pp. 238–56.

compensation. More substantively, Neumann could not accept Pollock's conclusion that 'with the autonomous market the so-called economic laws disappear'.[54] This assumption, after all, did amount to a departure from Marxism in its traditional guise. It followed that the crises and potential collapse of capitalism could no longer be explained on economic grounds. Neumann's insistence that the working class would have a role to play in the downfall of the Nazi regime bordered on the obsessive. 'Even the most self-centred worker', he claimed,

> will, almost every day, come up against the question why so developed an industrial apparatus as the German has to be kept together by terror. Unlimited productive power, terror, and propaganda cannot create National Socialism among the workers. On the contrary, the workers are more likely to move along revolutionary syndicalist lines, to evolve ideas of sabotage and of direct action, ideas that were frowned upon by Social Democrats and Communists alike, but which might be considered by them as the sole means of asserting man's dignity within a terroristic system.[55]

The working class might currently be too weakened by the combined impact of propaganda and terror to shake off the Nazi yoke under its own steam but ultimately, it was still the crucial factor. *Behemoth* ends with the following statement: 'The flaws and breaks in the system and even the military defeat of Germany will not lead to an automatic collapse of the regime. It can only be overthrown by conscious political action of the oppressed masses, which will utilize the breaks in the system.'[56]

Pollock's emphasis lay on the regime's integrative capacity and its welfare state elements. In 'Is National Socialism a New Order?', which began life as a paper given at Columbia,[57] Pollock explained that the role of the individual in National Socialism differed entirely from that of the liberal market subject:

---

54   Pollock 1941a, p. 201.
55   Neumann 1942, p. 179.
56   Neumann 1942, p. 389.
57   As Pollock noted, his text was 'the last in a series of five public lectures delivered at Columbia University by the Institute of Social Research during November and December 1941'. The other lectures were: 'State and Individual under National Socialism' (Herbert Marcuse); 'Private Property under National Socialism' (Arkadij Gurland); 'The New Rulers in Germany' (Franz Neumann); 'The Legal Order under National Socialism' (Otto Kirchheimer). Pollock 1941b, p. 440 n1.

> Property and income are no longer the foremost determinants of the individual's social position. Capitalists and labor are organized in one all-embracing organization, the Labor Front, and fused ideologically in the people's community. ... Social power, prestige, and honor now depend decisively upon one's place in the government and party hierarchies. The relation between property, income and social power has thus been radically altered. Money alone gives only limited power or (as in the case of the Jews) no power at all.[58]

When it came to the Nazis' ability to garner the support of the majority of unorganised workers, Pollock's assessment was far more realistic than Neumann's. He had abandoned the class-theoretical frame of reference and instead turned his attention primarily to questions of social psychology. Assuming that the categories wage, price and profit, while still significant, were no longer decisive driving forces, he turned instead to the ways in which psychic needs were met. 'The National Socialist regime', he wrote, 'has, more than any other form of government, unleashed the most brutal instincts of the individual'.[59] By lifting sexual and social taboos more generally, the regime had compensated individuals for their loss of autonomy and, at the same time, linked its sexual liberalisation to the politicisation of sexual relations. As the liberal distinction between private and public became a thing of the past, individuals were disconnected from their families and traditional values. This allowed them to be integrated fully into the *Volksgemeinschaft*. The regime's antisemitism featured only in passing in Pollock's discussion as one of numerous elements constituting the psychopathology of the 'Third Reich'. One of the opportunities for 'the release of instincts and impulses' the regime offered individuals, Pollock explained, was directed 'against the enemies and scapegoats of the regime' and took the form of 'cruelty against the weak and helpless (Jews, feeble-minded and "unfit" persons)'.[60]

In terms of the division of labour within the institute, psychological questions did not fall within the remit of Pollock the economist, and he generally erred on the side of caution in these matters by deferring to the trained psychoanalyst Fromm and, following his departure, to Adorno, Löwenthal and Marcuse. Yet he was only too aware of the fact that his analysis of National Socialism remained incomplete as long as he undertook it only from a political and economic vantage.

---

58   Pollock 1941b, p. 444.
59   Pollock 1941b, p. 448.
60   Pollock 1941b, p. 449.

This was also demonstrated by the first research proposal on antisemitism that was drafted by the institute, with Pollock's participation, in 1941 and published in the state capitalism issue of the journal. The draft stated that the research project 'will combine historical, psychological, and economic research with experimental studies'.[61] In February 1942, institute members met with potential sponsors of the research project. Along with a number of expert's reports and the draft proposal, they presented a supplementary statement that clearly reflected Pollock's state capitalism thesis. Under the heading, 'Our basic assumptions', it explained in rather wooden English that

> (1) Anti-Semitism is no accident. It is deliberately used to make social transformation more palatable to large social groups. ... (2) Our society is undergoing a profound transformation from liberal laissez-faire to centralized control. This process involves the rapidly progressing concentration of economic power and the gradual elimination of small business and independent professions. (3) This progress also involves profound socio-psychological changes. ... With his life increasingly dependent upon centralized agencies, every individual will feel that he is a mere object in the hands of forces beyond his control.[62]

It would be hard to overlook the parallels between this document and the gist of Pollock's two essays on state capitalism, and it is hardly surprising that Pollock was involved in the negotiations when the American Jewish Committee agreed, in 1943, to fund the research project on antisemitism. He was concerned not only with the empirical aspects of the research but, in close cooperation with Paul Massing, also worked on the development of a theory of 'political antisemitism' that went on to shape the first two sections of 'Elements of Anti-semitism', the final completed section of Horkheimer and Adorno's *Dialectic of Enlightenment*.

Pollock had maintained a close exchange with Massing, who rejoined the institute in 1942, more or less since his arrival in the United States. Pollock owned both Massing's account of his concentration camp experience and his prescient analysis, *Hitler Is No Fool*, published in 1939 with a general readership in mind. In *Hitler Is No Fool*, Massing emphatically stressed the need finally to take the Nazi's genocidal antisemitism seriously. 'Anti-Semitism is an

---

61 Institute of Social Research 1941, p. 124.
62 Institute of Social Research, 'The Political Function of Anti-Semitism. Supplementary Statement to the Research Project on Anti-Semitism, December 15, 1942', Horkheimer Archive, University Library Frankfurt/Main, MHA IX 92.7, pp. 19–20.

integral part of National Socialist doctrine. The Jew bears the same relation to Hitler's Aryan as Hell does to Heaven. This is exactly what is new in Hitler's anti-Semitism.'[63] Writing just after the November Pogrom of 1938, at a time when not only most leftists still minimised the significance of antisemitism on the assumption it was no more than an antiquated propaganda trick, Massing grasped the import of the Nazis' modernised, apocalyptic and, to use Saul Friedländer's terminology, redemptive antisemitism.

At the time, the members of the institute had not even begun to grasp the significance of the Nazis' antisemitism. In the 1930s, antisemitism was not a central concern nor even much of a concern at all for the critical theorists. In the volumes of the institute's journal that came out in New York prior to 1939, antisemitism in its own right featured not even in a book review. Not that a great deal of literature on the topic was being published but one would have expected what did come out to be of interest to the institute. Be it Peretz Bernstein's *Der Antisemitismus als Gruppenerscheinung* (1926, translated as *Jew-Hate as a Sociological Problem* and *The Social Roots of Discrimination*), Samuel Blitz's *Nationalism: A Cause of Antisemitism* (1928), Alexander Stein's *Adolf Hitler, Schüler der 'Weisen von Zion'* (Adolf Hitler: Student of the Elders of Zion, 1936) or even *Der neuzeitliche Antisemitismus und die 'Protokolle der Weisen von Zion'* (Modern Antisemitism and the Protocols of the Elders of Zion, 1935) by Boris Nikolaevsky with whom Pollock had collaborated for several years on the publication of Marx's works – none of these titles were reviewed.

The constellation bordered on the ludicrous. Most of the members of the institute were directly affected by antisemitic persecution and yet they refused to consider the Nazis' anti-Jewish hostility as anything more than a subordinate and epiphenomenal issue. In some ways, National Socialism's banality was the problem. It was so fundamentally predicated on the juxtaposition of friend and foe, of the *Volksgemeinschaft* and the enemies of the people, that the monstrosity of the constant and all-encompassing declarations of enmity detracted from the threat of antisemitism in its own right. The members of the institute knew, of course, that the regime targeted all Jews and not merely those who happened to be its political opponents. Yet before the war this did not lead them to reflect on distinctions between the various kinds of 'enemies of the people'. Paul Massing was the first to grasp just how central antisemitism was to National Socialism.[64] Hence, when the institute finally did embark on histor-

---

63   Billinger 1939, pp. 170–1.
64   Worrell 2009, p. 630.

ical and theoretical research on modern antisemitism, *Hitler Is No Fool* made him a desirable collaborator.

During the final years of the war, Massing was Pollock's closest collaborator. Just how close their cooperation was is demonstrated by the numerous notes and drafts they produced together.⁶⁵ On this issue too, the institute maintained an internal division of labour. Massing and Pollock were expressly tasked with research on political antisemitism while other colleagues focussed on cultural, religious, sociological and psychoanalytical aspects. For Massing and Pollock the lead question was:

> What precisely is the *political role* of antisemitism? What are the political conditions in the state that call for its use; what forces in the nation turn to it; what task is it assigned to fulfill? What historical aspects of the social position of the Jew casts him for this role?⁶⁶

Pollock's theoretical contribution to the understanding of antisemitism found its clearest expression in a paper he gave at the annual gathering of the Women's International League for Peace and Freedom (WILPF) in Washington D.C. in April 1944. It bore the title, 'Political Antisemitism'. In it, Pollock formulated his insights in the form of six (albeit lengthy) theses. Political antisemitism, he argued, was a novel form of hostility towards Jews distinct not only from medieval anti-Judaism but also from the racial antisemitism of the nineteenth century. While 'the motives of religious, economic, or general-cultural order may be sufficient to explain certain Antisemitic attitudes in the past', Pollock explained, 'they do not give us a satisfactory explanation for the readiness of large groups to accept totally inconsistent Antisemitic propaganda at its face value.'⁶⁷ This remark built on an idea formulated in an earlier preparatory paper for a joint meeting of the institute with the AJC in May 1943: 'It is impossible to detect in Nazi Antisemitism any logic, continuity or purpose of its own.'⁶⁸ While previous forms of hostility towards Jews drew on a kernel of truth, no matter how rudimentary, National Socialist antisemitism was entirely

---

65   See, e.g., Friedrich Pollock, 'Structural Analysis of a Hypothetical Situation in USA where Antisemitism in its "political" variety would be used as a main weapon for destroying the democratic system', Horkheimer Archive, University Library Frankfurt/Main, MHA IX 100, 2.
66   Institute of Social Research, 'Draft. Report I', March 1944, Horkheimer Archive, University Library Frankfurt/Main, MHA IX 119b, 6.
67   Pollock 2016, p. 208.
68   Joint Meeting AJC, May 7, 1943, 4: 'Problems involved in the Study of the Dynamics of Antisemitism in Germany (Massing)', MHA IX 100.

pathological in nature. This questionable contention bore some similarity to Hannah Arendt's line of argument in the essay on Dreyfus she first published in 1942 and later integrated into *Origins of Totalitarianism*.[69] Both Pollock and Arendt sought to throw the psychopathology of the new order into sharp relief by contrasting it to forms of antisemitism that had in some way supposedly still been 'rational'. To make things worse, both of them in fact went on to rationalise antisemitism as a *means* – deployed to destroy the democratic order – and precisely not as an end in itself. 'The manipulators', Pollock told the WILPF delegates, 'use the existing Antisemitic attitude for their own political purposes'.[70] Needless to say, this was no theoretical basis suited to facilitate any genuine comprehension of the systematic annihilation of European Jewry of which the members of the institute had been aware since the summer of 1942 at the latest. In what way was the murder of millions of Jews supposedly a means to an end rather than an end in itself?[71] The aforementioned internal paper expressly asked, 'What is the purpose of the most recent extermination against Jews in Eastern Europe?' Massing answered his own question by arguing that 'The cold-blooded murder of two million Jews, at this moment, was the answer of the Party to any attempt of German "moderate" groups to seek an understanding with England and America.'[72] The heading of the seventh thesis Pollock presented to the WILPF delegates likewise read: 'Mass Murder of Jews as a Means to Discredit the Conservative Groups in Germany'.[73]

Another aspect of Pollock's line of argument was more compelling. Just as state capitalism was no longer predicated on the individual as the basic social unit and instead merged the collective and the state, he argued, so too antisemitism 'was transformed from an attitude, based on personal convictions, to an institution of Nazi statesmanship'.[74] Not unlike Arendt in her treatment of Eichmann, Pollock sought to play off the SA's antisemitism of conviction against the supposedly 'synthetic' and 'strictly impersonal' antisemitism of the SS. Yet he was right in stressing that the institutionalisation of antisemitism undertaken by the Nazi state was something entirely new. Eichmann's so-called Jewish Section was part of Himmler's Reich Security Main Office, 'a new type of specifically National Socialist institution' with a staff of 3,000 devoted solely to

---

69 Arendt 1942; Arendt 1951.
70 Pollock 2016, p. 206.
71 See Gerber 2017.
72 Joint Meeting AJC, May 7, 1943, 4: 'Problems involved in the Study of the Dynamics of Antisemitism in Germany (Massing)', MHA IX 100.
73 Pollock 2016, p. 207.
74 Pollock 2016, p. 208.

'repelling or exterminating an enemy defined in völkisch terms.'⁷⁵ Antisemitism, then, was not an ideological complement but integral to the National Socialist system. This may seem a common place today but at the time, it was an original insight.

The institute's insights rarely reached the wider public, however. The breakthrough came only with the publication of the *Studies in Prejudice* Series in 1949/50. Alongside the best-known volume, *The Authoritarian Personality*, in which Adorno was heavily involved, the series also included Massing's monograph, *Rehearsal for Destruction: A Study of Political Anti-Semitism in Imperial Germany*.⁷⁶ While Pollock was intimately involved in the earlier study, *Antisemitism Among American Labor*, whose 1,400 pages of results were ultimately never published, his role in the *Studies in Prejudice* project was purely administrative. *Antisemitism Among American Labor* was funded by the Jewish Labor Committee (JLC) and, as the title indicates, focussed specifically on the Marxists' ostensible revolutionary subject: the workers.⁷⁷ Extending the focus to workers in the United States where Horkheimer, Pollock and Adorno feared antisemitism too might become hegemonic, the study amplified the results of Fromm's earlier research on German workers. Pollock was responsible for Part Five of the study. According to his later recollections, the results were so depressing

> that the Jewish Labor Committee would not let us publish the study. That's how awful the findings were. It turned out that antisemitism was more widespread among workers, especially among the war workers, than one could possibly have imagined.⁷⁸

The study was nevertheless a worthwhile exercise. Not only was Pollock able to gather valuable experience with US-American social research techniques. With its grant of $13,000 (equivalent to more than $250,000 in today's money), the JLC funded the project so generously that Pollock, as the institute's financial director, was able to employ 30 researchers and engage 270 volunteers, offering many of them a desperately needed lifeline.⁷⁹ The study also helped Pollock

---

75 Wildt 2009, pp. 9, 164.
76 Massing 1949.
77 Institute of Social Research, *Antisemitism among American Labor*, Volumes 1–4, documents, Horkheimer Archive, University Library Frankfurt/Main, MHA IX 146.1, 146.2–146.5. See Ziege 2009, pp. 180–228; Collomp 2011.
78 Ernst von Schenck, interview with Pollock and Horkheimer, transcript, 1965/66, Horkheimer Archive, University Library Frankfurt/Man, MHA X 132a, p. 128.
79 Ziege 2018, p. 190.

see more clearly that antisemitism was by no means a purely European phenomenon but also gaining ground in his new country. In the United States it was not yet too late and still worth putting up a fight to prevent the barbarism from spreading further. He no longer envisaged returning to Germany, even if Hitler were toppled. He had become an American and was now principally committed to preventing the triumph of fascism in the USA.

CHAPTER 10

Dinner at the White House

In the spring of 1941, Horkheimer and his wife moved to California, where they settled in Pacific Palisades, a western district of Los Angeles. Horkheimer was finally going to work on the long-planned book on dialectics (*Dialectic of Enlightenment* later evolved from this endeavour). The history of Pacific Palisades is inextricably linked to that of the Californian film industry that featured so prominently in Horkheimer and Adorno's 'philosophical fragments'. Beginning life as the Inceville film studio, where Western movies were filmed until 1922, Pacific Palisades rapidly grew into a district in its own right. As early as 1926, 250 families already lived there. Given its ideal location between Santa Monica, Malibu and Brentwood and its relatively temperate climate, it soon acquired the reputation of being the 'Californian Riviera'.[1] In the 1930s, it emerged as one of the most significant sites where German and, especially, German-Jewish émigré intellectuals settled.

> Along with the adjacent neighbourhoods of Brentwood – where Arnold Schoenberg, Theodor W. Adorno and Fritz Kortner found refuge – and Santa Monica – where Fritz Lang, Bertolt Brecht and Heinrich Mann found a home – Pacific Palisades was seen as a 'new Weimar on the Pacific', as 'Weimar under Palms', both in the sense that significant minds congregated between the mountains and bay of Santa Monica in a small area comparable to the Weimar of Goethe's time; and in the sense that among the émigrés who gathered here were some of the most prominent exponents of the Weimar Republic, the democratic Germany the Nazis had so brutally crushed when they took power in 1933.[2]

That the émigrés lived cheek by jowl in Pacific Palisades dawned on Horkheimer as soon as he bought his property on D'Este Drive. Determined to get the estate agent to agree to half of the asking price, Horkheimer was amazed when the agent instantly consented, and asked why. 'I had two properties', the agent responded, 'and I have sold the first for a very good price, so I thought: let this man have the other'. When Horkheimer inquired who his solvent new neighbour was,

---

1 See the – albeit antisemitically inflected – account in Wagner 1935, pp. 128–38.
2 See Blubacher 2011, p. 9.

it turned out that it was Thomas Mann. So we came to live close to each other and often went for walks together where I learnt many instructive and beautiful things. He told me a lot about his work and frequently read to me. I can only say: we may not always have seen eye to eye, but we got on wonderfully.[3]

Of course, this kind of harmony was not universal. The opening scene of Josef von Báky's *Der Ruf* (The Last Illusion, 1949), based on a script by (and starring) Horkheimer's Californian neighbour Fritz Kortner, impressively highlighted the conflicts within this close-knit émigré community whose members differed considerably in character, politics and cultural orientation. It was the very specific constraints of exile that placed a conservative such as Thomas Mann at a soiree also attended by prominent Communists such as Hanns Eisler and Bertolt Brecht. Horkheimer now joined this illustrious circle. Marcuse and Adorno soon followed him to the West Coast. Pollock and Löwenthal meanwhile stayed in New York where Pollock's workload only increased. On the institute's stationery, Pollock's status now changed from Assistant Director to Acting Director.

Horkheimer had chosen not him but Adorno as the co-author of his long-planned magnum opus. Nothing suggests that Pollock was jealous of Adorno. He felt that Löwenthal was underhanded and increasingly disliked him, radically disagreed with Neumann on crucial political issues and fell out with Grossman.[4] Yet he held Adorno in enormous esteem. Pollock later recalled that Horkheimer and Adorno enjoyed a strong mutual resonance unavailable to him

> because Adorno is much more intelligent than me. I am intelligent enough to be fully aware of this. This has nothing to do with some kind of inferiority complex, it is simply a fact. I would not want to swap with him, nor would Horkheimer want him in my role, but this does not change the fact that he is extraordinarily smart and owns an extraordinarily productive receptive capacity, i.e., he is able, when Horkheimer hints at an idea, to draw it out, and I mean on the spot. This is a skill I do not possess, I frequently find it difficult to follow Horkheimer's line of thought, I am often resistant, and it can take a while until I convince myself that there is something in it after all.[5]

---

3 Horkheimer 1985f, p. 472.
4 Kuhn 2007, p. 186.
5 Ernst von Schenck, interview with Pollock and Horkheimer, transcript, 1965/66, Horkheimer Archive, University Library Frankfurt/Man, MHA X 132a, p. 186.

Theodor and Gretel Adorno settled just a few minutes by car from Max and Maidon Horkheimer, and Adorno now grew into an established role alongside Horkheimer. As a result, he also grew closer and became increasingly friendly with Pollock. Even so, while there was always a room reserved for Fritz, now Fred, in Horkheimer's house, the same did not hold true for Teddie. For all their mutual emotional attachment, Adorno and Horkheimer were primarily congenial interlocutors and colleagues, and Pollock maintained his role as best friend and life partner. The account of his daily routine Horkheimer gave in a letter he wrote to Paul Tillich in the summer of 1942 reflects this:

> In the morning, Pollock and I go for a short walk, then I study intensely before writing notes and drafts, in the afternoon, I usually see Teddie to work on the final text. Occasionally, I also meet Marcuse to discuss his sections. The evening belongs to Pollock and sometimes to Weil.[6]

Although Pollock came to California every couple of months, he found the separation hard to bear and sought to distract himself by picking up with old acquaintances. He occasionally met with Lili and Siegfried Kracauer, for example, who now lived in Manhattan too.[7] He regularly spent time with Adolph Löwe and Paul Tillich, not only at their fortnightly circle. They went on short excursions to the countryside where Pollock occasionally rented a horse. He had learnt to ride as a soldier and, aside from his walks with Horkheimer, horse riding seems to have been the only physical exercise he undertook to compensate for the strain of his endless office hours.

The friendship between Pollock and Löwe – which, as we saw, harked back to their youth – intensified in the 1940s. They met frequently in New York and occasionally went on holiday together.[8] On one of their trips, staying at Bar Harbor (Maine) in July 1943, Pollock drew an affectionate, humorous and penetrating sketch of Löwe. Pollock's caption read 'Colonel Lowe in mufti' (i.e., in civilian clothing) and poked fun at Löwe who had recently met a delegation of high-ranking militaries at the White House. The drawing bears witness to Pollock's skills as an attentive and acute observer.

Two years after his wife's death, Pollock began to embark on occasional romantic adventures again. These included an unfortunate affair with Felix Weil's third wife Lucille Weil, née Jakobowitz. She too originally came from

---

6 Max Horkheimer to Paul Tillich, 12 August 1942, Horkheimer 1996a, p. 313.
7 Friedrich Pollock to Siegfried Kracauer, 10 November 1941, Deutsches Literaturarchiv Marbach, Kracauer Papers, 72.2835/4.
8 Krohn 1996, p. 144.

Stuttgart. In 1936, she fled to New York where she was barely able to make ends meet as a shop assistant and hat model. Horkheimer, who knew her from back home, recommended her as a private secretary to Weil who promptly fell in love with and, in 1939, married her. More interested in fast cars and fashion than books, she had a hard time fitting in with his intellectual friends and associates. So great was her interest in cars that she even took driving lessons, which was still quite unusual for women at this time. Two years into the marriage, their relationship was on the rocks, principally because Felix Weil had already fallen in love with yet another, infinitely more urbane woman, Helen Knopping. Not even divorced from Lucille, he was already planning his next wedding.[9] Horkheimer and Pollock were not impressed. They liked Lucille with whom Maidon Horkheimer in particular had become friendly, and they were pretty fed up with Weil's womanising. They were also concerned that Weil's chaotic private life was getting in the way of his work for the institute and would prevent him from submitting his contribution to the dialectics book.[10] Weil trusted his friends' advice not only in financial matters but also in affairs of the heart, and Horkheimer decided that Pollock should mediate and try to save the Weils' marriage.

Pollock and the Weils thereupon went on a short trip to the Catskills in upstate New York. Yet instead of effecting a reconciliation, Pollock himself now fell in love with Weil's delightful third wife. While Felix Weil was busy studying, Pollock and Lucille went on long walks or rambling in the forest. His advances flattered her, and she soon began to flirt back.[11] They continued to see each other after their return from the Catskills, and Pollock 'began to take her out, introduce her to theatres and museums, sought to make a woman of the world out of her. They embarked on an affair or, to be more precise, an amour fou.'[12] When Weil found out, far from reprimanding his friend, he reached an understanding with Pollock. Horkheimer was aghast. 'The idea of Fritz and Lucille entering into a relationship to bring her back to you was disgraceful from the outset. Once Fritz and you had jointly been this foolish, further misguided suggestions hardly come as a surprise.'[13] The newest misguided suggestion in question was Pollock's plan to marry Lucille.

Pollock rented a small studio apartment for Lucille and suggested that they would move to a larger residence following their marriage. Yet in the end, they

---

9   Max Horkheimer to Friedrich Pollock, 4 October 1941, Horkheimer 1996a, p. 184.
10 Max Horkheimer to Felix Weil, 10 March 1942, Horkheimer 1996a, p. 276.
11 Leo Baeck Institute New York, Weil Family Collection, AR 11 781, Personal Histories II, p. 49.
12 Roßkamp 2002.
13 Max Horkheimer to Felix Weil, 10 March 1942, Horkheimer 1996a, pp. 273–8, p. 277.

did not marry, perhaps because Horkheimer – who felt that 'Fritz should not fall in love with the wife of his friend, let alone with Lucille' – vetoed the plan; perhaps because Pollock himself had second thoughts.[14] Lucille felt betrayed and subsequently characterised Pollock as 'a terrible liar and coward'.[15]

Pollock lived in Morningside Heights on the Upper West Side, in the immediate vicinity of Columbia University. In 1944, the institute rented an apartment in the same building at 90 Morningside Drive as its new office, entangling Pollock's life even more intimately with the work of the institute. He gave papers, attended meetings, was responsible for the institute's correspondence, read reports and proofs, took care of the books and sought as best he could to keep the show on the road. His conviction was waning, however. For many years, the journal was crucial to the institute's work, holding its members and associates together, their political differences and geographical dispersal notwithstanding. Its termination was a grave blow, and Pollock, Löwenthal and Horkheimer discussed the possibility of closing the institute altogether but, having given the matter careful consideration, decided that the risks involved in doing so were too great. Colleagues who taught elsewhere often depended on their formal affiliation with Columbia. More importantly, without this affiliation it would doubtless have been even more difficult to secure the external research funding on which the institute depended more than ever.

There was no ignoring the institute's disintegration, however. Franz Neumann and Otto Kirchheimer had moved to Washington to work for the Office of Strategic Services (OSS), the US military's foreign intelligence service, where Herbert Marcuse, after an initial six-month stint at the Office of War Information, joined them in the spring of 1943.[16] Involved in what was effectively a form of enemy reconnaissance, they now made a practical contribution to the war effort against Nazi Germany. This was a matter of considerable pride and prestige and close to Pollock's heart too. As we saw, he had advised the National Planning Board long before any of his colleagues would likely have condoned working for the military intelligence service of a capitalist state, yet now, his naturalisation in 1940 notwithstanding, his advances were rejected by the intelligence services because he was still on an FBI watchlist.

In June 1943, confronted with rumours that the FBI was going after the institute's members and intended to ensure Neumann and Marcuse were sacked, Pollock turned to the former senator for Utah, William H. King, whom he had

---

14   Max Horkheimer to Felix Weil, 10 March 1942, Horkheimer 1996a, pp. 273–8, p. 276.
15   Leo Baeck Institute New York, Weil Family Collection, AR 11 781, Personal Histories II, p. 49.
16   See Neumann, Marcuse and Kirchheimer 2013; Marcuse 1998.

met at a reception.[17] Writing to Horkheimer on the day, Pollock described King as 'remarkably young for a man of 80, conservative, a vehement proponent of state law vs. central control, a critic of the New Deal and mates with everyone, including Edgar Hoover'.[18] The following day, Pollock was able to report that neither the institute nor any of its members were being investigated and that there was no cause for concern.[19] King had spoken not to Hoover but to the renowned legal scholar Edward Levi, who served as special assistant to the US Attorney General during the war (and who later, as Attorney General under Ford, severely curtailed the powers of the bureau). The ensuing political intervention apparently also led to Pollock's file being expunged. A few weeks later he received an official invitation to serve as an advisor to the economic section of the OSS.[20]

Among the forms Pollock was now required to complete was an application for security clearance for 'highly confidential assignments'. While he did receive an employment contract after some months, unlike Neumann, he was initially refused any kind of security clearance. Either Pollock himself or somebody else at the OSS would not let the matter rest, however. The relevant file includes a hand-written note of April 1944, stating that it had been 'decided just to "sit" on the case for a month or two longer with the thought that it would die a natural death.' It evidently did not, and on 5 June the security office informed the civilian personnel office that,

> As a result of further investigation and consideration, we are hereby withdrawing our recommendation for a security disapproval issued 14 March 1944 and substituting an approval which has been limited by the Secretariat to the following conditions which it will be the responsibility of the branch head to enforce in the event Subject is employed.
> 1. He should not have access to any 'Top Secret' material.
> 2. He should not have access to 'Confidential' or 'Secret' material relating to the operational as distinguished from the intelligence functions of OSS. The methods we use in collecting intelligence would be regarded as operational.

---

17 Friedrich Pollock, 'Memorandum No. 46, 14. Juni 1943', Horkheimer Archive, University Library Frankfurt/Main, MHA VI 33, 451.
18 Friedrich Pollock to Max Horkheimer, 23 June 1943, Horkheimer Archive, University Library Frankfurt/Main, MHA VI 33, 431 r.
19 Friedrich Pollock to Max Horkheimer, 24 June 1943, Horkheimer Archive, University Library Frankfurt/Main, MHA VI 33, 432.
20 Friedrich Pollock, 'Memorandum No. 2, 19. September 1943', Horkheimer Archive, University Library Frankfurt/Main, MHA VI 33, 374.

3. Before employment, the branch head should consult this office in order to be thoroughly familiar with Subject's history and background so that he can be governed accordingly in his future relations with Subject.[21]

These very substantial limitations notwithstanding, Pollock was nevertheless exceedingly well informed. His relations to Neumann had markedly improved and even become friendly since his move to Washington, and Neumann kept him up to date. Even more importantly, Pollock had become politically extremely well connected. He was one of the founders of the Research Bureau for Post-War Economics, an organisation that submitted expert reports and proposals for post-war economic policies to the White House.[22] More significant yet were his appointments as advisor to the Board of Economic Warfare and the War Production Board created by executive order in 1941/42.[23] Pollock was only too pleased to be able to contribute to the – increasingly promising – war effort at least in this way.

The dinner invitation he received from Eleanor Roosevelt in February 1943 in many ways marked the culmination of his political engagement.[24] As First Lady, she was not only the wife of the president but an unusually popular figure in her own right. If in different ways, she was just as active politically as her husband. She gave interviews and held press conferences on political topics and, in her national syndicated column, 'My Day', which she began to publish in 1936, reported on her meetings with a broad range of social groups, representative bodies and charitable associations. All this was highly unusual for a First Lady and earned her a good deal of criticism too. Yet most US citizens viewed her as a collective mother figure and greatly revered her. Pollock was, of course, one of hundreds who received such dinner invitations from Eleanor Roosevelt, yet for him, it was an extraordinary honour.

Together with Adolph Löwe, Pollock had met with the First Lady in late January 1943 and evidently impressed her. In a confidential letter to Horkheimer ('not for the files'), Pollock reported that he had stolen Löwe's thunder.[25] The

---

21 National Archives and Records Administration, Joint Chief of Staff, OSS, Record Group 226, Personnel Files 1942–1945: Frederick Pollock, ARC 2183 363. See also Franz Neumann to Max Horkheimer, 30 November 1943, in Horkheimer 1996a, p. 515.
22 National Archives and Records Administration, FDR Library, Records of the War Refugee Board, 1944–45, Box 30, Folder 11, Research Bureau for Post-War Economics, 000717.
23 See Katz 1987, p. 445.
24 Eleanor Roosevelt to Friedrich Pollock, 3 February 1943, Fondo Friedrich Pollock, Università degli Studi di Firenze, 2.2.1, doc. 1.
25 Friedrich Pollock to Max Horkheimer, 23 January 1943, Fondo Friedrich Pollock, Università

meeting lasted until midnight and Roosevelt was so impressed that she invited Pollock and his associates to meet her husband and present their proposals for the post-war order to him personally. Pollock suggested it would make more sense for him to meet with Vice President Henry A. Wallace first to prepare the meeting with FDR, and the First Lady agreed.[26]

Horkheimer, who shared in the honour of the invitation vicariously, congratulated Pollock in English:

> I wish to tell you that the invitation by which you have been honored, was a real satisfaction for Maidon and for myself. You know, I don't overestimate successes particularly when there is only a very slight chance that they may have any tangible consequences. But in this case, I seriously think that we ought to be very grateful. It was a great experience and whatever will come out or not come out of it you have the right to be proud of it. I told you more than once how much I would give if I were offered the opportunity to listen in on conversations of historical importance. By the fact of your invitation a little bit of that wish has come true.[27]

Pollock's subsequent assessment was more restrained:

> I wrote you a post card telling you that the dinner was 'great fun'. This is true – in a way. On the other hand, I was seldom so depressed as when I left the beautiful house my hosts are living in. Depressed because the whole situation is do desperate and the people who are supposed to cope with it are so utterly inadequate. ...
>
> When I left the house, I had a sensation of being completely emptied. Not because the invitation was not a 'success'. But to the contrary: it came out better than could reasonably be expected. But because everything appeared so futile, so utterly inadequate. On the one side lies the future of humanity, on the other all the forces of evil forming a more and more streamlined coalition ... and between both these well meaning but basically helpless people.[28]

---

degli Studi di Firenze, 2.2.1, doc. 13. The letter is written in code. *Prima facie*, it reads like an account of a regular business dinner. Pollock changed the names of the officials and referred to the administration as the 'corporation'.

26 On this meeting, see Pauck and Pauck 1976, pp. 204–5; on a more critical note, see Graf 2013.
27 See Max Horkheimer to Friedrich Pollock, 10 February 1943, in Horkheimer 1996a, pp. 420–5, pp. 420–1.
28 See Friedrich Pollock to Max and Maidon Horkheimer, 7 February 1943, Fondo Friedrich

A further meeting with Eleanor Roosevelt took place in June 1943, this time over lunch at the Roosevelts' New York home at 29 Washington Square. Pollock, Tillich, Löwe, Hans Staudinger and a colleague from the Selfhelp committee spent some three hours with the First Lady, explaining their position on post-war reconstruction. 'As desert strawberries from Mr. Morgenthau's farm were served', Pollock noted after the lunch. 'They were outstanding. So was the hostess.' He recorded the outcome of the gathering as follows:

> Mrs R. urgently asks 'the group' to do the following:
> 1. Write a program for European reconstruction.
> 2. Write in so simple and two-syllable words an[d] brief sentences that even a congressman will be able to understand it.
> 3. Appeal to the selfinterest of the average man. Explain how the peace will affect him. Show that a humanitarian and just peace is 'good business' under t[w]o points of view: it will help to overcome depression here in USA and save our children from world war III.
> 4. Explain that a not so harsh treatment is not motivated by 'Gefühls-duselei' [soppiness] which would be unjustifiable after what the Germans have done, but by cold reasoning, how to avoid the next world war. It is most necessary to get a reasonable assurance of 'peace in our time' even if the Germans should get a better treatment than they deserve.
> 5. Show the alternatives etc. most clearly and illustrate them from past experience. The memory of the public is very short.
>
> Such a manuscript would be discussed, first between the President and Mr. Wallace and later, so she hopes, between both of them and 'the group'. The language should be simple because the President too wants to grasp quickly and without re-searching what is meant ... More complicated theoretical explanations should be postponed until the discussion has started.[29]

This was how politics worked. Eleanor was an excellent teacher when it came to the art of diplomacy. If one wanted to secure political agreement one needed to make one's cause attractive to those on whose support one depended. Moral objections and appeals to universal values achieved little in this sphere.

Pollock, Università degli Studi di Firenze, 2.2.1, doc. 2. In this letter, also labelled 'confidential', Pollock refers to the Roosevelts as Thérèse and Ernest Carol.

29 Friedrich Pollock, 'Memorandum No. 43', 7 June 1943, and 'Luncheon Meeting', 10 June 1943, Horkheimer Archive, University Library Frankfurt/Main, MHA VI 33, 477, 459, 460–1.

While it is unclear what Pollock and his colleagues ultimately submitted, a 'Tentative Worksheet for a Discussion on European (foremost German) Reconstruction' of 11 January 1943 gives us an indication of Pollock's thinking on the matter.[30] He identified six conceivable post-war regimes: 'a) autonomous revolution b) revolution under Russian control c) catholic fascist solution d) constitutional monarchies e) reactionary American occupation and reactionary coalition government f) enlightened American occupation and welfare collectivism.' He explicitly stated that options a) and b) did not merit consideration. He pointed to Metternich's increasingly crisis-prone system as evidence for the fact that option c) would offer 'a temporary peace only'. Given that the document was only an outline, it did not explain why option d) was no solution either, but it obviously made precious little sense in the German case.

This left only two options: reactionary or enlightened occupation. The paper suggested that the former would succeed only in the short term. The paper expressly referred to the Austrian-American Social Democrat Egon Ranshofen-Wertheimer, who held an adjunct position in International Affairs at the American University and advised the State Department. He had recently published a widely discussed book with the title, *Victory is Not Enough – A Strategy for a Lasting Peace*.[31] In it, Ranshofen-Wertheimer made the case for a 'realistic' foreign policy based on the insight that only the victorious powers' enduring threat of force would be able to ensure that peace prevailed in the long run. Enlightenment and rational insight were attractive goods, but the League of Nations had demonstrated that they could not be relied upon. Ranshofen-Wertheimer thus presented the preliminary outline of what could become the policy of deterrence that took centre stage during the Cold War.

To Pollock's mind, this approach fell short because it offered no perspective for the democratisation of society in the vanquished European nations that was the centre piece of the benevolent and 'enlightened' occupation the institute envisaged. Once Nazism was defeated, there would be no groups in Germany capable of initiating and driving the democratisation process, hence such forces would need to be carefully created and fostered. The United States would need to oversee the development of trade unions, educational institutions and decentralised local administrations. The institute envisaged a fundamental restructuring of the German state and a comprehensive programme of public enlightenment – just the kind of reconstruction and reeducation policy the

---

30 'Tentative Worksheet for a Discussion on European (and foremost German) Reconstruction', 11 January 1943, Horkheimer Archive, University Library Frankfurt/Main, MHA XXIV 8, 1.
31 Ranshofen-Wertheimer 1942.

United States initially did pursue in Germany until Ranshofen-Wertheimer's realism won the day and the goal of substantive denazification was radically pared down to placate the Germans.[32]

In early 1944, Pollock was back at the White House to discuss the drafted programme. This time, FDR was in attendance again.[33] Friedrich Pollock – the leftist social critic and former Marxist who hid Communists involved in the Bavarian Soviet Republic in his flat in Munich; who attended the celebrations marking the tenth anniversary of the October Revolution in Moscow as an official guest and who collaborated with the Soviet Marx Engels Institute for several years; several of whose colleagues were Soviet spies and who until recently was himself on the radar of the FBI – was now engaged in face-to-face discussions with the president of the United States; a constellation surely owed to the very specific circumstances of the Second World War.

Pollock's friends and acquaintances could hardly fail to notice all this, and he was the subject of much gossip, especially among the German émigré community in Los Angeles, many of whose members regularly gathered in Brecht's house for tea or at the Feuchtwangers' cocktail parties. When Pollock began to sermonise about the state of the world at one of these gatherings, the listeners quickly split into friend and foe. A diary entry by Horkheimer's neighbour Thomas Mann from October 1945 may convey a sense of the course of such gatherings:

> Dinner party to mark [Alfred] Neumann's fiftieth birthday with Peter Pr.[ingsheim], Leonh. Frank, Mrs Horkheimer, Dr. Pollack. Champagne and lobster, fillet, fruit flan. Conversations about matters nuclear, America & Russia, the state of capitalism, Europe's path to Socialism. As for America, the question whether in the case of a downturn after the boom of the next 3–5 years civil war or an external war loom. Evidently no suggestion of an immediate pre-emptive war against Russia.[34]

Pollock loved such occasions. He disliked public appearances and only reluctantly gave public lectures, but he thrived in closed groups – be they committees or cocktail parties. Some greatly respected and admired him, others intensely detested him for his conduct on such occasions. The composer Hanns Eisler, for example, who had been friendly with Adorno since they were young men, could not stand Pollock and suggested to Brecht that Pollock and his associates would

---

32   See Fait 2004; Rauh-Kühne 2004.
33   Krohn 2017, p. 173.
34   Mann 1986, p. 264. I am grateful to Dirk Heißerer for this reference.

provide a wonderful foil for the material Brecht had collected for his planned *Tui Novel*.³⁵ This certainly appealed to Brecht who had nothing but contempt for the institute. In August 1941, he wrote in his journal: 'at a garden party ... i met the twin clowns horkheimer and pollock, two tuis from the frankfurt sociological institute. horkheimer is a millionaire, pollock merely from a well-off background, which means horkheimer can buy himself a university chair "as a front for the institute's revolutionary activities" wherever he happens to be staying'.³⁶ Writing to Karl Korsch towards the end of 1941, he explained that he now met Horkheimer and Pollock only at parties and social gatherings and, 'the Tui Novel aside', had little use for them.³⁷

Brecht created the acronym tui by dissecting and reassembling the word intellectual as tellect_ual_in. For Brecht, intellectuals had sold out. They were pitiful opportunists who, in their utter helplessness, sought favour with the powers that be, and the 'Frankfurtists' were the worst kind of tuis.³⁸ In material from the 1930s and 1940s and especially in his play, *Turandot oder Der Kongreß der Weißwäscher* (Turandot or The Whitewashers' Congress) of 1953, they were, as Hans Mayer too has confirmed, the barely disguised butts of his mockery.³⁹ In the play, a version of Pollock featured as the Economics Tui who asks, 'Ladies! How can we make a success of business?' and answers:

> Take a look in my book, and for just a yen you too can find out what the science of economics has to say about it:
>
> Imagine business isn't going well –
> The big fish keep me wriggling in the dark.
> Why then I scratch my last remaining hairs out
> And ask how I can get to be a shark.
> I know what folk endure to earn their bread
> And, for their pains, they get it up the butt.
> They're good for nothing, or they're good for fleecing –
> I know the score – and so I take my cut.⁴⁰

---

35 Buono 1976, p. 77; Glahn 2019.
36 Brecht 1993, p. 161.
37 Bertolt Brecht to Karl Korsch, September 1941, in Brecht 1990, p. 339.
38 See [Anschauungsunterricht für ein neues Sehen der Dinge], in Brecht 1992, pp. 304–5. It is evident from the underlining in his copy that Brecht read Pollock's essay 'Bemerkungen zur Wirtschaftskrise' very carefully. See Wizisla 2007, p. 359.
39 Mayer 1992, p. 62.
40 Brecht 2013, pp. 176–7.

Like the Medicine Tui and the Love-Life Tui, the Economics Tui is ridiculous rather than menacing. The portrayal of Munka Du, a Great Tui, was less charitable yet. At the Tui congress, he gives a speech emphatically extolling the value of freedom that is quite intentionally devised to draw attention away from the actual relations of power and domination. He is eventually decapitated and his head is mounted on a spike. Both the German and British editors of the play concur that Munka Du bears 'caricatural traits of Theodor Adorno'.[41]

Not least given that the institute was still supporting him financially, Korsch was rather more well disposed towards Pollock and his colleagues. Pollock later recalled that, in the United States, Korsch was allowed nowhere near the institute

> because we knew that Korsch is a troublemaker who ends up quarrelling with everyone, [and who] was awfully loquacious. If one asked him a question, he would go on forever; on the other hand, we respected him as a man of integrity and someone who knew his stuff when it came to Marxism – theoretical and practical Marxism.[42]

From a letter he wrote to the council communist Paul Mattick back in 1938, we know that Korsch, conversely, greatly valued Pollock, both as a scholar and a human being. By contrast, he was unimpressed by Löwenthal's and Neumann's intellectual abilities, though he appreciated their personal integrity as authors. In terms of their convictions, all the members of the institute were 'without exception, to varying degrees, anti-Stalinists', but in the current situation (1938) they shied away both from directly confronting party Communism and from nailing their flag to what for Korsch was the only true and valid form of Marxism.[43] Pollock continued to feel some sympathy for the anti-Stalinist yet still revolutionary Marxist Korsch in the 1940s but theoretically they had grown far apart. Pollock was now rarely concerned with Marx and tended to be preoccupied with American industrial sociology and standard economic research literature – the sort of literature Korsch, Mattick and Brecht contemptuously dismissed as 'vulgar economics'.

All of them were intrigued by Aldous Huxley's dystopian bestseller *Brave New World* of 1932 which continued to be an important point of reference for Pollock for the remainder of his life. In the summer of 1942, Pollock participated

---

41 Kuhn and Constantine (eds.) 2013, p. 250; Wege 1992, p. 412.
42 Ernst von Schenck, interview with Pollock and Horkheimer, transcript, 1965/66, Horkheimer Archive, University Library Frankfurt/Man, MHA X 132a, p. 125.
43 Karl Korsch to Paul Mattick, 20 October 1938, in Korsch 2001, pp. 682–5, p. 684.

for several weeks in an informal seminar on the theory of needs with Brecht, Eisler, Ludwig Marcuse, Günther Anders and several other institute members that focussed on *Brave New World* and addressed the possibility 'that capitalism might be capable of meeting all basic needs'. In line with his concept of state capitalism Pollock assumed this was so and asked whether one could still speak of domination, should he be right. 'If capitalism can abolish need, what then distinguishes socialism from capitalism?', he asked provocatively.[44]

What was emerging here were the outlines of the concept of the administered world of which Adorno in particular became a prominent proponent after the war. Would not a system capable of accommodating all material needs and interests curtail freedom? Do creativity, individuality, autonomy and the arts not depend on the tension that arises when needs are not or only partially met? 'Will human beings still pursue higher goods if they are full? What is there, once the hunger is satisfied?'[45] The Brecht faction was outraged and maintained that one could only really begin to think once one was no longer hungry. In the end, the participants could only agree to disagree.

Back in New York, Pollock met with Löwe and Tillich in May 1943 for a historiosophical symposium that reflects Pollock's stance more clearly, given its far less polemical character. The point of departure for their discussion was the question of whether the course of history was in some way predetermined and to what extent the decisions of individuals influenced its unfolding. For Pollock, the former assumption was simply theological. It was surely not preordained that history would descend into barbarism as it now had. What, then, were the decisive forces that channelled historical contingency in one direction or another? The second part of the question was even more specific: who was responsible for the barbarism? Did it spring from individual criminal acts or a more universal malignancy? Did it make sense to identify individual culprits when dealing with historical events? 'How significant are individuals' actions', Löwe asked. 'How would history have unfolded if Hitler had not attacked? What would have happened to England if the Blitzkrieg had been resumed a few months later with a better equipped Luftwaffe?'[46]

Responding to these counterfactual scenarios, Pollock doubted that 'much would have changed in all these cases. Napoleon would have been able to ship

---

44 [Zu einem Referat über das Verhältnis von Bedürfnis und Kultur bei Aldous Huxley: Diskussion], in Horkheimer 1985a, p. 574.
45 [Zu einem Referat Ludwig Marcuses über das Verhältnis von Bedürfnis und Kultur bei Nietzsche], 14 July 1942, in Horkheimer 1985a, p. 568.
46 'Symposium Lowe-Tillich-Pollock on Philosophy of History', 31 May 1943, Horkheimer Archive, University Library Frankfurt/Main, MHA VI 33, 486.

landing troops across but unable to defend their supply lines against the British navy. Kerensky's government would have been toppled by radical forces sooner or later. Even if Hitler had continued his assault on England and postponed the invasion of the Soviet Union, he would probably still have lost the war.'[47] Much depended

> on the status of the subject responsible for fatal decisions. For an individual, a single mistake may indeed prove fatal and entirely alter the direction of his life. When it comes to a large country like Germany, this is much less likely, and it certainly does not hold true for the history of Europe or the globe.

Pollock was still convinced that material relations determined the course of history but, unlike conventional Marxists, he assumed that its course was subject to some measure of contingency, give that it had no inherent telos. This explained why the world had been able to descend into barbarism but also made it impossible to foresee what might transpire once humankind's basic needs were universally met and no one needed to fear for their existence anymore. This brought him back to Huxley's account of what he interpreted as state capitalism. On this occasion, his assessment was much more optimistic than it had been in the Californian debate: 'Until now, human beings have never been given the opportunity to develop fully. One knows from the world of technology that the more conducive the surroundings and the easier life is, the more human qualities in the narrower sense develop.' Given that 'the social climate of the class society basically destroys everything that is deserving and capable of affection', human beings had as yet never really 'stood a chance'.[48]

As Löwe noted at a gathering in January 1945, these discussions rarely led to any kind of satisfactory conclusion.

> Our situation resembles that of the old Jewish tale of the two quarrelling parties before the rabbi. The first party makes its case, and the rabbi says: you are right. The opponent makes his case, and the rabbi says: you are right. Thereupon a third party takes issue with this contradiction, and the rabbi says: you too are right.[49]

---

47 'Symposium Lowe-Tillich-Pollock on Philosophy of History', 31 May 1943, Horkheimer Archive, University Library Frankfurt/Main, MHA VI 33, 489.
48 Ibid.
49 Horkheimer et al. 1994, p. 299.

Even so, for Pollock, whom his administrative burden constantly threatened to bury alive, these debates were an essential lifeline.

When such opportunities arose, he would speak not only about economics, but also about theology, the relationship between theory and praxis or the New Woman. As we saw, Pollock and Horkheimer were great Ibsen enthusiasts in their youth. Given that his work radically questioned established gender roles, they enjoyed a broad reception among first-wave feminists. While his own treatment of women was profoundly patronising in practice, it went without saying that, as a progressive thinker, he was a staunch feminist in theory. What Pollock had to say on the matter certainly impressed Hannah Tillich who, at some point in 1943, wrote to him to let him know,

> just how much your seminar paper and your conversation in the car (*this I am sure you will have forgotten*) helped me and how wonderful and comforting it is to me that individuals of your kind and personality are working on the problems of our tumultuous age .... After the seminar, I said to Paulus: You can prepare a sculpture of Fred Pollock for Riverside Church (next to Einstein)[.] He is the *only* theologian among you ... who has the courage to take a fresh psychological *and* moral look at human beings from the vantage of economic necessities and in terms of the ways in which they are shaped by these necessities ... and what really moved me was, of course, the issue of the New Woman ... Time and again, when it came to my difficulties with Paulus, I have said ... we are not wrong at all ... it is just marriage with its economic dependencies and absurd and confused assumptions that is lethal or at least threatens to suffocate us.[50]

Not that Pollock was always a success when called upon in a pastoral capacity. He was frequently too sober in his response to display genuine empathy with his interlocutors. In his ultimately neither completed nor published memoirs, Felix Weil referred to 'Pollock's friendly smile' but then suggested that it was to some degree deceitful.

---

50 Hannah Tillich to Friedrich Pollock, incomplete letter, 1943, Horkheimer Archive, University Library Frankfurt/Main, MHA VI 33, 462. The tympanum of the (originally) interdenominational Riverside Church, inaugurated in October 1930, displays dozens of sculptures of both religious and secular figures, including philosophers and scientists. As the *New York Times* reported on 14 September 1930, 'Professor Albert Einstein of Berlin, propounder of the theory of relativity, is the only living one of the world's great to have his likeness carved with images of Christ, the angels and saints in stone on the tympanum of the doorways of the Riverside Church, 122d Street'. Tillich frequently preached at Riverside Church. See Graf 2017, p. 41.

'For Pollock', Weil wrote, 'I was a rich boy whom one would be able to teach a lot if one struck the right note; or, to be more precise, the right notes. The ones that resonated with me were scientific Marxism and friendship.'[51] As we saw, Weil's memoirs, written in the early 1970s, need to be taken with a considerable pinch of salt. Leaving the numerous factual errors to one side, Weil's account of his dealings with the institute was permeated by a profound sense of betrayal. He was no longer involved with the institute whose establishment he had initiated, and his politics were now far removed from those of his late friends. For him, their shift from Marxism to Critical Theory was simply a matter of treachery. Above all, he felt that he and his contribution had not received the credit they were owed, and he therefore set about making Horkheimer and Pollock look bad. Even so, Weil's claim that Pollock could seem two-faced cannot simply be dismissed out of hand. His honesty and sincerity are not in doubt, but it is clear that neither did he always tell the whole truth. The only person with whom he dared speak openly about everything – something he had not been able to do even with his wife – continued to be Horkheimer. Yet here he was, separated from Max and Maidon, far removed from the *île heureuse*. It was high time to leave New York and move to the West Coast.

---

51   Felix Weil, 'Erinnerungen (Fragment)', Institute for the History of Frankfurt, S 5/421: 'Weggefährten'.

CHAPTER 11

Return?

Germany's total capitulation had already come into force in the night of 8/9 May 1945 when it was ratified, some minutes later, by the heads of the German armed forces at the headquarters of the Red Army in Berlin-Karlshorst. Following the deployment of atom bombs over Hiroshima and Nagasaki, the Japanese too capitulated, and the Second World War was finally over. On 14 August, two million individuals poured on to Times Square and the streets of New York to celebrate VJ Day with abandon. 'We experienced that joy, it was a Friday evening', one contemporary recalled, 'jubilation broke out all over the country'.[1] For many, the famous photograph of a sailor and nurse kissing, taken by Alfred Eisenstaedt and published on the cover of *Life* magazine a fortnight later, has come to symbolise this joy as the slaughter finally ended. For just a moment, the world seemed to stand still. Many felt as though they were waking up from a horrendous nightmare.

This momentous historical caesura also animated Pollock's brother Hans, now Juan, to get in touch again. In his first post-war letter, posted in Buenos Aires on 15 May 1945, he asked his big brother to let him know how he was. 'Perhaps you will be able to spare an hour and tell us about the last year, your work, your travel and how you are.' So much had happened in the previous year, Juan noted.

> The victory in Europe will soon bring peace and see Nazi Germany held to account for all its crimes. Hopefully the judges will be guided by ... humane principles and rid humankind of these murderers. How dreadful has the fate of individuals in these concentration camps been and how grateful must we be to have been spared all this.[2]

Friedrich Pollock's reaction was muted. Not only did he rarely have time to write, he was also suspicious of his brother's suddenly rediscovered sense of

---

1 'Hundreds of couples re-enact historic kiss celebrating end of WWII on Times Square', *ABC News*, 15 August 2015, https://www.abc.net.au/news/2015-08-15/hundreds-of-couples-re-enact-famous-kiss-celebrating-end-of-wwii/6699624.
2 Juan Pollock to Friedrich Pollock, 15 May 1945, Horkheimer Archive, University Library Frankfurt/Main, MHA XXIII 22, 222.

family. Hence, Juan Pollock rarely received more than terse answers to his direct questions, and in English at that. For example, Juan Pollock sent his brother a moving account of the fate of the Loewenstein family with whom he and his family had shared their accommodation in Amsterdam. Apart from their daughter 'Ilse, her mother and her sister's seven-year-old child', they had all been murdered.[3] Pollock's oddly detached response read:

> The story you tell me about the fate of the Loewenstein family is, unfortunately, very typical. I have arranged for the sending of three food packages to the addresses indicated by you. I have not received the bill, as yet, but if they don't cost substantially more than $15 – I will charge them to your '50th birthday account'.[4]

This was a reference to Pollock's previous inquiry as to what he might give Juan on this occasion.

> I reck my brain to find out what little birthday gift might give you some fun, but I know so little about your personal hobbies that I came to no conclusion, can't you help and let me know what you would like to have? Havanna cigars (if the Argentine import duties are not prohibitive) or books in which you are particularly interested, or what?[5]

Yet Juan was far more interested in personal information than any gifts:

> You want to give me something for my birthday, I am happy to accept, but no Havannas, they are no longer appropriate, nor books; what I would like to ask you for is something much more personal. Fritz, you yourself write, 'but I know so little about your personal hobbies'; you're one to talk. how little do I know about you and your life, your successes and disappointments, I know nothing, nothing other than that I have a brother who made it possible for me to flee Europe and save myself. I do have a wish, it will cost you an hour a month. Send me a few lines each month, telling me something about your life, your work, so I know I have a brother in an

---

3   Juan Pollock to Friedrich Pollock, 13 August 1945, Horkheimer Archive, University Library Frankfurt/Main, MHA XXIII 22, 216.
4   Friedrich Pollock to Juan Pollock, 26 July 1945, Horkheimer Archive, University Library Frankfurt/Main, MHA XXIII 22, 217–18.
5   Friedrich Pollock to Juan Pollock, 8 September 1945, Horkheimer Archive, University Library Frankfurt/Main, MHA XXIII 22, 215.

emotional sense too. Call me sentimental, but it would mean a great deal to me ...⁶

Of course, for Pollock, an hour each month was a great deal of time. It seems unlikely in the extreme that he would have wanted to share his 'successes and disappointments' with anyone other than Horkheimer and he probably considered his brother's request an imposition. 'It is very kind of you that you have asked me to write a kind of autobiography for you', he wrote. 'There is not so much to tell. With one single exception, my personal life has been undeservedly happy and successful taking into consideration what happened in the outside world in the seven years since we have not seen each other.'⁷ Evidently, however fortunate he may have considered himself otherwise, he was still not entirely over the 'one single exception', his wife's death.

Pollock had spent most of the summer of 1945 in California but was now back in New York where he encountered the collective sigh of relief that pervaded the city. He was tasked with bringing the institute's relations with Columbia and a number of other organisations to an amicable conclusion. After that, he too would move to California. Not that he had any specific notion of what lay ahead but he knew he was about to begin an entirely new chapter in his life.

Pollock was now 51. For his fiftieth birthday, Horkheimer and Adorno had presented him with the original version of *Dialectic of Enlightenment*, which they dedicated to him. His own contribution to its production, both theoretical and practical-administrative, had been considerable. That his theory of state capitalism in particular had shaped the book in important ways is immediately evident from the preface. Take the statement, clearly echoing the Huxley debate, that, 'while individuals as such are vanishing before the apparatus they serve, they are provided for by that apparatus and better than ever before'.⁸ Similarly, in the culture industry chapter, there is a reference to the survival of 'a piece of the circulation sphere otherwise in the process of disintegration' that clearly reflected Pollock's account of the transition from the free-market economy to an organised form of capitalism.⁹

Yet just as important as his theoretical input was the fact that, by running the institute virtually single-handedly in New York, he had given Horkheimer and

---

6 Juan Pollock to Friedrich Pollock, 13 August 1945, Horkheimer Archive, University Library Frankfurt/Main, MHA XXIII 22, 216.
7 Friedrich Pollock to Juan Pollock, 8 September 1945, Horkheimer Archive, University Library Frankfurt/Main, MHA XXIII 22, 215.
8 Horkheimer and Adorno 2002, p. xvii.
9 Horkheimer and Adorno 2002, p. 104.

Adorno the space needed to devote themselves wholly to their work on the text. For this reason too it was entirely appropriate that they dedicated the finished product to him. Yet now that this truly foundational text had been published, Pollock felt old for the first time. In a sense, he only now came to appreciate just how exhausting the previous couple of years had been. Yet then Felix Weil's cousin, Carlota Weil (1905–1983), who was organising an arts programme for disadvantaged children at the Manhattan Day Care Center, stepped into his life.[10] They had known each other way back in Frankfurt but only now, 20 years later, did she catch his eye as an attractive woman. The decision to court her put a new spring in his step. Carlota, who was eleven years younger than Pollock, had one failed marriage to her name and was independently wealthy. She owned 20 per cent of the shares in the Weil grain business that was still worth millions.[11] Felix Weil later accused Pollock of having courted Carlota only for her money but there is little to support this claim. He was in love with her. He may not have been swept up by unbounded passion and frenzied desire, but he relished her company and they both enjoyed going out to the theatre, to exhibitions or on occasional shopping trips. Pollock had been interested in fashion since his childhood, when he gawped at the items on offer in his parents' store, and he shared this fascination with Carlota. He always wanted to know about the newest trends (a proclivity he may also have shared with Lucille). Yet Carlota was much more urbane than Lucille, nor were there any reasons why they should not date. They became a couple and soon married. The wedding took place on the downlow in New York on 14 February 1946.

Pollock and Horkheimer now needed to negotiate what the new *intérieur* should look like and what Carlota's role within it would be. Previously, they had assumed that Pollock would simply move in with Max and Maidon Horkheimer. This was now no longer an option, and it was decided that the couple, drawing on Carlota's fortune, should acquire a property close to the Horkheimers. As the decision-making process advanced, Horkheimer admonished Pollock:

> It is obvious that everything depends on your and my personal relationship. If there is not the slightest doubt that everything in our practical lives is subordinated to the fulfilment of our original aims, the efforts which Carlota will have to make will be meaningful and gratifying to herself. If there is the slightest wavering or guilt feeling on your part with

---

10 See Carlota Weil, A Program of Art Education, New York, 1946, Fondo Friedrich Pollock, Università degli Studi di Firenze, 3.1, doc. 1. I am grateful to Nicola Emery for this reference.
11 Heufelder 2017, p. 99.

> regard to this effort, the natural resistance which is necessarily present in anyone who enters a new situation such as this one will find a hundred rationalisations. She will be led into challenging the whole form of existence which she is supposed to enter. Her function which is to enable you to fulfill your own task in our life, will appear to her as unreasonable and unjust instead of a help and a cure for her own difficulties whatever they may be. Your responsibility to make it easy for her to understand is great and you will certainly not get very far with that socalled democratic common sense which is neither democratic nor common sense.[12]

Horkheimer thus clarified that the covenant they had entered into as adolescents in Stuttgart and elevated to the status of a religion in Brussels, London and Manchester, continued to take precedence over anything as profane as a marriage. There was only one role Carlota could conceivably play within their arrangement: it was up to her to offer her husband unconditional support without getting in his way. She would be in no position to place demands on Pollock, let alone would her relationship with Pollock trump his friendship with Horkheimer. 'What Carlota should understand', Horkheimer decreed, 'is the following: you and I have been friends with divided functions but a common task'.[13] Pollock needed to impress on Carlota that nothing would be allowed to jeopardise their joint project. There is nothing to suggest that Horkheimer's admonishing, borderline hectoring tone in any way surprised or irritated Pollock. They were in full agreement, and it seems highly unlikely that Carlota was left in any doubt about Pollock's expectations – although, in the event, as opposed to Dée and Maidon, she did not consistently conform to her assigned role. 'In general', Horkheimer wrote,

> all this will be the same after your marriage. The fact that you are so to speak leaving the family for which you had assumed a large part of responsibility, makes it necessary that a few personal matters are defined. For example, you have naturally always shared the house whenever we decided that we should both stay here. As far as you yourself are concerned, this will never change. However, as I said before, it would be foolish to attempt a symbiosis of the two married couples in question. The

---

12   Max Horkheimer to Friedrich Pollock, 7 May 1946, in Horkheimer 1996a, pp. 722–7, pp. 723–4.
13   Max Horkheimer to Friedrich Pollock, 7 May 1946, in Horkheimer 1996a, pp. 722–7, p. 724.

main reason why the house was built was to create a place for my particular work for which you felt as much responsibility as I did. It would neither be correct nor good psychology if you would lead Carlota to believe that the house is partly your property. You do not have to go into details, but I think you must tell her that your individual right to live here is based on our personal relationship. ... The clearer you make the point, the less resentment will arise.[14]

To be sure, given all the sacrifices Pollock had accepted in the interest of their cause in recent years, Horkheimer was pleased that his friend had found a wife but ultimately, Carlota did not fit into his vision of their covenant and he merely tolerated her presence.

In the summer of 1946, the newlyweds moved to Santa Monica where they lived in a property on San Vicente Boulevard, located ten minutes by car from the Horkheimers' residence. Horkheimer treated Carlota courteously but without genuine warmth. She remained an outsider and she knew it. In 1949, she expressed her frustration in her diary, noting sarcastically that Horkheimer was neither her husband nor her professor or her first friend.[15] It was particularly bad when Pollock was on the road, and her loneliness and anguish eventually evolved into a serious depression. In 1949, Pollock bought her a small dog in the hope that it might cheer her up.[16] The dog did offer her some solace but for the most part, she vacillated between periods of melancholy withdrawal and short spells of overwrought excitement. Time and again, she implored Pollock to devote more time to their shared life as a married couple:

> Please, Fred, tell me what you think. You are utterly human in your life, after all – and not some jaundiced individualist. You yourself don't want to lead the life you led prior to your first marriage and later on – no home of your own and instead lots of girlfriends, you're just not that sort of person. ... You are my husband, after all – the warmest and most cheering husband I could imagine or want.[17]

---

14   Max Horkheimer to Friedrich Pollock, 7 May 1946, in Horkheimer 1996a, pp. 722–7, pp. 724–5.
15   Carlota Pollock, Diary, May–June 1949, Fondo Friedrich Pollock, Università degli Studi di Firenze, 2.1.3, doc. 2.
16   See Margot von Mendelssohn to Friedrich Pollock, 13 June 1949, Horkheimer Archive, University Library Frankfurt/Main, MHA VI 36, 8.
17   Carlota Pollock to Friedrich Pollock, May 1949, Fondo Friedrich Pollock, Università degli Studi di Firenze, 2.1.3, doc. 3.

Alas, the latter was hardly true, given that Pollock never envisaged prioritising his marriage over his covenant with Horkheimer.

The new constellation was not exactly straightforward, then, but it nevertheless marked a new beginning for Pollock. He was greatly relieved to be able to give up several of his New York commitments. He left the *Aufbau* advisory board and resigned as president of the Social Studies Association. Conversely, he took on new roles in Los Angeles. He became chair of the Hacker Psychiatric Foundation based at the eponymous psychiatric clinic in Beverly Hills, named for the Austrian-American psychoanalyst Frederick J. Hacker, and established to facilitate joint research projects with the institute. At the same time, he entered into negotiations about the possibility of the institute becoming affiliated with the University of California (UCLA). This seemed a good option, but the discussions dragged on.

As a scholar, he was preoccupied with political aspects of the post-war order and, above all, with the likelihood (or lack thereof) of long-term peace in Europe and Asia. He feared from the outset that the looming Cold War might turn hot from one day to the next. He was particularly interested in Korea which, after the war, was divided into two occupation zones, one Soviet, the other American. In 1950, just five years after the end of the Second World War, the dispute over who was the legitimate successor state to the old empire precipitated a proxy war pitting the United States against the People's Republic of China which had been created the year before and was aligned with the Soviet Union. The three-year war cost four million lives and led to the establishment of the two current, mutually hostile Korean states.

In the years leading up to the war, in which the USA played a decisive role, Pollock noted that the structures of the American war economy were largely still in place. He identified signs of what he called a preparedness economy, a concept he had developed in 1940 in an article for the renowned *American Economic Review* to characterise the transition to a war economy.[18] The Fair Deal of FDR's successor Harry Truman followed on from the New Deal and extended the remit of the welfare state yet further. In principle, Pollock sympathised with this policy, but he saw only too clearly how inextricable it was from what was, to his mind, a latent war economy.

In addition, he was interested in the structures of distribution at the micro level because he wanted to ascertain how exactly the appropriation of social wealth transpired when the market was largely subordinated but not replaced by a comprehensive form of central planning. It turned out that the actual

---

18   Pollock 1940.

degree of planning was not as extensive as Pollock had expected it would be under democratic state capitalism. Consequently, the Mafia and the trade unions they controlled had joined forces with the monopoly capitalist cliques and stepped in to undertake the distribution of wealth. Since the 1930s, the market was increasingly being replaced by organised crime which exploited the interventionist state by abusing its social programmes. For Pollock, this proliferation of organised crime within legal structures and institutions was so significant that he identified it as a central problem in the post-war economic development. On 11 September 1949, Thomas Mann noted in his diary:

> Buffet dinner with K.[atia] and Golo at Eva Herrmann's .... Afterwards listened to Pollak's account of the American business by coercion and trust system. Incredible that anyone can still refer to 'free enterprise' with a straight face when the proprietor of even the smallest drugstore knows otherwise.[19]

Horkheimer and Pollock had worked on a transhistorical racket theory in the late 1930s that was also enshrined in *Dialectic of Enlightenment*.[20] The term racketeering had become common currency during the prohibition years. It initially referred to the extortion of protection money but increasingly came to denote all forms of illicit business from drug trafficking and illegal gambling to bribery and prostitution. In the context of Critical Theory, the term racket was appropriated to denote a social group or constellation that ruled predominantly by resorting to force and stuck together for as long as the participants were able to secure a worthwhile share of the spoils.[21] The concept served as a substitute for the category of class which, in their determination to bring Marxist theory up to date, they sidelined as obsolete. An aphorism Horkheimer wrote in 1942, 'Geschichte der amerikanischen Arbeiterschaft' (History of the American Working Class), summed up their position:

> The historical path of the proletariat led to a crossroads: it could become a class or a racket. Racket meant privileges within national borders, class meant world revolution. The leaders relieved the proletariat of the decision and chose the racket.[22]

---

19 Mann 1991, p. 125.
20 See Fuchshuber 2019.
21 Horkheimer 1985b, p. 287.
22 Horkheimer 1985c.

On this reading, class was identified with a form of transnational struggle against oppression of which precious little was left. Instead, trade unions haggled for a slice of the national pie. Akin to Lenin's castigation of the labour aristocracy, Pollock and Horkheimer characterised the leaders of the labour movement as racketeers. In the context of an interventionist state, they required a legal title confirming their racket membership. 'With it [the legal title] the state as the universal signatory confirms that its owner belongs to a racket and is thereby integrated into the system.'[23] Only those who could demonstrate their membership in one of the rackets – trade unions, legal, medical and industrial associations, academic and political cliques – were still able to share in society's wealth. In his notes, Pollock succinctly defined the racket as follows: 'an organization of "in's" whose privileges are as such reserved for themselves, and, to a minor degree ... for the "protected" group. Privileges and access to them [are] defended with nails and claws against the "outs"'.[24] The independent entrepreneurs who, in the liberal era, had competed with each other on the market, were superseded by tightly organised interest groups that demanded absolute loyalty. In a second step, Pollock and Horkheimer detached the concept from this specific historical context and established it as a transhistorical paradigm of domination.

There are obvious references in Pollock's unpublished papers to his translation of class theory into racket theory. These include apparent equations such as 'history = struggle of rackets' and 'classless society = society without rackets'.[25] But these efforts were about more than a straightforward exchange of terms. In contrast to the dualistic concept of the class struggle, rackets existed 'in all social strata. The *struggle* transpires not merely between capitalists & workers, but *equally* within both groups.'[26] The owners of capital were 'one racket only'.[27]

It is hardly surprising that Pollock increasingly perceived of the institute as a kind of counter-racket. It bore strong structural similarities to the racket – a conspiratorial closed group predicated on uniformity and loyalty – yet was needed as a refuge only because human society was in such a dire state. The

---

23 Horkheimer 1985b, p. 289.
24 Friedrich Pollock, 'Notes, to be followed up', Horkheimer Archive, University Library Frankfurt/Main, MHA XXIV 55, 18.
25 Friedrich Pollock, 'Theory of the Racket', Horkheimer Archive, University Library Frankfurt/Main, MHA XXIV 55, 15.
26 Friedrich Pollock, [Geschichte ist eine Geschichte der Ausbeutung], Horkheimer Archive, University Library Frankfurt/Main, MHA XXIV 55, 11.
27 Friedrich Pollock, 'Theory of the Racket', Horkheimer Archive, University Library Frankfurt/Main, MHA XXIV 55, 15.

creation of a 'society free of exploitation and rackets that grants everyone equal opportunities' would also render the counter-racket of the institute obsolete. In a sense, this was the utopian core of Pollock's political theory.[28]

Given its desolate state, the institute no longer offered any great protection, raising the question of how the continued existence of the extended family – Max and Maidon, Fred (and his tolerated plus one Carlota) and, increasingly, Teddie and Gretel Adorno too – might best be secured in the long term. They created a private investment fund and took out several life insurances, all the while discussing where they might live most securely in future. As far as the quality of life was concerned, California was clearly the preferred option. Yet in light of the mounting globally relevant tensions in Asia Pollock questioned just how secure the West Coast would really be. Yet what was the alternative?

In October 1946, a new and totally unexpected option came into play. The new vice chancellor of the Goethe University in Frankfurt, Walter Hallstein, wrote a short letter to Pollock and Weil in their capacity as joint chairmen of the Society of Social Research, inviting them to return to Frankfurt.[29] Now best known as a prominent foreign politician and the inaugural president of the European Commission, Hallstein was a legal scholar and former POW who returned to the university following his release by the US authorities in November 1945. He was elected vice chancellor the following year. Not a member of the Nazi party, he had joined various other Nazi organisations including the associations for legal practitioners and university teachers to avoid harming his career. From 1942 until his capture by US forces in northern France in 1944, he had served as a lieutenant in the Wehrmacht. No proactive supporter of the regime, he was enough of a conformist to hold on to his professorship in Rostock until 1941, when he secured a chair in Frankfurt. Following a meeting with Hallstein in New York in 1949, Horkheimer described him to his wife as 'a crafty, unscrupulous man who, like all Germans in leading positions, reminds one of the Hitler regime. ... Hallstein was in a pretty good mood. Oblivion and ice-cold deceit are what the heirs of the Nazis do best.'[30]

Pollock rejected the option of returning to Germany out of hand, but Horkheimer was not so certain. He at least wanted to know what an offer from

---

28 Friedrich Pollock, [Geschichte ist eine Geschichte der Ausbeutung], Horkheimer Archive, University Library Frankfurt/Main, MHA XXIV 55, 11.
29 Walter Hallstein to Friedrich Pollock and Felix Weil, 17 October 1946, in Horkheimer 1996a, pp. 765–6, p. 765.
30 Max Horkheimer to Maidon Horkheimer, 9 May 1949, in Horkheimer 2007, pp. 273–4 (translation amended).

Frankfurt would entail. Soon after Hallstein's note he received a sobering letter from Franz Neumann, sent on his return from Germany where he led the OSS contingent involved in setting up and gathering evidence for the Nuremberg Trials. 'Germany is worse today than in 1945', Neumann wrote.

> One gets a sense of total hopelessness and utter intellectual and political stagnation. In 1945, one could still imagine that something new might grow – in 1946, one finds only the old in a state of profound decay. ... Greetings go like this: 'How are you?' 'Thank you, very democratic.' This sort of thing illustrates what people truly think.

Yet reports of this kind did not deter Horkheimer. As well informed as ever, Neumann was also aware of the fact that 'Dr. Hermann Brill, junior minister in the Hessian ministry of science, wants to rebuild the institute.'[31]

Presumably for tactical reasons Horkheimer waited several weeks before responding to Hallstein's communication. He and his colleagues would 'carefully reconsider all the issues pertaining to an academic role in post-war Germany'.[32] To this end, they needed additional information, notably regarding the curriculum, student numbers and teaching staff. The requested information was promptly provided, along with a letter of encouragement from Fritz Karsen whom the institute had funded in 1938/39 and who now served as Chief of Higher Education and Teacher Training in the US military government. Given his role as director of the AJC's Department of Scientific Research, Horkheimer next consulted John Slawson, the committee's executive vice president, and his own departmental associate director Samuel H. Flowerman. Horkheimer suggested a research project on public opinion in Germany, undertaken under the auspices and with the support of the AJC, that would also allow him to explore the opportunity of establishing a branch of the institute in Frankfurt. In his response, Flowerman explained in no uncertain terms that the AJC had neither the capacity to undertake such a study nor did it seem a worthwhile project, given similar research was already being undertaken by other institutions and the military government itself. Moreover, while the institute could make a serious impact in the United States, its efforts would ultimately be wasted in Germany. 'Personally', Flowerman wrote, 'I despair very much of creating, through

---

31 Franz Neumann to Max Horkheimer, 31 October 1946, in Horkheimer 1996a, pp. 767–9, p. 737. See Perels 2001; Salter 2020, pp. 197–218.

32 Max Horkheimer to Walter Hallstein, 21 November 1946, in Horkheimer 1996a, pp. 771–2, p. 771.

academic sources in Germany, a climate which might help a portion of the younger generation to return to humanity.'[33] Horkheimer, though grateful for Flowerman's forthright response, disagreed with his 'radical pessimism'. Even so, he clarified,

> As far as a Frankfurt branch of the Institute is concerned, it is only natural that no member of ours here would care to stay there. The thing we have in mind would be to appoint one of our former associates over there. We might think, e.g., of our friend Dr. [Hans Klaus] Brill who was in charge of our branch at the École Normale Supérieure up to 1941 and who managed to survive during the occupation, and there are others to whom we feel similar loyalties.[34]

It is palpable from the relevant correspondence how the idea of re-establishing the institute slowly but gradually took hold of, and developed in, Horkheimer's mind. He came to think of the plan as a belated victory over the Nazis who had gone to such lengths in trying to root out all critical thought. Not that what had happened could ever be put right again, yet that was no reason to surrender to barbarism. Millions had given their lives to vanquish National Socialism and Horkheimer felt that he owed it to them to contribute to the attempt to create a democratic Germany. The re-establishment of the institute would be an important first step in this direction. Knowing how strongly Pollock was opposed to the idea of returning to Germany, Horkheimer was very reticent in broaching the issue with him. Having discussed the matter at great length, they eventually agreed to consider the option of opening a branch in Frankfurt, provided this did not require them to be physically present in, let alone move to, the city.

Reassured, Pollock and his wife embarked on an extended Latin American vacation. Originally, their prospective itinerary had included a trip to Buenos Aires, giving Pollock an opportunity to meet his new mother-in-law, Carlota's widowed mother Helena 'Hella' Rosenthal de Bernecker, and to see his brother Juan for the first time in almost a decade. In particular, he looked forward to meeting his niece Liselotte (Lilo) again whom he had last seen when she was still studying in Paris.[35]

---

33 Samuel H. Flowerman to Max Horkheimer, 5 February 1947, in Horkheimer 1996a, pp. 783–5, p. 784.
34 Max Horkheimer to Samuel H. Flowerman, 15 February 1947, in Horkheimer 1996a, pp. 787–9, p. 788.
35 See Pollock's instructions for Horkheimer's trip to Paris in November 1935 (including

Yet what Pollock considered a breach of trust on the part of his brother Juan got in the way of the planned reunion. In February 1946, he informed his brother that he had remarried and suggested he and his new wife would be visiting Buenos Aires the following year. 'Her Argentine family doesn't like me particularly', he noted, 'but I can assure you that this is mutual. They haven't known a thing about our intention to marry and will hear it by the same airmail'.[36] Within a matter of days, he received a response from Buenos Aires:

> Dear Fritz, You cannot imagine how overjoyed we all were when your letter arrived earlier today. I was already in the workshop when Idel called, Lilo was constantly interrupting and, at first, I couldn't understand what was going on. Fritz, I send you and Carlota my sincerest congratulations.[37]

For Juan, the fact that his brother had finally shared such personal news with him weighed just as heavily as the news themselves. It seemed to signal the resumption of intact fraternal relations after the many years of hardship and loss. Given his refined upbringing and the fact that he lived in the same city as his new relatives, he felt it was his duty to call on Carlota's mother with a bouquet and a congratulatory note. She was not in at the time but found Juan's flowers and card on her return and informed Pollock about his brother's visit. Pollock was apoplectic. When he reprimanded his brother for what was, as he saw it, this massive interference in his personal life, Juan responded, not without a note of irony:

> Dear Frederick, when I received your letter of 12 April, I had to smile with amusement. You're still the same petulant brother Fritz you were thirty years ago. Individuals really do not change, and that holds true for my big brother too. ... On the issue itself, I have the following to say in my 'defence': When the letter concerning your marriage arrived, I was still in bed but gradually getting better. I understood full well what you meant when you remarked that your new family was not particularly fond of you. It was clear to me that my role would be entirely passive. However, a few weeks later, various parties began to ask why I had not introduced myself

---

Liselotte's address) and Friedrich Pollock to Juan Pollock, 1 August 1950, Horkheimer Archive, University Library Frankfurt/Main, MHA VI 31, 12a and XXIII 22, 132.

36 Friedrich Pollock to Juan and Ida Pollock, 14 February 1946, Horkheimer Archive, University Library Frankfurt/Main, MHA XXIII 22, 212.

37 Juan Pollock to Friedrich Pollock, 20 February 1946, Horkheimer Archive, University Library Frankfurt/Main, MHA XXIII 22, 207.

to Mrs. Bernecker given that she, after all, as an elderly lady, could hardly come and congratulate me first. When Lilo and Paul were asked similar questions, I decided to do what good manners dictated. Mrs. Bernecker was on a trip, and we were due to leave a few days later, ... hence the flowers and congratulatory note. Your mother-in-law responded with a thank you note remarking that we should meet following her return after Easter. Nothing more has occurred since.[38]

Pollock was not convinced, and it did not help that his brother did then meet with Hella Bernecker. 'Mrs. Bernecker just wrote that you had seen her', he noted in a peevish letter to Juan on 14 May 1946, 'so you know everything about our life here, given that Carlota reports to her mother faithfully every week'. He added brusquely that 'A trip to Argentina is not on our schedule for 1947 and in 1948, it is more likely that we shall cross the Atlantic than the Southern Pacific.'[39] In the event, the first post-war meeting of the Pollock brothers took place only in May 1948.[40]

Horkheimer meanwhile continued to prepare for his trip to Germany. He was still pursuing the option of the AJC funding an empirical study in Germany that would offer him an opportunity to persuade the military government to involve the institute in its reeducation programme.[41] An invitation to give a number of lectures as a visiting professor in Frankfurt provided a hook on which to hang this proposal. In late April 1948, Horkheimer set sail for Europe. He initially spent three weeks in Paris. From there he travelled to Zurich, where his interlocutors included the erstwhile member of the covenant, Suzanne 'Suze' Neumeier. It was from Switzerland that Horkheimer openly broached, for the first time, the possibility of settling permanently in Europe again. 'You will no doubt sense already', he wrote to Pollock,

> that Europe is making quite a considerable and, on balance, positive impression on me. For all the horror that has occurred here and still looms and the in some respects horrendous conditions I cannot ignore the fact

---

38   Juan Pollock to Friedrich Pollock, 5 May 1946, Horkheimer Archive, University Library Frankfurt/Main, MHA XXIII 22, 205.
39   Friedrich Pollock to Juan and Ida Pollock, 14 May 1946, Horkheimer Archive, University Library Frankfurt/Main, MHA XXIII 22, 200.
40   See Friedrich Pollock to Margot von Mendelssohn, May 1948, Horkheimer Archive, University Library Frankfurt/Main, MHA VI 36, 102r.
41   These plans found expression in a detailed memorandum Horkheimer submitted to Slawson in February 1948: 'Re: German re-education and suggestions for an investigation on the spot', in Horkheimer 1996a, pp. 919–24.

that I understand people's speech, facial expressions and gestures here. ... Not for a single moment do I forget the past and one is constantly reminded of it anyway ... but even so, this is the ground from which grew not just the evil but also the good. All this has little to do with the question of where one lives. I preferably want to live where the conditions are most conducive to saying what needs to be said. If one leaves the money to one side that is obviously California.[42]

Horkheimer was clearly prevaricating and seemed increasingly comfortable with the idea that he might have to stay in Germany for up to a year in order to take care of their interests. These included the issue of compensation for their expropriated house in Kronberg. In the last week of May 1948, he entered Germany for the first time in fifteen years. He stayed for more than a month of very mixed feelings. Everything reminded him of the Nazis, and he was repulsed by the slippery conformists who sought to ingratiate themselves with him; but he was also able to meet old associates and was delighted to be able to speak freely with the students. Reticent in his correspondence with Pollock, he poured his heart out to Maidon, writing pages and pages about his experience.

In early July, Horkheimer travelled to Paris to attend a two-week UNESCO seminar that led to the publication of the edited collection, *Tensions That Cause Wars*.[43] Only now did he write to Pollock in greater detail (and in French). He still considered 'Germany the most expansionist and dangerous country in Europe', he explained, but he nevertheless felt that 'it would be good to live in Europe for several years'.[44] They would be able to achieve much more here than in the United States. In Europe, there were numerous individuals 'who need us and whom we therefore need too'. He therefore intended to rent or buy a small house in the south of France where they would be able to live and work, returning to Germany only during term time.

Pollock was not best pleased. He had only just had a house built at Latimer Road 21 in Pacific Palisades where he lived in the immediate vicinity of Hanns Eisler and Aldous Huxley. He had married and shed many of his onerous New York commitments – and now he was suddenly expected to move to the south

---

42 Max Horkheimer to Friedrich Pollock, 17 May 1948, in Horkheimer 1996a, pp. 967–9, p. 967.
43 See Horkheimer 1950. When the re-established institute seemed likely to host a UNESCO institute in Frankfurt, Hannah Arendt's best friend, Anne Mendelsohn-Weil, contacted her to debate how this might best be prevented. Library of Congress, Washington DC, Arendt Papers, 010882.
44 Max Horkheimer to Friedrich Pollock, 4 July 1948, in Horkheimer 1996a, pp. 1000–2, pp. 1000–1.

of France. It hardly helped that Horkheimer made all these decisions on his own as though they did not affect him too. When Horkheimer finally returned to California in August, they discussed the matter at great length. Given Pollock's objections and the more distanced vantage he had now that he was back, Horkheimer agreed to reconsider his plan.

At the end of January 1949, Horkheimer led the German authorities to believe that an agreement was within reach, yet Pollock still urged him to reconsider. A memorandum they agreed on 21 March stated unambiguously: 'We appreciate that this decision is one of the most difficult in our life because it means that we relinquish in perpetuity the opportunity to re-establish the institute in Germany and thus fulfil the tasks the Nazis prevented us from undertaking.'[45] Instead, they wanted the institute to be affiliated with, and reactivated under the auspices of, a prestigious US university, as it previously had been in New York. Following preparatory negotiations, Pollock had opted, as we saw, for the University of California, Los Angeles (UCLA) with whom an agreement seemed in reach. Yet on 30 March, Pollock and Horkheimer agreed on a new memorandum detailing reasons 'for the revision of the provisional decision of 21 March 1949 regarding the rejection of the invitation from Frankfurt University'.[46] One consideration was that Adorno might still return to Germany in which case the institute would lose one of its principal members. Another problem was that their rejection of the offer would be irrevocable, yet Horkheimer wanted to keep his options open. The following day, they wrote two mutually contradictory memoranda. The first, signed only by Pollock, definitively rejected the option of returning to Germany. 'The reasons for a revision of the tentative decision of 21 March given in the memorandum of 30 March are evidently partisan and reflect a momentary mood rather than a reasoned consideration of the risks attached to either option.'[47] Yet the second memorandum stated that Horkheimer would spend the summer semester teaching in Frankfurt. Here, the main consideration was that they should not burn their bridges. 'This consideration', they agreed in the characteristic pseudo-legal jargon of their friendship agreements, 'was previously formulated in the memorandum of 30 March, page 2, under #1.'[48]

---

45 Friedrich Pollock and Max Horkheimer, 'Memorandum', 21 March 1949, in Horkheimer 1996b, pp. 16–18, p. 16.
46 Friedrich Pollock and Max Horkheimer, 'Memorandum', 30 March 1949, in Horkheimer 1996b, pp. 18–20, p. 18.
47 Friedrich Pollock and Max Horkheimer, 'Memorandum' (I), 31 March 1949, in Horkheimer 1996b, pp. 20–1, p. 20.
48 Friedrich Pollock and Max Horkheimer, 'Memorandum' (II), 31 March 1949, in Horkheimer 1996b, pp. 21–2, p. 21.

It seems improbable that the two friends actually agreed on both of these mutually contradictory memoranda on the day. More likely, they recorded their continued dissent. Pollock was as convinced as ever that returning to Germany was a mistake. He wanted to stay in the United States where, in contrast to Horkheimer and Adorno, he had come to feel genuinely at home. 'I can well imagine,' he teased Horkheimer, who was already in New York, on 15 April 1949, 'how everyone is badgering you to exploit every possible opportunity in Germany. Yet I have not heard a single new argument from you that would provide grounds to "reconsider" our *decision*.'[49] Apparently, he genuinely failed to appreciate that Horkheimer had made up his mind months ago and that 'their' decision was really just his. While he nevertheless agreed to join Horkheimer in Frankfurt to steer the negotiations about a possible reestablishment of the institute in Frankfurt, he was very clear that he personally would not return to Germany on any kind of permanent basis.

Pollock arrived in Frankfurt in mid-May 1949 and stayed for four weeks. He wrote a detailed, essentially private report on this first stay in the land of the perpetrators, 'Eindrücke aus Frankreich und Deutschland' (Impressions of France and Germany). He prefaced the report by clarifying that 'the following notes are designed for a small circle'. They would be of no interest to those 'who have already been to Europe since the war or who are not specifically connected to the author'. He did not explain what kind of specific connection he had in mind, perhaps this was a reference to the collective experience of the Jewish émigrés.[50] Arriving from Paris, he had expected Frankfurt to lie in ruins and was surprised that 'the majority of familiar buildings' had survived. 'From a distance, Kaiserstraße looks the same as it did in the past. The trees sport the green of May, the familiar tram carriages that now look a little comical (because they are so small) run as though nothing had happened.' The complexion of the city's inhabitants was surprisingly healthy, and they certainly did not look famished. They 'strut around. They are better clothed than the local population in Paris and fastidiously dressed, many men wear gloves and people running around without a hat (like me) are in the minority.'[51]

Yet appearances were deceptive. When he took a closer look on a walk through the Old City, he noticed that many buildings were in fact mere fronts

---

49 Friedrich Pollock to Max Horkheimer, 15 April 1949, in Horkheimer 1996b, pp. 27–8, p. 27. The word 'reconsider' was written in English in the original.
50 Friedrich Pollock, 'Eindrücke aus Frankreich und Deutschland. Frankfurt vom 19.5.1949 bis 17.6.1949', Fondo Friedrich Pollock, Università degli Studi di Firenze, 2.1.3, doc. 1, p. 1.
51 Friedrich Pollock, 'Eindrücke aus Frankreich und Deutschland. Frankfurt vom 19.5.1949 bis 17.6.1949', Fondo Friedrich Pollock, Università degli Studi di Firenze, 2.1.3, doc. 1, p. 3.

with little more than debris behind them. Owing to the strict admission criteria, the students in Frankfurt – as opposed to their peers in Göttingen or Erlangen – had 'a strong democratic bent', yet Pollock suspected that 'a considerable measure of cynicism lies behind their open-minded manner and the thoughtful way in which they treat all issues'. His assessment of their parents was no less gloomy. 'The older people are pretty much as we thought they would be. From top to bottom, the middle classes are characterised by their desperate determination to recover their status, nationalism seems to be drastically increasing, there is a lot of self-pity, and they muster the utmost resistance when it comes to acknowledging what transpired under the Nazis, let alone, their own share in the responsibility.' Denazification had evidently failed, Pollock concluded, given that the bulk of the old regime's beneficiaries, 'having paid a small fine', continued to hold significant positions.

What he evidently did not encounter was antisemitism on any significant scale. The people were free of any fanaticism and, in a strange way, apolitical, he noted. As a result, one could do absolutely anything with them. An ordinary taxi driver who was an enthusiastic Nazi just a few years ago might very well be 'an equally reliable Social Democrat' now. Pollock stressed that he did not want to give the impression 'that I consider the German population to be particularly benign. One may think so when one hears them speak some affable Frankfurt idiom or some other southern German dialect, but history clearly demonstrates the opposite.' In short, as he put it in a letter to Horkheimer's secretary Margot von Mendelssohn, he found Germany 'extremely interesting and *extremely* exhausting'.[52]

To be sure, the negotiations he led in Frankfurt were strenuous, but it is clear from the report that Pollock took a good deal of time to explore post-war West Germany, almost as though he were a sociologist undertaking field work. He took the tram and travelled by third class rail to have an opportunity to talk to ordinary citizens; he moved from a luxury hotel into a plain guest house; and he cruised the black market and shops in downtown Frankfurt, all to gain as objective a sense of the country and its population as possible. Occasionally, he was overcome by his awareness of the fact that he had only narrowly escaped the horror that had transpired here. 'On one of our first days here', he wrote,

> we were in the Börsenkeller, which is a middle-class restaurant today. I observed the patrons. They all looked extremely innocuous, their clothing

---

52 Friedrich Pollock to Margot von Mendelssohn, 16 May 1949, Horkheimer Archive, University Library Frankfurt/Main, MHA VI 36, 18.

was a little shabby, but they were meticulously kempt and spotless, and then I suddenly imagined for a moment what the same scene with the same people would have looked like five years ago; what many of them would have looked like in party uniforms and sporting party insignia, and what they would have done to me, had they known that I was sitting among them as a Jew. Yet it really takes such fantasies to see through the present that superficially seems so harmless and peaceful.[53]

Pollock rarely referred to himself as a Jew. Yet here, in the land of the perpetrators and their accomplices, he could not avoid the insight that, regardless of his religious affiliation or lack thereof, he existed 'among them as a Jew'. Little wonder, then, that, as his correspondence with Horkheimer bears out, his stay in Germany made him feel no more positively about returning to Germany than before. His experiences essentially confirmed his misgivings.

In a joint memorandum of late April 1949, concluded before they left for Germany, they had agreed that they would begin to sort out their 'existence in accordance with our principles' as soon as Horkheimer returned from his semester in Frankfurt. Each would henceforth spend no more than one day a week undertaking administrative tasks. Trips would need to be mutually approved. The concluding fifth paragraph of the memorandum reiterated the core ideals underpinning their covenant: 'Given our pessimistic assessment of the *extérieur*, we consider it entirely possible that the trip [to Germany] will not be a success. We resolve even now not to consider this a failure and instead to seize on it in order to begin the planned new life in L.A. with even greater conviviality and fortitude.'[54]

One can only assume that Pollock hoped Horkheimer's visiting professorship in Frankfurt would not be a success. If it was, remaining in the United States would no longer be an option. The outcome is well known, of course. Horkheimer was a big success not only in Frankfurt but also at the other universities where he gave one-off lectures, and Pollock was forced, against his own better judgement, to return to the land of the perpetrators. In January 1950, he gave his friend carte blanche 'to determine the length of his stay, the date of Teddie's return, the question of whether Maidon, Gretel, Fred and Carlota should

---

53   Friedrich Pollock, 'Eindrücke aus Frankreich und Deutschland. Frankfurt vom 19.5.1949 bis 17.6.1949', Fondo Friedrich Pollock, Università degli Studi di Firenze, 2.1.3, doc. 1, pp. 8–9. The Börsenkeller was a prominent public house and function room frequently used by political and professional associations for annual meetings etc.

54   Friedrich Pollock and Max Horkheimer, 'Memorandum', 30 April 1949, in Horkheimer 1996b, pp. 28–9, p. 29.

travel to Frankfurt this spring, based on his evaluation of his new experiences.'⁵⁵ They still needed to agree formally on whether to return to, and stay in, Germany permanently, but the decision had to all intents and purposes been taken. Pollock now suggested that he was 'neither for nor against Germany'. Above all, he wanted the spatial separation between them to come to an end. After months, indeed years of tortuous anguish he let Horkheimer have his way.⁵⁶

---

55 Friedrich Pollock and Max Horkheimer, 'Memorandum', 9 January 1950, in Horkheimer 1996b, pp. 90–1, p. 91.
56 Friedrich Pollock to Max Horkheimer, 9 February 1950, in Horkheimer 1996b, pp. 109–10, p. 109.

CHAPTER 12

New Old Germany

Utterly inconceivable as it had seemed to him only a short while ago, once he realised he could no longer avoid returning to Germany, Pollock began to feel more pessimistic about his planned life in Los Angeles. Whether this was merely a rationalisation in light of his having been unable to persuade Horkheimer otherwise or genuinely reflected his assessment of the changing political situation, as he claimed, is a moot point. Either way, by the summer of 1950, Pollock's enthusiasm for California had largely dissipated. On 25 June, the Korea War he had anticipated for some time became a reality. Given that it was a proxy war in which the United States were heavily implicated, he feared that the West Coast might be affected by the hostilities. As he wrote to Horkheimer in Frankfurt, 'It seems to me that Korea means that America will develop into a veritable preparedness economy and that the atmosphere in the most exposed locations – and Los Angeles incl. Santa Monica (Douglas Aircraft) is definitely one of them – will become hard to bear.'[1] Consequently, he suggested retreating to a city further inland and proposed Boulder (Colorado).

Horkheimer rejected this proposal, explaining that he would rather spend two years in Germany and then return to California. Pollock, who assumed that another world war – which would obviously devastate Germany too – was on the cards, considered this too risky and took precautionary measures 'for the not entirely inconceivable case ... that we (i.e., you and I and our wives) have to flee Los Angeles'. As he wrote on 28 July 1950, he did not believe that

> the threat of a world war has passed for the time being; in fact, it may have increased. As soon as there is an indication that L.A. or other large cities might be attacked from the air, a mass exodus will begin. It will then be very difficult to find a suitable refuge further inland unless one has prepared in advance. To avoid having to tell myself later that I acted negligently I have joined a group of Jewish-German businessmen and professionals who intend to buy a motel with 20 units in one of the mountain states. Each member of the group will own one unit and have the right to move in whenever they want .... I have signed up for one unit each for you [i.e., Horkheimer and his wife] and us [i.e., Pollock and his wife].[2]

---

1 Friedrich Pollock to Max Horkheimer, 17 July 1950, in Horkheimer 1996b, pp. 153–6, p. 154.
2 Friedrich Pollock to Max Horkheimer, 17 July 1950, in Horkheimer 1996b, pp. 167–8, p. 167.

From today's vantage, Pollock's concerns may seem paranoid. Yet in the turbulent immediate post-war years it was indeed hard to foresee what lay ahead. More importantly perhaps, it needs to be borne in mind that Pollock had experienced once before how a threat all too readily dismissed by many one day had become a matter of life and death the next. This was not an experience he would ever forget.

In September 1950, having prepared for the worst, Pollock too made his way to Frankfurt, still on the assumption that his sojourn in the city might be merely temporary. He had a good sense of what awaited him in Germany, both from his earlier trip and from the restitution negotiations he and Horkheimer had begun the year before. As far as the house in Kronberg, which was technically owned by Maidon, was concerned, they were forced to settle, not least since the new owners were in no position to offer any meaningful compensation. The case concerning compensation for the suitcase factory that had been forcibly auctioned off was still pending. The proceedings were protracted and throw a telling light on the cynicism and malice of the supposedly reformed beneficiaries of the Nazi regime.

Prima facie, the case was straightforward enough. Julius and Hans Pollock owned 97 per cent of the shares in Nördlinger & Pollock. During the Great Depression, the enterprise got into trouble and was forced to take out loans in 1932 and 1934, respectively. As its losses increased, it was no longer able to service the loans, the bank foreclosed and the property and factory building were auctioned off in August 1935. Thus, the Württembergische Landessparkasse (State Savings Bank of Württemberg) was able to acquire the property as well as the machines and other inventory perfectly legally for 150,000 Reichsmarks. The following year, the bank sold the assets on to the municipality of Stuttgart for 205,000 RM, making a handsome profit.[3] To make things worse, in 1941, a court in Amsterdam, where Hans Pollock had sought refuge, insisted that he was required to repay an additional 150,000 RM.

Yet 'the Nazi directors of the Landessparkasse' had in fact 'intentionally brought about' the financial difficulties of the enterprise.[4] Hans Pollock was only forced to sign up to the second loan of 1934 with its extremely unfavourable terms because

---

3 See Jewish Restitution Successor Organization to Amtsgericht (Magistrates' Court) Stuttgart, 8 December 1950. State Archive Ludwigsburg, FL 300/33 I Bü 19516, doc. 7/8. For further details, see Huber 2019, pp. 66–74.
4 Friedrich Pollock to Juan Pollock, 5 July 1949, Horkheimer Archive, University Library Frankfurt/Main, MHA XXIII 22, 176–7; Landgericht (District Court) Stuttgart, Wiedergutmachungskammer, 12 June 1951, State Archive Ludwigsburg, FL 300/33 I Bü 1958, doc. 9.

one evening at dinner time, three gentlemen from the L[andes-] Sp[arkasse] [turned up], one name Stutzmann or something like that, one in ss uniform, the other in brownshirt, and demanded that I hand over all relevant N & P documentation and the share certificates I kept in my cabinet. I handed over the documents and share certificates but was refused a receipt. The next day, the papers were returned but neither the share certificates nor, despite my complaint, a receipt; this was rejected on the grounds that they were merely being held in trust for me.[5]

The share certificates were never returned, the bank had simply stolen them.

Yet the bank flatly denied this and turned the tables on the Pollock brothers, tormenting them with constant demands that they pay 150,000 DM to cover the loan. Juan Pollock was literally penniless when he arrived in Argentina. With a lot of hard work he was able to establish a small workshop in which he and a limited number of staff once again produced suitcases. The fact that the bank, far from refusing to acknowledge the injustice he had suffered, instead sought to harm and humiliate him yet further, affected Juan Pollock badly, and the fear of once more losing everything struck terror in his heart. The older brother vowed to undertake everything within his power to ensure that 'the gentlemen in Stuttgart do not endanger the existence you have so arduously created for yourself in Buenos Aires'.[6] Friedrich Pollock himself had already lost all hope that he might ever be compensated, rightly so, as it turned out. He never received a penny of his late father's considerable fortune.

In the end, the case of the family business was also settled. The Landessparkasse and the municipality relinquished their ridiculous claims and, in turn, the Pollock brothers and the Jewish Restitution Successor Organization (acting on behalf of the Nördlingers who had still owned the three per cent of shares in the company not held by the Pollocks) agreed not to pursue the restitution case any further.[7] Juan Pollock's dogged pursuit of compensation for the curtailment of his professional development and lost earnings eventually led to a belated success of sorts. In 1960, he was awarded 'a monthly pension of 600 Deutschmarks for the period from 1 November 1953 to 31 March 1959 and of DM 630 from

---

5 Friedrich Pollock to Juan Pollock, 23 January 1950, Horkheimer Archive, University Library Frankfurt/Main, MHA XXIII 22, 155.

6 Friedrich Pollock to Juan Pollock, 5 July 1949, Horkheimer Archive, University Library Frankfurt/Main, MHA XXIII 22, 176–7.

7 Public Session of the Wiedergutmachungskammer I–II in Stuttgart, 23 April 1953, State Archive Ludwigsburg, FL 300/33 I Bü 19516, doc. 12/13.

1 April 1959 for life as well as a compensation payment of DM 7200'.[8] In 1965 – 20 years after the war had ended! – the Internal Restitution Authority awarded him DM 7,640,51 as compensation for his expropriated private assets.[9]

It was clear to Pollock from his attempts to seek restitution that the Germans were unwilling to bear any responsibility for what had transpired between 1933 and 1945 and that they were determined, even after 1945, to cover up their own crimes and everyone else's complicity. Nor was there any sign of contrition. The *Volksgemeinschaft*, in short, was no spectre of the past but continued to function in a barely concealed form. Many of the shiny new democrats who claimed to have maintained their dignity throughout had been complicit in, or at the very least benefitted from, the National Socialist regime of terror, war and genocide. This insight only intensified Pollock's sense of solidarity with those who had been persecuted by the regime and those who had tried to help them. When relatives or friends reported that individuals who had helped them were now in dire straits, he promptly arranged for them to receive care packages or small amounts of money.

The reconstruction of German democracy did not have the same priority for Pollock as it did for Horkheimer and Adorno. He understood the need for re-education, of course, but he also felt that after the many years of valiant hard work, they had well and truly earned the right to take a step back and live their lives as they saw fit. Yet nothing could have been further from Horkheimer and Adorno's mind. They were busier than ever as they paved the way for the official inauguration of the re-established institute on 14 November 1951.

Although Adorno, who also returned in 1949, was now the deputy director, Pollock continued to function as the institute's *éminence grise*. Jürgen Habermas, who joined the institute as a research fellow in 1956, recalls Pollock often standing behind Horkheimer's chair in meetings in a way that some students found intimidating.[10] It was undoubtedly Horkheimer and Adorno who were decisive in shaping the intellectual profile of what now increasingly came to be known as the Frankfurt School but in the initial years following the institute's re-establishment, Pollock also maintained a considerable presence. Few knew what exactly his role or biographical background were, but it was palpable that there was a special bond between him and Horkheimer that set him apart from the other members of the institute. As Monika Plessner, who joined

---

8   RA Dr. Sturm (solicitor) to Juan Pollock, 2 August 1960, Horkheimer Archive, University Library Frankfurt/Main, MHA XXIII 22, 105.
9   Oberfinanzdirektion (State Finance Directorate) to Verwaltungsamt für Innere Restitution, Munich branch, 5 October 1965, State Archive Ludwigsburg, FL 300/33 I Bü 9846.
10 Conversation in Munich on 24 June 2017.

the institute in September 1952, later recalled, it was Pollock, 'Horkheimer's oldest friend and the only one he addressed with Du', who welcomed her.

> As an economist and financial expert, he was his majordomo. A man of athletic build with large hands, everything about his demeanour marked him out as the born guardian. Bouncy and noiseless in his crepe-soled shoes (all the rage at the time), he guided me through the building.[11]

In the summer semester of 1951, Pollock took up his position as professorial fellow again and began to lecture on 'Modern Economy and Society: Structural Transformations' (summer semester 1951) and the 'Theory and Practice of the Planned Economy' (winter semester 1951/52).[12] In the summer semester of 1952, he was appointed to a personal chair and lectured on 'Problems of the Planned Economy'.[13] Drawing on his familiarity with cutting-edge research in the United States, he also offered tutorials in research methods for beginners (summer semester 1952) and advanced students of the social sciences (summer semester 1953), respectively.[14] In the winter semesters of 1952/53 and 1953/54 and the summer semester of 1954, he was granted leave to take care of the institute's affairs in the United States, allowing him to accompany Horkheimer during his tenure as visiting professor in Chicago. Even so, there was no suggestion that they would be returning to the USA permanently any time soon. Both Pollock and Horkheimer went to considerable lengths, however, not to lose their US citizenship.

The research method tutorials were the fruit of discussions within the institute regarding its first empirical research project now it was back in Frankfurt, a study of German public opinion commissioned and funded by the US High Commissioner for Germany, John McCloy. Pollock and Adorno took the lead on this project. Officially, Adorno acted as the principal investigator, but it was Pollock who was responsible for the publication of the results. Following the years spent in the United States and the major empirical studies undertaken there, Pollock and his colleagues were well versed in the respective advantages and

---

11   Plessner 1995, p. 61.
12   *Personen- und Vorlesungsverzeichnis der Johann Wolfgang Goethe-Universität Frankfurt am Main, Sommersemester 1951*, p. 62; *Personen- und Vorlesungsverzeichnis der Johann Wolfgang Goethe-Universität Frankfurt am Main, Wintersemester 1951/1952*, p. 64.
13   *Personen- und Vorlesungsverzeichnis der Johann Wolfgang Goethe-Universität Frankfurt am Main, Sommersemester 1952*, pp. 26, 67.
14   *Personen- und Vorlesungsverzeichnis der Johann Wolfgang Goethe-Universität Frankfurt am Main, Sommersemester 1952*, p. 67; *Personen- und Vorlesungsverzeichnis der Johann Wolfgang Goethe-Universität Frankfurt am Main, Sommersemester 1953*, p. 73.

drawbacks of relevant research methodologies, yet Adorno and Pollock were still not entirely satisfied with the methods they had previously developed and deployed. Principally, the question of how one might best extrapolate robust generalisations from individuals' responses continued to vex them, not least, given that they were uneasy about the extent to which questionnaires and individual interviews genuinely reflected the full spectrum of opinions anyway. Psychological mechanisms such as repression, resistance and projection were hard to pin down by empirical means and could be identified only by means of qualitative evaluation. This, in turn, raised complex hermeneutical questions transcending the material itself. It was as though an insurmountable chasm separated the theoretical work from the material, threatening to invalidate both.

Its own pioneering work in this field notwithstanding, the institute's members never abandoned a healthy degree of scepticism regarding the ultimate reach of empirical research of this kind. This had nothing to do with some brand of metaphysically motivated anti-positivism. As Adorno expressly acknowledged in his essay, 'Scientific Experiences of a European Scholar in America', they learnt a great deal from their cooperation with social scientists in the United States.[15] Insofar as Critical Theory was fundamentally predicated on experience, it was dependent on empirical data, yet the data first needed to be deciphered. It was at this juncture that the critique of positivism and its assumption that data spoke for themselves came into play. In order to make sense of empirical data one not only needed to reflect constantly on one's methodology but also depended on extra-empirical stimuli. One needed a concept of society and its workings and a theory of the life of the soul capable of affording some insight into the functioning of the individuals who form society. One needed to be armed with theories both of the political and of the economy of the soul to read empirical data properly.[16] One needed a command, drawing on Marx and Freud, of the mechanisms, laws and dynamics governing individuals from within and without if one wanted genuinely to comprehend what they articulated.

When it came to gauging German public opinion so soon after the end of the war, an additional problem arose. How might one take account of the impact of National Socialism and the ways in which it had deformed individuals in their social and psychological makeup? Given individuals' intimate entanglement in the Volksgemeinschaft that was now setting itself in scene as a collective vic-

15   Adorno 1969.
16   I have adopted the term economy of the soul from Krug 2016, p. 45.

tim of fate, Adorno and Pollock decided that it made little sense for the study to home in on the isolated individual. It was little more than a hypothetical construct in this context. Consequently, they sought to focus on individuals in familiar group situations in which they would feel sufficiently secure to express their true sentiments. To be sure, this brought with it its own pitfalls, given that individuals might be swayed by peer group pressure, yet to Pollock and Adorno this seemed, on balance, a price worth paying, given that they saw no other way of gaining a genuine sense of German popular opinion.

In the winter of 1950/51, 151 groups comprising an average of fourteen members each, were convened.[17] In total, 1,635 individuals were questioned. The members of each group either knew each other already or belonged to the same social group (farmers, unemployed, refugees etc.) It was hoped that this would enhance a climate of trust. To the same end, the groups were convened in locations with which they were already familiar. The meetings began with a tape recording of a fictitious letter supposedly written by a US or British officer called Colburn or Colburne, read with an English or American accent, depending on the origin of the occupation forces in the location in question, and presented to participants as being authentic. The letter discussed various issues including the persecution of the Jews, German guilt, the Allied victory and democracy. It frequently precipitated, without any further intervention, animated and occasionally emotional discussions among the participants. Only in a second phase did the researchers themselves intervene, reiterating and rigorously defending the claims laid out in the document. There was nothing particularly provocative about the letter, it merely reflected what many UK and US officers presumably did think:

> I can say many good things about the Germans. They are hardworking and only rarely insubordinate. They are clean and orderly, and many give the impression of being intelligent. Of course, I do not know to what extent they are independent or just repeat what they have heard elsewhere. I do not find any indication of unusual crudeness and cruelty, but nor are there many indications that they have taken to heart what was done to people under Hitler. ... Despite the past calamity, many think of themselves as better and more capable than us. They do not want to hear anything of the fact that Hitler started it. ... They are still hostile toward the Jews and use the DPs in particular as a pretense for one-sided judgments. Only very few openly admit that they were Nazis, and those admitting it are often

---

17   For the following, see Walter-Busch 2010, pp. 134–7.

not the worst ones. ... The risk is that, tomorrow, they will again follow a Hitler or Stalin, and will still believe that such a strong man will represent their interests best.[18]

When all the minutes of the group discussions had been gathered up – the typescript ran to 6,000 pages – and evaluated, the findings essentially bore out the claims of the fictitious letter. Pollock edited and wrote the introduction to the report. *Gruppenexperiment* (Group Experiment) was published in 1955 as the second volume in the institute's new publication series, *Frankfurter Beiträge zur Soziologie* (Frankfurt Contributions to Sociology). Both in methodology and content, the study was a milestone in the development of the social sciences in Germany. For the first time, the illusion of a democratic consensus in the early Federal Republic (West Germany) was punctured with empirical means. By distinguishing between public and private popular opinion, it demonstrated that the authoritarian personality type idealised by the Nazis continued to impact democracy. The Germans were nowhere near as reformed as they claimed, the study concluded.

None too surprisingly, this conclusion met with considerable opposition. In 1957, the *Kölner Zeitschrift für Soziologie und Sozialpsychologie* (*Cologne Journal of Sociology and Social Psychology*) published a 'critical appraisal' by Peter Hofstätter. Established in 1948 by René König, himself a former émigré, this was arguably the most significant sociological periodical in the early Federal Republic. Hofstätter was an Austrian military psychologist who had just assumed a chair in political psychology at the Social Science Academy in Wilhelmshaven. A member of the Nazi party, he served in the war ministry from 1937 to 1942 and the justice ministry from 1943 until the end of the war. His criticism of Pollock and his colleagues was, by any conventional standard, extraordinarily brutal. Intent on proving that the Germans were still Nazis, they had pre-programmed the outcome by using the fictitious letter. By expecting participants to 'shoulder the horrors of Auschwitz', Pollock and his colleagues had knowingly demanded the impossible. The study's findings needed to be turned from their head onto their feet. It was the former Jewish émigrés who were prejudiced against the Germans and therefore manipulated their communication with them in a manner that backed them into a corner. This was not scholarship, it was, for the most part, 'simply an exercise in excoriation'.[19] One can well imagine the unease of the former Nazi now masquerading as a

---

18 Pollock, Adorno et al. 2011, pp. 177–8.
19 Hofstätter 2010, p. 195 (translation amended).

democrat at a study that 'essentially seeks to unmask'.[20] For Hofstätter, then, as Wolfgang Bock has put it, the *Gruppenexperiment* 'was indeed a study in prejudice – albeit in the prejudice of its authors'.[21]

It fell to Adorno to write a rejoinder for the same issue of the *Kölner Zeitschrift für Soziologie und Sozialpsychologie*. Adapting a Heine quotation, he wrote that 'one should not speak of the noose in the house of the hangman, lest one be suspected of resentment'. The Germans were really in no position to reprimand those who reminded them of their crimes. The 'horrors of Auschwitz', Adorno pointed out, had already been 'shouldered', namely by the victims, not 'by those who, to their own detriment and that of their country, do not want to face up to the truth.'[22]

The findings of the group experiment, criticism such as that articulated by Hofstätter and, not least, the failed restitution cases convinced Pollock that he was not going to devote his remaining years to Germany's democratic reconstruction. He made no effort to regain his German citizenship and constantly wanted to know from Horkheimer when they would finally be able to leave. His priority was still the creation of a solid basis for the realisation of his covenant with Horkheimer. Global political developments were one crucial factor; where they would best be able to work undisturbed was another. Working, in this context, always meant: making a contribution to the merging of theory and practice to which their covenant aspired. From this vantage, the institute in Frankfurt did more to prevent than foster their work. It was a burden that made the implementation of the covenant's goals more difficult. A memorandum of September 1951 reiterated their commitment to the creation of a micro utopia in which 'the laws of society shall not apply'.[23] Theirs was still a very practical utopian commitment.

Adorno's collection of aphorisms, *Minima Moralia*, which was published in the same year, might in part be understood as a critique of the ideas underpinning Horkheimer and Pollock's covenant. The sixth aphorism in particular, 'Antithesis', would seem to disavow their vision of dispensing with the laws of society on the micro level. 'The nonconformist', Adorno wrote, 'runs the risk

---

20 Hofstätter 2010, p. 194 (translation amended).
21 Bock 2018, p. 438.
22 Adorno 2010, p. 208 (translation amended). Adorno's famous formulation inverted Heinrich Heine's earlier objection, in his polemic against Ludwig Börne, that, '"In the house of the hanged ... one does not talk about ropes"'. It was directed at Börne's polemic against baptized but, to his mind, insufficiently acculturated Jews. The implication was that, despite being baptized, Börne too continued to bear Jewish traits (Heine 2006, p. 22).
23 Friedrich Pollock and Max Horkheimer, 'Memorandum', 8 September 1951, in Horkheimer 1996b, pp. 218–20, p. 218.

of assuming he is better than the others and abusing his critique of society as an ideology to serve his own private interests. While groping to turn his own existence into a flimsy image of true existence, he should bear this flimsiness in mind and know what a poor substitute the image is for true life.'[24]

In its radical negativity, Adorno's aforementioned infamous contention that 'Wrong life cannot be lived in the right way',[25] is central to Critical Theory. Yet understood as an ideological statement it turns apologetic. If one interprets it to mean that nothing can be done to combat existing injustices because the untrue is all-pervasive, it would follow that it did not matter what one did. Adorno's negativity needs to be understood as an expression of polemical hyperbole designed to provoke a response. His concept of society only *seems* to collapse into seamless immanence. Inspired by Benjamin's Messianism, Adorno believed that humankind could step out of this immanence at any point and create a truly human society. Yet reliance on this Messianic potential became counterproductive and harmful when utopian concepts of a better society were elaborated upon and openly propagated. Since human beings were always beholden to the existing order, their positive utopian concepts were invariably at risk of simply extending the very order they sought to transcend into the future and thus betraying the actual, concealed but constantly present utopian potential.[26]

This line of thought was very close to Horkheimer's interpretation of the prohibition of the image which, for him, rooted Critical Theory in Judaism. Yet he never applied his version of the ban on elaborated utopian visions to his own utopian covenant with Pollock. For him, Critical Theory and the utopian inflection of their covenant, *intérieur* and *extérieur*, seem to have coexisted without destabilising each other or, rather, the *intérieur* was supposed to create the preconditions for a future utopian transformation of the *extérieur* too. Yet this was a secret that must not be revealed. Consequently, the hope for reconciliation was ultimately rooted in faith in the good. This was the motivation inherent in the theoretical considerations that motivated Horkheimer's post-war turn to theology and Judaism. In addition, he felt compelled by the experience of being persecuted as a Jew to avow his Jewishness – especially in the land of the perpetrators.[27]

Pollock's thought did not acknowledge any such religious vanishing point. Still an 'Israelite' as a student, Pollock's personnel file in Frankfurt identified

---

24   Adorno 2005, p. 26 (translation amended).
25   Adorno 2005, p. 39 (translation amended).
26   See Adorno 1967; Machunsky 2014.
27   Boll 2013, esp. pp. 358–61.

him as a 'dissident' (the pre-1945 term for those not affiliated with any of the recognised religious denominations).[28] As far as he was concerned, people would lead better lives and be happier if the state systematically catered for their basic needs. The constant fear of losing one's existence and the unrelenting pressure to compete would dissipate and the ideals he and Horkheimer had to go to such lengths to realise for their *intérieur* would automatically come to govern the *extérieur* as well. In this sense, Pollock was more political than Horkheimer. Yet he was also criticised for this stance. In the aforementioned memorandum of September 1951, Horkheimer suggested that Pollock's anti-transcendental political rationalism betrayed a lack of imagination and a form of conformism that inclined him to 'take the position of the world when push comes to shove'. These traits reflected an obsessional neurosis whose impact could be neutralised only if Pollock learnt systematically to 'distrust his own instincts and judgements'.[29]

Pollock's disaffection with his current circumstances seems to have reached some sort of crisis point in the spring of 1954. This is indicated by the memorandum of 30 April in which he and Horkheimer set themselves a deadline of early August finally to stop 'muddling through' and make definitive arrangements guaranteeing 'optimal opportunities for work, political and financial security and agreeable living conditions'. The memorandum outlined three options: firstly, they could return to the United States; secondly, both of them could move to a location in Switzerland or France, in which case Horkheimer would apply for German citizenship while Pollock maintained his US citizenship for the time being; thirdly, they could stay in Germany, in which case they might either both become German citizens or Pollock might try to attain Austrian or Liechtensteinian citizenship and Horkheimer would try to keep his US passport.[30]

In the event, they failed to meet their own August deadline, but they did come to a decision in October 1954. During a stay in the posh spa resort of Baden-Baden they again discussed the issue at great length and eventually agreed that they would move to Switzerland. They would seek full retirement or an early release from their duties and both become German citizens.[31] Finally,

---

28   'Pollock, Friedrich', in Heuer and Wolf (eds.) 1997, pp. 291–4, p. 291.
29   Friedrich Pollock and Max Horkheimer, 'Memorandum', 8 September 1951, in Horkheimer 1996b, pp. 218–20, p. 219.
30   Friedrich Pollock and Max Horkheimer, 'Memorandum', 30 April 1954, in Horkheimer 1996b, pp. 266–7, p. 267.
31   Friedrich Pollock and Max Horkheimer, 'Memorandum', 30 October 1954, in Horkheimer 1996b, pp. 282–3, p. 283.

Pollock would be able to share his life with Horkheimer in a secluded location in the way he had envisaged for so long. He immediately started searching for the perfect location.

Not that this definitively resolved the issue. The option of returning to the United States continued to feature in their thoughts as a serious alternative for the remainder of their days. In 1952, Horkheimer's name was tacked on to a private bill initially submitted to help Werner Richter who had returned to Germany and become vice chancellor of the university in Marburg and was therefore in a similar position. The two men were granted the right to keep their US citizenship, provided they returned to the country permanently within two years (i.e., by 1954).[32] Following confirmation from the State Department that he indeed needed to meet this requirement,[33] Horkheimer took up a visiting professorship at the University of Chicago in 1954, which he held until 1959. In 1955, a private bill designed to lift this stipulation for Horkheimer and his wife was referred to the Committee of the Judiciary but died there, (officially) due to lack of time. Horkheimer continued to return to the United States every two years until Schneider *v.* Rusk, 377 U.S. 163 (1964) finally removed the requirement to reside in the United States for all naturalised citizens.[34]

In 1957, Pollock and Horkheimer finally moved to Montagnola in Ticino. Now in their sixties, it was here that they had decided to spend the rest of their lives (world politics permitting). They had spent sixteen years in the United States, followed by seven years in Frankfurt that were repeatedly interrupted by often lengthy stays abroad. Pollock then spent his final thirteen, Horkheimer his remaining sixteen years in Montagnola. In this light, the commonplace that Pollock and Horkheimer returned to Germany after the war seems rather questionable.

---

[32] 'An Act for the Relief of Professor Werner Richter and Professor Max Horkheimer', Private Law 1023 – July 18, 1952, https://www.congress.gov/82/statute/STATUTE-66/STATUTE-66-PgA213.pdf.

[33] See Adorno and Horkheimer 2006, p. 69.

[34] Schneider *v.* Rusk, https://tile.loc.gov/storage-services/service/ll/usrep/usrep377/usrep377163/usrep377163.pdf.

CHAPTER 13

Automation

In times of war, needs must, and during the Second World War enormous funds flooded into numerous, often long-standing research and development projects that promised, if channelled appropriately, to be of immediate benefit to the war effort. A frequently cited case in point is the Electronic Numerical Integrator and Computer, ENIAC, developed under the auspices of J. Presper Eckert Jr. and John W. Mauchly to help with the calculation of ballistic trajectories. Completed in the final year of the war, it was, for a decade, the only fully electronic computer in use in the USA and provided an important platform for the development of programming.[1]

This, in turn, paved the way for the utilisation of computers in industrial production processes. They allowed for increased batch quantities to be produced using significantly less and less skilled labour and made administrative services simpler and more efficient. Conversely, engineers and other technical staff were all the more hotly sought-after. It was not long before the term automation made the rounds, denoting the creation of closed production systems in which human labour potentially became superfluous. Ultimately, it was envisaged, only a small number of technicians and supervisors would be required to run and oversee the computers and robots.

A veritable second industrial revolution seemed to be unfolding, raising numerous issues first debated in the United States where it had progressed the furthest. From there, the debate spread to Europe. In June 1955, a conference with the title, *The Automatic Factory: What Does it Mean?*, organised by the Institution of Production Engineers (GB), took place in Margate.[2] At the same time, the German trade union movement became increasingly concerned about the impact of automation.[3] John F. Kennedy's Manpower Development and Training Act of 1962, providing millions for the retraining of skilled workers rendered redundant by automation, clearly indicated that the massive structural impact of automation was now universally acknowledged.

Needless to say, Pollock, as the institute's economist – and prognostician – was highly alert to these far-reaching developments. His contribution to the

---

1 See Haigh, Priestley and Rope 2016.
2 *The Automatic Factory: What Does it Mean? Report of the Conference Held at Margate, 16–19 June 1955* (London: Institution of Production Engineers, 1955).
3 See, for example, Matthöfer et al. 1956.

first volume of the institute's new publication series, a Festschrift to mark Horkheimer's sixtieth birthday, was an 80-page essay on 'Automation in USA: Betrachtungen zur "zweiten industriellen Revolution"' (Automation in the USA: Reflections on the 'Second Industrial Revolution'). Pollock distinguished between 'Automatisierung' (the regular German term for automation) and 'Automation'. The former encompassed the individual automation measures, the latter the outcome of the process overall. For Pollock, automation in this comprehensive sense amounted to a new mode of production in which human labour became, potentially at least, entirely redundant. 'In the operation, direction and supervision of machines, "automation" as a production technique seeks to replace human labour by machines to such an extent that not a single human hand touches the product in the course of the entire production process.'[4]

While the subject had previously been treated in entrepreneurial and engineering periodicals and, as Pollock expressly acknowledged, in science fiction literature, his was the first substantive scholarly analysis of automation published in German. At the time, one of the few points of reference, in terms of a sociological analysis of automation, was the extraordinarily prescient *Problémes humains du machinisme industriel* by Georges Friedmann, a former assistant of the institute's Paris branch. First published in 1946, an English translation, *Industrial Society: The Emergence of Human Problems of Automation* came out in 1955.[5] Pollock published his scholarly magnum opus, *Automation. Materialien zur Beurteilung der ökonomischen und sozialen Folgen* (Automation. A Study of its Economic and Social Consequences) with the Europäische Verlagsanstalt the following year.[6]

It became his greatest success. Never before had he encountered anything close to the level of attention he now drew, both public and academic. He suddenly received endless invitations from conference organisers, gave television interviews and was consulted by trade unions interested in his assessment of economic developments. A comprehensively updated edition of the book, adding a further 100 pages, was published in 1964 and re-issued again in 1966. These two editions ran to 14,000 copies in total. Additional editions were brought out by the Büchergilde Gutenberg and other trade union licensees.[7] The book was translated into Italian (1956), English (1957), French (1957), Dutch (1957), Spanish (1959) and Japanese (1959), and it featured prominently in Ger-

---

4 Pollock 1955, p. 80.
5 Friedmann 1955.
6 Pollock 1957.
7 I am grateful to Johannes Platz for this information.

man publications of record such as *Der Spiegel* and the *Frankfurter Allgemeine Zeitung*. In 1964, a special issue of *Der Spiegel* on the topic called Pollock 'Germany's leading scholar of automation'. It quoted him as insisting, against the proponents of the social market economy, 'that, for Europe, at least preparing for a planned economy is a matter of life and death'.[8]

Pollock also contributed to a widely discussed volume for a general readership, *Revolution der Roboter* (*Revolution of the Robots*).[9] The volume drew on a lecture series organised by the Circle of Social Democratic Academics in Munich, sometimes described by observers as a German version of the Fabian Society. Alongside Pollock, the authors included Fritz Erler, a close associate of Willy Brandt, and Alfred Weber. In his review of the book, published in the intellectually aspirational weekly, *Die Zeit*, Hans Gresmann paid particular (critical) attention to Pollock's contribution: 'In a fascinating contribution, the economist *Friedrich Pollock*, one of the few authorities on automation, seeks to demonstrate with scientific means that automation, if left to the caprice and whim of individual entrepreneurs, would inevitably lead to technological unemployment.'[10]

Pollock was indeed convinced that automation would render millions of workers redundant. To be sure, he acknowledged that the impact of the 'electronic brains' was not all bad, it was 'freeing the assembly-line worker from the soul-destroying drudgery of the conveyor-belt', yet it also led to 'an ever-increasing number of other workers ... drifting into equally dull and monotonous jobs'.[11] The crucial point, then, was not to let automation simply take its course but to find political solutions for the problems it inevitably entailed. At this juncture, Pollock's decades-old predilection for the planned economy came into play once again. Whether in its socialist or democratic variant, Pollock remained convinced that only a planned economy offered a solution to humankind's problems. It is this conviction that marks the fundamental constant across all of Pollock's scholarly and political works. As he wrote in *Automation*: 'The object of economic planning must be to integrate automation with a free and democratic society. Success in such planning would mean that the second industrial revolution could help to establish a social system based upon reason.'[12] Failing this, the world faced the consequences the founding

---

8   'Automation. Einzug der Roboter', *Der Spiegel*, 18.14, 31 March 1964, pp. 30–48, pp. 46, 48.
9   Pollock 1956. See Platz 2009.
10 Hans Gresmann, 'Revolution durch Roboter? Probleme, Prognosen, Programme – die Automatisierung erregt die Geister', *Die Zeit*, 19 July 1956.
11 Pollock 1957, pp. 26, 91.
12 Pollock 1957, p. 253 (translation amended).

father of cybernetics, Norbert Wiener, had presciently outlined: mass unemployment, the demise of numerous skills and professions and a massive economic crisis that, on Pollock's account, might well dwarf the Great Depression of the 1930s. Pollock's readership knew only too well what this meant: a renewed catastrophic economic crisis might very well spell the return of fascism.

Presenting his path-breaking monograph, *Cybernetics or Control and Communication in the Animal and the Machine*, to 'the world of Belsen and Hiroshima' in 1948, Norbert Wiener – whose father was a Jewish immigrant from Białystok of notable rabbinic lineage – expressed grave concerns that the new methods might be harnessed to serve tyrannical ends.[13] Pollock shared these misgivings. 'It may be worth at this point', he wrote,

> to draw attention once more to the risks involved in letting automation simply run its course, regardless of its social consequences, wherever private economic profit beckons because one fails to recognise the limits of the market economy's capacity for self-regulation. With an obliviousness akin to that of the sorcerer's apprentice those who do so might set in motion forces that no benign sorcerer will stop in time: the social upheaval that might be precipitated by an overly hasty introduction of automation would pave the way for a tyranny armed with unprecedented resources.[14]

Should computers be equipped with the ability to anticipate human conduct or calculate psychological response patterns, this would place totalitarian states on a whole new footing in terms of the techniques at their disposal when it came to the central task of 'moulding public opinion'.[15] For Pollock, what many considered the unprecedented manipulation of voters in the US presidential election of 2016 by Russian hackers would have been old hat. As he noted in the second, updated edition of 1964, the Democrats deployed high-powered computers in the 1960 presidential campaign to gauge potential voters' responses to various factors. This ability to make reliable predictions turned computers into a means of subjugation and the resulting transformation of voters into transparent consumers of political propaganda posed a substantial threat to democracy.[16] If the manipulation of the masses had progressed this far in the

---

13   Wiener 1948, p. 38.
14   Pollock 1957, p. 248 (translation amended).
15   Ibid.
16   Pollock 1964.

United States, where democracy was firmly established, Pollock dreaded to think what havoc it might wreak in countries with less stable democracies or none. He therefore took it upon himself to help avert this renewed totalitarian threat by alerting the world to it as best he could.

Far from sharing the enthusiasm of the US entrepreneur John Diebold, who is credited with coining the term automation, Pollock feared the emergence of a dictatorship of the experts. Drawing on Huxley once more, Pollock outlined what can only be described as a dystopian account of the automated society. 'At the top of the social pyramid we will find an *economic general staff* as the true master of both machines and men', he wrote.

> Only this relatively small group, together with its 'officer corps', will be able fully to grasp technical and economic processes and make economic policy decisions. ... Since everything seems to become calculable, such an elite engages in manipulation as a matter of course. It is likely to view the masses, who are undiscerning, easily swayed by the means of modern propaganda and assuaged by access to the swelling flow of consumer goods, with considerable contempt. The role of the *officer corps* in the army would be played in this society by the engineers, administrators, research staff and technicians versed in the handling of human beings. Right down to the officers' underlings, the members of this group need to own considerable specialist skills and be able to think for themselves.[17]

Yet the 'constructive imagination' of these officers too would be needed only until 'the machines construct new machines under their own steam'.[18] What Pollock was describing was the administered world he and his colleagues had begun to identify in their discussions of Huxley in the 1940s and whose conceptualisation featured in Adorno's *Negative Dialektik* (*Negative Dialectics*) and crucially shaped the New Left's reception of Adorno.[19]

It principally fell to Pollock to provide the underpinning in the realm of economic theory for Adorno's cultural philosophy and thus tie the works of the post-war era back to those of the 1940s. In this context, Pollock and Horkheimer now adjusted the racket theory to apply it to the domination of the experts.[20] The concept of the administered world entailed the assumption that closed groups of experts also monopolised access to social wealth. Unlike that of the

---

17 Pollock 1957, pp. 83–4 (translation amended).
18 Horkheimer and Pollock 1988a.
19 See Heerich 2007.
20 See, e.g., Horkheimer and Pollock 1988b.

fascists, their power was based not on brute force but on privileged knowledge that also found expression in their reliance on technical jargon. Only the initiated were able to join the elite.

In this respect too, Pollock looked to the United States where he felt that relevant developments had progressed the furthest. In fact, all his assumptions about future economic and social developments in Europe seemed to be predicated on the state of play in the USA. In this respect, he was not unlike Marx who assigned much the same role to England. Only rarely did Pollock take developments in Britain, Germany or the Soviet Union into account, although he did append a further section on automation in Europe to the second edition of the book. He also relied almost entirely on Anglo-American research literature. The guiding lights of his earlier intellectual endeavours – Marx, Engels, Hilferding and Lenin – were nowhere to be seen. Only initiated readers would sense their continuing esoteric influence on his thought, such as it was.

Pollock's research also shaped his teaching. In the winter semester of 1954/55, he lectured on the theory of full employment. A year later, he offered a course on 'The Second Industrial Revolution' and a tutorial on automation. Pollock's final lecture course, in the summer semester of 1956, dealt with 'The Economic and Social Significance of Automation in Production and Administration'.[21] He then took a number of sabbatical semesters. In 1959, he was at last promoted to a regular full professorship.

He was finally able to retire in 1964. In the intervening years, his teaching and administrative duties having been substantially reduced, he began to work on a new theory of productive labour that he was unable to bring to fruition. Among his papers are various notes, collected under the heading 'Marxist Problems', that range from excerpts to draft definitions and provisional outlines.[22] He wanted the envisaged book to cover three interconnected topics. Firstly, he was working on an extension of the concept of productive labour designed to incorporate the service industry, i.e., 'all human labour expended for goods and services that fulfil a social need'.[23] This was Pollock's response to the problem

---

21   *Personen- und Vorlesungsverzeichnis der Johann Wolfgang Goethe-Universität Frankfurt am Main, Wintersemester 1954/1955*, p. 87; *Personen- und Vorlesungsverzeichnis der Johann Wolfgang Goethe-Universität Frankfurt am Main, Wintersemester 1955/1956*, pp. 87–8; *Personen- und Vorlesungsverzeichnis der Johann Wolfgang Goethe-Universität Frankfurt am Main, Sommersemester 1956*, p. 93.
22   Friedrich Pollock, 'Marxist Problems', Horkheimer Archive, University Library Frankfurt/Main, MHA XXIV 87, 3.
23   Horkheimer and Pollock 1988c, p. 385.

that, as long as one limited the concept of productive labour to the production of material goods alone, it became increasingly inexplicable how the entire surplus value was supposedly being extracted from the labour of a constantly diminishing share of the workers. He was determined, in short, to develop a post-industrial labour theory.[24]

Secondly, Pollock was intent on formulating a critique of the canonical theories of imperialism developed by Lenin, Luxemburg and Grossman. '"Imperialist offensives"', he wrote, were triggered 'not by lack of m [surplus value] ... but (according to F.P.) by the absolute unavoidability of the alternative: expansion or regression'.[25] In other words: imperialism was not a form of spoliation resorted to by monopoly capitalism when it was in trouble but an innate feature of the capital relation. Money only acted as capital, after all, when it served the extraction of surplus value from labour. In a market economy the realisation of the surplus value transpired through the sale of produced goods. As automation rapidly inflated the mass of goods, so too the need for ever expanding markets arose. This rendered the search for new markets increasingly global and inclined states to secure markets with political or military means.[26] Where colonialism and classical imperialism had been based on the control of territories, imperialism was now all about access to markets.

Thirdly, Pollock intended his labour theory to offer a critique of Marx's anthropology which, as we saw, was of crucial import to Marcuse in particular. Pollock was critical of the vitalist resonances in Marcuse's call for a renewed anthropology and its compatibility with Heidegger's critique of technology. Pollock associated Marx's 'sensualist materialism' of the 1840s and its ahistorical essentialisation of labour as a human activity squarely with 'Marx before Marxism'. It predated the focus of Marx's mature thought on the specific form and function of labour in capitalism.[27] While sections of the New Left too began to idealise the working class in naïve – and, in the German case, as far as National Socialism was concerned, apologetic – ways, seeking to reinstate it as the revolutionary subject, Pollock remained firm in his scepticism. Following the Hard Hat Riot of May 1970, when 200 unionised construction workers attacked a student protest against the Vietnam War

---

24 See, e.g., Reckwitz 2017.
25 Friedrich Pollock, 'Marxist Problems', Horkheimer Archive, University Library Frankfurt/Main, MHA XXIV 87, 3.
26 See also Pollock's television interview of 15 July 1969, Horkheimer Archive, University Library Frankfurt/Main, MHA XXIV 174.
27 See Schmidt 1973.

and injured some 70 protesters, Pollock characterised the incident, in a letter to Martin Jay, as a 'symptom of what can be expected from the "proletarian"'.[28]

Pollock also returned to crisis theory. Moreover, he apparently intended to publish a volume of notes recording conversations with Horkheimer that he collated under the title *Späne (Swarf)*.[29] Now that he was free to focus on the world's problems as he saw fit, he was full of energy and enterprise. With his move to Montagnola the unsettling state of suspended animation between New York, Los Angeles and Frankfurt had finally come to an end. In 1959, following Khrushchev's infamous Berlin ultimatum, Pollock and Horkheimer did acquire an emergency residence in Stamford (Connecticut) that they kept until 1961. Yet this undertow of unease – typical of many former émigrés – aside, they felt well in Ticino. They loved the landscape and went on long walks or hiking almost daily, frequently spending the evenings together in one or other of their adjacent houses or their shared garden. As Nicola Emery has shown, they had paid considerable attention to the aesthetics of their new *intérieur*, discussing the architectural features of their new domicile at great length.[30] They occasionally hosted guests and continued to travel to Frankfurt, Los Angeles and Chicago, but they finally had plenty of time again to debate and analyse each other.

These mutual analyses have left some traces in *Späne*, mainly in the form of Horkheimer's assessments of Pollock. For example, a note from December 1963 treats their respective character traits. It refers to Pollock – who usually features a Y in the covenantal documents but in this case was identified as Z – as inclining towards 'negativism, i.e., only negative objects carry a libidinous charge. A wall separates conscious intention and action from the libido structure'.[31] In the minutes of a conversation in August 1962, Pollock holds forth on historical grounds against Horkheimer's contention that the Communist revolution would have been possible at any point in time, only to be told that he was a positivist in the vein of Wittfogel and Neumann.[32] They also discussed religion. Pollock maintained that neither traditional religion nor the 'Western substitute religions' such as socialism, communism or the bourgeois faith in progress were still credible.[33] Ultimately, people only cared about consumption and the

---

28 Friedrich Pollock to Martin Jay, 13 May 1970, Martin Jay private collection.
29 See Schmid Noerr 1988.
30 Emery 2023, Chapter 3.
31 Horkheimer and Pollock 1988e.
32 Horkheimer and Pollock 1988d.
33 Horkheimer and Pollock 1988g.

unabashed satisfaction of their needs. In this context, as in his private notes taken during the war, Pollock clearly veered towards nihilistic cultural pessimism.

His take on Judaism was no exception. Unlike Horkheimer, he considered it a 'terrible misfortune' that 'the Jews did not cease to be a people following the victory of the early medieval church and assimilate into their host peoples ... Innumerable individuals would have been spared untold suffering.'[34] Prior to the emergence of racial antisemitism it had still been possible to evade persecution by conversion but the instilled sense of being a separate people had obstructed this way out. Precisely what Horkheimer admired about Jewry – that it had stuck together, the 'utmost sacrifices' notwithstanding and despite lacking any 'hope of being rewarded' – irked Pollock. 'The Jewish tragedy', he wrote, 'which sprang from submission to a law inextricably linked to an ultimately alien tribal history bears testimony to the lethal impact of a tradition based on earliest childhood experiences.'[35]

Pollock's radical eschewal of imposed traditions, in this case the Jews' 'tribal history', seems to be diametrically opposed to Horkheimer's Messianism. For Horkheimer, it was precisely halakhah, Jewish law, that epitomised the dynamic spirit of Judaism and its quest for reconciliation. Of course, neither of them genuinely approached Judaism as a religion. For them, it was a tradition and, as Jews, they were forced to position themselves vis-à-vis this tradition, one way or another. Pollock had learnt in the course of his life that the one thing one could not do was ignore it. As a young man he had felt indifferent about his Jewishness, considering it a mere biographical coincidence. The National Socialists robbed him of this indifference, turning him, against his will, into a 'full Jew'. Thus, he was forced to reflect on his stance vis-à-vis his Jewishness in a context of persecution. Subjectively, however, although he differentiated between Judaism and Jewishness, his basic indifference survived the Shoah. Even in old age, he maintained that there was 'ultimately nothing very Jewish' about him, that he lacked any relation to Jewish ritual and felt no great affinity for Jewish thought.[36] In contrast to Henryk Grossman, whom he repeatedly credited with a 'talmudic' way of thinking, his own Jewishness, as he wrote to Martin Jay shortly before his death, did not extend beyond his ethnic origin.[37] Yet what are we to make of this?

---

34 Horkheimer and Pollock 1988f.
35 Ibid.
36 Ernst von Schenck, interview with Pollock and Horkheimer, transcript, 1965/66, Horkheimer Archive, University Library Frankfurt/Main, MHA X 132a, p. 164.
37 Friedrich Pollock to Martin Jay, 24 March 1970, Martin Jay private collection.

In 1960, because Horkheimer had been taken ill, Pollock was forced to give a formal address at the central ceremony to mark the tenth anniversary of the establishment of the Central Council of Jews in Germany, the official representative body of Jews living in West Germany. His performance on this occasion gives an indication of the complicated and tortuous nature of Pollock's attitude towards his own Jewishness. He copiously avoided any use of the word 'we', presenting himself as an objective social scientist speaking on issues of political education. Among the problems he identified was the stereotyping of entire groups ('"the" American, "the" Frenchman, "the" Jew'), which, he insisted, was equally problematic, regardless of whether the implications of the clichés deployed were assumed to be negative or positive.[38]

Acting as a reader for an edited collection on antisemitism, he chastised one of the contributors, the German-American economist Hans Wolfram Gerhard, as falling into the category of 'the antisemitic "Jew lover"' intent on 'being party to the (waning) pro-Jewish mode'. His text was a 'pointless ragbag of liberal economic theories and tidbits from economic history, assembled along the lines of: "Only the very best, Sir."'[39] His equal contempt for ostentatious philosemites and antisemites (suddenly a startlingly rare breed) may help explain the emergence of his interest in serious historical accounts of the Shoah. He was deeply impressed with Gerald Reitlinger's pioneering book, *The Final Solution*. Only this kind of exact reconstruction had the potential to circumvent stereotypes and lead to a differentiated understanding, he felt. When he wrote to Juan Pollock in 1961 that 'the horrors of the Nazi years' were 'inconceivable even now', he added: 'When you come over, I will let you, Hans, browse my small library on this topic. Women should not read these books, I have also asked Carlota not to look at them.'[40] Pollock evidently assumed that these accounts were too shocking for women to bear. When gifting an edition of Shoah-related documents to the nineteen-year-old student Emil Walter-Busch, who assisted him with the

---

38   Friedrich Pollock, 'Aufgaben und Grenzen der politischen Bildung. Festvortrag anläßlich der Feier des zehnjährigen Bestehens des Zentralrats', *Berliner Allgemeine. Wochenzeitung der Juden in Deutschland*, 15.38, 16 December 1960, p. 3.
39   Friedrich Pollock, 'Gutachten zu Professor Gerhard: Die wirtschaftlich begründete Judenfeindschaft', 1962, Horkheimer Archive, University Library Frankfurt/Main, MHA XXIV 93. The quotation at the end is a reference to the popular comical figure 'little Moritz', a fictitious Jewish schoolboy who regularly deflates the pomposity of the adults around him with curt responses. In this instance, set against the backdrop of the rise of the Nazis, his teacher asks him what he knows about the old Germanic tribes and little Moritz answers simply: 'Only the very best, Sir.' Gerhard's text was published all the same. Gerhard 1963.
40   Friedrich Pollock to Juan and Ida Pollock, 16 February 1961, Horkheimer Archive, University Library Frankfurt/Main, MHA XXIII 22, 100.

revised edition of *Automation*, his dedication read: 'For Emil Walter Jr., that he may gain a sense of what human beings are capable of in the mid-twentieth century'.[41]

In 1960, the municipal authorities in Stuttgart commissioned the city archivist Maria Zelzer to prepare a volume commemorating the city's former Jewish citizens.[42] To this end, she contacted various former Jewish inhabitants of the city, including Horkheimer and Pollock. In response, Pollock made a serious effort to ascertain what had happened to his own relatives. 'Please let me know', he wrote to Juan and Ida Pollock in February 1961,

> what dates you have for Sallie [Stern], Alfred F[ranck], Sigmund and Rösl [Nördlinger]. The year of deportation is of particular interest. These are, alas, not our only murdered relatives, but the people in Stuttgart are interested only in those who still lived in Stuttgart in 1933.[43]

The Pollock brothers' maternal uncle Alfred Franck, who became one of the suitcase factory's authorised signatories in 1914, was taken to Theresienstadt in 1942 and perished there within a fortnight.[44] Ida Pollock's half-sister Johanna Rothschild, née Joseph, perished in Theresienstadt a year later.[45] As we saw

---

41 Quoted in Walter-Busch 2010, p. 10.
42 Zelzer 1964.
43 Friedrich Pollock to Juan and Ida Pollock, 16 February 1961, Horkheimer Archive, University Library Frankfurt/Main, MHA XXIII 22, 100.
44 Theresienstadt Memorial, https://www.holocaust.cz/en/database-of-victims/victim/10589-alfred-franck/.
45 Theresienstadt Memorial, https://www.holocaust.cz/en/database-of-victims/victim/29723-johanna-rothschild/. Johanna Rothschild's daughter Bella Reich, née Rothschild, and her daughter Ingeborg were deported to, and murdered in, the Riga ghetto in January 1942. https://www.bundesarchiv.de/gedenkbuch/en1138132; https://www.bundesarchiv.de/gedenkbuch/en1138254. Johanna Rothschild's daughter Martha Bachenheimer, née Rothschild, and her son Stephan were deported to, and murdered in, Auschwitz in February 1943. https://www.bundesarchiv.de/gedenkbuch/en1047513; https://www.bundesarchiv.de/gedenkbuch/en1016698. Martha Bachenheimer's son Manfred was deported to, and murdered in, the Riga ghetto in October 1942. Martha Bachenheimer's daughter Ellen Ruth was deported to Theresienstadt in June 1943 and from there to Auschwitz, where she was murdered, in October 1944. https://www.holocaust.cz/en/database-of-victims/victim/4717-ellen-ruth-bachenheimer/. Johanna Rothschild's daughter Flora Voos, née Rothschild, her husband Heinz Voos and their children Walter and Doris were deported to Theresienstadt in September 1944 and from there to Auschwitz, where they were murdered in October 1944. https://www.holocaust.cz/en/database-of-victims/victim/35412-flora-voos/ ; https://www.holocaust.cz/en/database-of-victims/victim/35437-heinrich-voos/; https://www.holocaust.cz/en/database-of-victims/victim/35415-walter-voos/; https://www.bundesarchiv.de/gedenkbuch/en995973.

earlier, Rosa and Sigmund Nördlinger were murdered in Theresienstadt and Treblinka, respectively, in 1942, and Ida Pollock's mother Settchen Joseph in Auschwitz the following year.

Their exchange regarding the fate of their relatives brought Pollock and his Argentinian relations closer together again. Pollocks' letters, which, although he had begun to communicate with Juan in German again since his return to Europe, had nevertheless continued to be characterised by a notable frigidity ever since his brother's unauthorised contact with Carlota Pollock's mother, now took on a new warmth and their mutual trust palpably increased from one letter to the next. What Juan had hoped for in January 1945 – that they might be something resembling a family again – was finally coming true, at least in part.

CHAPTER 14

On Old Age

In May 1962, the Argentinian Pollocks came to Montagnola for two days. That was not a lot of time to get to know each other again after so many years, but Pollock enjoyed the visit. He was still not entirely at ease with his brother, but he got on extremely well with Ida and especially with his niece Lilo who was now 49. Pollock had reluctantly agreed occasionally to represent his brother's business interests in Europe and the United States. As a result, he sometimes had dealings with Lilo's husband, Paul Sommer, who was an investor in Juan Pollock's enterprise. They just about got on, but Pollock disliked Sommer who he felt treated Lilo badly and was often disrespectful towards Ida.

He took great delight in his great-nephew Peter, however, who, on his recommendation, had come to Switzerland to study and with whom he was subsequently in regular contact.[1] Unfortunately, Peter was not particularly happy in Switzerland. It was 'remarkable how Argentinian the German-Jewish children are', Ida noted in a letter to Pollock. To cheer Peter up she wanted to give him a copy of Martin Buber's book *Begegnung* (Meetings) for 'Chrismukkah' and she asked Pollock to get hold of it for her.[2]

The kind great-uncle who felt responsible for his family and brought his nieces and nephews gifts – this was certainly a new role for Pollock, not least, given that he himself had no children. He had no regrets in this respect but since his retirement he had little contact with younger people and lived in what one might well describe as a self-governed old people's home in an idyllic Swiss resort.[3] In one of their conversations, Horkheimer expressed his dis-

---

1 Friedrich Pollock to Juan and Ida Pollock, 25 July 1964, Horkheimer Archive, University Library Frankfurt/Main, MHA XXIII 22, 59.
2 Ida Pollock to Friedrich and Carlota Pollock, 10 November 1962, Horkheimer Archive, University Library Frankfurt/Main, MHA XXIII 22, 82.
3 One of their visitors in Montagnola was their long-standing friend (and Andrée Pollock's first husband) Julius Marx who did not return to Germany after the war. He spent the rest of his life in Zurich where he rebuilt his old business and once again became an extremely wealthy man. He was particularly well known for his promotion of the work of Georg Kaiser (1878– 1945), one of the most prominent Expressionist authors and playwrights who fled Germany in 1938 and died in exile in Switzerland. In his memoirs, Marx wrote: '*19 January 1967*: I spent the weekend with my friends in Montagnola near Lugano, Professors Horkheimer and Pollock, two men who are advanced in age yet still youthful in their aspirations. They live in two villas in Montagnola that resemble each other like twin sisters. The view reveals a panorama the likes of which I have rarely seen. It was as though Lake Lugano and the mountains behind

gust at the fact that, rather than 'bawling out what is bad' he was now 'a Jew of independent means with a German passport living in Ticino'.⁴ Pollock was more at ease with this situation, but it also changed him. He clearly felt the impact of advancing age. He was sick more often and took longer to recover. Writing to congratulate his brother on the occasion of his seventieth birthday, 'F. (Fred or Fritz, whichever you prefer!)' wrote, that Juan should not mind 'if old age takes its toll. It is, e.g., a widespread misconception that one needs less sleep in old age. This holds true only if one is entirely inactive, otherwise the opposite is the case (as I, much to my regret, am finding out in my own case).'⁵ When Otto Kirchheimer congratulated him on his own seventieth birthday, Pollock responded that it seemed 'strange to me that I have now entered my eighth decade, yet who am I to argue with the birth certificate. I certainly intend to do something worthwhile in my remaining years.'⁶

One of the areas to which he wanted to turn his attention was the sociology of old age, a field of study then still in its infancy.⁷ In 1958, the German broadcaster Süddeutscher Rundfunk ran a series of programmes on 'Old People in Our Age', to which Pollock contributed a lecture on 'Growing Old as a Sociological Problem'. He pointed out that rising life expectancy would lead to the older age groups forming an increasing share of the overall pop-

---

it were posing for me as I stood on the terrace of the philosopher's house.' Marx 1970, p. 250. In August 1966, Marx also joined the Pollocks and Horkheimers in the mountain resort of Flims for several days. In his memoirs, he reports the following: '22 *August 1966*: Yesterday I had a long conversation with Mrs Pollock, an intelligent, indeed, a wise lady. She advised that I should publish only a carefully chosen selection of my memoirs to avoid giving rise to all too many malicious attacks on me. We Jews did not have the right constantly to cause offence, even if we are motivated by the desire to ascertain and convey the truth.' Marx 1970, p. 210. That Pollock and Marx were in fairly regular contact is also borne out by the fact that, in 1965, Marx passed on a photograph of Georg Kaiser he had received from Pollock to the Academy of Arts in West Berlin (Julius Marx to Walter Huder, 20 October 1965, Akademie der Künste Berlin, Huder 987, https://archiv.adk.de/objekt/2076290). According to Nebel (1994, p. 100), a large painting of Marx's first wife Andrée took pride of place in his flat in Zurich. In his will, he bequeathed the painting to Pollock. Given that Pollock died almost to the day two months after Marx, it seems unlikely that the transfer of the painting ever took place.

4 Horkheimer 1988d.
5 Friedrich Pollock to Juan and Ida Pollock, 25 July 1964, Horkheimer Archive, University Library Frankfurt/Main, MHA XXIII 22, 55.
6 Friedrich Pollock to Otto Kirchheimer, 12 June 1964, SUNY Albany, M.E. Grenander Department of Special Collections & Archives, Otto Kirchheimer Papers, 1/127. The term 'birth certificate' is in English in the original.
7 See Wiese 1954, p. 29.

ulation while their 'social utility and ... status' decreased.[8] In 1900, merely seven per cent of the German population had been aged sixty or over. By 1950, that proportion had doubled, and it was anticipated that by 1957 roughly 20 per cent of the German population would fall into this category.[9] Pollock raised three principal concerns. Firstly, increasing automation would devalue the advanced skills of older, more experienced employees. Instead, 'youthful' attributes such as 'speed, versatility, a rapid grasp of new tasks' would take centre stage. Secondly, inflation had systematically wiped out the assets of the bourgeois middle classes in the years since the First World War. As a result, power and capital had come to be concentrated in 'ever larger capital conglomerates'. This meant that, in addition to no longer being able to rely on their advanced skills to shore up their status, old people were no longer able to depend on inherited assets either. Thirdly, the family had been transformed from a unit essentially geared to production into a much smaller community of consumers. As a result, intergenerational relations had become much looser and elder relatives were frequently encountered exclusively as a burden. 'This makes cohabitation, especially given the current housing situation, unbearable in ways that wholly undermine old people's esteem and status.'[10] This marginalisation led to boredom, loneliness and despondency as well as material and intellectual misery. Those of advanced age soon became physically and intellectually old too. In this sense, old people now were 'older' than their counterparts had been a century earlier. People who were redundant withered as individuals.

In political terms, there were two possible approaches to the issue. One could follow either the Social Democratic principle of solidarity or the conservative principle of subsidiarity. The former expected society as a whole to take care of, and integrate, its older members, the latter assumed that smaller social units – families or communitarian institutions – were better placed to take on this task. Empirical studies demonstrated that neither the young nor the old still looked to the intergenerational family as a suitable means of maintaining intergenerational solidarity. Social policies designed to reinvigorate the extended family for this purpose were therefore anachronistic and doomed. This left only social policies predicated on solidarity of the kind that were increasingly

---

8   Pollock 1958, p. 113.
9   In 2021, 29.3 per cent of the German population was older than 60. Statistisches Bundesamt, Bevölkerung nach Altersgruppen, https://www.destatis.de/DE/Themen/Gesellschaft-Umwelt/Bevoelkerung/Bevoelkerungsstand/Tabellen/bevoelkerung-altersgruppen-deutschland.html%20 (30 September 2022).
10   Pollock 1958, p. 117.

becoming the norm. Yet these too faced problems as automation reduced the numbers of employees able to pay into the social security system while the number of those in receipt of support rose. 'The liberating and solving potential' that attaches to old age 'just as much as the risk of isolation and growing lonesomeness can only be realised if society creates a meaningful and secure status for the older generation. It can presumably be constructed only on the basis of objectively required social functions and a protracted period of purposeful preparation.'[11]

Pollock had his doubts as to how robust and resilient the principle of solidarity would prove and saw no prospect of a better organised social order that would genuinely improve the lives of older people. Far from it. The more younger Germans sought to shake off the legacy of National Socialism (or what they assumed that legacy to be), the more youthfulness would trump old age. For many in the post-war generation that has entered the history books as the 'generation of '68' and a generation of revolt, the previous generations embodied a harmful German tradition that led directly to Hitler. To sustain this vantage, they ignored everything that was youthful, dynamic and subversive about National Socialism and instead identified all forms of conservatism and any kind of attachment to tradition with 'fascism', thus eschewing all the hard questions a serious engagement of the Nazi past would have needed to address – which is, of course, precisely what made this approach so compelling.[12] Given the obvious parallels between the increasing prioritisation of younger employees and their specific traits and characteristics in the economic process and the ire the anti-authoritarian revolt of the young directed at the old and decrepit, Pollock instantly recognised that theirs was in fact a conformist rebellion.

Marking Pollock's seventy-fifth birthday with a laudatory article in the *Frankfurter Allgemeine Zeitung* in 1969, Horkheimer stressed that his friend was 'the opposite of an apologist of violence', placing him radically at odds with the militant arm of the APO (the so-called extra-parliamentary opposition). 'To hypostatise the revolution', Horkheimer wrote, 'and affirm it as an absolute goal in countries where freedom currently has an abode', would be as alien to Pollock 'as a profession of faith in Hitler or Stalin'.[13] Members of the institute certainly maintained relations with leading APO figures but the extent of the student movement's identification with the Frankfurt School has generally

---

11   Pollock 1958, p. 127.
12   See Aly 2008.
13   Horkheimer 1969.

been exaggerated.[14] Among the activists were many who distanced themselves from the more academically focussed second generation of critical theorists that included scholars such as Jürgen Habermas, Herbert Schnädelbach and Albrecht Wellmer. They were desperate to find a shortcut to practical political solutions and liked to think of themselves as the 'third generation'. Pollock, Horkheimer and Adorno viewed this primacy of praxis with great scepticism. 'Once again', Adorno lamented in a text that he wrote just before, and that was published in *Die Zeit* nine days after, his death in 1969, 'the antithesis between theory and praxis is being misused to denounce theory'. He pointed to the concrete example of a student whose 'room was trashed because he preferred to work rather than join in actions' and on whose 'wall was scrawled: "Whoever occupies himself with theory, without acting practically, is a traitor to socialism."'[15]

While Adorno had direct dealings with the revolting students and knew the leaders of the APO personally, Pollock and Horkheimer now rarely came to Frankfurt. Even so, Pollock obviously registered what the radical students were making of the Critical Theory he had helped develop. Their reappropriation of Marx's critique of political economy, often accompanied by sympathies for the Soviet Union, would certainly have reminded Pollock of his own youthful enthusiasms. Yet these were no longer the 1920s. In the meantime, the show trials, the Hitler-Stalin Pact, the Second World War, the civil wars in China, Korea and Vietnam, not to mention the Shoah, had taken place. One could no longer draw out the Marxist tradition as though none of this had occurred. This kind of Marxism was not only ahistorical, it also ignored the failure of the labour movement when confronted with the greatest catastrophe in human history.[16] Now, in the late 1960s, one could only continue with the kind of orthodox reconstruction of Marx's thought to which Pollock himself had made a significant contribution with his doctoral thesis of 1923 by ignoring its historicity. Contemporary Marxism and obliviousness to history went hand in hand. This also explains why he repeatedly urged the removal of Marxist terminology from a prospective new edition of *Dialectic of Enlightenment* for which there was enormous demand among the students. In 1961, he had still expressed his misgivings about republishing the book at all, suggesting that only select sections should be reissued. By the late 1960s, this position was no longer tenable since numerous pirated editions of the book were already in circulation.[17] An author-

---

14   See Kraushaar 1998.
15   Adorno 1998b, p. 263.
16   Lenhard 2016c.
17   Friedrich Pollock to Max Horkheimer, 24 January 1961, in Horkheimer 1996b, p. 502.

ised Italian edition with 29 revisions by Pollock came out in 1966 and in 1969, *Dialectic of Enlightenment* was finally reissued in an authorised German edition with minor revisions.

How astute Pollock's assessment of the students' ahistorical reading of Marx was is demonstrated not least by the case of the prominent SDS (Socialist German Student Federation) member Hans-Jürgen Krahl (b. 1943), arguably one of the intellectually most gifted leaders of the student movement. He was one of Adorno's doctoral students and concerned himself in great detail with the thinkers that also preoccupied his supervisor: Kant, Hegel, Nietzsche, Freud and, above all, Marx. Yet their assessments of political reality differed considerably.[18] Detlev Claussen, who also studied with Adorno and Horkheimer and was one of Krahl's fellow activists, has lamented the inclination of the 'third generation' to 'level the experience of National Socialism into a dangerously flat concept of fascism' that it applied in a flippant and overly loose manner.[19] While Claussen expressly exempted Krahl from this critique, a close reading of Krahl's version of Critical Theory illustrates the degree to which his experiential background – radically distinct from that of Pollock and his peers – shaped his vantage on the world. Having previously advanced a similar critique in an article published in the leftist daily, *Frankfurter Zeitung*, a week after Adorno's death,[20] Krahl, in a radio debate about Adorno broadcast by Hessian public radio in December 1969, vehemently criticised the 'cognitive constraints' that, according to Critical Theory, followed from 'the experience of fascism'. These constraints engendered the erroneous assumption in the critical theorists 'that collective praxis is necessarily destructive of consciousness, that through collective praxis class morphs into mass.' The ignorance betrayed by Krahl's suggestion that the former émigrés were in the grip of a 'regressive fear of expressions of practical resistance' was not only juvenile but also potentially antisemitic.[21] Jews had more than ample grounds to associate revolution with anti-Jewish violence, after all. It was no coincidence that Krahl and his peers perpetually spoke of fascism rather than National Socialism. If 'Auschwitz' did get a look in, then almost invariably as a metaphor for the generic horrors of late-capitalist modernity.[22]

---

18   On Krahl's interpretation of Marx, see Hoff 2009, pp. 37–8.
19   Claussen 1985, p. 66.
20   Krahl 1975. A clipping of the article is among the Pollock papers held in Florence: Fondo Friedrich Pollock, Università degli Studi di Firenze, 2.2.4, 11.
21   Krahl 2008, pp. 300, 303.
22   See Claussen 2005, pp. 35–50. In an email of 28 January 2020, Claussen argues that Krahl was an exception in this respect. For him, Auschwitz was not just a metaphor but a very

For many of the radical students, Pollock, Horkheimer and Adorno were simply conservative and/or defeatist 'elders'.[23] Reporting on a teach-in in Frankfurt with Rudi Dutschke, the best-known figurehead of the student movement, Hilke Schlaeger – then a *Zeit* editor, she was soon to emerge as one of West Berlin's most prominent (feminist) broadcasters – wrote: 'Their students have long since started to look at the "elders" whom they consider "lacking in resolution and too timid" with nothing but contempt.'[24] Three weeks later, Kai Hermann suggested in the *Zeit* that the students' current idol, Herbert Marcuse, given his lack of 'ideological asceticism and revolutionary optimism', would likely soon share the fate of Habermas, Horkheimer and Adorno who, despite being 'the father figures of the young German left only yesterday, have since been retired'.[25]

In addition to the generation gap, a number of political factors contributed to the alienation between the young leftists and their academic teachers. These included the former émigrés' identification with the United States. It tended to make them staunch supporters of West Germany's western integration and led some of them to be ambivalent in their assessment of the Vietnam War. As the New Left turned on Israel following the Six Day War, the student movement also found itself at odds with the solidarity of many Jewish academics with the Jewish state.[26] Critical of Zionism as an ideology, Horkheimer nevertheless supported Israel in various ways.[27] Although neither of them ever visited the state, Pollock too was well disposed towards Israel. He refrained from publicly criticising Jewish nationalism and certainly had no time for the students' antizionism, not least given that he rejected the Leninist concept of imperialism underpinning it anyway. In the aftermath of the terror attack carried out by the PFLP on a school bus on route between Avivim and Dovev, two north-

---

real occurrence that irrevocably undermined his faith in the notion (also in its traditional Marxist guise) that history was ultimately guided by reason.

23 The German term 'alter Herr' can mean simply elderly gentleman, but it is also the term for former student fraternity members who stay on the books but are no longer actively involved in the life of the fraternity. There seems to be no direct English/American equivalent, hence the use of the term elder. The student movement radically distanced itself from the student fraternities (Burschenschaften, studentische Verbindungen), given that they were traditionally – and largely still are – hotbeds of extreme nationalism, antisemitism and far-right politics.

24 Hilke Schlaeger, 'Rundherum voll Ungeduld. Auch die westdeutschen Studenten entdecken nach und nach ihre Rolle in der Gesellschaft', *Die Zeit*, no. 28, 14 July 1967.

25 Kai Hermann, 'Das Idol der Berliner Studenten. Doch die Blumen für den Philosophen Herbert Marcuse beginnen schon zu welken', *Die Zeit*, no. 29, 21 July 1967.

26 See Schmidt 2010.

27 Lenhard 2017.

ern Israeli agricultural communities close to the Lebanese border, on 22 May 1970, in which nine children and three adults were murdered, Pollock wrote to Martin Jay that his only consolation was Ben Gurion's assertion that in Israel, one needed to believe in miracles to be a realist.[28] Roughly at the same time, an SDS delegation travelled to Jordan where, on some accounts, they attended a Fatah training camp.[29] The chasm that gaped between the founding fathers of Critical Theory and the young rebels could barely have been more profound.

The year 1968 had not yet passed before parts of the student movement began to evolve into Marxist-Leninist cadre parties, initiating the transition from the anti-authoritarian to the 'proletarian' phase of the revolt.[30] Pollock did not live to see what the plethora of new parties and so-called K groups that were formed in the early 1970s got up to but he certainly realised, at the end of his life, that the anti-authoritarian movement was going through a process of disintegration.[31] Its descent into Maoism and Stalinism disappointed him, to be sure, but it also vindicated yet again his decision to retire to Ticino.

Meeting statutory requirements, Pollock's house in Montagnola was equipped with an air raid shelter, just in case,[32] but rarely in his life had he felt as safe as he did in his mountain refuge overlooking Lage Lugano. As a retired German professor, he drew a handsome pension, and he could safely assume that his financial worries lay in the past. Of course, this retreat from the immediate cut and thrust of the public sphere also drew some flak. In 1962, in his introduction for the new edition of his *Theorie des Romans* (The Theory of the Novel) published by Luchterhand the following year, Lukács famously applied his own earlier comments about Schopenhauer (in *The Destruction of Reason*) to Adorno and, by extension, to Pollock, Horkheimer and their other former émigré colleagues. 'A considerable part of the leading German intelligentsia', he wrote, 'including Adorno, have taken up residence in the "Grand Hotel Abyss"

---

28 Friedrich Pollock to Martin Jay, 16 July 1970, Martin Jay private collection.
29 On this episode, see Kraushaar 1998, p. 446. It should be noted that Detlev Claussen vehemently disputes this version of events. In an email of 21 January 2020, he writes: 'As an eyewitness, I can confirm: the SDS delegation did not travel to a "terror camp", nobody underwent "military training" nor was it requested. The factfinding mission visited Fatah institutions in Jordan. ... To save costs, the group from Frankfurt, along with other international visitors, stayed under canvas in a camp (not a training camp).'
30 See Benicke 2010. The still existing German Marxist-Leninist Party (MLPD), established in 1965, was less successful among students.
31 For the context here, see Koenen 2001.
32 This is evident from a detailed plan by the architect Peppo Brivio in Nicola Emery's private collection.

which I described in connection with my critique of Schopenhauer as "a beautiful hotel, equipped with every comfort, on the edge of an abyss, of nothingness, of absurdity. And the daily contemplation of the abyss between excellent meals or artistic entertainments, can only heighten the enjoyment of the subtle comforts offered." [33] Lukács's mockery soon found favour not only with the radical students but with mainstream commentators too. The journalist Jochen Steinmayr, born in 1926 and a graduate of an extremely selective private school created and run directly by the Nazi party in Feldafing where, in 1942, a subsidiary camp belonging to the Dachau camp complex was established on the same property as the school, is a case in point. In an article with the title, 'Die Revolution frißt ihre Väter' (The Revolution Devours Its Fathers), published in the weekly *Der Stern* in 1969, he derided the now retired founders of the institute who had turned their backs on their students and 'moved away to fashionable Lugano'.[34]

In May 1970, in light of the 'massive conflicts between Adorno and the student movement and Horkheimer's dissociating himself from it', Claus Grossner (who later rose to prominence as an investment banker and philanthropist), writing in *Die Zeit*, proclaimed the 'end of the Frankfurt School'.[35] This was more than Pollock, now in his seventy-sixth year, was willing to countenance and he sent a letter of protest to the editors of the *Zeit*. He was particularly irked by Grossner's suggestion that Horkheimer had become a conservative in old age who, in the spirit of Paul VI's encyclical of 1968, *Humanae vitae*, opposed oral contraception. Alas, Pollock's defence of Horkheimer did little to dispel the specific accusation. The new means of contraception undoubtedly marked a significant form of progress, he conceded, yet it was important to take note of 'what needs to be sacrificed to this progress'. Horkheimer, he explained, had wanted to point to a diminution of love that would result from this innovation, a diminution 'that it would be pointless to want to prevent but of which one should at least be aware'.[36] In this respect, Pollock and Horkheimer's position

---

33 Lukács 1971b [1963], p. 22. The original formulation reads: 'So Schopenhauer's system, well laid out and architecturally ingenious, rises up like a modern luxury hotel …' (Lukács 1980, p. 243). Lukács first expounded the concept of the grand hotel abyss in 1933 (Lukács 1984) in a text not published at the time, in which he essentially presented it as the intelligentsia's counterpart to Social Democracy's 'social fascism'. As we saw, Schopenhauer was an extremely important point of reference for Pollock and Horkheimer.

34 Jochen Steinmayr, 'Die Revolution frißt ihre Väter', *Stern*, 21.11, 11 February 1969, p. 28. The word 'fashionable' was written in English in the original.

35 Claus Grossner, 'Frankfurter Schule am Ende', *Die Zeit*, no. 19, 8 May 1970.

36 Friedrich Pollock, 'Leserbrief', *Die Zeit*, no. 20, 15 May 1970.

indeed bore a striking resemblance to the encyclical's insistence on the inseparability of intercourse as a mark of love (*significatio unitatis*) from intercourse for the purpose of procreation (*significatio procreationis*).³⁷

Not that Pollock and Horkheimer were on a crusade for the 'bourgeois patriarchal family', as an outraged article in the *Stuttgarter Zeitung* claimed.³⁸ Yet against the backdrop of the Nazis' criminal eugenics and euthanasia campaigns they felt that the impact of new forms of contraception required careful consideration. Pollock's work on automation stressed the extent to which the production process was rendering ever more individuals economically redundant, given that machines and robots were able to do their jobs in a more reliable and cost-efficient manner. It seemed oddly fitting – and concerning – that human procreation was now being optimised in decisive ways too.

In this sense, this new, highly efficient form of contraception was an instrument of domination. It offered yet another means of suppressing any kind of spontaneity that might get in the way of automated production processes. Intercourse was robbed of its unpurposiveness, becoming instead a means used either to achieve pure pleasure or to procreate. In both instances, sex was instrumentalised and consequently dehumanised. This process could be stopped only by insisting on its unpurposiveness and unconditionality. The encyclical insisted that '[this] love is human and therefore both of the sense and of the spirit'. It was therefore

> a product not only of natural instinct and inclinations [*affectuum*]; it also and primarily involves an act of free will. Through this act of free will [the spouses resolve] that their love will not only persevere through daily joys and sorrows but also increase. Therefore it is especially important that they become one in heart and soul, and that they obtain together their human perfection.
>
> Next, this love is total [*pleno*]; that is, it is a very special form of personal friendship whereby the spouses generously share everything with each other without undue reservations and without concern for their selfish convenience. One who truly loves his spouse not only loves her for what he receives from her but also for her sown sake.³⁹

---

37 'Humanae Vitae' 1991, p. 281.
38 Günther Mehren, 'Die Welt des Paschas. Horkheimers Apologie in Zürich', *Stuttgarter Zeitung*, 23 November 1970, quoted in Eitler 2009, p. 187.
39 'Humanae Vitae' 1991, p. 278.

The relationship between Pollock and Horkheimer may not have been a marriage nor was it sexual in nature, and yet the encyclical's remarks would well describe their covenant – if one leaves aside the commandment of procreation.

Pollock, Horkheimer and Adorno all consciously decided not to have children. Each had established a form of kinship with their closest friends and associates. Of course, this meant that their 'families' would cease to exist when the friends died. For obvious reasons, Pollock had never been a great fan of the idea that sons and daughters should step into their parents' shoes. Even so, as he grew older, he did wonder what his legacy would be after his death. In his eulogy for Franz Neumann, who died of injuries sustained in a car crash while on holiday in Switzerland in 1954, Pollock noted that believers might rely on a higher being to put a terrible blow such as Neumann's death right again. For nonbelievers, by contrast, life after death lasted only as long one was remembered by one's loved ones. As long as one of their group was still alive, Pollock vowed, Neumann would not be forgotten.[40] He picked up this theme again almost a decade later in the eulogy for his mother-in-law, Hella Bernecker, this time, rather remarkably, giving the idea a specifically Jewish twist. 'The notion of hell and heaven was alien to traditional Jews', he explained. 'The worst punishment *we* know of are not the torments of hell, it is banishment from the hearts of other human beings. Of all the curses flung at Spinoza, "you will not be remembered" was the gravest' (emphasis added).[41] Yet who would remember the non-Jewish Jew and godless materialist Friedrich Pollock?[42] Since there would be no heirs in the conventional sense once the other members of this 'family' had died, he would have to find other ways of securing his legacy.

One possibility was obviously the creation of a substantial body of scholarly work that might last. As the aforementioned corpus of notes and excerpts demonstrates, Pollock continued to work tirelessly on his labour theory in his final years. It was supposed to form the heart piece of a comprehensively

---

40 'Friedrich Pollock am Grab von Franz Neumann', in Erd (ed.) 1982, p. 22.
41 Friedrich Pollock, 'Grabrede auf Hella Bernecker', 9 April 1963, Fondo Friedrich Pollock, Università degli Studi di Firenze, 2.1.2. Readers may recall that Spinoza was one of Pollock's first philosophical encounters in Brussels. Ironically, the *herem* (statement of excommunication) against Spinoza did not in fact contain this specific formulation (the phrase there is 'the Lord shall blot out his name from under heaven'). Pollock's formulation, 'nicht gedacht soll Deiner werden' is identical with the wording in Leopold Zunz's translation of the *Tanakh*. It is also almost identical with the first line of a poem by Heinrich Heine, 'Nicht gedacht soll seiner werden', which is in fact a more precise rendering of the relevant scriptural passage (Ezekiel 21, 37).
42 On the well-rehearsed trope of the non-Jewish Jew, see Deutscher 1968.

renewed critique of political economy, a kind of cutting-edge post-Marxism. This was no mean aspiration but would have made for a truly fitting legacy.

Yet Pollock wanted not only his scholarship but his life too to be remembered. His intense preoccupation with issues of life writing indicates that he was preparing to put his house in order. It was no different for Horkheimer who was, of course, a much more prominent figure. In his quest for a suitable biographer, Horkheimer gave a succession of interviews about his life. Pollock was frequently present and was able to provide valuable additional information, given how much of their lives they had shared. The first published biography of Horkheimer, a biographical essay based on numerous interesting documents and written by the journalists Helmut Gumnior and Rudolf Ringguth came out with Rowohlt in 1973, soon after Horkheimer's death.[43] It is still well worth a read. The following year, Horkheimer's former assistant, Alfred Schmidt, published an introduction to Horkheimer's philosophy.[44] A second biography, written by Maimon Maor, followed in 1981.[45] Other important works of importance to my own work have been published since.[46] What concerns us here is that both Horkheimer and Pollock were keen, in their final years, to ensure that appropriate accounts not only of their life's work but also of their lives would be forthcoming.

This has made my task easier in some respects. The detailed interviews with Ernst von Schenck that Wiggershaus also used extensively, are a case in point. Given the dearth of documentation regarding the earlier periods of their life – not least, given that they were forced to leave virtually everything behind when they fled Germany – these interviews are of crucial significance. Yet one also needs to bear in mind the extent to which they are shaped by various forms of self-stylisation. When Pollock criticises Horkheimer's conservative lifestyle, for example, he is not only teasing his friend but the two of them are in fact putting on a performance. There is a clear dramaturgy to scenes such as the following:

> POLLOCK   I don't really understand why you still write in German cursive.
> HORKHEIMER Because the transition to Latin script was too practical and functional, to which I didn't want to conform. I would say that

---

43   Gumnior and Ringguth 1973.
44   Schmidt 1974.
45   Maor 1981.
46   Stirk 1992; Rosen 1995; Abromeit 2011.

the fact I didn't go along with this marks the distinction between us. One could [describe] this distinction between us precisely in terms of my not going along with this; it is the same with my wearing suspenders and a waistcoat. It is just the same. There are innumerable such things. It is just the same with his not wearing suspenders as a matter of course, the occasional exception aside.

POLLOCK   I never wear suspenders.

HORKHEIMER   And when they were abolished, he abolished them too. Originally, he wore suspenders too and originally, he wrote in German cursive too. But then, when one switched over to the other script, he went along with it, and I refused to go along with either.[47]

Thus, they set in scene a juxtaposition that contrasted Horkheimer, the insistent, slightly eccentric traditionalist who kept alive elements of a lost bourgeois civilisation, to Pollock, who went with the flow, wore crepe soles and belts and wrote in a way that readers born after 1945 would find more accessible. Similar juxtapositions also characterise the *Späne* project. Pollock artfully crafted it as a work of autobiography. 'Fred's gravity is demonstrated positively by his loyalty to us', one of the aphorisms explains, even though, 'taking air travel and shaving cream into account, he probably belongs to the other generation.'[48] Pollock not only dressed stylishly, then, but also used shaving cream, abandoning the shaving brush, and preferred aeroplanes to boats.

All this brings with it the risk of our only ever seeing Pollock through Horkheimer's eyes when it may well be that Horkheimer's assessments of his friend sometimes tell us more about himself than they do about Pollock. Nor can there be any suggestion that Horkheimer's autobiographical novellas offer us an accurate account of the events they portray. Even so, they do offer us some insight into the youthful Horkheimer's feelings and thoughts and his sense of his interaction with Pollock.

With the papers they left at the time of their death we are on more reliable ground. Yet here too we need to be careful. The Pollock who not only preserved but also, at least in part, ordered the thousands of items – letters, notes, manuscripts, typescripts, all manner of miscellanea – was the ageing social critic keen to secure his legacy. Adorno's concept of the 'message in a

---

47   Ernst von Schenck, interview with Pollock and Horkheimer, transcript, 1965/66, Horkheimer Archive, University Library Frankfurt/Main, MHA X 132a, p. 12.

48   Horkheimer 1988c, p. 47.

bottle' of which one would never know whom it might reach also holds true for Pollock's papers. He archived them in the hope that somebody would one day find the message.

At the end of his life, Pollock was unexpectedly able to help shape his legacy in at least one respect. When writing his biography of the institute, *The Dialectical Imagination*, Martin Jay, then aged 25, not only visited the two friends in Montagnola but also sent Pollock the draft prior to publication. Pollock both read it attentively and annotated it copiously.[49] Not that Jay, who had a wealth of sources reflecting varying vantages at his disposal, accepted all his suggestions, but Pollock's annotation throws an interesting light on the way in which he himself might have approached the task of writing a history of the institute and, by implication, his own. We may confidently assume that it would hardly have looked like this book, yet Pollock would hopefully show it the same forbearance he showed Jay's book, divergences of interpretation notwithstanding.

On 16 December 1970, Friedrich Pollock died of stomach cancer in Montagnola. Just months earlier he had still hoped that he might recover sufficiently to continue working. 'By the way', he wrote to Jay on 22 August 1970, having annotated about a third of his draft, 'a very thorough examination in a leading Swiss hospital informed me that my illness is painful but not dangerous and will in due time disappear. *Pazienza* they say in Italy.'[50]

---

49   See Jay 2020.
50   Friedrich Pollock to Martin Jay, 22 August 1970, Martin Jay private collection.

Epilogue

I am typing these lines in the recently renovated café on the ground floor of the Artists' House in Stuttgart. The exhibition spaces, studios and workshops are located on the upper floors. In 2018, an exhibition by Christian Flamm engaged with the history of this institution established in 1978. Two floors were left entirely empty and on the ground floor, Flamm placed dozens of white paper rolls resembling construction plans never carried out that have long since completely faded. On a table in the centre of the room stood a model, approximately 50 cm in height, of the building's façade. Behind the façade one saw only a vague representation of the foundation walls leading nowhere. The stark white walls and low ceiling of the elongated room lent it a strangely constricted and oppressive air, its brightness notwithstanding. So many people have gone in and out of here that the stone floor is smooth as glass. The upper floors looked much the same. Here, Flamm had reconstructed the walls at the centre of the room, 1.5 metres thick, that were originally installed in 1978 so exhibits could be attached to them.

Of course, the history of this building, which is instantly recognisable as a former factory, began long before it became the Artists' House.[1] It was in these elongated halls that hard-working employees once produced suitcases bearing the Nord-Pol logo, the logo of Nördlinger & Pollock. To this day, vintage enthusiasts may occasionally find leather cases with the logo, showing an ice bear standing on a suitcase in front of a stylised globe, on eBay. Yet the business and its erstwhile owners have disappeared. Like archaeological finds, the suitcases and ammunition pouches occasionally recovered from dusty attics seem to connect us to a past that has long since passed.

The factory once owned by the Pollocks is now a site of communication, art and creativity. Nothing recalls how the building is connected to this book. The same holds true for other sites I visited to gain a sense of Pollock's surroundings. The house in Freiburg where he was born was demolished after the war. His grandparents' house in Wiehre has survived. Ironically, it is located across the street from the offices of ça ira in Freiburg, the current publisher of Pollock's collected works.

It is much the same in Stuttgart. The house on Reinsburgstraße has disappeared. The villa on Lessingstraße still stands and is as impressive as ever, but its surroundings have changed radically. Pollock's residence in Munich has

---

1   Huber 2019. I am grateful to Hans Dieter Huber for sharing this study with me prior to its publication.

gone. The property where it once stood now forms part of the perimeter of the American Consulate – it has, rather fittingly, become extraterritorial and part of the United States, as it were. The unimaginative neoclassical architecture on Odeon Square that Pollock and Horkheimer were able to see from their window, looking across the Hofgarten as they watched the Freikorps hunting revolutionary workers, by contrast, survived the bombing raids of the Second World War. Thousands of tourists come each day to take photos of the Feldherrnhalle (Field Marshal's Hall), in many cases probably without knowing any more about it than that it is somehow connected to Hitler.

The house in Kronberg and Horkheimer's villa in Montagnola still stand. In Montagnola, the new owners have even preserved part of the original *intérieur*: the original bookcases (though not the books) are still in place as is the old typewriter in the study. The spacious patio overlooks the garden in which Ernst von Schenck, Matthias Becker and Martin Jay once interviewed Horkheimer against the backdrop of the mountains and palms surrounding Lake Lugano. On the left, a tree of almost 30 metres overlooks the garden. At the level of the patio, it has formed two separate trunks. It sounds so corny that one hardly dares mention it, but the double-trunked tree standing directly on the boundary between the two properties seems emblematic of the covenant of friendship between Pollock and Horkheimer. Pollock's former villa has not survived. A wealthy Russian had it demolished and replaced it with an eyesore of a high-security compound. Two servile moors stand guard at the gate which bears the inscription Il Principe. Like their previous residences in New York and Los Angeles, the properties in Montagnola were in prime location, and it has been a long time since two professors, no matter how established and well placed, would have been able to acquire them.

What remains? The traces of history inevitably fade, much like tombstones that are symbols of mourning but also remind us of the past and allow us to recall those who have died. In this sense we might consider this book a tombstone for Friedrich 'Fred' Pollock, designed to ensure that not just the name and dates inscribed on the actual tombstone in the Jewish cemetery in Bern – located less than 100 metres from Maidon and Max Horkhheimer's headstone – but his life, thoughts, fears, hopes, actions, weaknesses and strengths too are remembered.

    Prof. Dr.
    Friedrich Pollock
    1894–1970
    ה' נ' צ' נ' ה'

There are two mistakes in the rendering of the traditional blessing, 'May his soul be bound up in the bond of eternal life' (based on 1 Samuel 25, 29), on Pollock's tombstone. The first letter should be not a ה but a ת, the penultimate letter should be not another נ but a ב. Perhaps the (possibly Christian) stonemason was responsible for the errors. Perhaps the two friends were trying to tell us something that we have yet to decipher.

Chronology

1894	Pollock is born in Freiburg/Breisgau.
1900	Registration of Nördlinger & Pollock OHG.
1910	The Pollocks move to Stuttgart.
1911	Pollock befriends Horkheimer.
1912–1915	Business apprenticeship including stays in Brussels, London, Manchester and Paris.
1915–1918	Military service, stationed in Ludwigsburg.
1918–1919	Pollock witnesses the Revolution in Munich, he completes the university admission qualification as an external candidate and begins to study economics and politics in Munich.
1919–1923	Move to Kronberg/Taunus, Pollock continues his studies in Frankfurt/Main and Freiburg.
1921	Nördlinger & Pollock goes public (all the shares are held by the two families, however).
1923	Pollock completes his doctorate in politics and co-founds the Institute of Social Research.
1924–1928	Joint director (with Felix Weil) of the Marx Engels Archive Ltd.
1926	Publication of *Sombarts 'Widerlegung' des Marxismus* (Sombart's 'Refutation' of Marxism).
1927	Invited to attend the festivities marking the tenth anniversary of the October Revolution, Pollock spends a month in Moscow.
1928	Pollock completes his postdoctoral qualification.
1928–1931	Following Grünberg's incapacitation, Pollock serves as acting director of the Institute of Social Research.
1929	Publication of Pollock's postdoctoral thesis, *Die planwirtschaftlichen Versuche in der Sowjetunion, 1917–1927* (*The Attempts to Construct a Planned Economy in the Soviet Union, 1917–1927*).
1930	Pollock's mother Elisabeth Pollock dies. The institute opens a branch in London.
1931	Max Horkheimer is appointed director of the Institute of Social Research, Pollock as his deputy.
1932	Establishment of the Société Internationale des Recherches Sociales in Geneva with Pollock as director.
1933	Hitler is appointed chancellor, the house in Kronberg and the institute are expropriated, Pollock's academic teaching licence and Prussian citizenship are revoked.
1934	Pollock moves to New York.

1934–1949	Pollock serves as assistant director of the International Institute of Social Research in New York.
1935	Pollock marries Andrée Woog.
1936	Pollock's brother Hans Pollock, his wife and mother-in-law flee to Amsterdam.
1937	Pollock's father Julius Pollock dies.
1939	Andrée Pollock dies of cancer. Pollock's German citizenship is revoked.
1940	Pollock is naturalised in the United States.
1941	Publication of Pollock's programmatic essays on state capitalism.
1943	Pollock meets FDR at the White House.
1943–1945	Pollock acts as a consultant for various government agencies.
1946	Pollock marries Carlota Weil.
1949	First post-war stay in Germany.
1950	Pollock temporarily returns to Frankfurt/Main.
1951	The Institute of Social Research is reconstituted in Frankfurt/Main.
1951–1958	Pollock holds a personal chair for economics and sociology at Frankfurt University.
1955	Publication of *Gruppenexperiment. Ein Studienbericht* (*Group Experiment*)
1956	Publication of *Automation. Materialien zur Beurteilung der ökonomischen und sozialen Folgen* (*Automation: A Study of its Economic and Social Consequences*).
1957	Move to Montagnola (Ticino).
1958	Pollock is appointed to a full professorship of economics and sociology at Frankfurt University.
1963	Pollock retires.
1969	Maidon Horkheimer and Theodor W. Adorno die. Pollock is awarded Frankfurt's medal of honour and the Bundesverdienstkreuz (West German Order of Merit).
1970	Pollock dies of cancer in Montagnola.

Archives

Bayerisches Hauptstaatsarchiv, Abt. IV: Kriegsarchiv (Bavarian State Archive, War Archive)
Folgeeinrichtungen der Bayerischen Armee (Bavarian army, successor institutions)
Personenbezogene Akten (personal files).

Brandenburgisches Landeshauptarchiv Potsdam (Brandenburg State Archive, Potsdam)
Geheime Staatspolizei und Konzentrationslager, Rep35G KZ Oranienburg (1933–1950), 3/22/1 Schutzhaft namentlich genannter Häftlinge, Buchstabe M (Gestapo and Concentration Camp Oranienburg, Named Prisoners in Protective Custody, Letter M).

Deutsches Literaturarchiv Marbach
Autorenkonvolut Ernst Bloch (Ernst Bloch Papers).
Nachlass Siegfried Kracauer (Siegfried Kracauer Papers).

Hoover Institution Stanford
Wittfogel Papers.

Institut für Stadtgeschichte Frankfurt am Main (Institute for the History of Frankfurt)
Felix Weil, 'Erinnerungen (Fragment)', S 5/421.

Landesarchiv Baden-Württemberg. Hauptstaatsarchiv Stuttgart (State Archive Stuttgart)
Kirchenein- und -austritte Freiburg im Breisgau (church membership files Freiburg).
Personenstandsregister der jüdischen Gemeinde in Freiburg im Breisgau (Register of Births, Deaths and Marriages, Jewish Congregation Freiburg).

Landesarchiv Baden-Württemberg. Staatsarchiv Freiburg (State Archive Freiburg)
Handelsregistrierung S. Pollock, G 540/5 (commercial register registration S. Pollock).
Landesamt für Wiedergutmachung: Außenstelle Freiburg, Personalakten (State Restitution Bureau: Freiburg Branch, Personal Files).

Landesarchiv Baden-Württemberg. Staatsarchiv Ludwigsburg (State Archive Ludwigsburg)
Amtsgericht Stuttgart, Akten des Schlichters für Wiedergutmachung Stuttgart, FL 300/33 1 Bü (Stuttgart Magistrates' Court, Files of the Stuttgart Restitution Arbitrator).
Finanzamt Heilbronn, Steuerakten jüdischer Bürger 1913–1977 (Finance Directorate Heilbronn, Jewish Citizens' Tax Files).

Handelsregistrierung der Firma Nördlinger & Pollock, F303/11 Bü 344 (Commercial Register Registration Nördlinger & Pollock).
Kartei der Stuttgarter Passakten (Register of Stuttgart Passport Files).

Leo Baeck Institute New York
Auerbach Family Collection, AR 11 847, III/56.
Selfhelp for German Refugees Collection, 1937–1977, AR 4002.
Toni and Gustav Stolper Collection, AR 11 781, Personal Histories 11.

Library of Congress
Hannah Arendt Papers.

National Archives and Records Administration (NARA), Washington DC
242.15 Microfilm Copies of Records Filmed at the Berlin Document Center (BDC), T355, Name Index of Jews Whose German Nationality Was Annulled by the Nazi Regime, roll 7.
Franklin D. Roosevelt Library, Records of the War Refugee Board, 1944–1945. General Correspondence, Box 24, Folder 1: Selfhelp for Emigres from Central Europe; Box 30, Folder 11, Research Bureau for Post-War Economics, 000 717.
Joint Chief of Staff. Office of Strategic Services. Record Group 226, Personnel Files 1942–1945: Friedrich Pollock, ARC 2183 363.

New York Municipal Archives
New York City Marriage Records, 1829–1940, FHL microfilm 1,674,299.

Martin Jay Private Collection, Berkeley
Pollock's annotation of the typescript of The Dialectical Imagination.
Correspondence with Friedrich Pollock.

Nicola Emery Private Archive, Montagnola
Casa Pollock Construction Plans.

Schweizerisches Bundesarchiv (Swiss Federal Archive)
Schweizerisches Auswanderungsamt und Auswanderungsbüro. Überseeische Auswanderungen aus der Schweiz 1910–1953 (Swiss Emigration Bureau. Overseas Emigration from Switzerland).

State Archive Munich
Staatsanwaltschaften 1939, Gerichtsverfahren gegen Tobias Akselrod (Prosecution Services 1939, Proceedings Against Tobias Akselrod).

Staatsanwaltschaften 2296, Gerichtsprozess gegen Anton Aschauer (Prosecution Services 2296, Trial of Anton Aschauer).

Stadtarchiv Freiburg im Breisgau (Municipal Archive Freiburg)
Hinterlassenschaftsakte Salomon Pollock, H. Nr. 18904 (Probate File Salomon Pollock).

SUNY Albany, M.E. Grenander Department of Special Collection & Archives
Otto Kirchheimer Papers.

Università degli Studi di Firenze, Biblioteca Umanistica
Fondo Pollock.

Universitäts- und Stadtbibliothek Frankfurt am Main, Archivzentrum, Max-Horkheimer-Archiv (University and Municipal Library Frankfurt, Max Horkheimer Archive)
Nachlass Max Horkheimer, Na 1 (Max Horkheimer Papers).
Nachlass Friedrich Pollock, Na 2 (Friedrich Pollock Papers).

Universitätsarchiv Freiburg im Breisgau (University Archive Freiburg)
B 44: Studentensekretariat, Exmatrikelbücher (1884–1938), 51/655 (Student Registry, Deregistration Registers).

Zentralarchiv der Ludwig-Maximilians-Universität München (Ludwig Maximilian University Munich, Central Archive)
Belegblätter der besuchten Veranstaltungen (Student Course Registrations).
Studentenkartei (1914–1935) (Student Register).
Personenstandsregister Winter-Halbjahr 1918/19 (Student Register, Winter 1918/19).

References

Abromeit, John D. 2011, *Max Horkheimer and the Foundations of the Frankfurt School*, New York: Cambridge University Press.

Adorno, Theodor W. 1967 [1942/51], 'Aldous Huxley and Utopia', in *Prisms*, translated by Samuel and Shierry Weber, Cambridge, MA: MIT Press, pp. 95–117.

Adorno, Theodor W. 1969, 'Scientific Experiences of a European Scholar in America', translated by Donald Fleming, in *The Intellectual Migration: Europe and America, 1930–1960*, edited by Donald Fleming and Bernard Bailyn, Cambridge, MA: The Belknap Press of Harvard University Press, pp. 338–70.

Adorno, Theodor W. 1998a [1965], 'Offener Brief an Max Horkheimer', *Die Zeit*, 12 February 1965, https://www.zeit.de/1965/07/offener-brief-an-max-horkheimer, in *Gesammelte Schriften*, Darmstadt: Wissenschaftliche Buchgesellschaft, pp. 155–63.

Adorno, Theodor W. 1998b [1969], 'Marginalia to Theory and Praxis', in *Critical Models: Interventions and Catchwords*, translated by Henry W. Pickford, New York: Columbia University Press, pp. 259–78.

Adorno, Theodor W. 2005 [1951], *Minima Moralia: Reflections from Damaged Life*, translated by Edmund Jephcott, London: Verso.

Adorno, Theodor W. 2010 [1957], 'Reply to Peter R. Hofstätter's Critique of Group Experiment', in *Guilt and Defense: On the Legacies of National Socialism in Postwar Germany*, translated and edited by Jeffrey Olick and Andrew J. Perrin, Cambridge, MA: Harvard University Press, pp. 197–209.

Adorno, Theodor W. et al. 1950, *The Authoritarian Personality*, New York: Harper.

Adorno, Theodor W. and Walter Benjamin 1999, *The Complete Correspondence, 1928–1940*, translated by Nicholas Walker, Cambridge: Polity.

Adorno, Theodor W. and Max Horkheimer 2003, *Briefwechsel*, Volume 1, Frankfurt/Main: Suhrkamp.

Adorno, Theodor W. and Max Horkheimer 2004, *Briefwechsel*, Volume 2, Frankfurt/Main: Suhrkamp.

Adorno, Theodor W. and Max Horkheimer 2006, *Briefwechsel*, Volume 4, Frankfurt/Main: Suhrkamp.

Adorno, Theodor W. and Siegfried Kracauer 2020, *Correspondence*, translated by Susan Reynolds and Michael Winkler, Cambridge: Polity.

Alcock, Antony 1971, *History of the International Labour Organization*, New York: Octagon.

Alexander, Stephan 2000, *'Communazis': FBI Surveillance of German Emigré Writers*, New Haven: Yale University Press.

Alexander, Susanne 1985, 'Marxistische Arbeitswoche 1923', in *Beiträge zur Geschichte der Arbeiterbewegung*, 27, 1: 53–4.

Aly, Götz 2008, *Unser Kampf 1968 – ein irritierter Blick zurück*, Frankfurt/Main: Fischer.
Anderson, Perry 1976, *Considerations on Western Marxism*, London: Verso.
Appel, Michael 1992, *Werner Sombart. Historiker und Theoretiker des modernen Kapitalismus*, Marburg: Metropolis.
Arendt, Hannah 1942, 'From the Dreyfus-Affair to France Today', *Jewish Social Studies*, 4, 3: 194–240.
Arendt, Hannah 1951, *Origins of Totalitarianism*, New York: Harcourt Brace.
Arendt, Hannah 1968a, 'Walter Benjamin. I. Der Bucklige', *Merkur*, 22, 238: 50–65.
Arendt, Hannah 1968b, 'Walter Benjamin und das Institut für Sozialforschung – noch einmal', *Merkur*, 22, 246: 968.
Arendt, Hannah 2007 [1943], 'We Refugees', in *The Jewish Writings*, edited by Jerome Kohn and Ron H. Feldman, New York: Schocken, pp. 264–74.
Backhaus, Hans-Georg 1997, 'Anfänge der Neuen Marx-Lektüre', in *Dialektik der Wertform. Untersuchungen zur marxschen Ökonomiekritik*, Freiburg/Breisgau: ça ira, pp. 9–40.
Bajohr, Frank and Michael Wildt (eds.) 2009, *Volksgemeinschaft. Neue Forschungen zur Gesellschaft des Nationalsozialismus*, Frankfurt/Main: Fischer.
Bast, Jürgen 1999, *Totalitärer Pluralismus. Zu Franz L. Neumanns Analysen der politischen und rechtlichen Struktur der NS-Herrschaft*, Tübingen: Mohr Siebeck.
Behrend, Manfred 1998, 'Der Wandschirm, hinter dem nichts geschieht. Bildung, Tätigkeit und Ende der ersten deutschen Sozialisierungskommission', in *Beiträge zur Geschichte der Arbeiterbewegung*, 40, 4: 18–35.
Benanav, Aaron 2020, *Automation and the Future of Work*, London: Verso.
Benda, Julian 1928, *The Treason of the Intellectuals*, translated by Richard Aldington, New York: W. Morrow.
Benicke, Jens 2010, *Von Adorno zu Mao. Über die schlechte Aufhebung der antiautoritären Bewegung*, Freiburg/Breisgau: ça ira.
Benjamin, Walter 1991a [1939], 'Meine Beziehungen zum Institut', in *Gesammelte Schriften*, Volume 5.2, pp. 1174–5.
Benjamin, Walter 1991b, *Gesammelte Schriften*, Volume 2.3, Frankfurt/Main: Suhrkamp.
Benjamin, Walter 1999 [1931], 'A Short History of Photography', translated by Edmund Jephcott and Kingsley Shorter, in *Selected Writings*, Volume 2.2, Cambridge, MA: Belknap Press of Harvard University Press, pp. 507–30.
Benjamin, Walter 2000, *Gesammelte Briefe*, Volume 6, edited by Christoph Gödde and Henri Lonitz, Frankfurt/Main: Suhrkamp.
Billinger, Karl 1935, *Fatherland*, New York: Farrar & Rinehart.
Billinger, Karl 1939, *Hitler Is No Fool*, New York: Modern Age Books.
Blubacher, Thomas 2011, *Paradies in schwerer Zeit. Künstler und Denker im Exil in Pacific Palisades*, Munich: Sandmann.
Blum, John Morton (ed.) 1973, *The Price of Vision: The Diary of Henry A. Wallace, 1942–1946*, Boston: Houghton Mifflin.

Bock, Wolfgang 2018, *Dialektische Psychologie. Adornos Rezeption der Psychoanalyse*, Wiesbaden: Springer.

Boeckmann, Staci Lynn von 2004, 'The Life and Work of Gretel Karplus/Adorno: Her Contributions to the Frankfurt School', PhD Thesis, University of Oklahoma.

Böhm-Bawerk, Eugen 1884, *Kapital und Kapitalzins. Erste Abteilung: Geschichte und Kritik der Kapitalzinstheorieen*, Innsbruck: Wagner'sche Universitäts-Buchhandlung.

Böhm-Bawerk, Eugen 1890, *Capital and Interest: A Critical History of Economical Theory*, translated with a preface and analysis by William Smart, London: Macmillan.

Boldyrev, Ivan and Martin Kragh 2015, 'Isaak Rubin: Historian of Economic Thought During the Stalinization of Social Sciences in Soviet Russia', *Journal of the History of Economic Thought*, 37, 3: 363–86.

Boll, Monika 2013, 'Max Horkheimers zweite Karriere', in *'Ich staune, dass Sie in dieser Luft atmen können'. Jüdische Intellektuelle in Deutschland nach 1945*, edited by Monika Boll and Raphael Gross, Frankfurt/Main: Fischer, pp. 345–74.

Braunstein, Dirk 2011, *Adornos Kritik der politischen Ökonomie*, Bielefeld: Transcript.

Brecht, Bertolt 1990, *Letters, 1913–1956*, translated by Ralph Manheim, London: Methuen.

Brecht, Bertolt 1992, *Werke. Große kommentierte Berliner und Frankfurter Ausgabe*, Volume 21: *Schriften* 1, Berlin, Frankfurt/Main: Aufbau, Suhrkamp.

Brecht, Bertolt 1993, *Journals, 1933–1955*, translated by Hugh Rorrison, London: Methuen.

Brecht, Bertolt 1998, *Werke. Große kommentierte Berliner und Frankfurter Ausgabe*, Volume 29: *Briefe* 2, Berlin, Frankfurt/Main: Aufbau, Suhrkamp.

Brecht, Bertolt 2013 [1953/54], *Turandot or The Whitewashers' Congress*, translated by Tom Kuhn, in *Collected Plays Eight*, London: Bloomsbury, pp. 128–93.

Brenner, Michael 2022, *In Hitler's Munich: Jews, the Revolution, and the Rise of Nazism*, translated by Jeremiah Riemer, Princeton: Princeton University Press.

Breuer, Stefan 1985, 'Horkheimer oder Adorno: Differenzen im Paradigmenkern der kritischen Theorie', in *Aspekte totaler Vergesellschaftung*, Freiburg/Breisgau: ça ira, pp. 15–33.

Buckmiller, Michael 1988, 'Die "Marxistische Arbeitswoche" 1923 und die Gründung des "Instituts für Sozialforschung"', in *Grand Hotel Abgrund: Eine Photobiographie der kritischen Theorie*, edited by Gunzelin Schmid Noerr and Willem van Reijen, Hamburg: Junius, pp. 141–82.

Bukharin, Nikolai 1918, *Programm der Kommunisten (Bolschewki)*, Leipzig: Franke.

Bukharin, Nikolai 1920 [1918], *Programme of the World Revolution*, Glasgow: Socialist Labour Press.

Bunge, Hans and Hanns Eisler 2014 [1975], *Brecht, Music and Culture: Hanns Eisler in Conversation with Hans Bunge*, translated by Sabine Berendse and Paul Clements, London: Bloomsbury Methuen Drama.

Buono, Franco 1976, 'Die drei Kongresse der Tuis', in *Brechts Tui-Kritik. Aufsätze, Rezensionen, Geschichten*, edited by Wolfgang Fritz Haug, Karlsruhe: Argument, pp. 53–89.

Campani, Carlo 1992, *Pianificazione e teoria critica. L'opera di Friedrich Pollock dal 1923 al 1943*, Naples: Liguori.

Chaloupek, Günther 1996, 'Long Term Economic Trends in the Light of Werner Sombart's Concept of Spätkapitalismus', in *Werner Sombart (1863–1941). Social Scientist*, edited by Jürgen Backhaus, Volume 2, Marburg: Metropolis, pp. 163–78.

Chaloupek, Günther 2019, 'Karl Pribram (1877–1973). Ökonom und Pionier der österreichischen Sozialgesetzgebung', *Wirtschaft und Gesellschaft*, 45, 3: 403–19.

Clausing, Kathrin 2005, *Leben auf Abruf. Zur Geschichte der Freiburger Juden im Nationalsozialismus*, Freiburg/Breisgau: Stadtarchiv Freiburg im Breisgau.

Claussen, Detlev 1985, 'Hans-Jürgen Krahl – Ein politisch-philosophisches Profil', in Hans-Jürgen Krahl, *Konstitution und Klassenkampf. Zur historischen Dialektik von bürgerlicher Emanzipation und proletarischer Revolution*, Frankfurt/Main: Neue Kritik, pp. 65–70.

Claussen, Detlev 2005, *Grenzen der Aufklärung. Zur gesellschaftlichen Genese des modernen Antisemitismus*, updated edition, Frankfurt/Main: Fischer.

Claussen, Detlev 2008 [2003], *Theodor Adorno: One Last Genius*, translated by Rodney Livingstone, Cambridge, MA: The Belknap Press of Harvard University Press.

Collomp, Catherine 2011, '"Anti-Semitism among American Labor": A Study by the Refugee Scholars of the Frankfurt School of Sociology at the End of World War II', *Labor History*, 52,4: 417–39.

Debacher, Karl-Heinz 1988, 'Geschichte der jüdischen Gemeinde Rust', in *Schicksal und Geschichte der jüdischen Gemeinden Ettenheim – Altdorf – Kippenheim – Schmieheim – Rust – Orschweier*, edited by Historischer Verein für Mittelbaden, Ettenheim: Historischer Verein für Mittelbaden, pp. 399–435.

Deutscher, Isaac 1968 [1958], 'The Non-Jewish Jew', in *The Non-Jewish Jew and Other Essays*, edited by Tamara Deutscher, London: Oxford University Press, pp. 25–41.

Diehl, Karl 1916, *Theoretische Nationalökonomie*, Volume 1: *Einleitung in die Nationalökonomie*, Jena: Gustav Fischer.

Diehl, Markus Albert 2005, *Von der Marktwirtschaft zur nationalsozialistischen Kriegswirtschaft. Die Transformation der deutschen Wirtschaftsordnung 1933–1945*, Stuttgart: Steiner.

Dietzel, Heinrich 1895, *Theoretische Socialökonomik*, Leipzig: Winter.

Diner, Dan 1993 [1988], 'Reason and the "Other": Horkheimer's Reflections on Anti-Semitism and Mass Annihilation', in *On Max Horkheimer. New Perspectives*, edited by Seyla Benhabib, Wolfgang Bonß and John McCole, Cambridge, MA: MIT Press, pp. 335–63.

Dolfe, Alwin [Adolf Lewin] 1891, *Der ewige Jude. Eine Ansprache an Viele, wenn nicht an Alle*, Trier: Maas.

Drechsler, Nelly 1990, *Ohne Scham. Lebensbericht der Nelly Held*, edited by Marianne Krumrey, Potsdam: Brandenburgisches Verlagshaus.

Dubiel, Helmut 1975, 'Kritische Theorie und politische Ökonomie', in Friedrich Pollock, *Stadien des Kapitalismus*, Munich: C.H. Beck, pp. 7–19.

Eitler, Pascal 2009, *Gott ist tot – Gott ist rot. Max Horkheimer und die Politisierung der Religion um 1968*, Frankfurt/Main: Campus.

Eitz, Thosten and Isabelle Engelhardt 2015, *Diskursgeschichte der Weimarer Republik*, Hildesheim: Olms.

Emery, Nicola (ed.) 2018, *Automazione e teoria critica: A partire da Friedrich Pollock*, Milan: Mimesis.

Emery, Nicola (ed.) 2023, *For Nonconformism: Max Horkheimer and Friedrich Pollock: The Other Frankfurt School*, Leiden: Brill.

Engels, Friedrich 2010 [1877], *Anti-Dühring. Herr Eugen Dühring's Revolution in Science*, in *Marx Engels Collected Works*, Volume 25, London: Lawrence & Wishart, pp. 5–309.

Erd, Rainer (ed.) 1982, *Reform und Resignation. Gespräche über Franz L. Neumann*, Frankfurt/Main: Suhrkamp.

Evans, Richard J. 2004, *The Coming of the Third Reich*, New York: Penguin.

Eykman, Christoph 1989, 'Manfred George und der Aufbau: Ihre Bedeutung für die deutsche Exilliteratur in den USA', in *Deutschsprachige Exilliteratur seit 1933*, Volume 2, edited by John M. Spalek and Joseph Strelka, Bern: Francke, pp. 1385–1402.

Fait, Barbara 2004, 'Supervised Democratization: American Occupation and German Politics', in *The United States and Germany in the Era of the Cold War, 1945–1968*, edited by Detlev Junker, New York: Cambridge University Press, pp. 57–64.

Flechtheim, Ossip K. 1969 [1948], *Die KPD in der Weimarer Republik*, Frankfurt/Main: Europäische Verlagsanstalt.

Franck, Wolf 1935, *Führer durch die deutsche Emigration*, Paris: Éditions du Phénix.

Friedmann, Georges 1955 [1946], *Industrial Society: The Emergence of Human Problems of Automation*, Glencoe: Free Press.

Fromm, Erich 1984 [1929], *The Working Class in Weimar Germany: A Psychological and Sociological Study*, edited by Wolfgang Bonß, translated by Barbara Weinberger, Leamington Spa: Berg.

Fuchshuber, Thorsten 2019, *Rackets. Kritische Theorie der Bandenherrschaft*, Freiburg/Breisgau: ça ira.

Gangl, Manfred 1987, *Politische Ökonomie und Kritische Theorie. Ein Beitrag zur theoretischen Entwicklung der Frankfurter Schule*, Frankfurt/Main: Campus.

Gangl, Manfred 2016, 'The Controversy over Friedrich Pollock's State Capitalism', *History of Human Sciences*, 29, 2: 23–41.

Geheran, Michael 2020, *Comrades Betrayed: Jewish World War I Veterans under Hitler*, Ithaca: Cornell University Press.

Gerber, Jan 2017, 'Gedichte nach Auschwitz. Die Kritische Theorie und der Holocaust', *Jahrbuch für Antisemitismusforschung*, 26, pp. 253–76.

Gerhard, Hans Wolfram 1963, 'Die wirtschaftlich argumentierende Judenfeindschaft', in *Judenfeindschaft. Darstellung und Analysen*, edited by Karl Thieme, Frankfurt/Main: Fischer, pp. 80–125.

Glahn, Philip 2019, 'Brecht, the Popular, and Intellectuals in Dark Times: Of Donkeys and "Tuis"', in *Philosophizing Brecht: Critical Readings on Art, Consciousness, Social Theory and Performance*, edited by Norman Roessler and Anthony Squiers, Leiden: Brill, pp. 121–44.

Gödde, Christoph and Henri Lonitz 2006, 'Das Institut für Sozialforschung/Gretel Adorno, Adorno und Horkheimer', in *Benjamin Handbuch. Leben – Werk – Wirkung*, edited by Burkhardt Lindner, Stuttgart: J.B. Metzler, pp. 92–106.

Graf, Friedrich Wilhelm 2013, 'Paul Tillich, die Roosevelts und das Ehepaar Trude Pratt Lash und Joseph P. Lash. Mit einer unbekannten Traupredigt Paul Tillichs', *Zeitschrift für Neuere Theologiegeschichte*, 20, 2: 278–301.

Graf, Friedrich Wilhelm 2015, 'Februar 1932, Party bei den Tillichs. Reale Dialektik in Frankfurt', *Zeitschrift für Ideengeschichte*, 9, 4: 111–20.

Graf, Friedrich Wilhelm 2017, 'Paul Tillich im Exil', in *Paul Tillich im Exil*, edited by Christian Danz and Werner Schüßler, Berlin: De Gruyter, pp. 11–77.

Grossman, Henryk 2021 [1929], *The Law of Accumulation and Breakdown of the Capitalist System, Being also a Theory of Crises*, translated by Jairus Banaji and Rick Kuhn, in *Works*, Volume 3, Leiden: Brill.

Grünberg, Carl 1924, *Festrede gehalten zur Einweihung des Instituts für Sozialforschung an der Universität Frankfurt a. M. am 22. Juni 1924*, Frankfurt/Main: Werner u. Winter.

Gumnior, Helmut and Rudolf Ringguth 1973, *Max Horkheimer in Selbstzeugnissen und Bilddokumenten*, Reinbek: Rowohlt.

Haffner, Sebastian 1972, *Failure of a Revolution: Germany, 1918–19*, translated by Georg Rapp, New York: Library Press.

Hahn, Joachim (ed.) 1992, *Friedhöfe in Stuttgart*, Volume 3: *Pragfriedhof, Israelitischer Teil*, Stuttgart: Klett-Cotta.

Haigh, Thomas, Mark Priestley and Crispin Rope 2016, ENIAC *in Action: Making and Remaking the Modern Computer*, Cambridge, MA: MIT Press.

Hecker, Rolf 2009, 'Dawid Borisowitsch Rjasanow (1870–1938)', in *Bewahren, Verbreiten, Aufklären. Archivare, Bibliothekare und Sammler der Quellen der deutschsprachigen Arbeiterbewegung*, edited by Michael Schneider, Bonn: Friedrich Ebert Stiftung, pp. 258–67.

Heerich, Thomas 2007, 'Autologische Spiegelung der Verwalteten Welt: Friedrich Pollock (1894–1970)', in *Das Feld der Frankfurter Kultur- und Sozialwissenschaften vor 1945*, edited by Richard Faber and Eva-Maria Ziege, Würzburg: Königshausen & Neumann, pp. 107–20.

Heine, Heinrich 2006 [1840], *Ludwig Börne: A Memorial*, translated by Jeffrey L. Sammons, Woodbridge: Boydell & Brewer.
Heißerer, Dirk 2008 [1993], *Wo die Geister wandern. Literarische Spaziergänge durch Schwabing*, Munich: C.H. Beck.
Hepp, Michael 1985, *Die Ausbürgerung deutscher Staatsangehöriger 1933–1945 nach den im Reichsanzeiger veröffentlichten Listen*, Volume 1, Munich: Saur.
Herres, Jürgen 2018, *Marx und Engels. Porträt einer intellektuellen Freundschaft*, Ditzingen: Reclam.
Heuer, Renate and Siegbert Wolf (eds.) 1997, *Die Juden der Frankfurter Universität*, Frankfurt/Main: Campus.
Heufelder, Jeanette Erazo 2017, *Der argentinische Krösus. Kleine Wirtschaftsgeschichte der Frankfurter Schule*, Berlin: Berenberg.
Hielscher, Friedrich 1954, *Fünfzig Jahre unter Deutschen*, Hamburg: Rowohlt.
Hilferding, Rudolf 1933, 'Zwischen den Entscheidungen', *Die Gesellschaft*, 10, 1: 1–9.
Hilferding, Rudolf 1981 [1910], *Finance Capital: A Study of the Latest Phase of Capitalist Development*, edited by Tom Bottomore, from translations by Morris Watnick and Sam Gordon, London: Routledge & Kegan Paul.
Hoff, Jan 2009, *Marx global. Zur Entwicklung des internationalen Marx-Diskurses seit 1965*, Berlin: Akademie Verlag.
Hofstätter, Peter R. 2010 [1957], 'On Group Experiment by F. Pollock: A Critical Appraisal', in Theodor W. Adorno, *Guilt and Defense: On the Legacies of National Socialism in Postwar Germany*, translated and edited by Jeffrey Olick and Andrew J. Perrin, Cambridge, MA: Harvard University Press, pp. 189–96.
Hoppe, Bert 2007, *In Stalins Gefolgschaft. Moskau und die KPD 1928–1933*, Munich: Oldenbourg.
Horkheimer, Max (ed.) 1936, *Studien über Autorität und Familie. Forschungsberichte aus dem Institut für Sozialforschung*, Paris: Félix Alcan.
Horkheimer, Max 1950, 'The Lessons of Fascism', in Hadley Cantril (ed.), *Tensions That Cause Wars: Common Statement and Individual Papers by a Group of Social Scientists Brought Together by UNESCO*, Urbana: University of Illinois Press, pp. 209–42.
Horkheimer, Max 1969, 'Friedrich Pollock. Glückwunsch zum 75. Geburtstag', *Frankfurter Allgemeine Zeitung*, 23 May, p. 32.
Horkheimer, Max 1973 [1940/42], 'The Authoritarian State', translated by Paul Breines, *Telos*, 15: 3–20.
Horkheimer, Max 1978 [1934], *Dawn & Decline. Notes 1926–1931 and 1950–1969*, translated by Michael Shaw, New York: Seabury Press, Continuum.
Horkheimer, Max 1985a, *Gesammelte Schriften*, Volume 12, Frankfurt/Main: Fischer.
Horkheimer, Max 1985b [1939/42], 'Die Rackets und der Geist', in *Gesammelte Schriften*, Volume 12, Frankfurt/Main: Fischer, pp. 287–91.

Horkheimer, Max 1985c [1942], 'Geschichte der amerikanischen Arbeiterschaft', in *Gesammelte Schriften*, Volume 12, Frankfurt/Main: Fischer, p. 260.

Horkheimer, Max 1985d [1964], 'Einsicht in die Gegenwart. Friedrich Pollock zum 70. Geburstag', in *Gesammelte Schriften*, Volume 7, Frankfurt/Main: Fischer, pp. 265–8.

Horkheimer, Max 1985e [1969/1974], 'Dokumente – Stationen [Gespräch mit Otmar Hersche]', in *Gesammelte Schriften*, Volume 7, Frankfurt/Main: Fischer, pp. 317–44.

Horkheimer, Max 1985f [1972/1976], 'Das Schlimme erwarten und doch das Gute versuchen [Gespräch mit Gerhard Rein]', in *Gesammelte Schriften*, Volume 7, Frankfurt/Main: Fischer, pp. 442–79.

Horkheimer, Max 1987 [1914], 'L'île heureuse', in *Gesammelte Schriften*, Volume 11, Frankfurt/Main, Fischer, pp. 292–328.

Horkheimer, Max 1988a, *Gesammelte Schriften*, Volume 14, Frankfurt/Main: Fischer.

Horkheimer, Max 1988b [1914], 'Krieg. Ein Briefwechsel', in *Gesammelte Schriften*, Volume 1, Frankfurt/Main: Fischer, pp. 21–64.

Horkheimer, Max 1988c [1949/52], 'Schwerkraft', in *Gesammelte Schriften*, Volume 14, Frankfurt/Main: Fischer, pp. 45–7.

Horkheimer, Max 1988d [1960], 'Überlegungen aus dem Frühling 1960', in *Gesammelte Schriften*, Volume 14, Frankfurt/Main: Fischer, p. 544.

Horkheimer, Max 1989 [1939], 'The Jews and Europe', in *Critical Theory and Society: A Reader*, edited by Stephen E. Bronner and Douglas M. Kellner, New York: Routledge, pp. 77–94.

Horkheimer, Max 1995a, *Gesammelte Schriften*, Volume 15, Frankfurt/Main: Fischer.
Horkheimer, Max 1995b, *Gesammelte Schriften*, Volume 16, Frankfurt/Main: Fischer.
Horkheimer, Max 1996a, *Gesammelte Schriften*, Volume 17, Frankfurt/Main: Fischer.
Horkheimer, Max 1996b, *Gesammelte Schriften*, Volume 18, Frankfurt/Main: Fischer.

Horkheimer, Max 2002a [1932], 'Notes on Science and the Crisis', translated by Matthew J. O'Connell, in *Critical Theory: Selected Essays*, New York: Continuum, pp. 3–9.

Horkheimer, Max 2002b [1937], 'Traditional and Critical Theory', translated by Matthew J. O'Connell, in *Critical Theory: Selected Essays*, New York: Continuum, pp. 188–243.

Horkheimer, Max 2007, *A Life in Letters: Selected Correspondence*, edited and translated by Manfred R. Jacobson and Evelyn M. Jacobson, Lincoln: University of Nebraska Press.

Horkheimer, Max and Theodor W. Adorno 2002 [1944/47], *Dialectic of Enlightenment: Philosophical Fragments*, translated by Edmund Jephcott, Stanford: Stanford University Press.

Horkheimer, Max and Friedrich Pollock 1988 [1955/56], 'Notizen zur Automation', in Max Horkheimer, *Gesammelte Schriften*, Volume 14, Frankfurt/Main: Fischer, p. 253.

Horkheimer, Max and Friedrich Pollock 1988a [1957/67], 'Der Fachmann und die totalitäre Gesellschaft'; 'Fachmann, Führer und die Vernunft'; 'Herrschende Klasse, die von Rackets beherrschte Klasse und die Rolle der Fachleute'; 'Der Fachmann', all in Max Horkheimer, *Gesammelte Schriften*, Volume 14, Frankfurt/Main: Fischer, pp. 318, 309, 334–5, 359.

Horkheimer, Max and Friedrich Pollock 1988b [1957/67], 'Das Wertgesetz und der Begriff der produktiven Arbeit', in Max Horkheimer, *Gesammelte Schriften*, Volume 14, Frankfurt/Main: Fischer, pp. 384–5.

Horkheimer, Max and Friedrich Pollock 1988c [1962], 'Es soll nicht sein. Ein Gespräch', in Max Horkheimer, *Gesammelte Schriften*, Volume 14, Frankfurt/Main: Fischer, pp. 545–6.

Horkheimer, Max and Friedrich Pollock 1988d [1963], 'Stichworte zur Beurteilung von zwei Charakteren', in Max Horkheimer, *Gesammelte Schriften*, Volume 14, Frankfurt/Main: Fischer, p. 547.

Horkheimer, Max and Friedrich Pollock 1988e [1969], 'Zwei Ansichten über das Judentum', in Max Horkheimer, *Gesammelte Schriften*, Volume 14, Frankfurt/Main: Fischer, p. 527.

Horkheimer, Max and Friedrich Pollock 1988f [1970], 'Ist die Fortschritts-Ideologie noch glaubhaft', in Max Horkheimer, *Gesammelte Schriften*, Volume 14, Frankfurt/Main: Fischer, p. 541.

Horkheimer, Max et al. 1994 [1945], 'Diskussion über Theorie und Praxis', 28 January 1945, in Erdmann Sturm, 'Paul Tillich und Max Horkheimer im Dialog. Drei bisher unveröffentlichte Texte (1942–45)', *Zeitschrift für Neuere Theologiegeschichte*, 1, 2: 275–304, 295–304.

Huber, Hans Dieter 2019, 'Als der Nordpol noch in Stuttgart lag. Die Firma Nördlinger & Pollock und die Reuchlinstraße 4b in Stuttgart', in *Künstlerhaus Stuttgart 40 Jahre 1978–2018*, edited by Hannelore Paflik-Huber, Stuttgart: av Edition, pp. 27–79, https://archiv.ub.uni-heidelberg.de/artdok/7258/1/Huber_Als_der_Nordpol_noch_in_Stuttgart_lag_2019.pdf.

Huhn, Willy 2003, *Der Etatismus der Sozialdemokratie. Zur Vorgeschichte des Nazifaschismus*, Freiburg/Breisgau: ça ira.

'Humanae Vitae' 1991 [1968], in *'Humanae Vitae' A Generation Later*, edited by Janet E. Smith, Washington, DC: Catholic University of America Press, pp. 272–95.

Ibsen, Henrik 1890, *Enemy of the People*, translated by Eleanor Marx-Aveling, in *Prose Dramas: Authorized English Edition*, edited by William Archer, New York: Scribner & Welford, pp. 103–237.

Ickes, Harold K. 1953, *The Secret Diary of Harold K. Ickes: The First Thousand Days, 1933–1936*, New York: Simon & Schuster.

Ikeo, Aiko 2014, *A History of Economic Science in Japan: The Internationalization of Economics in the Twentieth Century*, New York: Routledge.

International Institute of Social Research 1935, *A Short Description of Its History and Aims*, New York: International Institute of Social Research.

Institute for Social Research 1941, 'Research Project on Antisemitism', *Studies in Philosophy and Social Sciences*, 9, 2: 124–25.
Jacobs, Jack 2015, *The Frankfurt School, Jewish Lives, and Antisemitism*, New York: Cambridge University Press
Jahoda, Marie, Paul F. Lazarsfeld and Hans Zeisel 1972 [1933], *Marienthal: The Sociography of an Unemployed Community*, translated by the authors with John Reginall and Thomas Elsaesser, London: Tavistock.
Jay, Martin 1979, 'Kurt Mandelbaum: His Decade at the Institute of Social Research', *Development and Change*, 10, 4: 542–52.
Jay, Martin 1996 [1973], *Dialectical Imagination: A History of the Frankfurt School and the Institute of Social Research, 1923–1950*, Berkeley: University of California Press.
Jay, Martin 2020 [2015], '"The Hope That Earthly Horror Does Not Possess the Last Word": Max Horkheimer and *The Dialectical Imagination*', in *Splinters in Your Eye: Frankfurt School Provocations*, London: Verso, pp. 19–32.
Jenemann, David 2007, *Adorno in America*, Minneapolis: University of Minnesota Press.
Jünger, Ernst 2014 [1920], *In Stahlgewittern. Ein Kriegstagebuch*, Stuttgart: Klett-Cotta.
Kalchthaler, Peter 2017, 'Hans Ludwig Pollock', in *Freiburg im Nationalsozialismus. Begleitbuch zur Ausstellung des Augustinermuseums in Kooperation mit dem Stadtarchiv*, edited by Peter Kalchthaler, Freiburg: Michael Imhof, p. 94.
Katz, Barry M. 1987, 'The Criticism of Arms. The Frankfurt School Goes to War', *Journal of Modern History*, 59, 3: 439–78.
Katznelson, Ora 2012, 'Two Exceptionalisms: Points of Departure for Studies of Capitalism and Jews in the United States,' in *Chosen Capital: The Jewish Encounter with American Capitalism*, edited by Rebecca Kobrin, New Brunswick: Rutgers University Press, pp. 12–32.
Kautsky, Karl 1918, *The Dictatorship of the Proletariat*, translated by Henry J. Stenning, Manchester: National Labour Press.
Kellner, Douglas 1984, *Herbert Marcuse and the Crisis of Marxism*, Berkeley: University of California Press.
Koenen, Gerd 2001, *Das rote Jahrzehnt: Unsere kleine deutsche Kulturrevolution, 1967–1977*, Cologne: Kiepenheuer & Witsch.
Korsch, Karl 2001, *Gesamtausgabe*, Volume 8, Hannover: Offizin.
Kracauer, Siegfried 1930, *Die Angestellten. Aus dem neuesten Deutschland*, Frankfurt/Main: Frankfurter Societäts-Druckerei.
Kracauer, Siegfried 2012 [1938], 'Pollock, 12. April 1938', in *Werke*, Volume 2.2, Berlin: Suhrkamp, pp. 827–9.
Krahl, Hans-Jürgen 1975 [1969], 'The Political Contradictions in Adorno's Critical Theory', *Sociological Review*, 23, 4: 831–4.
Krahl, Hans-Jürgen 2008 [1969/71], 'Kritische Theorie und Praxis', in *Konstitution und Klassenkampf*, fifth edition, Frankfurt/Main: Neue Kritik, pp. 295–303.

Krause, Werner 1962, *Werner Sombarts Weg vom Kathedersozialismus zum Faschismus*, Berlin: Rütten & Loening.

Kraushaar, Wolfgang 1998, *Frankfurter Schule und Studentenbewegung. Von der Flaschenpost zum Molotowcocktail*, Volumes 1–3, Hamburg: Hamburger Edition.

Krohn, Claus-Dieter 1996, *Der philosophische Ökonom. Zur intellektuellen Biographie Adolf Lowes*, Marburg: Metropolis.

Krohn, Claus-Dieter 2017, 'Kairos und "Dritte Kraft"', in *Paul Tillich im Exil*, edited by Christian Danz and Werner Schüßler, Berlin: De Gruyter, pp. 143–77.

Krüger, Doris Maja 2015, 'Leo Löwenthal und die jüdische Renaissance in der Weimarer Republik', in *Das Kulturerbe deutschsprachiger Juden. Eine Spurensuche in den Ursprungs-, Transit- und Emigrationsländern*, edited by Elke-Vera Kotowski, Berlin: De Gruyter, pp. 249–62.

Krug, Uli 2016, *Der Wert und das Es. Marxismus und Psychoanalyse in Zeiten sexueller Konterrevolution*, Freiburg/Breisgau: ça ira.

Krull, Germaine 2015, *La vie mène la danse*, Paris: Édition Textuel.

Krysmanski, Hans Jürgen 2014, *Die letzte Reise des Karl Marx*, Frankfurt/Main: Westend.

Kucher, Primus-Heinz 2016, '"When the Facts About Auschwitz Came Through ..." Der traumatische Einbruch der Shoah in das deutschsprachige Exil in den USA', *Exilforschung*, 34: 17–35.

Kuhn, Rick 2007, *Henryk Grossman and the Recovery of Marxism*, Urbana: University of Illinois Press.

Kuhn, Tom and David Constantine (eds.) 2013, 'Notes and Variants: Turandot', in *Collected Plays Eight*, London: Bloomsbury, pp. 239–55.

Lash, Joseph P. 1982, *A World of Love: Eleanor Roosevelt and Her Friends*, Garden City, NY: Doubleday.

Lenhard, Philipp 2014, '"In den Marxschen Begriffen stimmt etwas nicht". Friedrich Pollock und der Anfang der Kritischen Theorie', *sans phrase*, 5: 5–16.

Lenhard, Philipp 2016a, 'Staatskapitalismus und Automation. Einblicke in die Kritik der politischen Ökonomie im Spätwerk Herbert Marcuses und Friedrich Pollocks', *Zeitschrift für kritische Theorie*, 42/43: 9–39.

Lenhard, Philipp 2016b, 'An Institution of Nazi Statesmanship: Friedrich Pollock's Theoretical Contribution to the Study of Anti-Semitism', *New German Critique*, 43.1, no. 127: 195–214.

Lenhard, Philipp 2016c, 'Abschied vom Marxismus. Friedrich Pollock, Franz L. Neumann und die Entstehung der kritischen Theorie des Antisemitismus im amerikanischen Exil', *Exilforschung*, 34: 148–70.

Lenhard, Philipp 2017, 'Reconstruction and Reeducation: Max Horkheimer und die deutsch-israelische Freundschaft, 1948–1973', *Naharaim*, 11, 1–2: 25–46.

Lenhard, Philipp 2019, 'Adornos letzte Postkarte', *Sinn und Form*, 71, 4: 567–70.

Lenin, Vladimir I. 1960 [1902], *What is to be Done? Burning Questions of Our Movement*, in *Collected Works*, Volume 5, translated by Joe Feinberg and George Hanna, Moscow: Progress, pp. 347–527.

Lenin, Vladimir I. 1964 [1917], *Imperialism, the Highest Stage of Capitalism*, in *Collected Works*, Volume 22, Moscow: Progress, pp. 185–304.

Lewin, Adolf 1890, *Juden in Freiburg i. B.*, Trier: Maas.

Lewin, Adolf 1909, *Geschichte der badischen Juden seit der Regierung Karl Friedrichs (1738–1909)*, Karlsruhe: Braun.

Liebner, Petra 2001, *Paul Tillich und der Council for a Democratic Germany (1933 bis 1945)*, Frankfurt/Main: Peter Lang.

Lorwin, Lewis L. and A. Ford Hinrichs 1934, 'National Planning – Digest of Report', in *National Planning Board. Federal Emergency Administration of Public Works. Final Report 1933–34*, Washington, DC: United States Government Printing Office, pp. 62–103.

Löwenthal, Leo 1980, *Mitmachen wollte ich nie. Ein autobiographisches Gespräch mit Helmut Dubiel*, Frankfurt/Main: Suhrkamp.

Lowenstein, Steven M. 2005, 'The Beginning of Integration, 1780–1870', in *Jewish Daily Life in Germany, 1618–1945*, edited by Marion A. Kaplan, New York: Oxford University Press, pp. 93–171.

Lukács, Georg 1971a [1923], *History and Class Consciousness: Studies in Marxist Dialectics*, translated by Rodney Livingstone, London: Merlin.

Lukács, Georg 1971b [1963], 'Preface', in *The Theory of the Novel*, translated by Anna Rostock, Cambridge, MA: MIT Press, pp. 11–23.

Lukács, Georg 1980 [1954], *The Destruction of Reason*, translated by Peter Palmer, London: Merlin.

Lukács, Georg 1984 [1933], 'Grand Hotel Abgrund', in *Revolutionäres Denken – Georg Lukács. Eine Einführung in Leben und Werk*, edited by Frank Benseler, Darmstadt: Luchterand, pp. 179–96.

Machunsky, Niklaas 2014, 'Dialektik der Resistenzkraft. Über die Ungleichzeitigkeit der Utopie', *Prodomo. Zeitschrift in eigener Sache*, 18, pp. 33–9.

Mallmann, Klaus-Michael 1996, *Kommunisten in der Weimarer Republik. Sozialgeschichte einer revolutionären Bewegung*, Darmstadt: Wissenschaftliche Buchgesellschaft.

Mann, Thomas 1986 [1944/46], *Tagebücher 1944–1946*, Frankfurt/Main: Fischer.

Mann, Thomas 1991, *Tagebücher 1949–1950*, Frankfurt/Main: Fischer.

Maor, Maimon 1981, *Max Horkheimer*, Berlin: Colloquium.

Marcuse, Herbert 1998, *Technology, War and Fascism*, London: Routledge.

Marcuse, Herbert 2005 [1932], 'New Sources on the Foundation of Historical Materialism', translated by Joris de Bres and John Abromeit, in *Heideggerian Marxism*, edited by Richard Wolin and John Abromeit, Lincoln: University of Nebraska Press, pp. 86–121.

Marcuse, Herbert 2009 [1934], 'The Struggle Against Liberalism in the Totalitarian View of the State', in *Negations: Essays in Critical Theory*, translated by Jeremy Shapiro, London: mayfly, pp. 1–30.

Marcuse, Ludwig 1960, *Mein zwanzigstes Jahrhundert. Auf dem Weg zu einer Autobiographie*, Munich: Paul List.

Marx, Julius 1939, *Kriegs-Tagebuch eines Juden*, Zurich: Verlag 'Die Liga'.

Marx, Julius 1970, *Georg Kaiser, ich und die anderen. Alles in einem Leben. Ein Bericht in Tagebuchform*, Gütersloh: Bertelsmann.

Marx, Julius 2013 [1939], 'Juden im Krieg. (Ich hatte einen Kameraden)', translated by Gesine Schröder, in *In der Ferne das Glück. Geschichten für Hollywood*, edited by Wolfgang Jacobsen and Heike Klapdor, Berlin: Aufbau, pp. 183–240, 445–51.

Marx, Karl 2010a [1867], *Capital. A Critique of Political Economy*, Volume 1, in *Marx and Engels Collected Works*, Volume 35, London: Lawrence & Wishart.

Marx, Karl 2010b [1894], *Capital. A Critique of Political Economy*, Volume 3, in *Marx and Engels Collected Works*, Volume 37, London: Lawrence & Wishart.

Marx, Karl and Friedrich Engels 1927, *Historisch-kritische Gesamtausgabe*, Volume 1.1.1: *Karl Marx, Werke und Schriften bis Anfang 1844 nebst Briefen und Dokumenten*. Im Auftrage des Marx-Engels-Instituts Moskau herausgegeben von D. Rjazanov, Frankfurt/Main: Marx-Engels Archiv

Massing, Hede 1951, *This Deception. The Story of a Woman Agent*, New York: Duell, Sloan and Pearce.

Massing, Paul W. 1949, *Rehearsal for Destruction: A Study of Political Anti-Semitism in Imperial Germany*, New York: Harper.

Matthöfer, Hans et al. 1956, *Gewerkschaftliche Beiträge zur Automatisierung*, Köln-Deutz: Bund-Verlag.

Mayer, Hans 1992, 'Institut für Sozialforschung und Collège der sociologie', in *Der Zeitgenosse Walter Benjamin*, Frankfurt/Main: Jüdischer Verlag, pp. 61–6.

McLaughlin, Martin 1985, *The Gefland Case: A Legal History of the Exposure of US Government Agents in the Leadership of the Socialist Workers Party*, Detroit: Labor Publications, Volume 1.

Mehring, Franz 1962 [1918], *Karl Marx: The Story of His Life*, translated by Edward Fitzgerald, Ann Arbor: University of Michigan Press.

Mikhaél, Éphraïm 1890, 'L'île heureuse', in *Œuvres: Poésie – Poèmes en prose*, Paris: Alphonse Lemerre, p. 102.

Mülder-Bach, Inka and Ingrid Belke 2012, 'Nachbemerkung', in Siegfried Kracauer, *Werke*, Volume 2.2, Berlin: Suhrkamp, pp. 827–84.

Müller, Tim B. 2010, *Krieger und Gelehrte. Herbert Marcuse und die Denksysteme im Kalten Krieg*, Hamburg: Hamburger Edition.

Mulder, Bertus 1991, *Andries Sternheim. Een Nederlands vakbondsman in de Frankfurter Schule*, Zeist: Kerckebosch.

Mulder, Bertus and Lolle W. Nauta 1990, 'Working Class and Proletariat: On the Relation of Andries Sternheim to the Frankfurt School', *Praxis International*, 9, 4: 433–45.
Nebel, Theobald 1994, 'Julius Marx. Ein jüdisch-schwäbischer Unternehmer aus Freudental', *Ludwigsburger Geschichtsblätter*, 48: 85–115.
Nenarokov, Albert P. 2011, 'Das Gespann Rjazanov – Nikolaevsky', *Beiträge zur Marx-Engels-Forschung* NSer., pp. 43–52.
Neumann, Franz L. 1942, *Behemoth: The Structure and Practice of National Socialism*, London: Victor Gollancz.
Neumann, Franz, Herbert Marcuse and Otto Kirchheimer 2013, *Secret Reports on Nazi Germany: The Frankfurt School Contribution to the War Effort*, edited by Raffaele Laudani, Princeton: University of Princeton Press.
Neumann, Friedrich Julius 1898, 'Wirtschaftliche Gesetze nach früherer und jetziger Auffassung', *Jahrbücher für Nationalökonomie und Statistik*, Ser. 3, 16, 1: 1–38.
Oppenheimer, Franz 1964 [1931], *Erlebtes, Erstrebtes, Erreichtes. Lebenserinnerungen*, Düsseldorf: Melzer.
Osterloh, Jörg 2017, '"Es wurde ja auch darüber geschrieben, in der Zeitung ..." Die Berichterstattung im Deutschen Reich über die Häftlinge der frühen Konzentrationslager', in '*... der schranklosesten Willkür ausgeliefert'. Häftlinge der frühen Konzentrationslager 1933–1936/37*, edited by Jörg Osterloh and Kim Wünschmann, Frankfurt/Main: Campus, pp. 317–48.
Pakushanis, Evgeny 2002 [1924], *The General Theory of Law and Marxism*, translated by Barbara Einhorn, New Brunswick: Transaction
Pauck, Wilhelm and Marion Pauck 1976, *Paul Tillich: His Life and Thought*, Volume 1, New York: Harper & Row.
Paulus, Jael 1984, 'Geschichte der Juden Badens – Ein Überblick', in *Juden in Baden 1809–1984. 175 Jahre Oberrat der Israeliten Badens*, edited by Oberrat der Israeliten Badens, Karlsruhe: Oberrat der Israeliten Badens, pp. 19–56.
Perels, Joachim 2001, 'Fast vergessen: Franz L. Neumanns Betrag zur Konzipierung der Nürnberger Prozesse. Eine Erinnerung aus Anlass seines 100. Geburtstags', *Kritische Justiz*, 34, 1: 117–25.
Platz, Johannes 2009, '"Revolution der Roboter" oder "Keine Angst vor Robotern"'? Die Verwissenschaftlichung des Automationsdiskurses und die industriellen Beziehungen von den 50ern bis 68, in *Enterprises et crises économiques au xxe siècle*, edited by Laurent Commalle, Metz: Centre de Recherche Universitaire Lorrain d'Histoire, pp. 37–59.
Plessner, Monika 1995, *Die Argonauten auf Long Island. Begegnungen mit Hannah Arendt, Theodor W. Adorno, Gershom Scholem und anderen*, Berlin: Rowohlt.
Pollock, Friedrich 1929, *Die planwirtschaftlichen Versuche in der Sowjetunion 1917–1927*, Leipzig: C.L. Hirschfeld.

Pollock, Friedrich 1930, 'Das Institut für Sozialforschung an der Universität Frankfurt am Main', in *Forschungsinstitute. Ihre Geschichte, Organisation und Ziele*, edited by Ludolph Brauer, Albrecht Mendelssohn Bartholdy and Adolf Meyer, Volume 2, Hamburg: Paul Hartung, pp. 347–54.

Pollock, Friedrich 1932a, 'Die gegenwärtige Lage des Kapitalismus und die Aussichten einer planwirtschaftlichen Neuordnung', *Zeitschrift für Sozialforschung*, 1, 1: 8–27.

Pollock, Friedrich 1932b [review on titles in the field of family sociology], *Zeitschrift für Sozialforschung*, 1, 3: 448–51.

Pollock, Friedrich 1933, 'Bemerkungen zur Wirtschaftskrise', *Zeitschrift für Sozialforschung*, 2, 3: 321–54.

Pollock, Friedrich 1936 [review of Sternberg, *Der Faschismus an der Macht*], *Zeitschrift für Sozialforschung*, 5, 1: 538.

Pollock, Friedrich 1940, 'Economics of War. Influence of Preparedness on Western European Economic Life', *American Economic Review*, 30, 1.2: 317–25.

Pollock, Friedrich 1941a, 'State Capitalism: Its Possibilities and Limitations', *Studies in Philosophy and Social Sciences*, 9, 2: 200–25.

Pollock, Friedrich 1941b, 'Is National Socialism a New Order?', *Studies in Philosophy and Social Sciences*, 9, 3: 440–54.

Pollock, Friedrich 1955, 'Automation in USA: Betrachtungen zur "zweiten industriellen Revolution"', in *Sociologica. Aufsätze, Max Horkheimer zum sechzigsten Geburtstag gewidmet*, edited by Theodor W. Adorno and Walter Dirks, Frankfurt/Main: Europäische Verlagsanstalt, pp. 77–156.

Pollock, Friedrich 1956, 'Die wirtschaftlichen und sozialen Folgen der Automatisierung', in *Revolution der Roboter. Untersuchungen über Probleme der Automatisierung*, Munich: Isar Verlag, pp. 65–105.

Pollock, Friedrich 1957 [1956], *Automation: A Study of its Economic and Social Consequences*, translated by W.O. Henderson and W.H. Chaloner, New York: Frederick A. Praeger.

Pollock, Friedrich 1958, 'Altwerden als soziologisches Problem', in *Der alte Mensch in unserer Zeit*, Stuttgart: Kröner, pp. 111–27.

Pollock, Friedrich 1964, *Automation. Materialien zur Beurteilung der ökonomischen und sozialen Folgen*, second, revised edition, Frankfurt/Main: Europäische Verlagsanstalt.

Pollock, Friedrich 1968, 'Zu dem Aufsatz von Hannah Arendt über Walter Benjamin', *Merkur*, 22, 242: 576.

Pollock, Friedrich 1984 [1932], 'Socialism and Agriculture', translated by Ben Fowkes, in *Paths of Development in Capitalist Agriculture: Readings from German Social Democracy, 1891–99*, edited by Athar Hussain and Keith Tribe, London: Macmillan, pp. 159–92.

Pollock, Friedrich 1995 [1935], 'Materialien für Neuordnung von Grundsätzen', in Max Horkheimer, *Gesammelte Schriften*, Volume 15, Frankfurt/Main: Fischer, pp. 380–9.

Pollock, Friedrich 2014 [1941], 'Die bessere Ordnung', in *sans phrase*, 5: 3–4.
Pollock, Friedrich 2016 [1944], 'Political Antisemitism', quoted in Philipp Lenhard, 'An Institution of Nazi Statesmanship: Friedrich Pollock's Theoretical Contribution to the Study of Anti-Semitism', *New German Critique*, 43.1, 127: 195–214, 204–12.
Pollock, Friedrich 2018a, *Gesammelte Schriften*, Volume 1, Vienna: ça ira.
Pollock, Friedrich 2018b [1923], *Zur Geldtheorie von Karl Marx*, in *Gesammelte Schriften*, Volume 1, Vienna: ça ira, pp. 23–127.
Pollock, Friedrich 2018c [1926], 'Sombarts "Widerlegung" des Marxismus', in *Gesammelte Schriften*, Volume 1, pp. 153–250.
Pollock, Friedrich 2021a, *Gesammelte Schriften*, Volume 2, Vienna: ça ira.
Pollock, Friedrich 2021b [1929], *Die planwirtschaftlichen Versuche in der Sowjetunion 1917–1927*, in *Gesammelte Schriften*, Volume 2, Vienna: ça ira, pp. 25–466.
Pollock, Friedrich, Theodor W. Adorno and Colleagues 2011 [1955], *Group Experiment and Other Writings*, translated and edited by Andrew J. Perrin and Jeffrey K. Olick, Cambridge, MA: Harvard University Press.
Postone, Moishe and Barbara Crick 1993, 'Critical Theory and Political Economy,' in *On Max Horkheimer: New Perspectives*, edited by Seyla Benhabib, Wolfgang Bonß and John McCole, Cambridge, MA: MIT Press, pp. 215–56.
Prellwitz, Jens 1998, *Jüdisches Erbe, sozialliberales Ethos, deutsche Nation: Gustav Mayer im Kaiserreich und in der Weimarer Republik*, Mannheim: Palatium.
Ranshofen-Wertheimer, Egon 1942, *Victory is Not Enough: A Strategy for a Lasting Peace*, New York: W.W. Norton.
Rathenau, Walter 1921 [1920], 'Über Produktionspolitik', *Das Tage-Buch*, 2.24–28, 18 June–16 July: 741–47, 771–4, 809–12, 840–3, 863–6.
Rauh-Kühne, Cornelia 2004, 'Life Rewarded the Latecomers: Denazification During the Cold War', in *The United States and Germany in the Era of the Cold War, 1945–1968*, edited by Detlev Junker, New York: Cambridge University Press, pp. 65–72.
Raulet, Gérard 1986, 'Kritik der Vernunft und kritischer Gebrauch des Pessimismus', in *Max Horkheimer heute: Werk und Wirkung*, edited by Alfred Schmidt and Norbert Altwicker, Frankfurt/Main: Fischer, pp. 31–51.
Reckwitz, Andreas 2017, *Die Gesellschaft der Singularitäten. Zum Strukturwandel der Moderne*, Berlin: Suhrkamp.
Regius, Heinrich [Max Horkheimer] 1987 [1934], *Dämmerung*, in *Gesammelte Schriften*, Volume 2, Frankfurt/Main: Fischer, pp. 309–452.
Reijen, Willem van and Jan Bransen 1987, 'Das Verschwinden der Klassengeschichte in der "Dialektik der Aufklärung". Ein Kommentar zu den Textvarianten der Buchausgabe von 1947 gegenüber der Erstveröffentlichung von 1944', in Max Horkheimer, *Gesammelte Schriften*, Volume 5, Frankfurt/Main: Fischer, pp. 453–7.
Riazanov, David (ed.) 1925, *Marx-Engels-Archiv. Zeitschrift des Marx-Engels-Instituts in Moskau*, 1, Frankfurt/Main: Marx-Engels Archiv.

Rieß, Rolf (ed.) 2019, *Arbeitsgemeinschaft zum Studium der sowjetrussischen Planwirtschaft*, Marburg: Metropolis-Verlag.

Rosen, Zvi 1995, *Max Horkheimer*, Munich: C.H. Beck.

Rosenthal, Jacob 2007, *Die Ehre der jüdischen Soldaten. Die Judenzählung im ersten Weltkrieg und ihre Folgen*, Frankfurt/Main: Campus.

Roßkamp, Simone 2002, '"Adorno war ganz schön hässlich." Von Stuttgart nach New York – das Leben der Lucille Weil', *Aufbau*, 68.11, 30 May, p. 12.

Roth, Joseph 1995 [1926], 'Der neunte Feiertag der Revolution', originally published in the *Frankfurter Zeitung* on 14 November 1926, in *Reise nach Rußland. Feuilletons, Reportagen, Tagebuchnotizen 1920–1930*, Cologne: Kiepenheuer & Witsch, pp. 172–6.

Roy, Samaren 1997, *M.N. Roy: A Political Biography*, London: Sangam.

Rubin, Isaac Ilyich 1973 [³1928], *Essays on Marx's Theory of Value*, translated by Miloš Samardźija and Fredy Perlman, Montréal: Black Rose Books.

Rueß, Susanne 2009, *Stuttgarter jüdische Ärzte während des Nationalsozialismus*, Würzburg: Königshausen & Neumann.

Sabrow, Martin 2016, *Erich Honecker. Das Leben davor 1912–1945*, Munich: C.H. Beck.

Salter, Michael 2020, 'The Visibility of the Holocaust: Franz Neumann and the Nuremberg Trials', in Robert Fine and Charles Turner (eds.), *Social Theory After the Holocaust*, Liverpool: Liverpool University Press, pp. 197–218.

Schmid Noerr, Gunzelin 1988, 'Editorische Vorbemerkung' (editorial preface to *Späne*), in Max Horkheimer, *Gesammelte Schriften*, Volume 14, Frankfurt/Main: Fischer, pp. 172–6.

Schmidt, Alfred 1973, *Emanzipatorische Sinnlichkeit. Ludwig Feuerbachs anthropologischer Materialismus*, Munich: Hanser.

Schmidt, Alfred 1974, *Zur Idee der Kritischen Theorie. Elemente der Philosophie Max Horkheimers*, Munich: Hanser.

Schmidt, Holger J. 2010, *Antizionismus, Israelkritik und 'Judenknax'. Antisemitismus in der deutschen linken nach 1945*, Bonn: Bouvier.

Scholem, Gershom (ed.) 1989 [1980], *The Correspondence of Walter Benjamin and Gershom Scholem, 1932–1940*, translated by Gary Smith and André Lefevere, New York: Schocken.

Scholem, Gershom and Theodor W. Adorno (eds.) 1994 [1966], *The Correspondence of Walter Benjamin, 1910–1940*, translated by Manfred R. Jacobson and Evelyn M. Jacobson, Chicago: University of Chicago Press.

Schrag, Peter 2019, *The World of Aufbau: Hitler's Refugees in America*, Madison: University of Wisconsin Press.

Schulz, Gerhard 1987, *Deutschland am Vorabend der Großen Krise*, Berlin: De Gruyter.

Sering, Paul [Richard Löwenthal] 1936, *Faschismus und Monopolkapitalismus*, n.p.: n.p.

Sichel, Kim 1999. *Germaine Krull: Photographer of Modernity*, Cambridge, MA: MIT Press.

Silberner, Edmund 1983, *Kommunisten zur Judenfrage. Zur Geschichte von Theorie und Praxis des Kommunismus*, Opladen: Westdeutscher Verlag.

Sönke-Schneider, Gregor 2014, *Keine Kritische Theorie ohne Leo Löwenthal. Die Zeitschrift für Sozialforschung (1932–1941/42)*, Frankfurt/Main: Peter Lang.

Sombart, Werner 1902, *Der moderne Kapitalismus*, Volume 1, Leipzig: Duncker & Humblot.

Sombart, Werner 1911, *Die Juden und das Wirtschaftsleben*, Leipzig: Duncker & Humblot.

Sombart, Werner 1914 [1911], *The Jews and Modern Capitalism*, translated by Mordechai Epstein, New York: E.P. Dutton.

Sombart, Werner 1924, *Der proletarische Sozialismus (Marxismus)*, tenth, updated edition, Jena: Gustav Fischer.

Sperber, Jonathan 2013, *Karl Marx: A Nineteenth-Century Life*, New York: Liveright.

Sternberg, Fritz 1926, *Der Imperialismus*, Berlin: Malik.

Sternberg, Fritz 1935, *Der Faschismus an der Macht*, Amsterdam: Contact.

Stirk, Peter M.R. 1992, *Max Horkheimer: A New Interpretation*, Hemel Hempstead: Harvester Wheatsheaf.

Thälmann, Ernst 1977 [1933], 'Aus dem Referat auf der Tagung des ZK der KPD in Sporthaus Ziegenhals', in *Ausgewählte Reden und Schriften in zwei Bänden*, Volume 2, Frankfurt/Main: Verlag Marxistische Blätter, pp. 345–57.

Tränkle, Sebastian 2013, 'Die materialistische Sehnsucht: Über das Bilderverbot in der Philosophie Theodor W. Adornos', *Zeitschrift für kritische Theorie*, 36/37: 82–109.

Ullrich, Anna 2019, *Von 'jüdischem Optimismus' und 'unausbleiblicher Enttäuschung'. Erwartungsmanagement deutsch-jüdischer Vereine und gesellschaftlicher Antisemitismus 1914–1938*, Munich: De Gruyter Oldenbourg.

Ulmen, Gary L. 1978, *The Science of Society: Toward an Understanding of the Life and Work of Karl August Wittfogel*, The Hague: Mouton.

Vatlin, Alexander 2014, 'Weltrevolutionär im Abseits. Der Kommissar der bayerischen Räterepublik Tobias Axelrod', in *Vierteljahrshefte für Zeitgeschichte* 62, 4: 513–36.

Voigt, Wolfgang 2016, 'Franz Roeckles Institute für Sozialforschung in Frankfurt. Politische Architektur in "sachlicher Zweckmässigkeit, ehrlicher Herbheit"', in *Franz Roeckle. Bauten 1902–1933*, edited by Marianne Hilti-Roeckle, Hanna Roeckle and Peter Zimmermann, Ostfildern: Hatje Cantz, pp. 49–65.

Wagner, Anton 1935, *Los Angeles. Leben, Werden und Gestalt der Zweimillionendstadt in Südkalifornien*, Leipzig: Bibliographisches Institut.

Wainstein, Albert L. 1931 [review of Pollock 1929], *Weltwirtschaftliches Archiv*, 34: 195–8.

Walter-Busch, Ernst 2010, *Geschichte der Frankfurter Schule. Kritische Theorie und Politik*, Munich: Wilhelm Fink.

Weber, Adolf 1907, *Armenwesen und Armenfürsorge. Einführung in die soziale Hilfsarbeit*, Leipzig: Göschen.

Weber, Adolf 1908, *Die Großstadt und ihre sozialen Probleme*, Leipzig: Quelle & Mayer.

Weber, Adolf 1910, *Der Kampf zwischen Kapital und Arbeit. Versuch einer systematischen Darstellung mit besonderer Berücksichtigung der gegenwärtigen deutschen Verhältnisse*, Tübingen: Mohr Siebeck.

Wege, Carl 1992, 'Turandot oder Der Kongreß der Weißwäscher: Zeilenkommentar', in Bertolt Brecht, *Werke. Große kommentierte Berliner und Frankfurter Ausgabe*, Volume 9: *Stücke 9*, Berlin, Frankfurt/Main: Aufbau, Suhrkamp, pp. 408–16.

Wegner, Armin T. 1979 [1930], *Fünf Finger über Dir. Aufzeichnungen einer Reise durch Rußland, den Kaukasus und Persien 1927/28*, Wuppertal: Hammer.

Weil, Felix 1921, *Sozialisierung. Versuch einer begrifflichen Grundlegung nebst einer Kritik der Sozialisierungspläne*, Berlin: Verlag Gesellschaft und Erziehung.

Weiss, Hilde 2006 [1940], *Soziologin, Sozialistin, Emigrantin. Ihre Autobiographie aus dem Jahre 1940*, edited by Detlef Garz, Hamburg: Dr. Kovac.

Wiener, Norbert 1948, *Cybernetics or Control and Communication in the Animal and the Machine*, Cambridge, MA: MIT Press.

Wiese, Leopold von 1954, 'Über das Alter', in *Spätlese*, Cologne: Westdeutscher Verlag, pp. 29–38.

Wiggershaus, Rolf 1994a [1988], *The Frankfurt School: Its History, Theories and Political Significance*, translated by Michael Robertson, Cambridge: Polity.

Wiggershaus, Rolf 1994b, 'Friedrich Pollock – der letzte Unbekannte der Frankfurter Schule', *Neue Gesellschaft/Frankfurter Hefte*, 41, 8: 750–6.

Wiggershaus, Rolf 2013, *Max Horkheimer. Unternehmer in Sachen Kritische Theorie*, Frankfurt/Main: Fischer.

Wildt, Michael 2009 [2003], *An Uncompromising Generation: The Nazi Leadership of the Reich Security Main Office*, translated by Tom Lampert, Madison: University of Wisconsin Press.

Wizisla, Erdmut 2007, *Die Bibliothek Bertolt Brechts*, Frankfurt/Main: Suhrkamp.

Worrell, Mark P. 2009, '"Es kommt die Nacht": Paul Massing, the Frankfurt School, and the Question of Labor Authoritarianism during World War II', *Critical Sociology*, 35, 5: 629–35.

Wyrwa, Ulrich 2017, 'Kritische Theorie und Antisemitismusforschung. Paul W. Massing und sein geschichtswissenschaftlicher Beitrag', *Jahrbuch für Antisemitismusforschung*, 26: 277–301.

Zelzer, Maria 1964, *Weg und Schicksal der Stuttgarter Juden: Ein Gedenkbuch*, Stuttgart: Klett.

Ziege, Eva-Maria 2009, *Antisemitismus und Gesellschaftstheorie. Die Frankfurter Schule im amerikanischen Exil*, Frankfurt/Main: Suhrkamp.

Illustrations

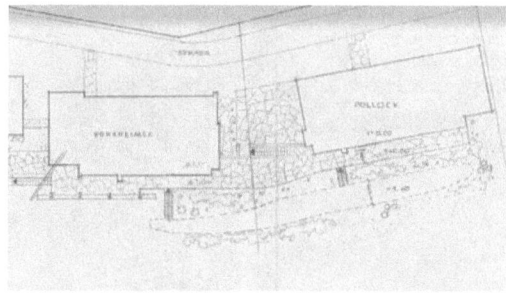

FIGURE 1
Groundplan of the Casas Horkheimer and Pollock in Montagnola
PRIVATE ARCHIVE NICOLA EMERY

FIGURE 2
Pollock's Birthplace in Freiburg
WIKIMEDIA COMMONS

FIGURE 3   Pollock's Gravestone on the Jewish Cemetery in Bern
PRIVATE ARCHIVE PHILIPP LENHARD

FIGURE 4
Lucille Weil
IN: DER AUFBAU 11 (30. MAI 2002), P. 12

FIGURE 5 Logo of the NordPol suitcase factory
EBAY.DE

FIGURE 6 Pollock's drawing of Adolph Lowe
STATE UNIVERSITY OF NEW YORK, ALBANY, ADOLPH LOWE PAPERS

FIGURE 7
Self-portrait, 1920
ARCHIVE CENTER OF THE
UNIVERSITY LIBRARY FRANK-
FURT AM MAIN

FIGURE 8   The Pollock Family, 1898
          UNIVERSITY LIBRARY FRANKFURT AM MAIN

FIGURE 9   The Pollock Family, 1902
UNIVERSITY LIBRARY FRANKFURT AM MAIN

FIGURE 10   The Pollock Mansion
UNIVERSITY LIBRARY FRANKFURT AM MAIN

FIGURE 11 Max Horkheimer and Friedrich Pollock as Soldiers
UNIVERSITY LIBRARY FRANKFURT AM MAIN

FIGURE 12
Friedrich Pollock, 1929
UNIVERSITY LIBRARY FRANKFURT AM MAIN

FIGURE 13
Max Horkheimer and Friedrich Pollock, 1928
UNIVERSITY LIBRARY FRANKFURT AM MAIN

FIGURE 14   Friedrich Pollock, early 1930s
UNIVERSITY LIBRARY FRANKFURT AM MAIN

FIGURE 15
Friedrich Pollock, early 1940s
UNIVERSITY LIBRARY FRANKFURT AM MAIN

FIGURE 16   Andrée and Friedrich Pollock, 1939
UNIVERSITY LIBRARY FRANKFURT AM MAIN

FIGURE 17   Group Photo of the First Marxist Work Week, 1923
UNIVERSITY LIBRARY FRANKFURT AM MAIN

FIGURE 18
Dée Pollock looks at the NYC skyline
UNIVERSITY LIBRARY
FRANKFURT AM MAIN

FIGURE 19
Carlota Pollock, 1948
UNIVERSITY LIBRARY
FRANKFURT AM MAIN

Index

Abromeit, John   viii
Adorno, Gretel (née Margarete Karplus)   104n21, 110, 163, 187, 196
Adorno, Theodor W. (also: Wiesengrund, Theodor)   3, 46, 49, 56, 58, 72, 77, 88, 91, 95–96, 104, 106, 108–110, 112, 114, 116, 120, 130, 133, 143, 147, 149–152, 154–155, 159, 161–163, 171, 173–174, 180–181, 187, 193–194, 201–204, 206–207, 214, 226–230, 232, 234
Akselrod, Tobias »Tuvia« (also: Axelrod, Tobias »Tuvia«)   36–37
Alexander, Eduard Ludwig   53
Alexander, Gertrud   52n39
Alexander, Susanne   52n39
Anders, Günther (also: Stern, Günther)   174
Arendt, Hannah   108–109, 128, 130, 158, 192n43
Arndt, Paul   42
Aron, Raymond   106, 110

Baader, Franz von   58
Bach, Johann Sebastian   14
Bachenheimer, Ellen Ruth   220n45
Bachenheimer, Manfred   220n45
Bachenheimer, Martha (née Rothschild)   220n45
Bachenheimer, Stephan   220n45
Backhaus, Hans-Georg   49
Bacon, Roger   38
Baeumker, Clemens   38
Báky, Josef von   162
Baudelaire, Charles   111
Bauer, Otto   37
Baumann, Erich. See Mandelbaum, Kurt
Baumann, Kurt. See Mandelbaum, Kurt
Bebel, August   27
Becker, Matthias   237
Benda, Julien   106
Ben-Gurion, David   229
Benjamin, Walter   3, 33, 106–112, 133, 152, 207
Bernecker, Helene »Hella« (also Helena Rosenthal de Bernecker)   189, 191, 232
Bernstein, Eduard   68
Bernstein, Peretz   156

Biehahn, Walter   64
Blitz, Samuel   156
Bock, Wolfgang   206
Böhm-Bawerk, Eugen von   43
Börne, Ludwig   206n22
Bonaparte, Napoleon   7, 63, 174
Borkenau, Franz   96
Bouglé, Célestin   110
Brandt, Willy   212
Brecht, Bertolt   109–110, 151, 161–162, 171–174
Brill, Hans Klaus   189
Brill, Hermann Louis   188
Brunner, Ernst Ritter von   31
Buber, Martin   222
Budge, Ella (née Mayer)   128
Budge, Henry   43
Budge, Siegfried   43, 128
Budich, Willi   36–37
Bukharin, Nikolai   39, 103
Butler, Nicholas Murray   110

Calvelli-Adorno, Maria   133
Chabrier, Emmanuel   22–23
Chagall, Marc   41
Chamberlain, Neville   141
Claussen, Detlev   vii, 227, 229n29
Cornelius, Hans   44, 120
Cosack, Konrad   38
Czóbel, Ernst   67

Daladier, Édouard   141
Diebold, Bernhard   122n10
Diebold, John   214
Diehl, Karl   41, 43
Dietzel, Heinrich   43
Dreyfuß, Mendel   5
Duncker, Hermann   57
Dutschke, Rudi   228

Eckert, John Presper   210
Ehrenreich, Lili. See Kracauer, Lili
Eichmann, Adolf   158
Einstein, Albert   176n50, 130
Eisenstaedt, Alfred   178
Eisler, Gerhart   59n63
Eisler, Hanns   59n63, 143, 162, 171, 174, 192

INDEX

Eisler, Hede. See Massing, Hede
Eisner, Else 33
Eisner, Kurt 31, 33, 34n33
Emery, Nicola 217
Engels, Friedrich 39, 52, 61–62, 65, 68, 72, 74–76, 90, 149, 215
Epp, Franz von 34
Epstein, Mordechai 77
Erler, Fritz 212
Evans, Richard 82

Farquharson, Alexander 110
Favez, Juliette 113, 145
Feinberg, Julia (also: Meyer, Julia) 79
Feuchtwanger, Lion 130, 171
Fischer, Ruth 59n63, 84
Flamm, Christian 236
Flowerman, Samuel H. 188–189
Fogarasi, Béla 53
Franck, Alfred 220
Franck, Elisabeth. See Pollock, Elisabeth »Elsa«
Franck, Marga (née Oppenheimer) 126
Franck, Michael 126
Franck, Wolf 125–126
Frank, Leonhard 171
Freud, Sigmund 42, 131, 203, 227
Friedländer, Saul 156
Friedmann, Georges 211
Fromm, Erich 57, 88, 95–96, 104, 106, 114, 154, 159
Fuchs, Eduard 59, 109, 109n33
Fuchs, Frida 109n33
Fuchs, Margarete 109n33

Gaister, Aron Izrailevich 64
George, Manfred 129
Gerhard, Hans Wolfram 219
Gerlach, Kurt Albert 51–52
Gerloff, Wilhelm 58
Goitein, Irma 78
Goldmann, Nahum 130
Goldstein, Kurt 42
Goldschmidt, Alfons 57
Göring, Hermann 102
Gorki, Maxim 54
Graf, Friedrich Wilhelm 74
Graf, Oskar Maria 129
Gresmann, Hans 212

Grossman, Henryk 55–56, 66–67, 94–95, 100, 106, 109, 141, 162, 216, 218
Grossner, Claus 230
Grosz, George 54
Grünberg, Carl 52–58, 61–62, 64, 68–71, 75, 78, 86–87, 91–92
Grzesinski, Albert 83
Guggenheim, Paul 106, 110
Gumnior, Helmut 233
Gumperz, Hede. See Massing, Hede
Gumperz, Julian 54, 57–59, 102, 104, 106, 114, 140
Gurland, Arkadij (also: Arcadius Rudolf Lang Gurland) 152

Habermas, Jürgen viii, 201, 226, 228
Hacker, Frederick J. 184
Halbwachs, Maurice 110
Hallstein, Walter 187–188
Harpe, Jean de la 110
Hausmann, Sebastian 38
Heck, Jakob 33
Hegel, Georg Wilhelm Friedrich 227
Heidegger, Martin 41, 77, 137–139, 216
Heine, Heinrich 73, 206, 232n41
Held, Ernst (also: Rosenbaum, Ernst) 79
Held, Nelly (also: Rosenbaum, Nelly) 53, 78
Hermann, Kai 228
Herrmann, Eva 185
Herzfelde, Wieland 59
Hess, Moses 78
Hielscher, Friedrich 100
Hilferding, Rudolf 44, 50, 90, 94n32, 135, 215
Himmler, Heinrich 158
Hindenburg, Paul von 97
Hirsch, Katharina von. See Weil, Käthe
Hirschfeld, Magnus 99
Hitler, Adolf 1, 83, 85, 97, 102, 130, 133–137, 140–141, 144–145, 147, 156, 160, 174–175, 187, 204–205, 225–226, 237
Hobbes, Thomas 48
Hoffmann, Johannes 34
Hofstätter, Peter 205–206
Honecker, Erich 135n7
Honigsheim, Paul 104
Hoover, J. Edgar 121, 166
Horkheimer, Babette 29
Horkheimer, Max passim
Horkheimer, Moriz 15, 24

Horkheimer, Rose Christine »Maidon« (née Riekher) 29, 34, 41–42, 60, 117, 123, 129, 131, 163–164, 168, 171, 177, 181–182, 187, 192, 196, 199, 237
Huch, Ricarda 33
Hürlimann, Martin 110
Husserl, Edmund 41
Huxley, Aldous 173, 175, 180, 192, 214

Ibsen, Henrik 19, 176
Ickes, Harold 146
Isaak, Bernhard 73

Jäger, Hans 62
Jacoby, Fritz 125
Jacoby, Paul 125
Jay, Martin E. vii–viii, 74, 217–218, 229, 235, 237
Joseph, Babette »Settchen« 124–125, 221
Joseph, Ida. See Pollock, Ida
Jünger, Ernst 28

Kahn, Sigmund 29, 122n10
Kaiser, Georg 222n3
Kamenev, Lev 102
Kant, Immanuel 20, 227
Karsen, Fritz 106, 188
Kautsky, Karl 34, 44, 50, 62
Kennedy, John F. 210
Kerensky, Alexander Fyodorovich 175
Khrushchev, Nikita 217
King, William H. 165–166
Kirchheimer, Otto 104, 106, 152, 165, 223
Klee, Paul 41
Knopping, Helen. See Weil, Helen
König, René 205
Korsch, Karl 50–53, 55, 57–58, 86–87, 136, 172–173
Kortner, Fritz 161–162
Koyré, Alexandre 95
Kracauer, Lili (née Ehrenreich) 55, 163
Kracauer, Siegfried 55, 57, 72, 90n19, 110, 144, 163
Krahl, Hans-Jürgen 227
Krull, Germaine 32–33, 35–37, 60
Krzhizhanovsky, Gleb M. 64n78

Lamm, Hans 122n10
Landauer, Eva 124

Landauer, Gustav 35
Landauer, Karl 95, 110, 124, 132
Landauer, Lina (née Kahn) 124
Landauer, Paul 125
Landauer, Suze 125
Lang, Fritz 161
Langerhans, Heinz 58, 78
Lash, Trude x
Lazarsfeld, Paul 89
Lederer, Emil 50
Leichter, Käthe 89, 110–111
Leichter, Otto 111
Lenin, Wladimir Ilyich 31, 39, 43–45, 51, 54, 65–66, 72, 90, 92, 102, 186, 215–216
Leontief, Wassily 88
Lessing, Gotthold Ephraim 14
Levi, Edward 166
Leviné, Eugen 36
Levit, Samuel »Mila« 37
Lewin, Adolf 6
Lewin, Shlomo 122n10
Liebknecht, Karl 59
Liefmann, Robert 41
Lorwin, Lewis L. 110
Lotz, Walther 38, 45
Löwe, Adolph (also: Lowe, Adolph) ix, 14, 42, 114, 163, 167, 169, 174–175
Loewenstein, Ilse 179
Löwenthal, Leo 21, 28, 57–58, 85, 95–96, 104, 106, 123, 143, 154, 162, 165
Löwenthal, Richard (also: Sering, Paul) 137
Ludwig, Emil 130
Lukács, Georg 44, 52–53, 59, 105, 229–230
Luxemburg, Rosa 43–44, 52, 54, 76, 216
Lynd, Robert 104

Mackauer, Clara 55
Mackauer, Wilhelm 95
Maier, Wilhelm 33
Mandelbaum, Kurt (also: Baumann, Kurt; Baumann, Erich) 57–58, 87, 106, 140
Mann, Golo 185
Mann, Heinrich 161
Mann, Katia 185
Mann, Thomas 33, 130, 162, 171, 185
Mannheim, Karl 114, 148
Maor, Maimon 233
Marc, Franz 32, 41
Marc, Maria 32

INDEX 277

Marcuse, Herbert   3, 75, 96, 104, 106, 114, 116, 137–139, 143, 151–152, 154, 162–163, 165, 216, 228
Marcuse, Ludwig   72, 174
Marx, Julius   30–31, 122*n*10, 222*n*3
Marx, Andrée »Dée«. See Pollock, Andrée »Dée«
Marx, Eva   73
Marx, Heinrich   73
Marx, Henriette (née Pressburg)   73
Marx, Karl   2, 21, 39, 43–45, 48–49, 57, 59–62, 65, 68, 71–80, 85–88, 90, 95, 105, 119, 134, 138–139, 146, 149, 151, 156, 173, 203, 215–216, 226–227
Marx, Levi   73
Marx, Moses   73
Marx, Samuel   73
Massing, Gustav   101
Massing, Hede (née Tune; later: Eisler; Gumperz)   59–60, 100–103, 150
Massing, Paul Wilhelm (also: Billinger, Karl)   57–60, 98–103, 150, 155–159
Mauchly, John   210
Maus, Heinz   134
Mayer, Gustav   52
Mayer, Hans   110, 114, 172
Mayr, Georg von   38
McCloy, John   202
Mendelsohn-Weil, Anne   192*n*43
Mendelssohn, Margot von   195
Mendelssohn, Moses   73
Meng, Heinrich Otto   110
Mennicke, Carl   114
Meyer, Gerhard   74, 79*n*32, 140
Meyer, Julia. See Feinberg, Julia
Mikhaël, Éphraïm   22
Mozart, Wolfgang Amadeus   14
Müller, Hermann   83

Nägele-Nördlinger, Alice   11
Napoleon. See Bonaparte, Napoleon
Neumann, Alfred   171
Neumann, Franz Leopold   77, 103–104, 106, 148–149, 151–154, 162, 165–167, 173, 188, 217, 232
Neumann, Friedrich Julius   43
Neumann, Sigmund   95
Neumeier, Suzanne »Suze«   22–25, 29, 41, 191
Niekisch, Ernst   100
Nietzsche, Friedrich   21, 77, 227
Nikolaevsky, Boris Ivanovich   62, 156
Nobel, Nehemias Anton   57
Nördlinger, Rosalia »Rösl«, »Rosa«   9, 127, 200, 220–221
Nördlinger, Sigmund   9–10, 127, 200, 220–221
Noske, Gustav   34

Oppenheimer, Arthur   52
Oppenheimer, Franz   42–43, 53, 58
Oprecht, Emil   110
Otten, Karl   58

Pashukanis, Evgeny   44
Paul VI   230
Pfemfert, Franz   38, 84
Plessner, Monika   201
Pollock, Alice (née Goldschmidt, later: Pons)   126–127
Pollock, Andrée »Dée« (née Woog; later: Marx)   28–31*n*23, 121–123, 130–131, 182, 222*n*3
Pollock, Carlota (née Weil)   181–183, 187, 189–191, 196, 219, 221
Pollock, Elisabeth »Elsa« (née Franck)   7, 26
Pollock, Emanuel (later: Pollock, Emil)   9
Pollock, Hans (later: Pollock, Juan)   7, 10, 12, 41, 69, 123–125, 128, 178–179, 189–191, 199–200, 219–223
Pollock, Heinz (later: Pons, Henry)   125–127
Pollock, Ida »Idl« (née Joseph; later: Stern)   12, 123–125, 220–222
Pollock, Isidor Louis (also: Pollock, Hans Ludwig)   7, 12, 126–127
Pollock, Johanna Dorothea Marie (née Prielipp)   9*n*21
Pollock, Julius   6–7, 9–12, 24, 26, 127, 199
Pollock, Karl   9*n*21
Pollock, Pauline   8
Pollock, Rudolf Gerhard Werner   9*n*21
Pollock, Salomon   8–10
Pollock, Walter (later: Pons, Walter)   125–127
Pressburg, Henriette. See Marx, Henriette
Pribram, Karl Eman   64
Pringsheim, Peter   171
Pupko, Elia   35

Radek, Karl 103
Ranshofen-Wertheimer, Egon 170–171
Rappard, William Emanuel 110
Rathenau, Walther 43, 50
Reich, Bella (née Rothschild) 220n45
Reich, Ingeborg 220n45
Reich, Wilhelm 95
Reitlinger, Gerald 219
Remmele, Hermann 84
Ricardo, David 43
Richter, Werner 209
Richter-Brohm, Heinrich 97
Riekher, Rose Christine »Maidon«. See Horkheimer, Rose Christine »Maidon«
Rilke, Rainer Maria 33
Ringguth, Rudolf 233
Riazanov, David Borisovich 61–64, 67–68
Röhm, Ernst 34
Roniger, Boris 87
Roosevelt, Anna Eleanor ix–x, 167–169
Roosevelt, Franklin Delano ix, 141, 146–147, 149–150
Roosevelt, Henry ix
Roosevelt, Ruth Josephine (née Googins) ix
Rosenstraus, Alice 18
Rosenzweig, Franz 57
Roth, Joseph 63
Rothenbücher, Karl 38
Rothschild, Johanna (née Joseph) 220
Roy, Manabendra Nath 55
Rubin, Isaak Ilyich 44, 87
Rückert, Friedrich 14
Rüdenberg, Adele 10
Rumney, Jay 104

Salomon, Adrienne (also: Kahn-Woog, Adrienne) 28–29
Salomon, Albert 95
Sander, August 33
Saussure, Raymond de 110
Schacht, Hjalmar 147
Schachtel, Ernst 89
Schenck, Ernst von 14, 115n57, 233, 237
Schiller, Friedrich 14
Schlaeger, Hilke 228
Schlesinger, Rose. See Wittfogel, Rose
Schmidt, Alfred 233
Schmitt, Carl 77, 100
Schnädelbach, Herbert 226

Scholem, Gershom 108, 110
Scholem, Werner 58
Schönberg, Arnold 161
Schopenhauer, Friedrich 20–21, 37, 77, 229–230
Schröder, Rudy 110
Schumann, Robert 14
Schumpeter, Joseph 43, 50
Selke, Rudolf 64, 78
Simon, Ernst Akiva 57
Sinclair, Upton 54
Slawson, John 188, 191n41
Sombart, Werner 9, 75–80
Sommer, Liselotte »Lilo« (née Stern) 12, 123, 189–191, 222
Sommer, Paul 124, 191, 222
Sommer, Peter 222
Sorge, Christiane 55, 60
Sorge, Richard 52, 55, 59–60
Spann, Othmar 80
Spengler, Oswald 152
Spinoza, Baruch de 20, 232
Stalin, Joseph Vissarionovich 60–61, 66, 133, 144–145, 205, 225–226
Staudinger, Else 115
Staudinger, Hans 169
Stein, Alexander 156
Steinmayr, Jochen 230
Stern, Emil 12
Stern, Ida. See Pollock, Ida
Stern, Liselotte »Lilo«. See Sommer, Liselotte »Lilo«
Stern, Sallie 220
Sternberg, Fritz 42, 53–54, 135–137, 139
Sternheim, Andries 89, 104, 106–107, 112–114, 124
Sternheim, Gholina 113
Sternheim, Leonard 113
Sternheim, Paul 113
Stolper, Toni 115
Strauß, Johann 14, 30
Sugimoto, Eiichi 86–88

Tawney, Richard Henry 100
Thälmann, Ernst 135
Thomas, Albert 85
Tillich, Hannah 74, 176
Tillich, Paul 42, 74, 110, 114–115, 163, 169, 174, 176

INDEX

Toller, Ernst   33–35, 99
Tolstoi, Leo   54
Trotsky, Leo   72, 103
Truman, Harry S.   184
Turgot, Anne Robert Jacques   43

Ulmen, Gary   98
Unterleitner, Hans   34

Vaisberg, Roman Efimovich   64
Venedey, Hans   110
Vivaldi, Antonio   14
Voos, Doris   220n45
Voos, Flora (née Rothschild)   220n45
Voos, Heinz   220n45
Voos, Walter   220n45

Wagner, Richard   14, 76
Walch-Lux, Katja   33
Wallace, Henry A.   ix, 168–169
Walter, Emil   110
Walter-Busch, Emil   219–220
Weber, Adolf   42–43, 50
Weber, Alfred   43, 212
Weber, Max   38, 43, 50
Wegner, Armin Theofil   63
Weil, Felix José   50–55, 59–63, 70, 85, 87, 107, 131n48, 163–164, 176–177, 181, 187
Weil, Helen (née Knopping)   164
Weil, Hermann   50–52, 54
Weil, Katharina »Käthe« (née Bachert; later: von Hirsch)   52, 131n48

Weil, Lucille (née Jakobowicz)   163–165, 181
Weiss, Hilde   56, 88
Weisser, Susanne   55
Wellmer, Albrecht   226
Westermann, Abrascha   101
Wiener, Norbert   213
Wiesengrund, Oscar   133
Wiesengrund, Theodor. See Adorno, Theodor W.
Wiggershaus, Rolf   3, 233
Wilbrandt, Robert   50
Windmüller, Else (née Jacoby)   125
Wittfogel, Karl August   52, 55, 57, 60, 79, 98–100, 106, 123, 131, 136, 145, 217
Wittfogel, Olga (née Joffe, later: Lang)   99–100n9, 106
Wittfogel, Rose (née Schlesinger)   55
Wolf, Walter   16
Woog, Andrée »Dée«. See Pollock, Andrée »Dée«
Woog, Raoul   29

Zelzer, Maria   220
Zetkin, Clara   52
Zetkin, Konstantin   52
Zinoviev, Grigori   51, 83, 102
Zörgiebel, Karl   84
Zunz, Leopold   232n41
Zweig, Stefan   33

www.ingramcontent.com/pod-product-compliance
Lightning Source LLC
LaVergne TN
LVHW091719070526
838199LV00050B/2465